A BLONDE
IN
AFRICA

Laura Resnick

THE RESNICK LIBRARY
OF AFRICAN ADVENTURES

Mike Resnick, Series Editor

http://www.abooks.com/africa

Publisher: Ralph Roberts
Vice-President/Operations: Pat Hutchison Roberts

Resnick Library of African Adventure
Series Editor: Mike Resnick

Managing Editor: Vivian Terrell
Production: Gayle Graham
Fulfillment: Barbara Blood

Editors: Gayle Graham, Ralph Roberts, Pat Roberts, Bill Resnick

Cover Design: **WorldComm®**
Interior Design & Electronic Page Assembly: **WorldComm®**
Photographs as indicated

10 9 8 7 6 5 4 3 2 1

Library of Congress Cataloging-in-Publication

Resnick, Laura, 1962—
    A blonde in Africa / by Laura Resnick.
            p. cm. -- (Resnick library of African adventure)
        ISBN 1-57090-030-2
        1. Africa -- Description and travel 2. Resnick, Laura, 1962- --
    Journeys--Africa.   I. Title.   II. Series.
    DT12.25.R47   1996
    916.04'329--dc20   96-23455
                                                                        CIP

The author and publisher have made every effort in the preparation of this book to ensure the accuracy of the information. However, the information in this book is sold without warranty, either express or implied. Neither the author nor Alexander Books will be liable for any damages caused or alleged to be caused directly, indirectly, incidentally, or consequentially by the information in this book.

The opinions expressed in this book are solely those of the author and are not necessarily those of Alexander Books.

Alexander Books—a division of Creativity, Inc.—is located at 65 Macedonia Road, Alexander NC 28701. Phone (704) 252–9515, Fax (704) 255–8719. For orders only: 1-800-472-0438. Visa and MasterCard accepted.

Alexander Books is distributed to the trade by Midpoint Trade Books, Inc., 27 West 20th Street, New York NY 10011, (212) 727-0190, (212) 727-0195 fax.

This book is also available on the internet in the **Publishers CyberMall.** Set your browser to **http://www.abooks.com** and enjoy the many fine values available there.

CONTENTS

INTRODUCTION
by Mike Resnick

Africa can cast a spell that makes Merlin look like an amateur. It can grab you from half a world away, pull you to its bosom, and as you spend your last night there prior to going home, you find that you miss it already. It has a way of simplifying things, of making you realize what's really important to you; and it can convince you that the very best part of yourself will remain there, waiting for you to return and redeem it.

It can also drive you crazy, and break your heart again and again.

It can show you beauties undreamed of, and horrors equally unimagined. It is vibrant with life, both human and animal, yet no continent presents such a constant and uncaring display of death.

It is also a place of inspiration. People who would never have considered writing under other circumstances have taken years out of their lives to put their African experiences down on paper.

And when a *real* writer comes face to face with Africa, you get such masterpieces as Ruark's *Horn of the Hunter*, Hemingway's *The Green Hills of Africa*, Blixen's *Out of Africa*, Markham's *West With the Night*, and Huxley's *The Flame Trees of Thika*.

Hunters get that urge, too, and have produced such memorable volumes as Lake's **Killers in Africa** (Alexander Books, ISBN 1-57090-013-2), and **Hunter's Choice** (Alexander Books, ISBN 1-57090-026-4), Jordan's *Elephants and Ivory*, Bell's *Karamojo Safari*, the works of Selous and Boyes and Lyell and Stigand and Percival, and many, many more.

It even affects writers of category fiction. I've written nine science fiction novels and 22 short stories set in Africa. Other science fiction writers such as George Alec Effinger, Robert Silverberg, John Crowley, and Gregory Benford have recently set stories there. Nor has it escaped the attention of mystery writers such as M. M. Kaye, Elspeth Huxley, and Karin McQuillan, and adventure writers from Edgar Rice Burroughs and H. Rider Haggard right up to Michael Crichton.

What you now hold in your hands is a book by an award-winning romance and science fiction writer, who found Africa just as fascinating as all those who went before her. I know her a little better than those other writers who came under Africa's spell. I ought to: I'm her father.

Laura Resnick has always been a traveler. She went to Sweden when she was 16. She majored in French and minored in Italian at Georgetown University, the better to make her way through the non- English-speaking world. By the time she was 25 she had lived in England, Sicily, and an Israeli *kibbutz,* and had visited close to a dozen other countries.

Then it became time to make a living. Writing wasn't her first choice, but when you've got the touch it's hard to ignore it, and she quickly became a successful romance writer, winning an award as Best New Series Writer.

Before long she had expanded into science fiction and fantasy as well, and in August, 1993, while she herself was evading pachyderms in South Africa's Addo Elephant Park, I accepted the Campbell Award, science fiction's "Rookie of the Year" award, for her. This came a month after one of her romance novels won a major award. (I think she was busy drowning in the Zambezi at that very moment.)

Laura chose to see Africa not as a hunter (almost impossible these days, unless you want only to see tiny portions of Botswana, Zimbabwe, and Tanzania), and not as a luxury tourist. Instead, she chose to become an Overlander, a hardy and not-all-that-rare breed of traveler which one constantly encounters in the most out-of- the-way places in the Third World.

This is the first book in the Resnick Library of African Adventure, either here at Alexander Books or in its previous incarnation at St. Martin's Press, that does not involve hunting. I chose to run it because, while there have been many accounts of people traveling across Africa in less than sumptuous style, there has yet to be a book that gives you a true picture of an Overlander's daily life.

Overland vehicles set out to tour obscure lands hundreds of times each year; they are becoming increasingly popular not only for students, but for retired men and women living on fixed incomes who nonetheless have a hunger to see the world. Well, there's one thing I can promise you: if you're considering becoming an Overlander, once you finish reading this book you'll know *exactly* what to expect.

For instance:

You'll learn just how many diseases you can catch in eight months, despite your innoculations.

You'll learn what it feels like to have an entire village go suddenly berserk and attack your party in the middle of the night.

You'll learn why it's a bad idea to pitch your tent where the previous party had been baiting lions.

You'll learn what it's like to join a pygmy tribe during a hunt.

You'll learn just how many times you have to bribe border guards into doing precisely what they are paid to do in the first place.

You'll learn what it's like to be arrested in a Third World country. In a few of them, in fact.

You'll learn Tanzanian economics, and why bread comes from Arusha on Thursdays.

You'll experience the thrill of having baby gorillas playing right in front of you.

You'll see an ancient ceremony in which the men of a West African village willingly plunge knives into their own bellies.

You'll travel a dirt road that wends its way through hundreds of live mines.

You'll plunge through the Zambezi's rapids and suddenly find yourself beneath the surface, looking desperately for your boat while downstream the crocs are looking just as desperately for an appetizer.

And you'll have no trouble understanding why, despite all this, there's a bonus section featuring Laura's return trip barely a year later.

Speaking as an editor and not a blood relative (another circumstance you'll never find in Africa), I think you'll find that this is a book filled not only with adventure, but with charm, wit, and insight.

Enjoy.

A FUGITIVE WITH A PSEUDONYM

Wearing crisp khakis and a dashing hat set rakishly askew on her golden hair, she casually hoisted her battered rucksack over one shoulder as she made her way through the airport, her slim figure drawing approving glances. She had an air of competence, of ready courage. ...

Yeah, I think that's how I'd have written the scene. (In case you haven't guessed, I've written a lot of romance novels.) But, of course, that's not how it happened. I *am* golden-haired, but I'm definitely not slim, and my figure only draws approving glances in Mediterranean outposts where men still like really Rubenesque women. My hat was packed away in my brand-new, oversized, overweight duffle, and when I finally put it on weeks later, someone would comment that it made me look like a crazed lepidopterist. As for my air of competence and courage... Frankly, I was out of my depth and terrified. And, as is my wont in such circumstances, I was babbling. For some reason, I felt compelled to tell my companions at the airport all about the medical supplies I had packed. As one of them later reminisced, "It included an entire operating theatre, enough drugs to rouse a corpse from the dead, and an injection of something or other which you seemed set on sticking into some poor sucker's buttocks at the first opportunity." (The last item was adrenaline, to be injected in case of allergic reaction). I don't think I made the best possible first impression on my fellow overlanders.

And what, I hear you ask, is an overlander? Well, I daresay that I am now a veteran example of this proud breed. Overlanders are people who travel from one place to another without leaving terra firma. To be a *true* overlander, the destination should be really far

This is me, wearing every item of clothing I own (that's My nightgown you're looking at), in Morocco's Atlas Mountains in February.

away from the point of origin (I went from the shores of northern Morocco to the Cape of Good Hope), the terrain should be very difficult, you should live outdoors the whole time, you must have several mysterious illnesses along the way, and you should come close to meeting your Maker at least once. *I*, I hardly need add, am a *true* overlander.

Overlanders go to remote places, travelling in a leisurely fashion, meeting locals and living simply. There is notable risk involved (yes, people die overlanding), since you often travel through poor, out-of-the-way, unstable countries, and frequently have to rely on your own resources and ingenuity.

Not having the money to buy my own overland vehicle, knowing nothing whatsoever about engines, and knowing no one else who wanted to cross Africa, I had decided to cross Africa with Guerba Expeditions, a British overland company. They provided the overland truck and a crew of three, and I was supposed to provide a willing spirit, a healthy body, and true grit (and money, too, of course). It seemed a fair trade.

I and my fellow overlanders met at Gatwick Airport in London in early 1993 and flew to Gibraltar, where the crew met us with the truck. I don't think I can overstate the importance of the overland truck. It was quite literally my home now. It was my sole means of transportation across the African continent. It was the source of all my necessities. My food, firewood, cooking gear, camping gear, medical supplies, money, and personal gear all lived in that truck.

So you can imagine my dismay when I saw how little it was; I had imagined an armoured 18-wheeler, not this two-axle truck. My first reaction was, "Surely *this* can't be the truck. It must just be our transport to the *real* truck." A Bedford truck with a custom-built body, it looked too small, insubstantial, and vulnerable to carry me and my companions across the Dark Continent.

Our expedition leader, however, looked and sounded exactly the way I thought a rugged, fearless, overland adventurer should; it was as if I'd written him into the role. Indeed, from that day forward I thought of him as Fearless Leader, though I never called him that aloud. However, the first thing Fearless did was unintentionally compound my anxieties by saying that although he, the co-driver, and the campmaster were the "relief crew," called in at the last moment, they were thrilled to be here and were sure we'd have a fine time. I didn't realize until two weeks later that this was a joke, so you could say that I got off to a bad start.

Anyhow, my muttered imprecations were ignored in the confusion and excitement of getting everyone on board with their duffles and backpacks as quickly as possible so we could go rumbling off to our first campsite. And by the time we reached camp – our first night was to be spent in Spain, before crossing the Straits of Gibraltar the next morning – I had more pressing matters to worry about. For one thing, a sign posted inside the truck warned me:

"YOU TRAVEL AT YOUR OWN RISK"

I did not find this wildly reassuring and felt that perhaps such comments could have waited until I was feeling stronger. In June perhaps (this was February). However, I suppose the company was just trying to reiterate one of the most memorable clauses in the contract I had signed with them:

> *ACCEPTANCE OF RISK. The client acknowledges that the nature of the trip is expeditionary and adventurous and... may involve a significant amount of personal risk.*

Sure, that word "significant" had given me pause at first, but then I thought, "Hell, I'm a *writer*. I deal with *agents* and *editors* and *reviewers*, so don't tell *me* about risk, buddy!" And so I'd signed the document and started getting my yellow fever and meningococcal shots.

Several months after doing so, I found myself huddling in a deserted disco at some Costa Del Sol campground in Spain and wondering what could have possessed me to come here. Fearless had pulled out the Michelin map of Afrique (*Nord et Ouest*) and was discussing our route between here and Nairobi – which was already too dangerous to follow as originally planned.

I had already received letters from Guerba about some of the problems facing us. Due to raids by Tuareg nomads in northern Mali and Niger, the southern Sahara was considered too dangerous to cross. Stories abounded of individual vehicles, and even small convoys, being attacked and seized, thus leaving the passengers stranded in the desert. Though there was a rather diverting story about one overland truck which was so decrepit even the Tuaregs didn't want it, most of the stories were far from amusing. Inevitably, a tourist was shot, which certainly dampened my desire to attempt the same route.

The Tuaregs, who are scattered across several Saharan nations, are desert nomads whose society has suffered terribly in recent decades. Though they have long sought political autonomy, the situation didn't escalate into serious violence until a few years ago. The drought which devastated this region of the world in the 1970s and 1980s destroyed most of the livestock upon which the Tuaregs were dependent for their livelihood. Then, with the collapse of oil prices in 1985, thousands of other Tuaregs lost their gainful employment. Poverty and bitter racial conflict led to the formation of various Tuareg rebel groups in 1990 which started attacking government targets. This inspired increasingly brutal government reprisals, until the violence escalated into a full-scale rebellion.

Travel became increasingly hazardous in this region. The border between Algeria and Niger was closed in 1992. The last overland truck (not a Guerba truck) to attempt a desert crossing had been robbed in June near the Algeria-Mali frontier. It seemed unlikely that the situation would change any time soon. Having originally intended to cross the Sahara by going south through Tamanrasset in Algeria down to Timbuktu in Mali, we would now have to find another way.

I was disappointed that I wouldn't go to Timbuktu. It seemed like the sort of thing I'd want to say when I was old: "Ah, yes, when I was in Timbuktu..." It's one of those exotic-sounding places whose names had rolled off my tongue ever since I was a child poring over the atlas and dreaming of faraway places: Timbuktu, Samarkand, Macao, Maracaibo, Port Said, Jaipur, Kashmir... Well, you know.

Since crossing the Sahara via Libya was an even less likely prospect than Algeria, we looked westward to Mauritania. No, no, not Mauritius. *Mauritania*, a desert country so remote and untouristed that my massive 1,100-page African guidebook contained only four and a half pages about it. Due to a separate violent conflict, that border had still been closed as recently as autumn 1992, but it appeared to have opened since then.

At the time, I didn't understand this kind of phrasing. It *appeared* to have opened? Come on, either it was open or it wasn't. (It took me months to learn that this is exactly the kind of westernized thinking that can bring on a migraine while travelling in Africa.)

Apart from this first hurdle of the desert-crossing, there was also trouble brewing in both Togo and Zaïre which concerned us, since our plan was to go south into West Africa, then travel southeast across central Africa toward Kenya and Tanzania.

On the map, Togo appears as a narrow finger of land between Ghana and Benin. It's such a little country, I assumed we could drive around it or something if necessary. But Zaïre, a vast country sitting smack-dab in the middle of the continent, presented more of a problem; the only way around its eastern border was a route through the Sudan — not exactly a less hazardous option that year. I recalled part of a ditty I'd heard my mother sing once or twice when I was a child: *They're ri-ot-ing in Af-ri-ca*. Apparently they still were. I wondered if I'd really cross Africa this year, after all.

We took the ferry across the Straits of Gibraltar the next day and disembarked at Ceuta, a tiny Spanish enclave on the northwestern tip of Morocco, just east of Tangier. It's one of the few small, obscure remains of the Spanish colonies in Africa. From there, we crossed the border into Morocco. A lot of border crossings in Africa take a full day, and some can even take several days, depending upon how bored, hostile, or greedy the border guards are. This, however, was an easy crossing (certainly easier than the time I arrived in Tunisia with a boatload of Sicilians in the middle of a hot August night several years earlier – but that's another story). I think Fearless gave one of the Moroccan border guards a cassette tape, and our passports were stamped and returned to us by sunset.

We camped that night in an olive grove somewhere in northern Morocco. For the next few weeks, camping all across Morocco and heading into the desert, I was pretty miserable. I mean, I'm a *writer*, and I had never done anything quite so butch. Living rough – eating, whizzing (urinating), washing, and traveling outdoors all day, and sleeping in pup tents at night – wasn't what I was used to.

So why, I hear you ask, did I decide to cross Africa in an overland truck, knowing full well what it would be like?

It was just something I'd always wanted to do. My dreams are not always in accord with my temperament.

Besides, at thirty, I had reached a crossroads. I had been writing professionally, full-time, for five years. I wrote a very particular kind of romance novel, known as category romance – the sort of books released by publishing houses like Harlequin and Silhouette, with uniform packaging and strict formats. I found it a rather rigid field,

with many rules about word length, story type, sexual content (usually lots and lots, by the way), language usage, and so on. One of the reasons I had begun my career with this type of fiction is that I had really needed the focus and discipline of such a tight structure when I was learning to write novels; but after having written ten such books under the pseudonym Laura Leone, I had grown to feel frustrated and stifled

The Dyers' Souk in Fez, Morocco.

by that same structure. Yet, despite the many short stories I'd been selling, I had encountered nothing but failure in all my efforts to break away and sell some other kind of novel.

I felt unhappy and burned-out. I wasn't even sure I wanted to go on writing anymore, and I certainly felt ready to do away with Ms. Leone. My personal life, too, seemed to have been stagnating for over a year. I spent several months trying to decide what to do next with my life, because I knew I needed to do something more drastic than just move to a new apartment or change my pseudonym. I needed to do something completely different, something I was even afraid of doing. After examining and discarding numerous courses of action, I decided that, while I had the time, freedom, and opportunity, I wanted to cross Africa overland – something I had fantasized about doing for ten years.

It was a serendipitous decision. The moment I decided to go, things started happening to facilitate my quest. For example, after a long, dry spell which completely depleted my bank account, I suddenly sold two books in one week, and the advance money offered to me was *precisely* the amount I had worked out I would need in order to go to Africa. So I accepted the offers, wrote my eleventh and twelfth category romances, and left the country.

I had travelled a lot and lived abroad, but I had never done anything remotely like this. Some of my friends, relatives, and acquaintances were envious. Others clearly thought I had gone insane. But they'd all be stunned into disbelieving silence if they could see me now, getting up at dawn to strike my tent, cooking breakfast over an open fire, going to the bathroom in the mud behind scrubby bushes while Moroccan goats watched with idle curiosity, washing my private parts with a bowl of ice cold water under the North African stars in February (and let's be very clear about this – it's *cold* in Morocco in February), and living cheek-by-jowl with some twenty people I hadn't chosen.

So far, to be honest... I *hated* it.

We stopped off to see the Roman ruins at Volubilis, which sort of reminded me of the ruined *City On the Edge of Forever* in the old *Star Trek* series. We bush-camped at a farm that night, and I lost my only roll of toilet paper when it rolled downhill in the dark. The farmer who'd given us permission to stay on his land spoke no French or English, but his hospitality crossed all language barriers. I glimpsed his wife a few times, hiding in the shadows like some wraith, watching us curiously but disappearing the moment she knew she'd been seen; few Moroccan women speak to strangers or even meet their eyes.

Temperatures continued dropping as we headed for Rabat. I had never been so cold in my life. I was wearing everything I had, and I still wasn't warm enough. When packing for the trip, it had never occurred to me that Morocco in mid-February would be colder than the salt mines of Siberia. I reminded myself again and again that I had known the trip would be tough at first, that I had mentally braced myself to have a hard time for the first few weeks. It didn't help much.

By day we rode through mountains and valleys of burnt umber and slumbering green, passing plump families in little wooden donkey carts, exotic veiled women, and men who looked elegant and timeless in their *djellabas* (kind of like kaftans with hoods). By night I hunched in a fetal position with only a roll mat between me and Mother Earth, waking from a shallow sleep every time roosters crowed (why do they crow at *night?*), dogs barked, goats wandered by, or strangers raised their voices near my tent.

Sometimes the strangers were my fellow overlanders, to whom I was not yet accustomed. Often, though, they were locals who had come to see what these strange Europeans were doing camping in their local groves or fields. Increasingly distressed by being on display from the moment I opened my tent flap at dawn, I was relieved when we reached Rabat and checked into an official campground on the outskirts of the city.

> (Diary entry, Rabat campground)
> *February 17th:*
> Rough morning. Alone in the tent, I kept feeling a tickling on my legs. After several searches in my sleeping bag, I discovered a big, fat, squirming, green caterpillar. Half the camp heard me shriek.
>
> One of my companions, a ghoulishly grinning woman, suggests that this is an easy beginning: next week, scorpions; the week after that, snakes.
>
> The toilets at the campsite are revolting. Heaps of diarrhea and stains inside, the floors wet and muddy, everything stinks. I'm sure I smell urine near the tent. And the noise around here at night!
>
> So much for official campgrounds.

The Algerians were now preventing travellers from going any further south than Tamanrasset, so Mauritania remained our only feasible option for crossing the Sahara. Hence, we had come to Rabat to get visas for Mauritania.

The Mauritanian Embassy in Rabat refused to give them to us.

Fearless said he wasn't accepting "no" as a valid and final answer from the Mauritanians, and he went back to their embassy to "try things." According to the embassy officials, "too many people" wanted to cross the desert via Mauritania now that it was the only viable route in all of North Africa.

I didn't get it. I mean, Mauritania is pretty far off the beaten path, and how many people cross the Sahara annually anyhow? Presumably we're talking about fewer people than, say, go to a Yankees game. But the Mauritanians were adamant: no visas. And if you want to know why one of the five poorest countries in the world turned away some twenty Westerners with pocket money, you'd have to ask them.

It was more than discouraging; it was a real Catch-22. The only way to get to Mauritania overland from Morocco was by crossing occupied Western Sahara – which the Moroccans would never give us permission to enter without proof that we would be allowed into Mauritania upon reaching the border.

I've known people to have less trouble getting into the Queen's annual garden party.

The Guerba office in England suggested that one possible solution to this impasse was to get the Mauritanian visas somewhere other than Rabat. With only about half a dozen Mauritanian embassies world-wide, inquiries seemed feasible.

With matters still unresolved, we went off to Fès for a few days to act like tourists. I liked the city a lot. About 350,000 people live in Fès's ninth century medina. With its narrow alleys, public fountains, dark bakeries, beautiful mosques, heavily-laden donkeys, and colorful *souks*, I felt like I was stepping into scenes from *Casablanca, Road to Morocco*, and *Mask of Dimitrios*. The city's atmosphere so overcame me that I found myself buying a double-knotted Moroccan carpet and shipping it home, while others bought blankets to keep them warm on those cold Moroccan nights. I later learned that I'd been a fool not to barter, since most of my companions had purchased their prizes for half the original asking price. It was an expensive lesson, and I never forgot it.

However, my favorite memory of this incredible city, which is both the religious and cultural center of Morocco, was our local *hammam*. That's a public bath house, segregated by gender. After a week of being cold and dirty, I sat on the tiled floors of big, steamy rooms where I was massaged with soap and had bucket after bucket of hot water poured over my head. I was in paradise. I thought about moving into the *hammam* permanently and letting the truck go south without me. It struck me funny, too, that in a country where the women were usually covered from head to toe, they were all comfortable and unself-conscious here, walking around stark naked, shouting,

The Cascades d'Ouzoud, a seldom-visited Moroccan waterfall.

bathing, scrubbing, gossiping, and even ululating.

I'd never thought about getting lost. I assumed that whoever was driving the truck – either Fearless or Chris, the co-driver—was somehow omniscient and knew exactly where he was going.

Heading from Fès toward Marrakech, we climbed higher and higher into the mountains on some twisty little road while I lounged in the roof seat and idly wondered where we were. The truck finally stopped and I heard Fearless's voice from below:

"We're lost," he called.

Ha-ha! What a kidder!

"Has anyone got a *detailed* map of Morocco?" he asked.

I sat bolt upright. A quick poll determined that no one had a better map.

We were able to determine our location before long, but it finally occurred to me that Africa's a pretty damn big continent, and even someone who'd been crossing it on and off for nearly a decade (as Fearless had) was often no more likely to know where he was going than I was. The lesson was to come home even more forcibly in the following weeks and months when I would sit in the cab with a map, trying to figure out where we were and where we needed to be.

We navigated most of Africa using Michelin maps 953 for North and West Africa, and 955 for Central and Southern Africa, plus the little sketch maps in *Africa on A Shoestring* or various *Rough Guides* to get around the cities. We did pretty well for the most part, especially in countries that only had a few roads to choose from, but it could get confusing when the map didn't correspond to reality (imagine that!).

Personally, I hated Marrakech, and I'm glad to have this opportunity to suggest you never go there. It's an attractive city, and there are certainly many points of interest, but I have seldom met so many unpleasant people in one place (excluding the weekday lunchtime rush in Manhattan). An adolescent shill literally spit on Pippa, our campmaster; someone else's pocket got picked; and a shopkeeper chased me down the street shouting that I was a "motherfucker" because I didn't want to buy any souvenirs. Our guide in the *souk* appeared to speak no English until he demonstrated a remarkable command of the vernacular by cursing me and Alison, an English woman, when we tried to leave a market stall where the merchant kept blocking our way and grabbing our arms (the guide would, of course, get a commission on anything we could be bullied into buying).

Nights were okay in Marrakech, when the Place Djemaa El Fna was filled with storytellers, magicians, and musicians, and you could sip delicious *café au lait* in cafés overlooking the square, then take a carriage ride back to the campsite. However, it was impossible for Westerners to be there without acquiring a self-appointed "guide," whose main function was to keep away all the other guides. I was never sure what to make of these men and boys. I didn't want to be abused for not giving money to someone whom I had repeatedly asked to go away, and I didn't believe the ones who claimed they didn't expect a tip. Why were they aggressively dogging every foreigner in sight (male or female) if not to earn a little money?

February 22:
Fearless has heard that apparently the Mauritanian Embassy in Algiers is issuing visas without a fuss. If this is true, we might send our passports to Algeria via special courier; this would be much quicker and less expensive than going ourselves. There also might be some possibility of obtaining visas for Mauritania from their embassy in Dakar, Senegal; someone from Guerba's head office is looking into this. And another overland driver stuck in Morocco has now gone back to Spain to get his visas in Cádiz. Meanwhile, we continue to wander Morocco, destination nowhere.

Me, eating sand and humming the "Lawrence of Arabia" theme in the Sahara.

WIND, SAND, AND STARS

amadan began with the new moon. This festival is the fourth pillar of Islam. It lasts for one month in the Arabian calendar and commemorates the revelation of the Koran to Mohammed. Muslims observe Ramadan by fasting, and for one long month they may not eat or drink between dawn and sunset; after sunset they may partake in moderation. For us non-Muslims, this meant that food might be hard to find in the middle of the day, which was when we usually did our marketing.

Although I find grocery shopping at home quite boring and generally only do it to get away from my accusing word processor, I really enjoyed marketing in Morocco. French is the main European language in North and West Africa, and since I spoke the most proficient French among my fellow overlanders, I did a lot of the translating for our campmaster, Pippa. She spoke very little French, although she had a pretty good grasp of numbers and quite a way with sign language. Fearless's French was excellent, and certainly much more adapted than mine to African accents and vocabulary. However, when Fearless was busy, I gradually started doing more and more interpreting for Pippa and others in the group, often thrusting my services on people who probably would have preferred to fend for themselves; but sometimes people actually requested my help, and I was very pleased when they did. I didn't seem to be good at anything else out here. I felt out of place, inadequate, and afraid I'd ultimately be unable to cope. It was nice to feel that, at least in this one way, I played a useful role in the group.

With everything still up in the air, we left Marrakech and headed into the mountains for a two-day trek in the High Atlas. I already knew that five months later I would have the opportunity to climb Mount Kilimanjaro in Tanzania, and I regarded this Atlas trek as forerunner of that thrilling six-day event.

Well, you know, I learned something very important up there on Mount Toubkal, the highest mountain in North Africa: I learned that I absolutely *hate* walking uphill all day long in freezing cold weather, especially when this torture is only relieved by moments of sheer terror when I think I'm going to plunge to my death in some rocky abyss in the middle of nowhere. It was worth learning this about myself before I made the mistake of plunking down over four hundred dollars to spend six whole days of my life this way on Kilimanjaro.

Fearless dropped us off at the village of Imlil, a sad-looking cluster of shops and cafés. This climbing center boasts a hostel or two, but most people apparently press on without stopping long, at least at that time of year. It was cold, and it would get even colder higher up, so I piled on layers of clothing, wriggling awkwardly inside the truck while stone-faced villagers frankly stared.

We met our guides (Mohammed and Hassan), loaded our sleeping bags onto donkeys, picked up our day packs, waved good-bye to Fearless and the truck, and started walking uphill to the Berber village of Arund, where we would spend the night. I have a guidebook to Morocco which says Arund is about an hour's walk from Imlil. But if you're the sort of person who's spent a lot of her recent life munching on Pepperidge Farm cookies while staring at the computer screen and trying to think up an ending to chapter seven, then it takes a little longer.

This same guidebook also mentions how "surprisingly undisturbed" village life remains around there; apparently the writer didn't notice the three dozen children who accost every foreigner in sight, and who beg with an aggression and persistence reminiscent of bull terriers and American politicians. The booty sought (by Berber children, I mean) is invariably a dirham (Moroccan money), a bic (pen), a bonbon, or a *cadeau* (gift).

Upon finally reaching Arund, I was shown into Mohammed's large home, where each guest bedroom had 4-6 couches; the Berbers in this area make a little extra income renting rooms and selling meals to trekkers. I sacked out for a little while before Hassan volunteered to take a few of us on a walk around the village.

You had to respect anyone who could carve a living out of those cold, rocky hills, beautiful though they were. I recalled some passage from *The Seven Pillars of Wisdom* where T.E. Lawrence says that Bedouin ways are hard for those born to them, and a living hell for those who are not; I figured the same could be said about the Berbers. We saw women carrying 25-kilo loads of firewood on their backs, bent so low they almost looked like donkeys. They sang wailingly as they trotted briskly up and down steep, rocky slopes, steadying themselves only occasionally with short, skinny sticks.

I unintentionally created chaos in the village by giving away the only two balloons I had brought with me, thus instigating a violent fight between half a dozen children. The incident left me with a confused feeling of self-disgust which I naively assumed could have been prevented if I'd had the forethought to bring enough balloons for everybody.

The village was small and stony and poor, but the views were beautiful, and the people all looked tough enough to beat the crap out of me. I scrambled around with some of the others for a while before I decided to call it quits and go back to Mohammed's house. I engaged several of my unsuspecting companions in my favorite card game: Oh, Hell! It is also know by such names as Screw Your Buddy and Oh, Shit! It's a mean, ruthless game and I gloated smugly about winning the first round. As night fell, the women of Mohammed's household brought us *tajine* and *couscous* for dinner, which we wolfed down by lantern-light. Then we went to bed early in our chilly, candle-lit rooms.

Quite uncharacteristically, I was one of the first to awaken the next morning. I went outside to a cement water basin whose sides were crusted with ice, and I washed my face and brushed my teeth, really proud of myself for this stupid effort. After breakfast, we separated into two groups – one fast, one slow – and hiked up to the village of Sidi Charamouche (need I even mention which group I chose to go with?) I found the hike sheer hell and felt all the more inadequate when I realized that our courteous guide, Hassan, was making this climb while observing the strict fasting laws of Ramadan; he didn't even drink water. But what really made me feel like a wimp was that while I huffed and puffed and flung myself to the ground for increasingly frequent breaks, he never drew a deep breath, nor even took his hands out of his pockets. Pride demanded that I achieve my goal – reaching the snow line – before breaking for lunch. Being no climber, I was proud of getting just that far without quitting. I slipped in the snow coming back down from Sidi Charamouche, though, and made an uncontrolled descent on my bum for over a dozen yards, while Hassan ran after me, shouting, "Stop! Stop!" as if I was doing this just to vex him.

February 27th:
We awoke early and cold on the road to Agdz, skirting the northern edge of the Sahara. My cough (which started the night after we came down from

Imlil) has gotten worse, my throat hurts, and I want only two things in life: warmth and sleep. Fat chance of either, though.

We may not actually be in the Sahara yet, but it sure feels like desert to *this* Ohio girl. Dust storms, dry rocky mountains, sandy plains, and then – suddenly – the unlikely sight of almond trees blossoming near some little water source.

We stopped for lunch in a flat, barren moonscape. The wind was whipping across the plain so strongly that we couldn't put the drinking cups out, and some of our wash basins blew away.

The wind actually got worse – I'm told it blew a tree over at one point, but I must have been dozing again, with my head down and my blanket pulled over it. A thick red dust, reminiscient of Sicily's *scirocco*, has blown fiercely around us all day. The entire truck, and everything in it, is coated with red dust. Even though I dozed on top of my sunglasses, they, too, were caked with dust when I put them back on. Dust everywhere – hair, skin, mouth, ears, eyes, clothes, cuffs, nose.

Searching for the town of Agdz, we were utterly lost by the end of this dusty day, and threw ourselves upon the mercy of some tiny village we stumbled across. Looking like refugees, we bedded down that night in a schoolroom – a square cement block with three lights and four windows.

Throat aching and chest burning, I wanted only to sit quietly in a corner and read *The Conquest of Morocco*. It, too, proved to be a demoralizing experience. I learned that one of my favorite movies, *The Wind and the Lion*, is wildly inaccurate. Hopelessly romantic, I'd always thought there was some degree of truth in it. But Sean Connery – sorry, I mean the Raisuli – was apparently just a bloodthirsty, ambitious skunk who never even captured *Mrs.* Perdicaris (Candice Bergen), but rather her husband and some other fellow.

Children hung around outside the truck, uttering the usual chants: *Donne-moi un dirham! Donne-moi un bic! Donne-moi un bonbon!* (Give me a dirham, a pen, a sweet!) Or just: *Donne-moi ça!* (Give me that!) This last would refer to anything you were touching, cleaning, carrying, or throwing away. Yes, even garbage. The day before, a group of children had dug up our buried rubbish as we started to drive away. A sobering sight, to see my garbage held up as a trophy, a prized new possession.

Sick, depressed, and disoriented, I wasn't equal to the conversation I was drawn into with some of the locals, young men (for women never approached us in Morocco) who had entered the schoolroom and curiously watched everything we did – cooking, laying down roll mats and sleeping bags, writing in our diaries.

Mohammed (I was starting to suspect that almost every man in Morocco was named Mohammed) and his friends were schoolteachers who were eager to exchange ideas. One of them, also named Mohammed (see what I mean?), was full of tough questions. He wanted my opinions on US policy toward Iraq and Israel. He loved Sadaam Hussein (*"Je l'aime,"* he said) and wanted to know why we were so in favor of the Jews and so opposed to the Arabs. My political ambivalence irritated him, and he wasn't very impressed with my vehement opinions on the whole Salman Rushdie affair, either.

Another of Mohammed's friends (named Hassan, the name parents in Morocco give boys whom they don't name Mohammed) suggested that there would eventually be an all-out war between the Western powers and the Arab world, brought about by the West's insistence upon treating so-called Third World nations as countries without nationality. I had trouble following Hassan's elaboration of this argument, though I thought he had a point.

The first Mohammed was cute and apparently just wanted to practice his French and English; he asked me about sports and other activities in my native city (unfortunately, I know even less about sports than I do about US policies in the Islamic world). However, his friends continued to ask questions which would give even Bill Clinton pause, insisting that I reflect thoroughly and immediately upon any question I claimed to be unable to answer – which was most of them.

The wind howled all night, and for some reason, I kept having to run outside to whizz. Cold and disoriented, I crept barefoot past my sleeping companions several times and let myself out of the schoolroom with a noisy *bang!* that kept waking them. With no idea where I was, and afraid of being unable to find my way back in the dark, I groped my way around walls and gates, relieving myself (I realized the next day) in the middle of the village's main square.

The sun was shining the next morning, as if yesterday's howling cataclysm had never occurred. One of the teachers, sloe-eyed and elegant in his *djellaba,* came into the classroom to wish us godspeed. Pippa decided that, as thanks for his hospitality, it would be fitting to present him with some school supplies we were carrying which had been donated by an English teacher who had once travelled on a Guerba truck. The Moroccan teacher seemed touched by the gift, and it was clear that even such simple items as pens and notebooks were much-needed here. He promised to write to the English teacher, eager to exchange ideas and tell her about life in the Sahara. He hoped to send a symbolic gift to her in England. His French was so clear and elegant that translating was ridiculously easy. For a few moments there, I fantasized that I was a simultaneous interpreter at an important state occasion. We all parted in a spirit of amity and goodwill. I felt all warm and fuzzy inside.

Then a child who had been present throughout the exchange tugged on my sleeve and said, "*Donne-moi un bic!*"

I pointed at a box of pens and snarled in French, "I've just given you thirty. Get lost, kid!"

The young man who beckoned me into a shop in Agdz (which we finally found the next day) didn't look like a white slaver, but when he led me into a little back room with a carpet-covered door, I decided that one can never be too careful, so I summoned Mark and Christine to join me. A Kiwi (New Zealander) couple about my age, they were my cooking partners. The first day of the trip, we had all divided up into teams for the various chores that had to be done on a daily basis. A team of two or three people would wash all the dishes after every meal for a day or two, then cook all the meals for a day or two, then have about a week off from these particular chores.

Mark was really, really tall, but his imposing size was mitigated by his gentle nature. Once, when he and Christine were bargaining for a souvenir, Mark misunderstood the French word *cadeau* (gift) and thought he was being asked to add a "cuddle" to the final payment; he cheerfully plunked down his money and gave the merchant a big hug.

Inside the shop's back room, we exchanged formal introductions with Aziz, a gorgeous young man dressed in flowing blue and white desert robes. He explained in elegant French that I had been approached because I had been observed to speak both English and French in the street; could he impose upon me to write a letter in English to a friend in Germany? I saw no reason why not, so Mark, Christine, and I accepted Aziz's offer of some mint tea. He waved a graceful, be-robed arm and invited us to sit on the carpets.

We chatted amiably for a while, with me translating between Aziz and my Kiwi companions. When asked about his background, Aziz referred to himself as a *café au lait*, explaining that he had a Tuareg mother and a Berber father. As a result of this parentage, he said, he always prepared mint tea in the Tuareg manner. I was to see this elaborate method of making tea performed several more times in southern Morocco, but never more hypnotically or gracefully than it was done that day, in that cheerful little room with carpets lining the floor and walls.

Our host – who really looked like one of my more outlandish adolescent fantasies – first boiled some water in a small teapot on a brazier. Then he poured a little water into a silver teapot, to which he also added tea leaves and bits of some plantlike thing he said was absinthe. I asked about the latter, since I remembered vague, alarming stories about it from one of my French Literature courses in college. The absinthe I had read about was a green liqueur flavored with wormwood, and it apparently drove people (and especially writers) insane if they drank too much of it. I think it was even eventually outlawed in France. For some reason, I associated this information with the half-mad nineteenth century poet Paul Verlaine, who shot his lover Arthur Rimbaud. All in all, the notion of ingesting any absinthe myself made me rather uneasy.

I didn't have to recount any of this garbled recollection to Aziz. My merely asking about the absinthe made him smile knowingly and launch into a cheerful explanation about it; apparently lots of people besides me took French Lit in college. The *small* absinthe, he insisted, promotes good health and fights fatigue. It's the *big* absinthe which is no good for you; using that stuff to make their liqueur is where the French went wrong. As he spoke, he used a knife to shave slivers of absinthe off a raggedy looking little twig which didn't look particularly health-giving to me.

"Okay," I said. When in Rome (or Agdz)...

There was a silver tray with several small glasses set in a semicircle on its shiny surface. He poured some tea into one of the glasses, then back into the pot. Then he poured lots of boiling water into the teapot and put it back on the brazier. Then he poured more tea into a glass. Then he transferred this liquid from one glass to another to another, until it had been in every glass on the tray. With a flourish, he then poured the glass of tea back into the pot and added sugar. A *lot* of sugar.

The tea boiled for a little while longer, and then there was a great deal more of pouring tea from one cup to another, again and again, as gracefully as a ballet dancer, as skillfully as a magician, until this ritual of pouring and re-pouring nearly put me in a trance. As near as I could understand the explanations to my questions about it, it was done for good luck – and good tea.

As he offered us cups of the steaming brew, which was both tangy and syrup-sweet, he spoke at length about a camel caravan he had travelled with all the way to Kenya during his "youth." His family, along with twenty others, had made this incredible journey to find new outlets for trade, and to acquire new goods. I wasn't sure if I believed him, but it was a charming story, and it used to be possible to get from Morocco to Kenya by camel, before political turmoil made such a venture crazier than walking through the Bowery after dark.

Anyhow, Aziz used the story to smoothly segue into pulling out a lot of jewelry and trinkets which he tried to sell us. When I said I had no money with me, he suggested we trade. I politely refused to trade the only valuable possession on my person – a wristwatch which was a gift from friends – and suggested we get down to the business of writing this letter to the friend in Germany. We did, and the letter was an improbable mixture of wishes for the German friend's improved health and questions about a carpet Aziz was apparently holding until he received instructions about its shipment. The letter had to be in English, since the German friend didn't speak French. Since French was Aziz's only European language, I wondered how they had communicated or become "friends" in the first place. When I saw Aziz disinterestedly fold the finished letter and return enthusiastically to the question of trading trinkets with us, I suspected the request to write the letter had merely been a ploy to get me – and my friends – into the shop. Still, it was an *effective* ploy, much better than the strong-arm tactics employed in Marrakech, and certainly more subtle than the urgent invitations one usually received elsewhere. I admired Aziz's ingenuity. And one certainly couldn't fault his hospitality; he had plied us with tea and charming stories and was unfailingly courteous in his attempts to sell or trade goods. I hoped his next letter-writer was more inclined than me to buy souvenirs. He was a nice guy.

We left Agdz and headed south, past M'hamid. We had agreed that since the depressing possibility existed that we'd never get to cross the Sahara after all, it would be a good idea to go and take a look at some real Saharan dunes while we had the chance. We were accosted by "guides" at M'hamid who would give no straight answer to any questions about which direction to go once the road disappeared. Finally, we took one such guide on board to assist us and drove out to the dunes.

I had never seen anything like it, except on the movie screen. We drove into a sea of sand: acres and miles of nothing but rolling, shifting hills and valleys of golden sand. We stopped just before sunset in a remote spot chosen by our guide where – what a coincidence! – a rather elaborate Tuareg tent was already pitched. I wasn't paying much attention, but I believe the tent- owner was a relative of our guide, and I think he had things to sell. I was too busy to care – pitching my tent in shifting sand on a windy winter evening was taking all of my concentration.

I couldn't say I really loved the desert – I love green things and water – but there was something awesome and starkly beautiful about that land of wind, sand, and stars. I found myself humming the theme of *Lawrence of Arabia* as I worked, choking and blinking furiously whenever sand got in my nostrils, throat, teeth, eyes, and ears.

Having played in the dunes, we drove to Zagora the following morning. I enjoyed more mint tea in another shadowy shop. I felt deeply embarrassed when, having urged my hosts to join me in a drink rather than just watch me, they reminded me it was Ramadan. When I put my cup down, though, they urged me to finish my tea, insisting that seeing someone else drink during the day strengthened their resolve and made them strong of heart. Then we engaged in some hard bargaining.

After chewing on and coughing up sand all night long, I had decided to buy a Tuareg veil. Though several other people on the truck had already done so, I had thought I would feel incredibly silly wearing one. But I now realized that it was the most practical headgear for the desert.

The famous indigo-dyed cloth of Tuareg veils stains the skin of Tuareg men's faces with continued wear; hence their nickname, the Blue Men of the desert. Of course, things have changed a lot in recent years, and genuine face-staining, indigo-dyed veils are becoming a rarity. However, my chosen veil was sufficiently indigo-colored to please me, and I felt ready to face another day of wind and sand in southern Morocco after I was shown how to wind it around my head, turban-like, and cover my face with its gauzy folds.

Nevertheless, the bitterly cold winds and my relentless illness – coughing, sore throat, and congestion – demoralized me completely by the time we reached Ouarzazate. The comfortable, elegant hotel at which we stopped for a drink only further depressed me, since it contrasted so painfully with the fragile tent and grubby campsite in which I would spend the night. Only the thought of the local *hammam* kept me going. And, for a little while, as I scrubbed my grimy body in that steamy bath house, I found a little piece of paradise.

We had all agreed, somewhere along the way, that we were willing to gamble that the rumors about the Mauritanian Embassy in Algiers were true, i.e. that they were willingly issuing entry visas; and by now, all other possibilities had failed to pan out.

Our plan, therefore, was to send Fearless to Algiers with our passports to see what he could accomplish. This meant that he still had to get an Algerian visa before he could go to Algiers – and quickly, too, in order not to lose more valuable time. The Algerian Embassy in London could issue a visa in two days, rather than the seven days it would take at the Algerian Embassy in Rabat. However, the attempt to send Fearless's passport to England by special courier had failed. The Moroccan government won't let unaccompanied passports leave the country, so the courier service refused to send it.

Luckily, Fearless then met an English family who were on their way home from their Moroccan vacation. They agreed to take his passport with them; someone from Guerba would meet them at the airport in England and take it straight to the Algerian Embassy in London. After being stamped with an entry visa, it would be sent back to Morocco by overnight courier, enabling Fearless to leave immediately for Algiers.

With the successful completion of this complicated scheme, Fearless packed a bag and parted company with us in Ouarzazate, off to Algeria to see what he could accomplish with this last- ditch effort. Ignoring Moroccan law (and hoping we wouldn't get caught doing so), we sent our passports with him, along with a "we the undersigned" statement permitting him to apply for visas on our behalf.

As we waved him off, I was painfully aware that I couldn't cash traveller's checks or leave Morocco until and unless he returned safely. I was understandably apprehensive. The overland driver who had gone to Cádiz, Spain in an effort to get Mauritanian visas had been held up for two days by the Moroccan authorities when he tried to leave the country with his group's passports. I imagined all sorts of potential problems, even with the passports well-concealed beneath the dirty laundry in Fearless's duffle.

Since there was nothing else we could do but wait, we headed off to Todra Gorge – which had the novelty of being a place I'd actually *expected* to go to while in North Africa. Gold, brown, tan, bronze, and copper-colored cliffs rise high above the rocky paths of the gorge, which are graced by date palms, trickling water, and grazing camels. It was restful there.

Well into the third week of the trip by now, I thought a lot about quitting. I felt lost and directionless, lonely for something or some*one* familiar, and already worn down by the physical conditions I had mistakenly thought I was prepared for. Living outdoors day and night, being constantly on the move, and doing without many of the things I was used to were even harder than I had expected. I wasn't having fun. I wasn't "growing and learning." I was barely hanging onto each day by the skin of my teeth, and I wasn't sure why I had ever thought any of this would be worthwhile.

I reflected on this during the quiet days we spent at Todra Gorge, wondering not only what I would do if I left now, having directed all my financial and personal resources to this journey, but also what I would say to all the people in my life who knew my plans for this year. Pride sometimes moves us more than the supposedly worthier motives of courage and commitment. It was my sheer dread of having to tell anyone that I'd failed that kept me in the saddle during those uncertain days.

While still in Morocco, quitting the trip would be a simple matter of getting dropped off with my duffle at a major town and catching a bus to Casablanca or Marrakech. From there, I could easily fly to England. But I knew that if, by some miracle, Fearless was able to obtain those Mauritanian visas in Algiers, we would be heading into some very remote areas. If we went south into occupied Western Sahara and Mauritania, there would be no turning back. I couldn't reasonably expect to find a good opportunity to leave until we reached Bamako, the capital of Mali, which would be weeks from now. Before Fearless came back, I had to decide for good whether or not I was in for the whole ride.

Not everyone, of course, was responding to all these new experiences the way I was. In fact, my impression at the time was that *no one* was. Mark and Christine certainly remember me being the one who struggled the most (and, alas, the most *vocally*) in those early weeks. And our fellow overlanders looked at me with puzzled frowns once in a while and said, "Why on earth did *you* ever come here?"

We were a mixed bag of people, though some would say I was more mixed than most. There was one other American, one Canadian, one Japanese guy, and the others were all Aussies (Australians), Kiwis (New Zealanders), or Brits. The Aussies and Kiwis called the Brits "Pomes," an old acronym for "*P*risoners *O*f *M*other *E*ngland," which was printed on the clothing of the British convicts transported to Australia so long ago, and which is now flung back in British faces by people who apparently figure their ancestors got the best end of the deal, after all.

Our ages covered nearly a forty year spectrum. The Boys were three English lads who would all be starting university in the fall, while Grace was a 57-year-old Scottish widow. The majority of people were clustered right around my age group, say 25-35. Some had come to see the world, some for the sheer love of travelling, and some, like me, were at a crossroads in their lives. Some had come out of fascination for Africa, while others seemed to have reasons uniquely their own: one person seemed to have come all this way just to get away from family, while another seemed to have come just to get laid.

The only thing I could say we all had in common is that we had each managed to earn, beg, borrow, or steal enough money to make the trip.

Two-thirds of the people on board were only going as far as Nairobi, nineteen weeks away from Gibraltar. A few were going as far as Harare, the capital of Zimbabwe. Two of us would eventually choose to go all the way to the Cape.

At the moment, though, I thought I'd be lucky just to make it from one end of Todra Gorge to the other.

As overland trucks go, the Guerba truck was very comfortable – though it took me some time to fully appreciate this. One of Guerba's fleet of over twenty similar trucks, it was a sturdy four-wheel drive Bedford with technical reinforcements that I never understood at all.

The body was customized. Inside, a series of long cushioned seats lined either side of the truck, facing inward, like a subway train. Our personal lockers – and some of the food lockers – were located beneath these seats. My locker, which contained all of my worldly goods, was about 12" wide, 14" high, and about 30" deep (half of which seemed to be taken up by my medicines and tampons).

There was sort of a long ledge behind both rows of seats, with more storage lockers underneath. Though the roof was solid, the truck was open-sided (with heavy plastic flaps which could be rolled down and secured at night or in inclement weather), offering an unrestricted view of the scenery.

There was a roof seat above the cab. Up to five people could ride up there, and at night it could be arranged into a bed. In front of the roof seat was a huge storage box for tents, roll mats, mosquito nets, and truck equipment. This all belonged to Guerba; I was only required to supply my sleeping bag and personal gear.

Most spare parts for the truck were stored beneath the floorboards in the back, while sleeping bags and day packs were stored overhead on shallow shelves running the length of the truck. Storage compartments were built into the outer sides of the truck to hold large pots and pans, water jerricans, a gas cooker, the long table upon which we prepared meals, and the fire equipment. There were two large diesel fuel tanks toward the front of the truck. Sand mats, used when we got stuck in sand or mud, were fastened to both sides of the body, and heavy tools such as picks, shovels, and axes were fastened to the back.

Almost everything – lockers, tools, storage areas – was secured with padlocks. We were each issued one key, which opened every padlock on the truck. I hadn't remembered to lock my own front door in five years, so I wore my key around my neck as a constant security reminder (and also so I wouldn't lose it).

We entered and exited the truck via a two-part door at the back. The bottom dropped down to provide stairs into the truck. Somewhere near the door there was always an old coffee can with six or eight trowels, the little hand shovels we used to dig a hole behind some bush when we felt the call of nature. Toward the far end of the truck, away from the door, there was a little table which folded up against the wall and could be pulled down to use for writing and card-playing. Directly above this was the library, a cabinet stocked with books.

We began most mornings by taking down our tents, eating a hot breakfast, packing up camp, and hitting the road. After some slow starts, this procedure eventually took about an hour. We'd stop again around midday, for a cold lunch and an hour's break. Then we'd try to make camp somewhere before sunset. We'd put up our tents, cook dinner, clean up, and have a discussion about plans for the following day.

After that, people might sit in the truck, which had internal fluorescent lights which could be used even when the engine wasn't running, and catch up on their diaries, read, or write letters. Others would sit around the dying campfire (which was usually dying because we were running out of firewood).

Personal hygiene, which was extremely important to me in those early days, was carried out in a somewhat time-consuming manner in the bush. In addition to big plastic basins for preparing food or washing dishes, we had small basins for personal washing. We treated the water with Chloromin T, a white powder so powerful that only a tiny match head of it was needed to purify a 25- liter jerrican. Drinking water was unlimited, but water for washing one's person was limited to one small basin per day – and considerably less than that whenever water was hard to get or running low. Hence, despite the warnings of doctors, mothers, and guidebooks, we frequently washed in rivers and streams.

Naturally, there were plenty of chores. I've already mentioned cooking and dishwashing. In addition, everyone had regular daily duties. These included cleaning the truck's interior; packing and unpacking the tents, roll mats, and mosquito nets in the roof box; keeping the food lockers clean; packing and unpacking the folding stools, table, cooking lights, pots, pans, and cooking utensils; and burying the rubbish every day. Two or three firemen rotated the duty of building fires every morning before dawn and every evening as soon as we stopped, as well as collecting and chopping firewood. Unskilled at building fires, afraid of axes and saws, and convinced I'd eventually wind up picking up a snake instead of a piece of firewood, I hadn't even considered volunteering for fire duty. So I wound up cleaning the truck on a regular basis.

When preparing for the trip, I had often wondered about that universal and delicate issue – going to the bathroom. Tramping into the bush and digging a hole in the dark was easy enough to picture, if somewhat daunting, but what would I do during the daytime?

There was a buzzer in the interior of the truck, right next to the door, and a code for using it: one buzz to stop, two to go, and three for a toilet stop. This was how we communicated with the people in the cab (which was big enough for the driver and two others). For three buzzes, the driver would stop when he came to a likely spot – someplace with boulders, trees, bushes, or anything else that might provide a bit of privacy. Although initially shy about buzzing for these toilet stops, practicality eventually overruled Western socialization, and we soon became very casual about buzzing whenever we needed to; and whenever someone had diarrhea, that could be so often that the extra stops threatened to delay our estimated arrival in Nairobi by several weeks.

When I decided to go on this trip, male friends and relatives asked me what I would do about natural disasters, tropical diseases, and political turmoil. Women are more practical and usually concentrate on those things over which they can conceivably have some control; the first question every woman asked was what I would do about tampons. I brought my own, obviously. Enough for at least six months. Laugh if you will, but *every* woman I ever saw loading her gear onto an overland truck had brought a lifetime supply of tampons. The real challenge, which I hadn't fully considered, was finding enough privacy to change one.

One of the more unique customs of daily life on an overland truck was flapping. Our first night on the road, right after dinner, Pippa explained that as the dishes were washed and placed on the drying rack, we would have to pick them up and flap them – wave them around in the air – to dry them. There were too many to let them drip dry, and we couldn't wait that long before packing them up anyhow. And drying them with dish towels was too unsanitary, since the towels got wet and moldy and couldn't be properly washed on the road.

So after every single meal, we lined up at the table, collected dripping dishes, and waved them wildly up and down, rhythmically back and forth, carelessly from side to side until they were dry, repeating the process until all plates, cups, dishes, pots, pans, cutlery, and utensils were clean, dry, and packed away. Over the months, many Moroccans, Malians, Zimbabweans, Ugandans, Tanzanians, and South Africans would watch this insane performance with baffled expressions, wondering what on earth could be the purpose of this energetic ritual. It was deeply weird.

Part of my depression, of course, was due to our lack of momentum. I had already been in Morocco longer than expected and still didn't know when I'd be leaving. We were basically wandering around, killing time. Without meaning to disparage the country, I *really* wanted to leave Morocco. I had always thought of it as being simply "on the way" to where I was going. But now I was starting to feel as if I'd never get anywhere, as if I would instead spend the rest of the year seeing every inch of Morocco. Erfoud, Tafilalt, Tinerhir, Zagora, Ouarzazate... Sure, they were exotic-sounding, but they really weren't making up for what I was increasingly convinced I'd have to miss. I'd wake up every morning, squint at my tent-mate, and ask, "Are we still in Morocco?" And now, as if Fate really had it in for me, we were going back to Marrakech, this time to wait for word from Fearless.

March 7th:

It's no great pleasure to be back in Marrakech. A man just followed me down the street, aggressively pestering me, and then abused me for not responding favorably, when I hadn't encouraged him in the first place.

We met when he jumped into my path shrieking, "Fish and chips! Fish and chips!" For some reason, a number of Moroccan men seem to think this is a surefire conversation opener. What am I supposed to say in reply, I wonder? "Salt and vinegar! Salt and vinegar!"

Anyhow, since I asked several times to be left alone, I don't know why he should feel it his right to—

WAHOOOOOOO!!!!!

Chris just came back from town with a message from Fearless at last. He got the visas! *WE'RE GOING TO MAURITANIA!*

NO MAN'S LAND

I was walking along the road to Essaouira, a southern coastal town in Morocco, when a police car approached me from the opposite direction. Since I was an unusual sight, with my blonde hair, foreign clothes, and crazed-lepidopterist hat, they stopped. One of the four policemen inside the car got out. He looked at me for a moment, then looked up and down the long, empty stretch of road. We were miles from anything except goat herds and olive groves.

Clearly bewildered by my presence here, he asked (in French) where I was going.

I explained that I was traveling with friends. They had stopped to eat lunch along the road, but I had decided to get some exercise and walk on ahead. When they finished lunch, they would recommence their journey in this direction and collect me along the way.

The policeman seemed to think I was lying, or at least nuts. Then, as I had feared would happen ever since Fearless's departure, the cop demanded to see my passport. It was still with Fearless, of course, who was on his way back to Morocco; we were to meet him in Essaouira in a few days and then all head south together. However, considering Moroccan law, I could hardly say that my passport had gone to Algeria without me, so I told the first lie that came into my head: "My passport is in Rabat, at the Ivory Coast Embassy, to get a visa." We had, in fact, left our passports at that embassy for a day when we'd been in Rabat, for that very purpose.

He lectured me about the impropriety of roaming around Morocco without my passport. I said that we had not wanted to waste several days just sitting in the campsite in Rabat. No! We wanted to see as much as possible of this beautiful, wonderful, hospitable country before we left. He looked skeptical and asked more about the truck that I "claimed" would join me within an hour. Realizing that it would look pretty bad if our stories didn't match, I tried hard to discourage him from stopping the truck and questioning the others.

"None of them understands a word of French," I lied. "You'll be wasting your time." In fact, several of group understood some French, and Alison and Sophie spoke it quite proficiently. Still, I babbled on in this vein for a while before the cops finally let me go.

I got a little worried when well over an hour had passed and there was still no sign of the truck. When it finally appeared and Chris stopped to let me on, we exchanged our news. The cops *had* stopped the truck and questioned them, interrogating the people in the cab separately from the people in the back. Everyone pretended not to understand a single word at first. When finally forced to an explanation about the missing passports, they all spontaneously said, "They're in Rabat!"

Chris told the same story in the cab. He even embellished and added, "At the Ivory Coast Embassy. To get visas."

Great minds think alike – and without even planning it. What smooth liars we were becoming. Even so, I was *very* glad to get my hands on my beautiful American passport when Fearless met us in Essaouira.

Essaouira is a lovely coastal town which has been a busy spot since the time of the Phoenicians. Eighteenth century battlements surround the Medina, the Kasbah, and the Mellah, and the dark alleys twist and turn beneath high arches without ever becoming grubby or threatening. More than any place I had ever seen, Essaouira reminded me of tales from *The Arabian Nights*. In the *souk* of the wood carvers, skilled craftsmen turned the rich wood of ebony, acacia, and thuja trees into fabulously beautiful trays, chess boards, boxes, chests, cabinets, and tables, inlaid with shells, mother of pearl, chunks of silver, and strips of copper. The port, where we bargained for fresh fish, was a lively exotic place where men in long robes dickered energetically over piles of fish as they were hauled up onto the docks. There were squirming eels, creeping crabs, long skinny fish that shone like tarnished silver, and plump speckled fish with full lips and lacy fins.

An elderly man approached me in the street one afternoon, politely asked about my health, and introduced himself. He told a sad story about his house burning down recently, then brandished a sealed, addressed envelope under my nose. This was a letter to a relative in America, he said, telling him about this disaster and asking for help. Could I possibly spare a few coins to pay for its postage to the United States? Well, since I had just been to the post office, I gave him a stamp instead. Looking a little perplexed, he thanked me and walked away. Months later I actually read about this man in a guidebook. The author reflects that it's a shame this con-man only approaches most people once, because he has a huge supply of really entertaining stories.

Reunited with Fearless and our passports, we now wasted no time but started heading south immediately (after tracking down Grace, the Scottish widow, who had gotten lost going for a whizz in a vast olive grove outside Essaouira). My ambivalent mood at last changed dramatically as we drove south along the coast for several days. We were finally *going* somewhere now – someplace I had never thought I would go, a place I felt certain I could never have gone on my own. At last, I was in for the whole ride.

The land grew harsher and emptier as we followed the coast south, and the westering sun set nightly over an endless azure sea. We travelled through Agadir and Tiznit, and then stopped in Tan-Tan. We were the first Guerba truck to ever attempt the route through Western Sahara and Mauritania, two of the poorest, emptiest nations in the world. We didn't know what conditions would be like in Mauritania, so it seemed best to prepare for any eventuality. We stopped at many local markets and began stocking up on everything we could conceivably need: food, condiments, fuel, extra jerricans, toiletries, medicine. I also laid in a extra supply of that most essential of Western amenities: chocolate.

March 11th:

We camped on a beach south of Tan-Tan last night, a huge empty expanse of sand between two enormous cliffs, with temperate water rolling into shore and waves crashing against the rocks. The rhythmic roar and murmur of the ocean lulled me into a deep, snug sleep. The climate's getting warmer as we head south (approaching the Tropic of Cancer!) I slept in a T-shirt last night – no trousers, no long johns, no blanket!

I explored the beach this morning and found rockpools with sea anemones, mussel beds, coral, and little fish. Seems like a festival of life after the past month, where I've mostly seen donkeys and camels.

Tan-Tan was a bleak, ugly town of squat cement buildings, sullen people, and many hungry beggars. We're heading south to Dakhla, to join a Moroccan military convoy which will guide us through the landmines between there and the Mauritanian border.

> Sophie commented today that this 10-metre
> wide stretch of road we're following south is now the
> only viable route across the entire Sahara desert, a place
> as big as the US. Try to imagine only *one,* road going
> across the US!

Although this was the only viable route, it was not without its
hazards, as you have probably gathered from the references to
military convoys and landmines.

Western Sahara was a Spanish colony until 1975. Then Spain
withdrew hastily from the region when King Hassan II of Morocco
launched his infamous Green March; 350,000 Moroccan citizens
"reclaimed" the entire region, carving it up between Morocco and
Mauritania. Since then, tens of thousands of Sahrawi people, the native
inhabitants of Western Sahara, have become refugees, making a long,
bloody trek across the desert and into southwest Algeria.

After the Spanish withdrawal, full-scale fighting soon broke out
between the Sahrawi independence movement, known as the Polisario
Front, and Moroccan and Mauritanian troops. Economically crippled
by the war, Mauritania gave up its claim to the area and withdrew in
1979. Morocco promptly occupied this territory, too, and continued
fighting with the Polisario throughout the 1980s. As a defence against
guerrilla raids on Moroccan targets, the Moroccans erected an enormous sand wall, longer than the Great Wall of China, complete with
radar and observation posts, which effectively sealed off most of the
territory.

The Polisario's small poorly supplied army of approximately
15,000 men relied on flagging financial support from the Algerians,
while the Moroccans spent more than one billion dollars per year to
occupy the territory with four-fifths of their national army. Finally, in
September of 1991, both sides signed a United Nations-sponsored
ceasefire agreement and approved arrangements for a referendum on
self-determination.

However, by the time I arrived in Western Sahara in March of
1993, very little actual progress had been made. There was a UN
force of three hundred military observers at Dakhla, and we saw a
few other UN vehicles and officials wandering around the territory, but that was all. None of the other proposed plans had been
enacted yet. One year after the scheduled referendum had failed
to take place, Western Sahara seemed to be an uneasy ceasefire
zone with an uncertain future.

I had never seen such a barren, desolate place. Sandstorms can
blow for ten days at a time across this wasteland of baked stone and

crumbling cliffs. The ground is so poisoned with salt that nothing grows except a few small, twisted shrubs. Centuries ago, the Berbers used the barren estuaries along the coast as salt pans, harvesting this valuable mineral and using it to purchase gold and slaves from the south. Now this rocky coast of sheer cliffs, sudden storms, magnetic anomalies, and unpredictable currents, is known as "the graveyard of sailors." We saw many wrecked ships, some of them enormous, rising above the sea or lying slain along the shore.

We stopped in Laâyoune, the capital of Western Sahara, and stocked up on rice, flour, chick-peas, lentils, oil, raisins, salt, onions, potatoes, fresh vegetables, and as much butter as we thought we could use before it spoiled (two kilos). On an individual basis, we bought biscuits, figs, chocolate, toilet paper, soap, shampoo, and lotion. Pippa launched a search for sugar, which none of the merchants seemed to have. We were just about to give up when we found someone with five kilos of white sugar in baseball-sized chunks, each one as hard as granite. We bought it, figuring we could pulverize or grate it. We also filled all our jerricans at a desalinization plant.

We camped on another seaside cliff that night. Despite everyone's warnings that I was being foolish, I perched my tent right on the edge of the cliff. I wanted to sit in my tent as I watched the sun set over the ocean, then hear the roar of the sea directly below me all night long.

I hadn't counted on the wind. When the wind comes across the Sahara, it gathers force for hundreds of miles. There's nothing out there to stop, soften, or mitigate it. Though I had secured my tent with rocks, the wind blew it over in the middle of the night anyhow, nearly carrying it – and me – straight off the cliff and into infinity. I was on my own, since my tent-mate was guarding the truck that night. I crawled out and ran around wildly in the dark, picking up every rock I could find and plunking it down on my tent. Sharp pebbles and stones stung my bare feet, and I was hideously aware of the many snake holes in that landscape. One guidebook cheerfully warns that the snakes and scorpions there are so deadly that there's really not much you can do to save yourself if you get bitten. The tent nearly blew away twice more during the night, and I dozed uneasily with my body wrapped round one tent pole while the other lay prostrate at my feet.

I confess that I wondered why so many people had spent so long fighting for this land. Presumably it has some strategic importance not immediately apparent to a blonde romance writer from Ohio. More significantly, I learned that Western Sahara has one major export product: phosphates. Apparently the country's phosphate mines are extremely valuable. The war, however, has prevented Morocco from reaping their full financial potential. Nevertheless, there's a 120-kilometer conveyor belt that carries minerals from Bou Craa, in the interior, straight to an enormous processing plant on the sea. The stuff is refined there, then loaded directly onto ships which carry it off to developed countries where it's made into soap, fertilizers, insecticides, and other products. The conveyor belt is so big and important that it's even on the Michelin map, depicted as a thick yellow line which outshines most of the nation's roads. We camped near this thing one night, on a cliff overlooking both the processing plant and a huge ocean freighter which was awaiting its cargo. It might have looked fairly normal in Gary, Indiana, but it looked positively surreal in that otherwise empty moonscape.

I am not a desert-lover, but presumably the Sahrawis are. More than fifty years ago, the French author Antoine de Saint-Exupéry wrote about the people of this nation: "I shall never be able to express clearly whence comes this pleasure men take from aridity, but always and everywhere I have seen men attach themselves more stubbornly to barren land than to any other... The nomads will defend to the death their great store of sand as if it were a treasure of gold dust." Or, as a Polisario fighter said in a 1993 interview with *Africa Report,* "As long as the Moroccans are on our land, we must fight to defend our people and our country."

March 14th:

We've finally reached Dakhla. Weird place. Lots of spanking-new government and administrative buildings, as well as places that look like schools and apartment buildings, line the road to the town. But the town itself is a drab huddle of low, dingy, white buildings which squat here at the edge of the world. Presumably all the spanking-new stuff was built by and for the occupying Moroccans.

Today Pippa and I bought camel meat in the market. People here are more likely to speak Spanish than French, and most likely to speak nothing but Arabic. My Spanish is almost non- existent, and we wound up bargaining in a bizarre combination of French, Spanish, English, and sign language. The meat was bloody and fly-covered and somewhat less than appetizing, but perhaps a barbecue will improve its appearance.

We're camped at the beach several miles out of town for the next three nights. Our papers are said to be in order, so we expect to join Tuesday's southbound convoy which will take us through the landmines to the Mauritanian border.

The wind here is incredible. I've weighted down my tent with veritable boulders, but the wind has blown it over anyhow and torn stake loops off the fly. Actually, the wind was making it flap so much that it was quieter after it fell down on top of me, so I grabbed another hour of sleep.

We filled up those three days with various activities, including searching Dakhla for firewood and bread. We washed our dirty laundry in salt water, then rinsed it sparingly with water from the jerricans. Oh, and remember the overland driver who'd gone back to Spain to get visas? He'd finally succeeded, and his truck (from another company) was camped nearby. Those overlanders must have been overjoyed, since they'd have had to go home if he'd failed. Since Guerba had contracted to pay the flight costs for any portion of our journey which couldn't be completed overland, I'd have had another option (i.e. flying straight to Bamako from Morocco) if we hadn't gotten those visas; but the other group would probably have had to end their journey in Morocco. As it was, we had spent our own money to send Fearless to Algiers, but judged the results well worth the expense. Those other overlanders now joined us around our campfire one night in Dakhla after we'd dined on camel steaks (stringy, tough, and flavorless).

Knowing the opportunity wouldn't come again, half a dozen of us visited the local *hammam* in town. Afterward, as I sat by a public road repairing one of my shoes, a Frenchman drove up in a blue Peugeot and frantically asked if I had seen his wife anywhere in Dakhla. I hadn't. His name was Alain, and he would be in Tuesday's southbound convoy, too – if he could find his wife in time.

Fearless invited one of the UN Military Observers stationed in Dakhla to come out to our camp to explain the UN's role here. His talk was interesting, though his warnings were a trifle alarming. When going south with the Moroccan convoy, he warned, we must *never* stray off the road. The warring factions here had salted this entire region with landmines, and no one knew the location of all the danger zones. In fact, a goat had just been vaporized a few hundred meters away from the UN base.

Right after dinner that night, a Moroccan official came to the beach and ordered us to come to town immediately to execute more formalities – this included presenting our passports and filling out more application forms for passage on the convoy. We reported to a dreary barracks and spent hours waiting around and repeating information over and over to a roomful of soldiers typing slowly on French manual typewriters in the middle of the night. I found the experience so surreal I wondered if I was dreaming. They finally let us go, with orders to be back in time for an early departure the following day.

I slept on the truck that night with Mark and Christine; it was usual for the current cooking crew to also be responsible for sleeping on board and guarding the truck. Mark snored, and I am notoriously intolerant of snoring. It's surprising he's not brain-damaged from all the times I kicked his head in the middle of the night during those months on the road. It was a cold and wildly windy night again, so we strapped down the roll-down sides of the truck, locked up the back door, and curled up on the long seats in our sleeping bags and blankets. I was so excited I didn't think I'd be able to sleep. I mean, convoying through a landmined ceasefire zone in North Africa – this was adventure!

In fact, I slept hard that night and was cranky and groggy (as usual) when Christine woke me up early the next morning to start breakfast for everyone. As ordered, we reported back to the military station right after breakfast, all packed and ready to go. As I would eventually learn to expect in such situations, they then made us sit around and wait for several hours without explanation.

We couldn't stroll away and explore the streets of downtown Dakhla (already known and thoroughly memorized during the past three days, anyhow), because the convoy could theoretically leave at any moment. Consequently, I had a good chance to study our companions on the convoy (in case you've ever wondered what kind of people are this desperate to drive across the Sahara) as we all wandered aimlessly from vehicle to vehicle. There was, of course, the other overland truck. There were also four young German guys travelling in a run-down green VW van with the credo "Afrika Tour '93" painted on its back window. Besides them, there was a German couple on motor cycles. A white Peugeot, which I came to think of as the Kamikaze Mobile, contained a French couple and (it seemed) all their worldly goods. Alain was there, too; he had found his wife. However, their paperwork was evidently not in order, and they were not permitted to go with us. Finally, there were three Italian men in three impressive-looking range rovers.

Considering the UN officer's advice about never leaving the road (which included insisting we answer any call of nature right next to the truck, and not modestly behind a boulder), as well as the fact that we would be travelling with a number of other vehicles, I had wisely had very little tea or water that morning. So I suppose that sheer nerves must explain my frequent need for a whizz throughout the course of the day.

My first emergency was right there in the streets of Dakhla. I approached the military compound and requested permission to use their toilet. In a country where many women don't even show their faces, my private bodily functions had to be discussed by four Moroccan soldiers and reported to their commanding officer before I was given an answer. I was finally told that it was "*interdit*" – forbidden; a fierce foreign female like myself was not allowed access to their facilities, even under armed guard. I made my request at the police station and was again denied. At the risk of holding everyone up, I wandered away from the waiting vehicles and started searching Dakhla for a toilet. The town doesn't boast many shops or coffee houses, and none of the ones I entered had a toilet, or even a hole in the ground, that I could use. Finally, in sheer desperation, I squatted in the dirt of a narrow residential street while one of my fellow overlanders kept a lookout for me. (I think only three total strangers saw me.) For days afterwards, no one seemed to take any of my opinions or suggestions seriously because I was, after all, the sort of person who whizzed in public streets. I was starting to lose my standards.

We all cheered excitedly when, led by a Moroccan military escort, the convoy finally pulled out of town. We might not have bothered cheering, had we known that we would sit for two more hours at a guard station just at the edge of town – for a customs inspection.

Then we drove only a little further before we stopped again, at a check point this time. Bored, I strolled over to the Italians and started chatting (I speak Italian). One of them was middle-aged, the other two fairly young. The youngest one was almost a caricature of an Italian gigolo; he had long curly hair, a red and white striped shirt, designer jeans, black boots, and a jaunty little scarf tied around his neck. He also kept fiddling with his crotch as if his pants were too tight. He vaguely told me he and his buddies were *in giro* – on tour – and had brought three vehicles because it made them feel secure; if one, or even two, broke down, they still wouldn't be stranded. I smiled blandly and nodded. It seemed likely that they were taking the vehicles south to sell them illegally. Though risky, such a scheme can be very profitable in sub-Saharan Africa.

We stopped a few more times during the day until the road finally turned away from the coast along which we had been travelling ever since Essaouira. The sun set, the night grew dark, the wind turned into a gale, and sand obscured our vision and gusted across our path until we could no longer see the road. I started having *Lawrence of Arabia* fantasies again – remember the scene when Peter O'Toole tries to rescue one of his Bedouin servants from quicksand during a sandstorm?

Since this region was off-limits to civilians without a military escort, we had meekly followed a Moroccan military vehicle all day down a clear, well-marked tarmac road in broad daylight. And now, as we struggled though a foot of sand on a road that had virtually disappeared in the dark raging night, the Moroccans decided to abandon us. We had reached the end of the occupied territory and were now entering an unoccupied no man's land which lay between us and the Mauritanian border – a border which still lay an unspecified number of kilometers ahead of us.

The soldiers gave us back our passports, into which our exit visas had been stamped, then waved us off, warning us (surprise, surprise) to stick to the road. "There are landmines," they added gravely. Of course, we couldn't even *see* the road, although little rockpiles (which we could sometimes see if we looked really hard) marked its edges. The ride got rougher, and in the back of the truck we were tossed around as if in a sailboat on stormy seas. The sand grew even deeper, and all of the vehicles, including ours, got stuck. We hopped out and pushed. The sand was so soft and deep, I was amazed our twelve-ton truck was making any progress at all – and not surprised that nobody else was, not even the range rovers. When we eventually reached slightly firmer ground, we stopped for the night.

Pippa and the cooking crew whipped up something for dinner, and we all tumbled into our sleeping bags without bothering to put up tents. Although we'd been warned not to venture off the road, I didn't fancy sleeping in the middle of it. I had this horrible image of the Germans' green van or the Kamikaze Mobile driving over my prone, sand-covered body in the dark. So I dragged my sleeping bag a few meters off the road before bedding down for the night. It was the first time I'd slept out in the open, under the African stars. All the constellations looked wrong, and I realized I was south of the Tropic of Cancer for the first time.

I dreamed it was raining, and for some reason I was standing out in it, getting soaked. I awoke to find it *was* raining. I couldn't believe it. It only rained about three times a year here. Why did it have to pick the one night I had no shelter? I crawled under the truck, where I spent the rest of the night wrapped around the back wheel in exhausted slumber.

March 17th:

This morning we found a rough tarmac road and headed toward the border. After only a few kilometers, we came to a road block. The Mauritanian border officials (i.e., two bored soldiers guarding a rubber and metal obstacle in the sand) took our passports and said we can't proceed until they are sent ahead to Nouâdhibou for approval. They added that our arrival during the final days of Ramadan will slow down the process, so we may be camped here for a week.

It just started raining again.

I couldn't understand why this was happening, since our visas were certainly in order. After having gone to such great lengths to attain them, it seemed insulting that they counted for nothing with the border guards. Fearless had spent days at the Mauritanian Embassy in Algiers, wheedling, cajoling, and arguing (since they, too, had initially refused us visas). In the end, he'd had to visit the embassies of the various nationals on our truck (United Kingdom, Canada, United States, Australia, New Zealand, and Japan) to get letters of recommendation for each of us. Typically, the US Embassy in Algiers refused to give Fearless a letter for me, even after being told that all the other embassies had already done so. Throughout the world, ordinary US citizens rank lower than cockroaches on the unwritten list of State Department priorities. Fearless just kept nagging them until, in the end, they gave him a letter admitting that, according to my passport, I existed. Can I ever thank them enough?

The other vehicles caught up to us by lunchtime and joined our refugee camp deep in the heart of nowhere. Bored, I took a walk back along the way we'd come the night before. For two hours, I didn't see a single thing. No people, animals, or insects. Nothing. Such remoteness never ceased to amaze me. I walked back and was nearing camp when another walker *did* spot something: about fifty landmines, some of them just a few feet off the road.

The guards had warned us not to walk in the dunes on the other side of the road because of the landmines there, but apparently they didn't know about these. The wind had only blown away their cover of sand the night before. Since different warring factions have planted landmines across Western Sahara over the past two decades, no one knows where all of the minefields are. We looked uphill and realized that the things I had vaguely thought were camelpats (as opposed to cowpats) were actually *more* landmines.

I felt a little queasy. It certainly gave the war a whole new reality in my eyes. It made all of us more respectful, too, of all those warnings we'd received. One of those landmines was closer to the road than my sleeping bag had been the night before.

March 18th:

Although we're rationing all washing water (one cup a day for bodies, and as little as is still sanitary for dishes), our jerricans won't last a week. The Mauritanians have promised not to let us die of thirst (what humanitarians). However, they won't let anyone take the truck across the border to fill up at a well. Instead, they've promised to send us a military truck carrying water – *if* they think we need it. I've a shrewd suspicion that their idea of much how much water we need may differ considerably from *my* idea.

Fearless says that the landmines reputedly have a detonation weight of two hundred pounds. He suggests we distribute our weight by crawling.

A handful of vehicles (our truck is on the right) stranded at the Mauritanian border and surrounded by land mines.

THIRSTY IN THE DESERT

When one of the guards finally told us we could leave the following morning, Fearless suggested he just let us go immediately. The guard refused, and they dickered for a while. The guard finally said if we all knelt at the side of the road and prayed to Allah, we could go right away. I thought this was a joke and was disconcerted later to see some of the other refugees actually doing it.

Nonetheless, we weren't released until the following morning. In the end, we'd only been delayed for three days, but with nothing to do, nowhere to go, and so many people around us, it had seemed longer to me, and I was now immensely relieved. The drive to the official border was another trek through heavy sand, and this is where the Kamikaze Mobile really earned its stars, flying madly across patches of sand as if trying to become airborne. Next time I buy a car, I'm going to look into Peugeots.

We were held for several more hours at the next border post, where the guards counted our cash and searched our vehicles. Then we made a beeline for the nearest well, where we filled all our jerricans under the speculative gazes of about forty camels.

We finally convoyed into Nouâdhibou that afternoon, a vast sea of miserable shacks and shanties. The police station, where we were ordered to go, was one of the few permanent structures we saw, along with a couple of anomalies across the street – a very expensive French pastry shop and an express courier service – obviously geared toward the foreigners who had to report to the police station.

Mauritania once enjoyed a lucrative trans-Saharan trade in gold, salt, and slaves between West Africa and the Mahgreb (Morocco, Algeria, and Tunisia), and it was the land from which the Moors (remember them?) initially came north to conquer and rule. But that was centuries ago. Today it's one of the five poorest countries in the world. Crops are only grown in a few oases and along a narrow strip by the Senegal River in the south, and Mauritania currently meets less than 10% of its own food needs. The country has been further impoverished by the war in Western Sahara and disrupted by internal racial problems between blacks and Arabs. And although slavery was finally officially abolished in 1980 in Mauritania, it's estimated that there are, in reality, still tens of thousands of slaves in this country.

The official currency is the ougiya, though I never saw more than a few coins and tattered bills loaned to me by my companions. The banks were all closed for the end of Ramadan, the hotels had no cash, and I had naively told the truth on my money declaration forms, so I didn't want to risk the black market.

The police in Nouâdhibou said we'd need more forms, papers, and stamps before we could go further south, so we camped at a beach outside of town for a couple of days while waiting for them. There were a couple of northbound overland trucks which had been camped there for nearly two weeks, waiting for permission to go north. (Months later, I heard that they never got it, and their trips ended there.) Having come up through Mauritania, they advised us we'd need a guide for the desert crossing from Nouâdhibou to Nouakchott, Mauritania's capital.

> *March 21st:*
> Quite a change from Morocco. Many more people here are black. The women are veiled but leave their faces uncovered. You see the women in public more than in Morocco, too – shopping, working, gossiping, etc. And the women are friendlier and bolder; they look you in the eye, smile, talk to strangers.
>
> Most people here are beautifully dressed, despite the obvious poverty of the country. The women's veils and robes are so bright and colorful, and the flowing yards of cloth in the marketplace are gorgeous. The men wear desert robes in shades of blue and purple, and many of them look fierce and wild.
>
> There are very few private cars, but one sees green taxis *everywhere.*

Our guide Ouenna came highly recommended. A thin, elderly man with a big turban and the high-strung energy of a terrier, he was to see us safely through the desert crossing to Nouakchott once we were allowed to leave Nouâdhibou. The first 3-4 hours of the trip went pretty well, despite the heat. We only had to stop and use the sandmats a couple of times. We had five of them; the long ones were heavy enough that I couldn't lift one by myself, and I'm a strong woman.

Then, just when the day seemed to be going really well, we drove straight into a bog.

I remember a simultaneous sensation of hitting something and sinking. Climbing out of the truck, I saw that we seemed to be sunk about two feet deep into a clay bog. Although I glared at Ouenna, since this is exactly the sort of thing one hires guides to *avoid*, I had to admit that the entire area (except for the part with our truck sinking into it) did look perfectly innocent.

The next twenty hours were pretty grim. When it became apparent we weren't going anywhere anytime soon, Pippa and the cooks started dinner. In yet another attempt to find some way to make camel meat palatable, she ground it up and cooked it in a sweet 'n' sour stew. I threw up halfway through dinner and went straight to bed, determined never to eat camel *or* sweet 'n' sour again as long as I lived.

I felt very guilty when I woke up the next morning and found out that some people (including Pippa) had stayed up till 3:00 am trying to dig out the truck. But it was still right where I had left it. We ate breakfast and got back to work.

De-bogging the truck involved digging out the wheels and axles with shovels, trowels, and hands. Then we jacked it up and put a solid foundation of rocks beneath the wheels, then lay a sandmat over the rocks for traction. Then we pushed it for a foot or two, stopping and recommencing the whole process all over again.

We got the rocks from a little stone hill about a quarter of a mile away. At my tent-mate's suggestion, a couple of the guys took our pick axes over there and turned the hill into a quarry, chopping up the bigger rocks and smaller boulders for our use. We used the plastic wash basins to carry our loads of rocks back to the truck, where we would then pack them into the earth beneath the wheels.

The other overland truck, which had shadowed us ever since Dakhla, drove straight past us, just a few yards away from where our truck lay mired. On their way to Senegal now, they laughed and waved. I said unprintable things.

We cheered wildly when the truck was finally free. Everyone was covered in wet clay, especially one woman who'd gotten stuck beneath the truck at a crucial moment. With water now being conserved for drinking, I scraped the clay off my legs with a trowel and climbed aboard, ready to go.

We did a lot of sandmatting now. When the truck got a little speed going, the overlanders were supposed to snatch up the

Pushing the truck through the Mauritania desert. (Photo by Christine Watson)

sandmats, run ahead of the truck, and throw them beneath the wheels again, keeping kind of a perpetual track underneath the truck. Christine and I made a noble effort, but kept falling down; those sandmats were *heavy*.

We were in serious desert here. Nothing as far as the eye could see. Big sky, lots of sand and rock, and the occasional withered acacia tree. Camel tracks now and then. The interior thermometer read 102 degrees, and the wind was like a baker's oven. It was so dry that my skin soaked up a third of a bottle of lotion one afternoon, and my bladder never even noticed the four liters of water I'd drunk.

This, I thought, was deep in the heart of nowhere. This was the most remote place I had ever been in my life, perhaps the most remote place I would ever go.

It was in this frame of mind that my tent-mate and I pitched our tent several hundred meters from the truck that evening and took off our clothes to have a good wash with our cup of water; who would see, after all?

The French Kamikaze Mobile and the three land-roving Italians all drove up, honking and waving. A little while later, a couple of Mauritanians wandered by to request water, since they were awaiting some repairs on their stranded vehicle.

Some remote.

It felt like a great victory to finally reach Nouakchott, the capital city of Mauritania, after it's having been just a spot on the Michelin map for so long. The ride into town was depressing: hundreds of shanties, overcrowded shacks, stinking garbage dumps, a dead donkey lying in the dirt road. The center of town, however, was a surprise after Nouâdhibou. There were modern buildings, wealthy homes, cars, some paved roads, a few stoplights, pharmacies, and many shops.

We camped at the beach, on the grounds of the Hotel Sabah – a small lodge with a large tent and a few thatched huts – where we had access to an ablutions block. I took my first shower since Todra Gorge, but instead of using the smelly, dirty toilet, I would just sneak behind the dunes with my trowel.

People were celebrating the end of Ramadan, so I went with Alison and our respective tent-mates for a walk along the beach at sunset to see the locals taking a stroll in their holiday glad- rags. We walked past a fine fleet of long, slim fishing boats, all individually painted in bright colors. Many people were out, enjoying the festive atmosphere, swirling the rainbow colors of their beautiful veils and robes. A friendly people with nice manners, they treated us to many smiles and no hassles whatsoever.

A group of teenage girls, so graceful and elegant in their veils and hairpieces and jewelry, thought Alison and I were "*très joliès*" and couldn't understand why we weren't married yet. One of them who didn't even look old enough for a *bat mitzvah* was planning her impending wedding.

That night I experienced the frustrations of travelling with a group. The proprietress of the Hotel Sabah, upon learning from Fearless that there was a woman among us who spoke French, invited me to her office for conversation and a drink (juice, since the Mauritanians are strict Muslims). A charming, well-educated, well-travelled woman of about fifty, she was eager to talk about Mauritania as it is perceived in the West. She insisted that the Mauritanian women have more rights than the women in Morocco, cited state programs founded to teach the illiterate majority of women to read and write, and said there is now a government ministry just for women's problems. She herself is twice-married with five children and owns and runs this hotel. Her husband does not assist or interfere; he has his own business interests. Wearing the veil, she told me, was a matter of choice not necessity.

I felt some skepticism about her blanket statements, since in every country, including my own, a wealthy, educated woman always has more rights – and more ability to invoke them – than a poor, ignorant one. However, she was a fascinating woman and I was deeply frustrated not to be able to accept her invitation to dine with her family Mauritanian style the following evening; we were leaving first thing in the morning.

Later that same night, two Peace Corps workers and a budget officer from the American Embassy joined me by the campfire. After we chatted for a bit, they started issuing invitations for me to come to the American Club and other places where I could meet ex- pats living and working here. I wanted to stay behind for a few days; but since we weren't even sure where we were going, I didn't feel very sanguine about my ability to rendezvous with the truck at a later date.

March 26th:

It's a long way from Nouakchott to here – wherever we are. We completed passport formalities in Timbedgha yesterday, then kept going south. Camped last night amidst mesas and huge boulders. A large herd of camels passed us at sunset, and the new moon after Ramadan rose in the west against a pink sky.

Temperatures here in the Sahel are over 100 degrees by day, and that's in the shade. The sun is so hot it burns the top of my feet *inside* my shoes. Wind, dust, and sand blows so heavily by day, I'm still wearing my Tuareg turban.

More signs of wildlife now – little animal tracks
everywhere I whizz or pitch the tent. And almost all the
people's faces I see are black now. Getting into sub-
Saharan Africa at last.

I was translating for Chris earlier today, and we got
sixty liters of water for free at a well where they usually
sell it. The local teacher explained that these people are
poor but generous and felt obliged to offer us the water
as a gift.

At Koumbi Saleh, we stopped off to see the ruins of what was once
a northern outpost of the great medieval Ghanaian Empire. There's
not a whole lot there in the way of ruins, and apparently no money to
excavate or preserve what *is* there.

The whole village turned out in force to greet us, however. I found
it disconcerting, in such a remote, undeveloped village, to immediately hear the words, *"Donnez-moi un Bic!"* (Give me a Bic!)

After clambering around the ruins, we were invited to meet the
mayor. A group of men guided us into what was apparently the city
hall, a squat, cool, dark, square building with three separate rooms –
a donkey had to be chased out of one of them. They swept out the dung
and dust. We waited for the mayor, but he never showed up. Instead,
these men demanded 10,000 ouguiya (over $20) per person from us
for the privilege of having looked at the ruins. Fearless always kept his
cool in situations like this. He explained that we had no money and
suggested they should make this fee clear before strangers look at the
ruins, not after.

We left in a near-riot of children crying, *"Donnez-moi un Bic!"*

Remember the Tuareg rebels? Well, they were getting pretty
active this far west, too. Or else, some bandits picked up on the
opportunity to get away with highway robbery and blame the Tuaregs.
There's one "major road" going south from Mauritania into Mali.
Tuareg raiders (or their imitators) had begun attacking vehicles so
regularly there that we decided it wouldn't be safe to use it. So we
dropped south farther west, on what was – according to the Michelin
map – a minor road.

When this minor road degenerated into nothing but a faint wheel
mark left by a donkey cart in the middle of the vast Sahel, we realized
we were quite lost.

One of the key differences between the Sahara and the Sahel is
that one occasionally stumbles across family settlements in the Sahel.

They're usually small groups of round thatched huts surrounded by a low fence made of ancient, spindly sticks. The people we saw here travelled by horse or donkey cart, dressed traditionally, and clearly didn't see many strangers. The women wore rings in their noses, the children wore nothing at all, and I saw more than one gloriously indigo-robed man wearing an elegant curved dagger at his waist. I couldn't imagine how these friendly, courteous people eked out a living here. I saw no crops growing and couldn't guess where their water came from.

Sitting in the cab with Fearless, I had by now accepted the fact that the map wasn't corresponding to the vast, empty, trackless reality which stretched before me. We were trying to find Nara, a town somewhere across the border. So every time we stumbled across someone in that endless scrubland, Fearless would stop and ask, "Which way to Nara? How many kilometres?"

People would point and smile encouragingly. When we asked where the road was, they'd point to a dusty patch of ground, which to *their* eyes apparently looked quite different from the dusty patches of ground all around it. The road was rough, and we made frequent stops for sandmatting. The heat was fierce, and we didn't know where we were.

Which way to Nara? How far?

One man told us we must retrace our steps.

"Then go right," the man said, pointing left.

"That's left," Fearless said. "*That's* right."

"Yes, yes! Go right," the man said, pointing left.

I would hate to tell you how long this went on before he finally concluded by telling us to then look for a *grande route* – a major road. We nearly missed it in the end: a dirt track amidst some yellowed blades of grass.

In this haphazard manner, we eventually entered Mali a day before we realized it, and we found Nara the following morning. It's a pleasant, attractive town of broad dirt streets and simple mud buildings with open courtyards. There was a really noticeable change in people here in black Africa; there were so many waves and smiles everywhere we went, so much laughter. And there were women everywhere – working, walking, gossiping, tending market stalls, and sitting in cafés. They were regal, erect, elegant women dressed in bright, flamboyant robes and fabulous turbans, carrying loads on their heads with stately grace. Many of the women were quite fat, and beautiful in their fatness in a manner unknown to Americans. They wore elaborately puffed sleeves and ballooning dresses which emphasized their size, their girth, and the amount of space they were entitled to take up.

The Grand Mosque, the largest mud structure in the world, in Djenné, Mali.

Chris and Pippa got me to translate a little black market money exchange at a local garage so we could stock up on much-needed supplies. I loved the food market in Nara, where cheerful, eager women looked me right in the eye and drove a hard bargain. Beautiful Sicula girls, with big beads woven into their shiny hair, followed us around the marketplace, as did many of the children. There was little or none of the now-familiar demand: "*Donne-moi un bic!*" As we surveyed the produce, I realized with pleasure how much our diet would change now, for here we bought mangoes, pineapples, yams, peanut butter, bananas, and many other typically West African foods, including some which I had never seen before.

We left Nara amidst many warm smiles and friendly waves. I had reached West Africa at last, and I felt truly welcome here.

I was feeling kind of poorly by the time we got to Mali. Dehydration was a problem which would last for several weeks in these hot, arid climes. Having never been out here before, we were urged, warned, and nagged to drink as much water as we could, even more than we wanted to, and to mix salt and sugar into our water once a day. (I prayed fervently that my salt tablets would last long enough to spare me from this revolting practice.)

We were living in hellish heat, and I don't know how Africans can ever accomplish anything in a lifetime spent in that climate.

There was no shade, no breeze, no cool drinks, no cold food, no fans, no air-conditioning, no relief of any kind, in temperatures over 100 degrees every day (and this was not yet the hottest season). The water we carried was as hot as tea by midday, and the purifying chemicals we used on it burned my mouth and throat at that temperature. I began vomiting regularly, and even the smell of our cooking fire made me sick.

If you're wondering how much weight I lost as a result, the answer is: none. So don't ever try to tell me life is fair.

The dirt roads we travelled on blew up clouds of red dust all day long. It lined the shelves and surfaces of the truck, permeated the seats (which we had to take out and beat like carpets at night, to reduce the risk of fleas) and coated every inch of our skin. We perspired a great deal, and instead of evaporating as it had in the desert, our sweat now mixed with the red dust to run down our faces, arms, and legs in runny streaks and broad smears of reddish-brown.

The Malians had built traffic-slowing bumps into their roads, mounds of red earth over which the truck would lurch awkwardly while we braced ourselves against the clammy feel of each other's skin. The bumps were effective speed-reducers, though; Fearless wryly estimated they'd add a week to our trip.

It was only now that I fully realized that I had done it — I had travelled across the Sahara! The first hurdle of my journey was successfully completed.

But I was to face hurdles in West Africa which I had never even imagined.

THE DOGGONE DOGON TREK

You would have to go far to find a more exotic or fascinating country than Mali. Despite the image many Europeans and Americans have of pre-colonial Africa as a wilderness peopled solely by isolated tribes awaiting the dubious blessings of Christianity and Westernization, Mali saw the rise and fall of three powerful and sophisticated native empires long before the French laid claim to it in the nineteenth century.

The Empire of Ghana (no relation to the current nation of Ghana) covered most of modern-day Mali and Senegal, and endured for 500 years before being destroyed in the late 11th century by Berber invaders. Within two centuries, the vast Mandinka Empire arose and grew wealthy on the trans-Saharan trade route. Gold, ivory, kola nuts, and slaves were transported north in exchange for salt – which, believe it or not, was so valuable that the West Africans traded it pound for pound with gold.

The Songhaï Empire arose during the fifteenth century and became even more powerful than the Mandinka Empire had been. It lasted for well over one hundred years, creating a professional army and a civil service with provincial governors. Timbuktu, already an important commercial and intellectual center, grew to over 100,000 citizens (about six times bigger than it is now). This golden age ended when Berber tribes (yes, them again) invaded from the north in the late 16th century. In addition, European ships began competing against the caravan trade routes by sailing down along the African coast, forever ending the heyday of the trans-Saharan trade – and beginning the rise of European dominance in West Africa.

Mali enjoyed brief prosperity after independence in 1960, but bad management exacerbated by periodic droughts whittled away at the

A little girl by the Niger River in Mali.

nation's economy. Mali's history since independence is depressingly similar to that of most other African nations – unsuccessful political and economic experiments, increased population, decreased food production, political instability and violence, riots and massacres – and today it is one of the five poorest countries in the world.

Bamako, Mali's capital, is a bustling, crowded, noisy, colorful, quintessentially African city (despite all the French colonial buildings) with a few tarmac – but mostly dirt – roads. An aggressive but friendly city, it is about to introduce me to a few hard lessons which I will take months to fully digest.

By day, we park the truck outside the Grand Hotel and set up shifts – two people to guard it at all times. After only five minutes, I realize that the Grand Hotel's parking lot is the popular gathering spot of every swaggering, shiftless young man and self-appointed "guide" in the entire city; and they will prove to be a nuisance for the duration of our stay.

Finding a bank is my first priority, since I need to change money. Several of us make our way through town in search of one, smiling at the friendly greetings which so many Malians automatically offer a white stranger. The heat seems to be baking my brains, but the bank we choose is mercifully air-conditioned. Also crowded, noisy, and chaotic. The concept of getting in line (or in a "queue," as my Brit, Aussie, and Kiwi companions call it) is primarily a European one. (And even in Europe it's got its limitations; I never learned to say "line" in Italian since, living in Sicily, I never saw one.)

We fill out the necessary forms, rub elbows with the ever- growing crowd, and – what else? – wait for a long time. Sophie is among the first to finally get her money. When I at last get to the counter, I am told that I will only be allowed to cash my travelers' checks if I can present the sales receipts – i.e. the receipts which American Express carefully instructs all purchasers to always keep separate from the checks (in case you're robbed, you must provide the receipts in order to get a refund).

I explain all this, first to a clerk, and finally to the bank manager. I don't want to walk through the streets of Bamako carrying those receipts. In fact, I'm hot, thirsty, nauseated, and cranky, and I just plain don't want to walk through the streets again. Period. Besides, at least one of my companions simply doesn't *have* those receipts and will be unable to get cash under this policy.

But the real reason I put up such a fight is that, not five minutes ago, Sophie cashed her travellers' checks without having to provide a receipt. And the inconsistency of this drives me *nuts*. I am determined not to endure more bureaucratic irrationality. Not today. So I point out this inconsistency to the bank manager in irritated French.

He denies it.

I point to Sophie, who waves, and repeat my statement.

The bank manager again denies that anyone in the bank has cashed a travellers' check without the sales receipt.

I point to the clerk in question, who is about ten feet away from us. "He's standing right there," I say. I look more closely. "In fact, he's doing it again right now. Just ask him."

"I don't need to ask him," the bank manager says. "Show me this person with the money."

"There she is!" I point again to Sophie, who waves.

Never taking his eyes off my face, the bank manager says, "Show me this person."

"There she *is*," I cry, pointing. "Look!"

"Show me who." He keeps his gaze fixed firmly on me.

I stomp my foot in frustration. "Ask your employee!"

"I don't need to ask him. What you say is impossible."

"Look! Look!" I insist, near tears with frustration. "He's doing it *again*. Right now! Just *ask* him."

I am blatantly ignored as the bank manager strikes up a conversation with someone else about completely unrelated matters and refuses to acknowledge my presence again. I want to throw myself on the floor and weep. Some of the overlanders, apparently alarmed by my mood, suggest we just give in. I babble about the illogic of the bank manager's behavior all the way back to the truck. "He wouldn't even *look* at Sophie! He wouldn't even *ask* his employee!" I will not be consoled or soothed. I want *logic,* order, linear thinking, and I want them *now!*

After digging out the required sales receipts from the nethermost portions of my personal locker, I am followed back to the bank by Alex, a swaggering, smirking, obnoxious young man whom it will take me half the day to get rid of.

There are still more delays when I return to the bank, and I wind up telling another clerk, after another bewildering discussion, that I am a *foreigner,* I don't *know* how things are done here, and she needs to *explain* to me what I must do, not just stare silently at me, waiting for me to do the right things.

This outburst produces a polite procedural explanation of almost military precision, and I wonder how much of the two and a half hours I have spent in the bank could have been eliminated if I'd thought of this approach sooner.

After this unpromising start, I enjoyed a couple of days wandering around Bamako's many lively and colorful markets, ate in public food stalls, sent postcards home, and replaced my decimated sandals with a beautiful pair that rubbed against my feet until they developed painful sores which took weeks to heal (so I shrewdly traded the shoes to Alison).

By night, we camped around the ruins of the Lido, a hotel on the outskirts of town, destroyed by fire during the mass riots of 1991. I slept alone on the second floor veranda of the ruined hotel, surrounded by flowering vines and trees full of singing birds.

At the bottom of the wooded hill, there was a beautiful pond, perfect for swimming, with rocks to dive off of. The little cascades running into it were enough to make me rationalize that this was *moving* water and therefore all right to bathe in (despite my doctor's frequent warnings to the contrary). Hot, dusty, and filthy, I threw caution to the winds and joined half a dozen of my companions swimming in the cool water. It was fabulous!

Then a small group of locals came along. An extremely old man who had no teeth and spoke almost no French warned me that this water had "jabla." I quizzed him, but the language barrier prevented me from learning what "jabla" was. The old man grew increasingly agitated, insisting we *must* get out of the water. The "jabla" was very bad, and several people had died from it – two only last year.

Yes, but what *was* it, I asked. A disease? A crocodile? An evil spirit? Drowning?

I never learned, but the old man's conviction that we would all die as a result of "jabla" convinced us to get out of the water. I spent the next week wondering what I was going to die of, and how soon.

Sadly, my pleasant sojourn in this vivid city with its friendly citizens ended on a very sour note. Alex, the obnoxious young man who'd followed me around my first morning in Bamako, stumbled across me and my tentmate while we were sitting in a café during our last half hour before leaving the city for good.

Uninvited and unwanted, he pulled up a chair and sat next to me, put his face in my face, and put his hand on my bare thigh. I was stunned and furious. Alex accused me of racism for not welcoming his attentions and pursued me down the street, shouting vicious insults about my face, figure, and skin color.

Furious that anyone would treat me this way, and even angrier at my own sense of helplessness – for I couldn't think of any way to deal with him besides *escaping* from him – I returned to the truck feeling upset and exhausted. Another of the young men who perpetually hung out around the truck tried to sell me something and wouldn't go away. When I continued to refuse, he started snarling (in English this time): "Fuck you, fucking shit, fuck your father, fuck you bitch."

March 31st:

These are shiftless young men, without prospects for employment, who pass their time preying on foreigners. Better to remember all the friendly, smiling, bustling, good-natured people who wished me well in Bamako.

We drove all the hot afternoon after that, and camped on the banks of the Niger River – where I did laundry and had a quick swim. Drove all day today. We had a disturbing lunch stop, as the omnipresent children went wild at our rubbish hole, like hungry sharks scenting blood, holding up empty food cans and used band-aids as trophies, gleefully clutching these prizes as they escaped from other small hands clawing and clutching at them.

What a gap separates us – can I understand someone on the other side of such a huge divide?

Camping on the banks of the Bani River tonight. After putting up the tent, I soaked in knee-high water with big, globby, green things floating in it. I was just so *hot!* And tomorrow we will drink that same water, with purifiers in it.

Now I sit outside my tent, writing this while a boy crouches forward, watching my every movement.

A few minutes later, Grace – in response to the eternal "*donne-moi un bic!*" – gave that boy a pen. Holding it in one hand, he came back over to me and started demanding mine. I pointed out that he already had one, that the lady had already given him one. He ignored these objections and kept demanding my pen. He wouldn't go away and he wouldn't shut up. In a fit of vicious ill temper, I took his pen away and gave it back to Grace. (I know, I know.)

She rectified the situation upon realizing that the boy wanted a *blue* bic, like mine, instead of the red one she had given him. Perhaps – I realized – because he'd seen me writing in blue and not red. Confused and ashamed, I turned away.

Can I understand someone on the other side of such a huge divide?

For my sins, I got dreadfully sick the next day, and wouldn't feel well again until after we'd left Mali. Extreme heat, too much sun, nausea and vomiting, headache, dehydration, sunburn, diarrhea, infected sores on my feet... Not surprisingly, I began to again fantasize about leaving the trip, daydreaming about my big bed and my quiet, cool, clean, *private* apartment. I daresay I was not pleasant company.

Djenné, a small mud-brick town in the Niger River Delta, is one of the oldest and most charming cities in West Africa. The porches of the mud and thatch buildings are lined with wooden columns, while the wooden doors and shutters are brightly decorated with paint and metal objects. The two-and-three-story buildings and the narrow streets keep the sun out, making Djenné just about the coolest place I had been since leaving Morocco. Like Timbuktu, Djenné reached its zenith during the 14th and 15th centuries, in the great days of the wealthy trans-Saharan trade.

Djenné has fared better than Timbuktu in recent years, however. Our guide Omar showed us around his city with pride. In order to encourage local crafts and discourage begging, a women's cooperative has been formed where women learn, among other things, to make batik wall-hangings for export and sale to tourists. Skilled male artisans practice centuries-old crafts for which this region is known – including making the huge 14-carat gold *kwotenai kanye*

earrings worn by the wealthiest Peule women. The biggest earrings
are so heavy that the tops must be bound with silk or wool to protect
the ear. (No, you don't see a whole lot of women around here wearing
them anymore.)

Djenné's most famous sight is, of course, the Grande Mosque,
built in 1905 to replace one which had been destroyed in the
nineteenth century. The largest mud structure in the world, it is
considered by many to be the world's best example of Sudanese mud
architecture. (Yes, keeping a mud building from disintegrating during
the rains is a big job.)

I had to leave my companions while they were watching a
silversmith at work; I was due back at the truck for guard duty. Omar
told a boy who'd been assisting him – a son or nephew, perhaps – to
guide me back through the labyrinth of streets. When we neared the
truck, I figured the kid was a real guide and so deserved a real tip. As
soon as I was seen handing him a few coins, we were promptly
attacked in another sharklike feeding frenzy, with children swarming
out of nowhere, scratching me as they scrabbled for the coins, tugging
on me, hitting each other, hitting my young guide – who seemed,
above all, to be afraid Omar would be angry that he'd "let" this happen
to me. The children were so wild that it took another adult – armed
with a stick – to get them off me. If they had been bigger, I'd have been
truly frightened.

As it was, I was just overwhelmed. *Can I understand someone on the
other side of such a huge divide?*

We split up after Djenné. We were headed for Mopti, and Fearless
had spontaneously bargained a good price for transportation there on
local pirogues (dugout canoes) for anyone who was interested. Unfortunately, however, I was feeling so generally awful that I was afraid I'd
be tempted to throw myself overboard if I spent two days in a crowded
pirogue on the river (which would have been more humiliating than
dramatic, anyhow, since I later learned that the river was so shallow
they often had to get out and *push* the pirogues). So I elected to go
to Mopti by truck, as did half a dozen other people were weren't
feeling well.

Mopti was built where the Niger and Bani Rivers flow together,
so river trade is, of course, immensely important to the town. The
waterfront is packed with brightly painted pirogues where all sorts
of people are constantly coming, going, trading, washing clothes,
and bathing.

One of the things that struck me all over West Africa, and
particularly in Mali, was how beautiful the women were. Here, in

one of the poorest nations in the world, it seemed that every woman wore beautiful, brightly colored fabrics sewn into bouffant sleeves, flattering flounces, and delicate pleats. A bright, elaborate turban decorated almost every woman's head. Their teeth – perhaps because of the lack of sugar in their diet? – were usually good, and their skin glowed with vibrancy under the African sun (while mine burned and peeled). They moved with stately, unhurried grace, babies strapped to their backs and heavy loads borne on their heads. I read somewhere that most African women can carry 75-100 pounds on their heads while journeying on foot over distances that would make your average Western health club nut whimper with despair. Having been there, I believe it.

We pulled up at Le Campement, a hotel which permitted us to camp in the yard and, for a fee, use the shower off the barroom. The moment we opened the back door of the truck, I nearly started crying. The back and sides of the truck immediately filled up with young men trying to sell us shirts, cassettes, jewelry, food, drinks, and guide services. From the moment we arrived till the moment we left, I never knew a moment of freedom from them.

> *April 2nd:*
> They are aggressive, like hounds in full cry, like swarming flies. There is no peace, no quiet, no privacy, and no respect here. Poverty has stripped them of dignity or manners; and I find, to my shame, that the sight of so *much* poverty strips me of my compassion.
> Around 9pm, too hot to sleep, Grace and I left the grounds and walked across the square to get something to drink at one of the stalls. Uninvited, two men who'd been hanging around the truck followed us. Losing my cool, I asked if they were criminals. They said no, they just wanted to accompany us. I pointed out that in my experience, men who silently follow women in the dark, uninvited and unwanted, intend them harm.
> They "assisted" us in buying soft drinks, followed us back to the truck, and took our empty bottles back to the vendor. No harm done, but I do *not* feel good will emanating from them. I feel preyed upon. I feel my understanding of courtesy and civility being perverted here.

Remembering how many times I'd already been wrong about things, I couldn't make up my mind about these young men hanging around Le Campement for the next few days, following me everywhere, watching my every move, interrupting my every thought. Then I met Louise, a sophisticated African woman who'd been born in Cameroon but who had been living abroad – mostly in France – for years. Extremely elegant in clothing she had made herself from local fabric, wearing a pair of gold *kwotenai kanye* earrings which suited her perfectly (but which looked bloody silly on me), she spoke excellent French and English, had written professionally, and was apparently involved in the business end of exporting African art and music to Europe. Approaching middle age, she had decided to come back to West Africa to live permanently and was still undecided about where she wanted to settle. And one evening in Mopti, she positively *made* my day:

> One of the obnoxious, intrusive young men who's been hanging out in the courtyard for the past two days swaggered up to our table, threw himself into a chair, and boldly interrupted our conversation with the usual bullshit, in English: "Hey, baby, you want to come dance with me? My name is Jean, I come from New York." And so on.
>
> Louise stared at him. "You have *interrupted* us," she said in English. He smirked at her. "Hey, baby. I'm just trying to share some African culture with you. What's the matter? You no like Africans?"
>
> Well, Louise took him to the carpet! It was a sight to behold. She let loose a furious torrent of French, which he understood much better than English, pointing out that she *is* an African woman, and that he shames himself and other Africans with this rude, obnoxious, disrespectful behavior that creates such a bad impression – interrupting people, insulting them, forcing his presence on them, getting abusive, preying on foreigners.
>
> To my utter delight, he bowed and scraped and apologized "*cent fois*" [one hundred times] again and again under this angry, articulate tongue-lashing from another African.
>
> This incident – and Louise's comments to me about how much she hated the atmosphere here at Le Campement – convinced me that I was right. This horrible behavior *isn't* okay, all right, cool, and "wonderfully African."

This incident didn't straighten out my problems, not by a long shot, but in a way, it was the first step in the long, long process of clearing my head and finding my own way through the wilderness of my confusion. I had been criticizing myself for letting some things (particularly *this* kind of thing) bother me more than it bothered some of my companions. There were even those among them who openly criticized me for feeling the way I did, and I took that hard, feeling I must be "doing it wrong" out here, that I was failing if I didn't respond to my surroundings the way someone *told* me I should respond.

Considering how little I usually care what others think, I guess my mental state is proof of just how *hot* it was in Mali.

In an improved state of mind, I was able to join Grace for a day on the town. A self-appointed guide joined us somewhere along the way and stuck to us like glue, even after I explained that we didn't want a guide and wouldn't tip him. Issa was eighteen (he looked about 13), spoke good French, had nice manners, and made it quite clear that he didn't expect a *cadeau* for accompanying us. (And our own manners dictated that we buy him a soft drink whenever we stopped for one, which was several times due to the heat.)

After a visit to the market (wherein, as one of the few shoppers present that day, I was pleasantly and ruthlessly charmed into buying a beautiful terra-cotta and silver necklace for about $20), we took a little pirogue ride, getting out at various points to see a Bozo fishing village, a Fulani encampment, and an abandoned Tuareg village where the Bella, their former slaves (I was told), now live. All the activity on the river as we floated up and down, all the different peoples, the Bamabara music blasting out across the water from some local club's loudspeakers... I once again felt like I was in a movie.

Then the rest of the gang arrived, full of tales about pushing the pirogues halfway to Mopti. They'd seen several snakes, and one even swam right between Chris's legs. Although they seemed to have had a fine old time, that final detail made me glad I hadn't joined them. I *hate* snakes. Me and Indiana Jones.

We headed off to Dogon country, which I found both exciting and disappointing. Although far off the beaten path and living a National Geographic life-style, the Dogons have by now been visited by many thousands of tourists, and the effects show everywhere.

A great deal has been written about the Dogon people, and if you're interested, I suggest you check out the experts rather than rely on me. Basically, the Dogons were animists who, around 1300 AD, started building their villages in the Bandiagara cliffs — yes, in the *cliffs* — to avoid be conquered and converted by Moslems.

Inevitably, lots of Dogons did convert to Islam (or even Christianity) over the years, and many of them now live back down on the ground. Even in those cases, however, they still keep small granaries and a few huts up in the cliffs. Their way of life, their agricultural system, their religious ceremonies, and their art are all the subject of much study and commentary. Being smart people, they quickly figured out that there's profit to be made in thousands of Europeans trekking into their country every year.

A few of us were invited to sleep on the flat roof of the chief's house that first night, awkwardly climbing up a "ladder" made out of a tree trunk; when I saw the *twig* I was supposed to shimmy up with my bedroll, I nearly chickened out – but pride pushed me onward. It was a nice night, actually, if rather noisy; with the moon nearly full now, this country was bright at night, so people stayed up later – as did the goats and chickens – talking and playing music.

Our guide, a half Dogon fellow with the improbable name of Pygmy, and his assistant Omar were tireless about accommodating our different needs and requests. Some energetic souls wanted to hike night and day; *some* of us would rather have jumped off one of those cliffs. So Alison and I joined a late morning (i.e. 6:00 am) hike to Yabatolu, where Pygmy showed us the Justice Shelter, with 8 pillars representing the first 8 Dogons; the ceiling is low to help you keep your cool during an argument – if you jump up, you hit your head. We climbed the cliffs up to a water source which dripped through the rocks; ignoring everything I had read and everything my doctor had told me, I fell upon it greedily, drinking all I could, filling my (by now empty) water bottle, and splashing my face. One thing I may have forgotten to mention is that Dogon country is undoubtedly the hottest place on earth.

We climbed higher then to visit an abandoned Dogon village, where there were living quarters, women's storage houses, the chief's hut, and so on. It seemed like a museum display, though Pygmy insisted that it wasn't well-preserved. No, indeed; the well-preserved villages were farther away. With the temperature now well above 110 degrees Fahrenheit and my water bottle once again empty, I concluded that I'd just have to forego some experiences and started staggering back to camp. My memory of that day is quite dazed and fragmented, although I do recall coming across Alison at one point, resting despondently under a twig that some local people might consider a tree. I snarled at her to get up and keep going, then continued to plod along without waiting to see if she did, afraid that if I stopped I wouldn't start again. She later told me that if I hadn't come along then, she might *still* be sitting under that tree, withered and mummified.

April 5th:

Since arriving, we have been constantly surrounded by children trying to sell or trade whistles,
rattles, and slingshots; staring, giggling, and grabbing. But mostly, they keep up a constant chant of,
"Madame? Madame? Cadeau? Cadeau?" and cry,
"Donne-moi ça!" [Give me that!] every time you touch
something.

They come to my tent and stare in while I'm
sleeping or changing (asking for gifts the whole while).
They stopped seeming like children to me after about
twenty minutes of this and now seem more like flies.

I don't like this intolerant reaction in myself,
especially not when some people, like Grace, deal so
patiently with it and make friends with one or two of
the children.

Even Grace's patience wore out in the end, though. I told an
older boy who kept following me around that I was fed up with all
of this. He promised me the children would all go home if we gave
them bonbons. Recognizing a true wheeler-dealer, I tried not to
laugh. But when I translated his answer for Grace, she told me, her
Scottish accent thicker than usual, that she had no intention of
giving in to such blackmail.

Living on Nuprin, salt tablets, and hot, chlorinated water, my
heat-stunned thoughts raced ahead to the Ivory Coast. Surely it
would be green and leafy there? Surely there would be more for
shade than the occasional dying twig? Surely it would rain, and I
could go dance naked in it?

INVISIBLE ELEPHANTS AND EVIL SPIRITS

The bored border guard said he'd let us cross quickly from Mali into the Ivory Coast, provided we could do something about his toothache. One of the overlanders donated a bottle of clove oil to the cause, and across the border we went. Within a hundred yards, the dirt road suddenly ended, to be replaced by a new, good, black, tarmac road with a white line running down the center. The best road I'd seen in all of Africa.

Suddenly there were cool drinks (*cool* drinks!) to be had, and even a little ice cream, if you were willing to pay about $3 for a mass-produced drumstick. We drove into greener and greener country – flowering plants, wildlife, big trees dripping with golden mangoes, noisy crickets, fluttering insects, deep grass, leafy bushes. It rained (*rained!*) twice in two days.

We picked up a guide for a day in Korhoga. He wore polyester pants and a silly hat and kept repeating that we were in "*deep* Ah-fri-ka now." I thought he was either drunk or having flashbacks to the '60s. He offered some very confused chatter about fetishism and animism, got incoherently fixated on totems for a while, and created an awkward situation when he took us into villagers' homes without their permission – or else without having paid them what they considered enough. He was a government-qualified guide, but I thought he seemed more like an unemployed game-show host.

Poor by any European standards, with a nose-diving economy, an enormous foreign debt, and a reckless destruction of the rainforests which threatens the environment, the Ivory Coast is still, along with Ghana, one of the two wealthiest countries in West Africa. It was certainly the wealthiest place I'd seen in quite a while, and the things

A village weaver in the Ivory Coast.

I wouldn't have noticed had I flown here straight from Europe were the things which now struck me like a slap in the face: vast agricultural plantations, paved roads, electricity, heavy industry, indoor plumbing, and cafés serving French pastries. Yes, there were still plenty of traditional villages, thatched roofs, dirt roads, and barefooted women on their way to market with a baby strapped to their backs and a load balanced on their heads – but those were normal sights by now.

We drove south to Yamoussoukro, President Houphouët-Boigny's hometown, where he built the Basilique de Notre Dame de la Paix (more or less a modern imitation of St. Peter's in Rome) at a cost of some $300,000,000. Big enough to seat about 7,000 worshippers, its annual maintenance costs over $1,000,000 (in a country where the annual per capita income is considerably less than $1,000).

It was pretty empty when I was there. Just a few other Europeans and some flies.

D'Azagny National Park, we were told by one of its representatives, was one of the few places in West Africa which could boast big game. We were assured of finding hippo and elephant in this seldom-visited park which lay well off the beaten path. It sounded good to us, so we decided to give it a whirl. We sought permission at a local village to camp overnight on their soccer field, planning to set out at dawn the next morning.

The village apparently got few or no tourists. The people all gathered around to watch us, but only a few of the children asked for *cadeaux*, and *no one* asked for a Bic. They all just seemed curious, interested, surprised, shy, and amused. I traded a brightly-colored Moroccan scarf for a necklace of seeds and beads that one of the young girls was wearing. It was an altogether friendly place.

On hot nights like this, many of us would often forego pitching a tent and instead hang a mosquito net from a tree or off the side of the truck. A dozen or so locals watched me with riveted fascination as I laid out my roll mat and sleeping bag beside the truck and tucked the mosquito net around my bedding. Convinced that while they obviously found *this* really interesting, watching me sleep was bound to be pretty dull, I climbed into bed, secured the mosquito netting, and closed my eyes, confident that they'd all go away now.

A half hour later, they were all still watching me with unblinking interest. It finally dawned on me that when you've got no television, no local cinema, no books, and no café or nightclubs, then watching a strange blonde woman from halfway around the world sleep inside this bizarre contraption she had set up probably *was* pretty interesting. So interesting, in fact, that it was worth staying up all night to watch.

Fortunately, at Fearless's request, the chief came along and insisted that they all call it a night and go home.

I awoke at 5am to find one of the overlanders peering down at me, chirping "wakie-wakie" in a thick Australian accent. I lashed out at him but got tangled up in my mosquito net.

The ride into D'Azagny took us down an endless, narrow track of road with branches slapping the sides of the truck and dropping red ants on us, causing screeches of "ant alert" to echo down the truck as we beat them to death with shoes, the broom, the woven fan I'd purchased in Korhoga, and our bare hands. We finally arrived at an abandoned lodge area of thatched round huts – all deserted and overgrown. Our guide claimed this desertion was temporary. "The pump broke," he explained. Personally, I thought it looked more like there'd been an H-bomb mishap.

We climbed out of the truck, and – following our guide like lambs to the slaughter – we then proceeded to hike some 12 kilometers through the tropical jungle in the heat of the day. We saw a lot of ants. We saw some mosquitoes. Saw a praying mantis. Got really excited at one point when we saw a millipede.

"Where are the elephants? Where are the hippos?"

"Oh, they're on the island," the guide said.

"What island?"

Crossing the bridge in D'Azagny Nationl Park, Ivory Coast.

"Well, there's an island, and we have to cross a lagoon to get there."

"Lagoon" and "swamp" are not synonymous, but language barriers are so confusing, aren't they? The swamp was vast, overgrown, and distinctly primeval looking – so, by the way, was the bridge. Almost a kilometer long, it was a narrow, winding plank bridge of hills, gullies, and suspicious-looking gaps, surrounded by swamp, trees, and tumbling palm leaves. It was so weak that we were instructed to cross it in groups of no more than five people at a time, being sure to maintain a distance of at least 50 meters between each group.

"They had better be very *big* elephants," I said. Then I fell through the bridge. I jumped and flailed so well that only my toes got wet, but everyone in the swamp heard my curses.

While waiting around at one point for the group ahead of us to finish crossing a particularly tricky stretch, Sophie got curious about the swamp's depth, which we assumed to be one or two feet. She measured it with a twig, but was unable to find the bottom. So I took the long, fallen branch of a palm tree and started lowering it into the swamp. Six feet... Eight feet... Ten feet... My branch disappeared and sank without a trace. I heard one of the planks snap in the distance.

No, I won't keep you in suspense. I'm not that mean. No one died in the swamp, and there were no hippos or elephants on the island. In fact, the most interesting sight on the island was watching Fearless squeeze half a gallon of sweat out of his T- shirt after we had hiked for another hour.

Once or twice the guide pointed at the mud and cried, "Elephant footprint!" just to keep us interested. But since there were no tracks, no elephant droppings, no broken tree branches, and nothing that seemed to have been eaten lately, I remained unconvinced – which offended him. He was the African guide, after all; I was just some blonde chick from Ohio. So I made much over the next millipede we found and agreed it was a shame that we never saw the invisible elephants.

My first letter from home arrived in Abidjan, the bustling capital city of the Ivory Coast. Motherly love is an amazing thing, since my mother wrote me at every *poste restante* address I had in Africa, and I know that she *hates* to write letters. My father (a science fiction writer who, like any professional writer, loves writing letters because it's a good way to be seen sitting at one's desk without actually having to work on the current book) wrote often, too, but his first letter went astray. Mom writes in swirling, ballooning, overlapping cursive, on *both* sides of sheets of see-through airmail paper, so it took me half a day to interpret her missive, especially since the tropical rain got to it while I was carrying it to the truck.

While the West African heat melted my flesh, Mom's letter explained that she hadn't been able to check inside my apartment for a couple of weeks because the locks were frozen. At least, she assured me, I could count on no one *else* being able to get in there, either. At the time she wrote the letter (some six weeks before I received it), my native Midwest was under nearly a foot of snow. Sweat mingled with rain on my skin as I caught up on family news.

Camped outside of vast, sweltering, urban Abidjan, we stayed at a quiet little campsite on the beach called the Waves of Vridi. Jean, the courteous proprietor, gave me an avocado from his plantation out in the country, where he and his family hoped to open a big campground.

My tentmate and I left the fly sheet off the tent that evening, hoping to catch a good breeze in the hot night as we stretched out naked atop our sleeping bags. Evelyn awoke when it started raining, but saw me sleeping peacefully by the back window and decided not to wake me. Some time later, I woke up drenched and, not being as kindhearted as Evelyn, kicked her awake. But the rain suddenly started coming down too hard for us to go out and put on the fly. Thunder, lightening, wind, torrential rain! Our tent starting flooding as rain poured through the screen at the back. My roll mat became a surfboard. We decided to abandon the tent. All our clothes were hanging out on the washline, and we had nothing to wear; and the campground, alas, was not a private place like the bush.

We wrapped ourselves in our sleeping sheets, held our roll mats over our heads, and ran barefoot to the door of the refreshments room. It was locked. *All* the doors at Vridi were locked tonight. Finally, clutching the remnants of our drenched, battered sheets and mats, we ran clear across the campground to the truck and pounded on the backdoor until the cooks let us in. I lay on the floor half the night, listening to rain and snoring, and remembering those oven-like days in Mali as my hair dripped cold beads of water down my skin.

Although the vast, bustling markets of Treichville, an area of Abidjan, are well worth visiting (and I was rather curious to see Africa's only ice skating rink, also located in Abidjan), we were really in the nation's capital to get more visas. Some people have expressed surprise that I didn't simply get all my visas before leaving the States. I might have, if we knew where we were going and when we would get there – which, of course, we did not.

In addition to having completely changed our proposed route across the Sahara, we still remained uncertain about whether or not we'd be able to enter Togo or Zaïre, both of which were still in a state of unrest. Aside from these uncertainties, we travelled at a pace determined by circumstances. Although we had a definite arrival date scheduled for Nairobi, we always had roughly two weeks leeway in our daily schedule; as long as we didn't seem to be too far behind where we vaguely "ought" to be, there was nothing to worry about.

Also, many African visas expire within a short period of time, so you've got to time your entry and exit into the country rather well. Benin's standard tourist visa, for example, is only valid for forty-eight hours. And although (as instructed by my American booking agent) I had gotten a visa for Cameroon prior to leaving home, I had already learned that it would expire before we ever reached Cameroon, meaning I was going to have to pay for another one.

We had now reached the point at which we *must* decide whether or not we were going to Togo; and if not, how we would continue our journey. Since finding a ferry to take the truck from Ghana to Benin was apparently impossible (like so many things in Africa), our only option seemed to be to spend a week driving north around Togo and through Burkina Faso, yet another of the world's five poorest countries (which also has the world's highest incidence of river blindness, a disease which has so afflicted the country that whole riverside villages have been evacuated because of it). Like everyone else, I had decided I'd prefer to go through Togo unless someone could convince me it was too dangerous.

The Economist, in an article printed just as I departed for Africa, referred to Togo as "Zaïre in miniature," which did not seem very encouraging. President Eyadéma, after a yearlong terror campaign against his political opponents, had regained his lost power in 1992. Though his northern tribe, the Kabyé, were a minority in Togo, accounting for less than 15% of the total population, they made up two thirds of the army and filled most government posts. Togo's majority tribes, the Mina and the Ewé in the south, hated Eyadéma – who, in turn, hated opposition. By the beginning of 1993, hundreds of people in this tiny country had already died in political violence, and thousands of people were fleeing across the borders into the neighboring countries of Ghana and Benin.

In January of 1993, Togolese security forces shot and killed 17 pro-democracy protesters in Lomé, the capital city. Less than a week later, 6 more people were killed during political riots. Another (estimated) 25,000 people fled the country by the end of the month. Then in late March, as we contemplated entering the country, gunmen raided the presidential compound in Lomé. President Eyadéma, often compared to Zaïre's President Mobutu (no, the comparison is not intended to be a flattering one), was unharmed, but his military chief of staff lay among the dead by the time the attack was over.

In response to the unrest, Ghana placed its military forces on alert. The Ghanaians insisted they had no intention of attacking

Togo, were only guarding against "any Togolese adventurism," and simply intended to assist Togolese refugees. Eyadéma, however, accused Ghana of "intolerable interference," "provocation," and deliberately attempting to destabilize Togo. Adding to this tension was the knowledge that Ghana's President Jerry Rawlings is a member of the Ewé tribe that dominates the south of Togo. (As you may already know, the political borders in Africa are a European legacy which generally ignore tribal boundaries.) Such ingredients frequently cook up wars here.

I was nonetheless counting on the general theory that, with a few exceptions, Africans don't want to kill Europeans, who are seen as being outside of their political and tribal conflicts, and who are a source of money, after all. Anyhow, every statistic I've ever read suggests that I'm a lot more likely to get shot in my own gun-happy country than almost anywhere else on earth. While the genuine Europeans travelling with me (all whites are referred to as Europeans in Africa, regardless of nationality) couldn't bolster their resolve with these grim reflections, they were nonetheless all intent upon maintaining our intended route.

However, a bewildering variety of responses met any inquiry about entering Togo. The British Embassy in Accra (Ghana's capital) said they didn't know the situation, despite the fact that "the situation" was roughly 100 miles from their door. The French Embassy in Abidjan said we could indeed go, but added helpfully that it wasn't safe. The Ghanaian Embassy in Abidjan said we couldn't go. Period.

In the end, we decided to go ahead and get those Togolese visas, and just see what happened when we finally reached the border. Meanwhile, we also needed visas for Ghana, the country which lay between us and Togo. The Ghanaian Embassy in Abidjan only did visa business on Mondays, Wednesdays, and Fridays. When asked if we could drop our passports and visa applications off on Tuesday and then pick them up Friday, the embassy officials responded with an emphatic negative. Visas could *only* be submitted or collected on Mondays, Wednesdays, and Fridays. Period. (So who says *I* was the only person in West Africa who needed to develop a little flexibility?)

We had better things to do with our time than sit around the country's sprawling capital waiting three days for visas. So Fearless stayed behind while we went into the hinterlands. And, as was always the case if he or Chris separated from the group to get visas or deal with other dull bureaucratic matters which we didn't feel like waiting around for, we covered his expenses for the duration.

I felt rather sorry for him, because not only was Abidjan hot, crowded, expensive, and rather unattractive, but we were heading for a wonderful adventure.

The annual Festival of Dipri takes place in Gomon, a small village north of Abidjan. Fearless had been to this festival once before and, realizing that this was about the right time of year, had made tireless inquiries ever since crossing the border from Mali to find out if we were in time to attend. Happily, we were; and with Fearless left behind in Abidjan, I now wound up doing most of the talking, French being the *lingua franca* (and official language) of the Ivory Coast.

Once a year the people of Gomon hold a 24-hour festival to chase evil spirits out of their village. The village must be sealed off for the rituals to work. Therefore, if you are in the village at the start of the festival, you may not leave; and if you are outside, you may not enter. Consequently, we were under some pressure to find Gomon before sunset, and neither the village nor the road leading to it were on our map. Sitting in the hot cab with Chris, I kept asking locals for directions once we were in the general area to which Fearless had directed us. Finally, while rolling down a little dirt lane in the bush, we came across a group of young men who, with broad smiles and cheerful conversation, assured us we were in the right place.

We found Gomon's soccer field (it seemed to me that every village in West Africa had a soccer field), and most of the overlanders began setting up camp while a small group of us went to seek permission to stay here and attend the festival. Every section of the sprawling village had its own *chef du quartier* (neighborhood chief), and we were obliged to visit (so it seemed) every single one of them. The rest of the afternoon was pleasant but rather confusing, since part of the festivities included the consumption of liquid hallucinogens (for lack of a better term), and everyone I encountered was feeling no pain. After greeting the various *chefs du quartier*, we must then find the *chef du village* to get permission to stay for the festival. Our self-appointed guide, whose name I took to be Nali (though I was never quite sure about this), insisted there was plenty of time to find the chief. Meanwhile, we wandered from house to house (many of which Nali claimed he owned) meeting people.

European languages were adopted as the official languages of African countries upon gaining independence since they (in theory) provided linguistic unity within a country's borders, free of tribal rivalry. Few Africans speak the European language at home, however,

A man stabs himself in the belly for the Festival of Dipri. Gomon, Ivory Coast.

and many never learn it. Since French is neither my first language nor the first language of anyone I met in North, West, or Central Africa, I was often uncertain about what was being said. And since Nali and all of my hosts were stoned out of their minds, I was even more confused than usual. Fortunately, the general gist of every conversation seemed to be that I, my chief (as I introduced Chris to everyone), and our friends were all welcome here and that the locals were thrilled to death that we had come in time for the festival.

In one of the family compounds (small buildings and shelters surrounding a beaten-earth yard), Nali introduced me to his mother. She and a bald man of about 35 were drinking some muddy-looking liquid from a calabash. I would be frankly shocked to ever see *my* mother as thoroughly wasted as Nali's was. As I approached them, urged on by Nali, the bald man seemed to have a hallucination and started shouting wildly at me. Since he looked like a heavyweight boxer, I think my panic was natural.

When he finally calmed down, he decided that Chris and I should drink some of the muddy liquid in the calabash. We declined. As he grew more insistent and his friends and family joined in the chorus, I ruthlessly tried to shift all responsibility for this onto Chris; but since they couldn't understand him, they focused on me as the target of their hospitality. Several of the men started to get angry as I, politely and with increasing desperation, kept resisting their "when in Rome" arguments. I didn't really mind the thought of seeing evil spirits rise from the ground, but the risk of intestinal parasites was enough to make me do some fast talking to get out of that one. I'd already drunk a fair amount of pretty disgusting, off-color, earthy stuff in Africa, but at least it had always had Chloramine T in it.

Mercifully, just when it seemed my hosts intended to force the stuff on me, everyone got distracted, and Nali fuzzily decided it was time to go onto the next *chef's* domain. We seemed to wander aimlessly for a while, taking a lot of long-cuts (rather than shortcuts). Recognizing a marshmallow when he saw one, Nali held Mark's hand; I was getting so tired of his conversation I'd have bitten him if he'd tried to hold mine. He didn't urge me again to drink anything, but he was very insistent that, rather than camping out at the soccer field, we should all camp at his house. I pointed out that there were too many of us.

"Besides," I added, seeing that this didn't compute, "my friends have already set up their tents and started cooking dinner."

This didn't compute, either.

We finally found a large pavilion where a group of sophisticated-looking university students from Abidjan were attending an academic lecture about the significance of the customs they would observe during the next 24 hours.

The *chef du village* turned up at that point. About 40 years old, muscular and squarely built, quite handsome and very dignified, he was traditionally dressed, with a colorful swath of material draped diagonally across his bare chest and trailing over his shoulder. He greeted us warmly and apologized for not having met us sooner. He graciously granted us permission to camp on the soccer field and observe the festival. He welcomed us, assured us we were at liberty to go wherever we wanted, and invited us to make ourselves at home here. He assigned a still-sober villager to see us back to our camp, then left us to go speak to the university students. He was, as Chris later said, "very chief-like" in every way.

Back at camp, Pippa had already had to string a rope around our small camp area, so thick were the crowds of children surrounding the truck and tents. Being children, they were mischievous and immensely curious, so much so that one of the chiefs decided to assign an elderly villager to roam around our camp and make sure the children stayed behind the rope. As Evelyn pointed out, the rope kept us in more than it kept the children out, and it seemed rather unfriendly; however, there didn't seem to be a reasonable alternative, short of letting a hundred children climb into the truck and tents for the next two days.

Nali turned up that night, even vaguer and more pupil-dilated than he'd been that afternoon. He'd come to lead us to his house, where we were all persistently and blearily invited to camp for the night. Since I was the interpreter, the other overlanders maliciously left *me* to deal with him. I finally told Nali that this was a democracy, and I couldn't possibly accept his invitation without holding a palaver with my friends, half of whom were wandering around the village at the moment. I made sure I was already in bed by the time he came back again.

Gomon must be one of the nicest villages in all of Africa. Not only was there no begging whatsoever the whole time I was there, but everyone greeted me, wherever I went, with such warmth and generosity that I was overwhelmed by the genuine goodness permeating the town. Although the festival began in the middle of the night and continued all day, we were never alone at our camp in the soccer field. While guarding the truck, I finally asked some of the children why they preferred watching us to watching the thrilling events of the festival.

"We are *Christians*," I was told with great dignity. Several children explained to me in strong terms that they do *not* participate in the festival. Like Jews at Christmas, they were making do while the whole village closed down for a festival which was not their own; and on such a day, what could be more interesting than a truckload of Europeans performing strange tasks in the soccer field? I had noticed several Christian churches while wandering around the village and wondered how much of the population had converted and whether this brought any tension to the community.

I observed no tension today, however, and will long remember the Festival of Dipri as one of the most vivid, exciting days of my life. The drums began to pound before sunrise, excitement permeated the air, and the chief called out to his people to chase away the evil as the sun rose.

April 14th:

I went into the village with Alison and Jenny after breakfast. There were many people observing the festivities – sitting on their porches, lining the streets, crowding into the public squares. There was a pavilion set up for dignitaries, full of well-dressed, prosperous-looking people. A lot of outsiders came to observe the festival, but we saw only a couple of other Europeans the whole day. There was also a marquis set up for mourners. We saw framed photos of the dead, and occasionally a woman would appear, carrying a photo and singing a mourning song.

There were large groups of men and women jogging around the village, carrying little spears and singing melodic, festive songs. There were big drums placed every so often along the dirt streets, and there were percussion groups set up in the public squares. With all the continual drumming and singing everywhere I went, it was quite a musical festival – it sounded like a movie soundtrack.

Everyone was dressed in white, and most people had painted themselves with white clay. Their eyes were fogged and glazed as they ran around, danced wildly, rolled on the ground, and squirmed in the red dust, their eyes rolling back in their heads as they writhed in spirit trances. Some people tore their clothes off as they danced. One very fat woman ripped off her blouse and ran around the main square in a hot-pink bra before falling to the ground and rolling in the dirt as she shrieked and babbled.

Men bit the heads off chickens and sprayed the blood on each other. Jenny swears she saw one man whizz into his hands and then drink his own urine. Another man swallowed an egg and passed it whole. Tradition has it that women at the festival cook eggs and bananas in their hands, though I never saw this.

The main event, of course, are the Sékékponé, a specially trained society of men who plunge knives into their bellies. Real knives, real blood. The wounds are flesh wounds, not disemboweling wounds, but it's still very impressive to watch. They stalk the village, full of passion and power, frequently stopping to rapidly inflict a series of shallow belly wounds on themselves. Their white shorts soak up the blood in vivid red stains. One man knelt before another and ecstatically drank the blood dripping down his belly.

I asked someone yesterday to explain the festival to me. After group consultation, I was finally told that I would understand when I *saw* it, that explaining it would do no good. Still baffled, I sought out some Ivoirian students who've come home to Gomon for today's festival, and I asked them to tell me what they could about it.

The stabbing, the students said, is to show power. It's not easy, they assured me (in case I had thought otherwise), not everyone can do it. *"Il faut demander permission aux vieux"*: you must ask permission of the old ones. I quizzed them and gathered that by "old ones" they meant ancestors or spirits. Anyhow, if you forget to ask, or if you're refused permission and do it anyhow, then you'll get hurt. (So don't try this at home.) If you have permission and power, then you can do it without getting hurt. In this way, the Sékékponé demonstrate their spiritual power.

There's also a question of shoes, the girls explained to me. Closed shoes protect your feet well, but sandals or bare feet make it possible for spirits from the ground to enter your body via your feet. Whether or not you wear shoes is an individual choice, they assured me; but this explained why several people had already advised me to wear my boots during the festival. And here I thought they were just worried about me getting muddy.

The festival ends when evil is conquered for another year and the witch doctor, dressed in all his impressive finery, comes out to bless the village toward sunset. Guarding the truck, Alison and I fell asleep in the stifling heat and missed this part of the festival, to my eternal regret.

While I was still guarding the truck, it started pissing down rain. Having abandoned the formality of the dividing rope as a lost cause, I huddled underneath the truck with a dozen Christian children waiting for the storm to pass, and getting dripped on the whole time. Afterwards, I couldn't find my boots (soft, ankle-high hiking shoes with deep treads). Good shoes are immensely valuable all over Africa, and remembering what the girls had told me about the additional spiritual protection they provided in Gomon, I feared they had been stolen. I started asking around and soon had cause to regret my momentary lapse of trust in these people; one of the children slid under the truck and retrieved my boots from one of the deep crevices behind the cab. While I was dozing during the rain storm, the children had been afraid that my boots, which were getting dripped on, would be damaged, so they'd hidden them in a dry place for me.

There was a village soirée that night to celebrate the successful conclusion of the festival. The village's two tiny discos blared music out onto the streets, where people milled around, ate, drank, and offered a smile to everyone they encountered. It was like Independence Day in some fabled Midwestern town where everyone still knows everyone and no one remains a stranger for long.

The next morning, Chris and I sought out the ever-busy *chef du village* to thank him for his hospitality. He, in turn, thanked us for coming to Gomon, invited us to come again someday, and expressed hope that God would care for us on our way to our next destination. Amidst many waves and smiles, we pulled out of Gomon and hit the road again.

After collecting Fearless and our passports in Abidjan, we stopped for a few days in Grand Bassam. The original French colonial capital, it's sort of a crumbling resort town now, a ghostly, half-abandoned remnant of a bygone era. Though we bobbed around in the sea for a bit, I had no intention of doing any real swimming here. The entire West African Coast is awash with dangerous currents and strong undertows. Six people had reportedly drowned in Grand Bassam just this month, and someone else was killed in the water beside our camp in Abidjan.

The heat was so intense that even the Ivoirians complained about it. I kept throwing up, and Grace became quite ill. The French couple who owned the little inn in whose garden we camped were very kind, giving Grace medicine and a cool room for free, giving me cold (and normally expensive) bottles of filtered water when I got sick. The Frenchwoman had been a Red Cross nurse in Ethiopia for a couple of years before coming to West Africa a quarter of a century ago. She talked at length about how heart- breaking it was to work in African hospitals: no money, medicine, supplies, staff, or support.

Interesting and warmhearted people, she and her husband had a ten-year-old African daughter whom they had found in the streets some three years earlier. To their great pleasure and relief, the adoption papers would be final in another five months.

Our final morning before leaving Grand Bassam for Ghana was spent at the local police station.

April 18th:

We woke up to discover there'd been a thief in the night. Sophie and Sue were sleeping in the truck. The thief crept in – apparently over the open sides – and took their sleeping bags (which were still rolled up, but had been placed to hold down the edges of the mosquito nets). The thief also took Sue's daypack, which had been resting between Sophie and Sue's heads as they lay stretched out on the floor (which is cooler at night than the seats). Sophie is amazed they slept through this, especially as she was awake most of the night scratching mosquito bites.

IF THIS IS THURSDAY, IT MUST BE BENIN

We made quite a hit at the Ghanaian border since Becki, one of the more eccentric overlanders, had shaved her head in Grand Bassam one night, leaving only a little mohawk running down the center of her skull. Although the French lady who owned the inn in Grand Bassam didn't think the style flattered Becki, the Ghanaian border guards *loved* it and quickly ushered us into their country. Passage through a police check point somewhere up the road cost one bic.

If you ever go to Africa, I recommend that you bring about 500 bic pens with you. Sometimes they're valued as a totem of Western education or a symbol of Western prosperity; the further into Africa you go, the more they're actually used in place of money, as if they were the cowrie shells or trade beads of another century. Bics bought us good will from border guards, armed police patrols, and scowling bureaucrats more times than I could count; as our journey progressed, we would eventually start trading them for food.

The main thing anyone should remember about bics, though, is not to give one away for nothing. Indeed, having travelled up and down the continent for almost 8 months, I firmly believe that very few things should be given away for nothing. More than our wealth, it is the longtime European habit of flinging a handful of bics — or candy or foreign aid — at a crowd of Africans that has convinced many of them that all food, money, and material wealth must come from Europeans, that they themselves should do nothing more than wait for the eternal handouts which have been the primary Western response to a continent struggling with the aftermath of a century of colonialism.

If you're like me, you were taught virtually nothing about Africa in school. This isn't the place to count on filling in those gaps in your education, but books like Thomas Pakenham's colonial history *The Scramble for Africa*, Blaine Harden's *Africa*, David Lamb's *The Africans*, and Patrick Marnham's *Dispatches From Africa* – to name just a bare few – are a good place to start if you really want to know why Africa is the way it is.

For now, it's enough to know that the colonial powers (mainly France, England, Belgium, and Portugal), upon withdrawing from Africa, left behind a bureaucracy which they had always ensured too few Africans were sufficiently educated to manage, national boundaries which didn't reflect the ethnic populations (can you say "Yugoslavia"?), and economic systems which remained reliant upon European good will.

Since that time, and often with good intentions, the ex-colonial powers have generally botched almost every effort to rectify matters. In addition, the entire continent was a hideous casualty of the Cold War, wherein the USA and USSR rushed in to make up for all the time they'd lost by not participating in the colonial era.

The end result is an entire continent on the brink of or already in the midst of economic, physical, environmental, social, and spiritual disaster. If I had to describe an entire continent of roughly one billion people – a ridiculous exercise, and one which I am frequently asked to perform for the benefit of people who will never get to go there or who don't even want to read about it – I'd say that most Africans are pretty likeable, as patient as Job, quite courteous, and fairly shrewd. And too many of them think that they're supposed to get whatever they need, now and forever, from foreign aid, religious charities, and Europeans' handouts.

I'm no bleeding heart liberal who thinks we must, come hell or highwater (and hell seems to be what's coming), make up for the injuries of the past. Nor am I smug cynic who figures Africans are a lot of lazy beggars who should be left to sink or swim. I can't imagine what the answer is to Africa's many and truly overwhelming problems; I've just become convinced that the so-called experts who've been busy making a botch of it for thirty years don't know, either. The saying about teaching a man to fish as opposed to simply *giving* him a fish has never been more true anywhere in the world than it is in Africa today.

Mort Rosenblum and Doug Williamson's *Squandering Eden* offers a few dozen mortifying examples of where the post-colonial era's good (and not so good) intentions have led us and the Africans – down that well-paved road to a destination that would make midday in Mali seem cool. There are also some positive examples cited in the book, and the authors try to point out alternate roads to a new future in Africa. Fortunately, there are those among the new generation of African leaders who know that, ultimately, it's up to the Africans. As Nigerian statesman Olusagen Obasanjo said: "I believe that for us in Africa, our salvation lies in our own hands and nowhere else."

Ghana, in 1957, was the first black African country to gain independence, and they remain understandably proud of this. Unfortunately, 25 years of political and economic corruption and decline followed independence. Finally, in 1979, a young officer named Jerry Rawlings led a military coup, executed three former heads of state, and staged elections. Then, keeping his promise, Rawlings relinquished his power. Dissatisfied with the direction of the new government, the enormously popular Rawlings staged *another* coup in 1981 – and stayed in power this time. As complex and contradictory as any African leader, Rawlings led Ghana toward economic recovery, and it was one of the two most prosperous nations in West Africa when I arrived in April of 1993.

The two names commonly applied to this part of the world – the Gold Coast and the Slave Coast – tell you what interested the Europeans powers in this region. The Portuguese began building forts here in the fifteenth century as they searched for gold, but they soon found that trading human flesh was even more profitable. The British, Dutch, and Danish soon entered the competition, and Africans were bought, branded, and loaded onto European slave ships for the next 250 years. It occurred to the British, sometime in the early 19th century, that maybe this wasn't such a Christian thing to do after all, and they finally outlawed slavery. My own country, of course, would take several decades and a civil war to follow suit. Among the legacies of the slave trade are some 75 European castles and forts slowly decaying along the coast in the damp heat of West Africa.

Ghana was the first country we had been to where English was the *lingua franca*. I compensated for the heat and my bad temper by telling Pippa I had done more than my fair share of marketing and bargaining, and I wouldn't go shopping with her in this country, not even when it was my turn. We'd had an embarrassing scene in Grand Bassam over a misunderstanding with a fishseller that wasn't even my fault (and after which I had promptly thrown up again), and I was currently feeling rather snappish about the whole notion of marketing.

Meanwhile, listening to spoken English in Ghana for a whole week vindicated me (at least in my mind) for all the conversations I'd had trouble following in French-speaking Africa; the accent, syntax, and vocabulary in Ghana were so different from American, British, or Aussie English that, despite its being my native language, I still had trouble understanding what was going on.

While certain British legacies were easily apparent in Ghana – language, cheddar cheese, brown sandwich bread, stark white ice cream squares, and roundabouts on the roads – I thought the missionaries seemed to have had the most startling effect. Religious pop music blared out of every tin-roofed, shoebox-size store, and the business names made me feel we'd taken the wrong road off the last roundabout and somehow wound up in the Bible Belt. A few of my favorites: God Will Help Auto Repairs; For Christ's Sake Electricians; The God Is Beauty Beauty Salon; In Him Motors; Peace and Love Hair Care; and the Not I But Jesus Fashion Center.

Public buses, taxis, and "bush" taxis are how many Africans get around (most of the rest walk). The mottos painted on Ghana's buses and taxis were less original than the shop names, but equally heartfelt: God's Time Is the Best Time; God Is Love; God Is King; and (on a dissenting note, I suppose) Jesus Is King. Bumper stickers encouraged us with messages like: "Don't give up, your miracle is on the way!" and "The devil has lost the battle!"

Since we never saw this kind of wild enthusiasm in the French speaking countries largely dominated by Catholic missions, I had to assume that Protestant missionaries just had the pithiest sayings. Born to a Jewish-Catholic marriage, I have always thought I had enough to contend with without delving into the intimidating array of Protestant worship.

Accra is a sprawling city of well over one million citizens. Most people there seemed bold, eager to talk, proud, and full of ideas; many of them seemed well-educated, most of them seemed busy, and there was very little begging here. It was a lively, bustling, often chaotic city. Chris had a habit of driving around roundabouts for so long that I once suggested we just put a tent up in the middle until he made up his mind, but the roads *were* confusing around the capital.

Out in the countryside, the roads were lined with the usual foot traffic of Africa (women with babies on their backs and loads on their heads), and the occasional fast-food stop. Fast-food African style, that is: roasting grasshoppers, rodents, duikers, and monkeys. Duikers are cute-as-hell little antelope. It was the monkeys that upset me, though. There was something about seeing a cooked primate that I found instinctively frightening. (A strict vegetarian, Alison was upset by all of these sights, but kept her own counsel and stayed out of sight.)

There was a public phone and fax station near our campsite outside Accra, and so I was able to call my parents (after several abortive attempts) and catch up on family news in a shouting, overlapping, round-the-world conversation. It was good to hear their voices, good to hear that family, friends, and apartment were all fine, and a relief to be able to tell them I was fine, too, since I didn't know how often my letters reached them. Ghana, my father had taken pains to inform me months earlier, was one of those places where they could legally lock me up for no reason and refuse to tell the American Embassy anything about me (as if the American Embassy would even bother to ask). I encountered no serious ill-feeling there, and certainly no threats of that nature; but I would have to say that Ghana wasn't a particularly lucky country for me.

We camped along the beaches most nights in Ghana. One morning, Sue and I decided to walk to the old slave trading fort at Elmina, which we could see about a mile distant on the coast. The beach there, which looked so lovely when we started out, is actually one vast public toilet. It was covered with feces and diarrhea end-to-end, not to mention a whole lot of garbage. We stumbled across at least a dozen men along the way who were each having a morning dump (a very unhealthy-looking one, to be as vague as possible about it), and we definitely seemed to be more embarrassed than any of them.

The slave forts, of which we saw a couple that week, are very sobering. At Elmina, I forgot about the sewage-laden beach as a courteous and articulate guide spent an hour or so leading us through the centuries-old castle. I think these visits were especially evocative for Alison, whose forbearers were shipped to Jamaica from one of these coastal forts, and whose great-great- great-grandmother may well have been one of the young women paraded forth on a walkway above a courtyard, where "civilized Christian white men" would nightly choose the prettiest ones to deflower. While the dungeons, holdings areas, and execution areas were all chilling, I was most forcibly struck by the chapels in these forts; buy and sell human beings Monday through Saturday, then go to chapel piously on Sunday to ensure your place in heaven. Go figure.

By the time we reached Kumasi, the ancient seat of the Ashanti kings (who were, by the way, great slavers who were quite annoyed with the British for outlawing the trade), my adventures in Ghana had produced crippling stomach cramps and simultaneous vomiting and diarrhea. The vomit was a green bile that smelled positively poisonous, and you'd close the book in disgust right now if I described the other. The symptoms reached their height that night. We were camping in some kind of state park set aside for traditional crafts workshops, musicians, and cultural activities. By day, it was a fascinating place. By night, we were warned not to go alone to the toilet blocks, a 5-10 minute walk away. Even if I'd felt like waking up grumpy overlanders half a dozen times that night, I could never have made the walk. I took a trowel from the truck and picked a spot behind one of the crafts shops, about fifty yards from my tent; I dug half a dozen holes there and used them periodically that night, vomiting at the same time – all in full view of several vagrants spending the night in the vicinity. On one occasion, I didn't even make it all the way to my spot.

It was quite possibly the most horrible night of my life. By morning, I was weak, drained, and demoralized. I lay under a tree and waited to die. Pippa – who's a nurse when she's not overlanding – gave me some stuff to help with the nausea, and I dosed myself up with all the stuff my doctor had prescribed for diarrhea. Yes, I thought longingly of home, of my bed, of air- conditioning, of cold water that didn't taste of earth or Chloramine T. But I realized that I had come too far to give up now, no matter how much I wanted to stay under that tree until I died. Besides, I wasn't the only one in this condition. Living so communally, we often tended to get the same illness from the same source, or else contract things from each other. So while I whined and complained and lay around in what I was sure were my death throes, I was well aware that a couple of my companions were suffering identical problems.

Illness was very hard on the road. Although we would pick up the slack for each other (camp chores like cooking, washing up, cleaning the truck, chopping wood, and building fires, as well as pushing the truck through mud, changing money, erecting tents, and so on), conditions were very uncomfortable for someone who was ill. We continued our pace, lived outdoors, and relied solely upon our own medicine chest and common sense – one seldom wants to deal with the medical facilities in much of Africa, for precisely the reasons described by the French innkeeper at Grand Bassam.

The sick stopped the truck as often as they needed to, were allocated enough space on the dusty seats to nap all day, and only did what work they felt equal to. Whatever had gotten into my system was now trying to get out just as fast and unceremoniously as possible, and I remember almost nothing of fabled Kumasi, or of approaching the notorious Togolese border.

But even after my stomach and intestines returned to normal, another vexing health problem continued to worry me: tropical ulcers.

When I first heard about tropical ulcers, I freaked out. I was in Mauritania and met a girl coming north on an overland truck that had come through the tropics. She had odd, round, shiny scars on her legs and arms. Being a shameless overlander full of vulgar curiosity and increasingly devoid of social graces, I asked what had caused those scars.

"Tropical ulcers," she said, and explained what they were.

I spent the next four nights sitting wide awake and freaking out while Evelyn slept peacefully. Alison and I would repeat what the girl had told us, feeding each other's horror about what awaited us in the tropics. Mark once tried to soothe me by saying I shouldn't pay too much attention to what the girl said because she had struck him as a sissy.

"But, Mark, *I'm* a sissy!" I cried, and returned to my fretting.

A tropical ulcer usually begins when you get a break in the skin: a simple mosquito bite, for example. I'm lucky in that insects don't like me much; someone once told me it may be because of my cool skin temperature (which makes me miserable in cold weather). However, I am quite clumsy; I kept falling down or walking into things, and I'd break my skin open that way.

Then, because it's always so hot and so *damp* in West and Central Africa, the cut can't dry out enough to heal. Imagine how long it would take a sore to heal if you kept it immersed in water all of the time. Moreover, there's bacteria everywhere in such a climate, particularly if you're living rough. Soon the cut becomes a gaping sore. The sore becomes increasingly infected, oozing puss and icky stuff (that's the technical term). No matter what you do, the sore keeps getting bigger and deeper and more infected, going through layers of flesh, sometimes down to the bone.

So, I hear you ask with bated breath, how do you treat these sores?

The antiseptic creams in our various personal first aid kits had failed to combat the problem (remember: you've got to find a way to *dry out* the sores in a constantly wet environment, so putting cream on them defeats the purpose). Then Fearless one day announced that there was "too much puss on this truck," and decided to do something about it.

Well, the first time I saw Fearless treat someone's sores, I literally ran away from camp so he couldn't get his hands on me, too, because he had this big Aussie guy screaming like a girl. (Have I mentioned that the sores are incredibly painful and sensitive?) You scrub them out till they bleed. You make them bleed in an effort to get rid of the infection. You do this every day with a stiff brush and any mildly antiseptic liquid (soap and treated water, if you can't find anything else). And if you have anything in your medical kit that you haven't already tried and found utterly ineffective, you slap it on there. When the sores heal over, as one of mine did, you have to cut open the skin and scrape the whole thing out, because often the surface will *appear* to be healed while the infection continues well below the surface, and this is very bad news. I used a penknife I'd stuck in the fire to cut mine open.

Yes! *Me!*

After running away that first time, I realized that the pain would be preferable to having my leg fall off, so I started scrubbing my sores every day. As absolutely disgusting and painful as it all sounds, the funny thing is that – like anything else – you get completely used to it after a while. I had these things on my legs for six weeks (at one point I had a couple that were so big the pain made me limp and my companions dubbed me "Woman of the Festering Leg"), and there eventually came a time when I scrubbed them out and treated them with no more thought than you'd give to filing your nails. No matter who you are, no matter what your normal life is like, you would do the same. Trust me on this.

Just as I was among the first to get tropical ulcers, I was the very first to be completely cured of them, too. You know what finally worked? Listerine! I found a bottle in Ghana, when I was looking (in vain) for some kind of antiseptic. Figured what-the-hell and started applying it to my sores. They cleared up in less than a month. Moreover, the Listerine helped a few other people's sores clear up, and it prevented me from ever getting any more. Many months and several thousand kilometers later, when the nights grew blustery again, my Listerine even stopped a few people's colds and sore throats before they could develop into anything serious. *Great stuff!* I'm never again leaving home without it.

By the way, these sores are not to be underestimated. One girl got so covered in them that she couldn't even sleep because of the pain during our last week before reaching Nairobi. Not even antibiotic shots and pills cleared it up, and her ever-multiplying sores wept copiously. She was covered in cotton bandages day and night, with puss running down her arms and legs. She wasn't finally well until more than three months after returning home. (I should add this is unlikely to happen to just anyone; the sores are much worse if you don't tend them assiduously as soon as they start appearing).

Of course, painful ugly sores aren't the worst thing you can get out there. There's Guinea Worm, for example, which can be carried in the water in some places (and which none of us, thank God, ever got). I met a Peace Corps worker, though, who was afraid she had it and was on her way to be tested. Really gross stuff! This worm is very thin and grows very long, up to a meter, inside your body. It finally emerges through a blister on the skin. Then you have to spend days (up to a month!) twining it around a matchstick bit by bit to remove it from your body. If you break it, it can rot inside you and (I was vehemently assured) kill you.

I'm not making this up.

Then, of course, there's bilharzia (snail fever), a disease caused by tiny blood flukes. My doctor warned me not to go anywhere near untreated water, not to even let it splash on my skin, as bilharzia can painlessly bore through unbroken skin. Depending upon where the blood flukes take up residence and lay their eggs, bilharzia can cause anything from malnourishment to painful death, and they can do it rather quickly or spend years debilitating you. There is no vaccine, and a safe, effective treatment was only developed recently. The vast Lake Victoria is lousy with bilharzia; when it comes to the larger bodies of water out there, most people know whether or not they carry bilharzia. We, however, spent months stumbling across obscure creeks, ponds, and swamps. I was pretty religious about not touching the water for the first month or so, but I lost all my principles (and sense, some would say) when the temperature skyrocketed, water for washing became unavailable, and I could either jump in a river or remain hot and filthy. If there was little water for washing bodies, then there was even less for washing clothes, and we relied on rivers for that, too. Still, I seem to have survived.

And when the challenges of nature seemed to awful too dwell upon, there were always the political problems to consider.

Upon finally reaching the Togolese border, the Rubicon of our West African sojourn, it turned out that the Togolese *were* letting people in via the Togo-Ghana border; the Ghanaians just didn't want to let people *out*. Nevertheless, for reasons which still elude me, we were allowed through – and were immediately accosted by black-marketers on the other side. The truck drove across the border, but for some reason, we had to *walk* across. Black-marketers shoved fistfuls of West African francs into my face, while customs officials watched impassively, ready to pounce on me if I made a transaction. Made vaguely uneasy by the immigration officials who repeatedly urged me not to be afraid, I entered the country.

I noticed that Lomé, the capital city, seemed rather empty; I've since read that nearly half of the city's population of 600,000 had fled since the beginning of the year. (Am I perceptive, or *what?*)

> April 24th:
> A city of grand, impressive French colonial build-ings and polished gardens, Lomé is nonetheless strange today. Pippa says it seems like a "refugee" city. It makes me think of Brixton [a poor district of London near which I used to live] after the riots. You can tell that something's not right here. All the banks and nearly all the shops are closed. The market is operating,

but there aren't many customers. I also notice the ratio of fresh fruit and vegetables compared to other goods (fabric, shoes, batteries) seems very low. Has transport from the countryside been disrupted?

We've been warned repeatedly about bandits – armed, dangerous, bold, and ruthless – and heard numerous stories of theft. Certainly one has the sense of law and order on the wane here. Indeed, I've so far seen only one soldier in all of Lomé, which seems very strange after more than two months of seeing armed soldiers everywhere I go. In fact, we dragged this soldier over to settle a market dispute after a fruitseller refused to give Pippa her change.

Bandits roam the beaches, and the owners of our beach campsite have pointed out the local bandits to us. We've been warned to keep all valuables locked in the truck, to leave nothing in our tents, to go nowhere alone, and not to talk to strangers.

Others in the group have said they feel uncomfortable. I can't say I feel "threatened," as the Togolese I've spoken with here all seem friendly. I am aware of the tension, though – which doesn't involve me but which could conceivably overcome me. Also, the vigilance required here could become very wearing, except that we can't stay long. As is typical of Togolese tourist visas, ours only last for 72 hours.

Meanwhile, our local bandits occasionally forget to be menacing. Mark organized a tug-of-war game on the beach this afternoon – the Brits against the rest of us. The bandits drew closer, wondering what we were up to. They cheered wildly during our first two matches, and got so caught up in the third one that one of them joined me on the rope when I was losing ground.

Though I went to the post office for my *poste restante* mail, most of it never reached me. Later in Nairobi, I would receive enticing letters from friends and family asking if I'd received the letters and notes they'd sent me in Lomé; one particularly frustrating letter mentioned a package containing chocolate someone had sent me there! But, having elbowed my way through the chaotic and panicky crowd at the post office in Lomé, I met a nasty civil servant at the *poste restante* window who refused to let me look through the mail, yet couldn't read well enough to do it herself. As a result, I had absolutely no doubt that a number of letters for me were stacked behind her, but there was nothing I could do about it. I picked up a few letters from friends in America and in Italy, and mostly read assurances that I wasn't missing anything terribly exciting while I was out here.

There were a couple of letters from some of my romance writing colleagues, too; friendly, cheerful, and full of professional news. I read them, and admitted to a little homesickness as I wrote in my diary that night, but also to something else. After everything I'd been through since leaving London in February, I found I was "also a little unwilling to get twisted into knots anymore over something as silly as romance novels and publishing-world angst."

Which isn't to say that romance novels are silly (or even that I have never since gotten caught up in publishing world angst). I'm not going to bite the hand that fed me for so long or sneer at the genre that's published so much of my writing. But, one night in riot-torn Togo, I looked back and recalled a day when I had fallen into despondency because my career of writing formula fiction wasn't going so well; and I no longer related to that person − even if I didn't know what I *did* relate to now.

I decided to forget my professional ambivalence by buying something in the famous fetish market outside of Lomé. The fetish market was even more deserted than the food market, so the sorcerers were eager to do a little business.

I bought a few things from a handsome fetish priest who looked rather like Levar Burton. I made sure he blessed my fetishes for me (thus making them useless to anyone else), before we settled on a price, which strengthened my bargaining position. (I had learned a thing or two since Morocco.)

Among the fetishes available, there was one to ensure safe travel, one to help you sleep well, another to protect you from poisoning, yet another to help you remember things, and so on. One which caught my attention was a stick you brew and give to a man for virility. Translating from the priest's tribal language directly into English, the interpreter's explanation lacked delicacy but not precision: "Man's prick gets very big and he can fuck many times. Maybe fifteen times in one night." Jenny, Sophie, and I considered ordering a job lot to take home.

Since Jenny decided not to buy anything in the end, she was kicked out of the hut since we were approaching a "sacred" moment: the point of purchase. I chose a little leather neck-pouch with a couple of cowrie shells sewn on it, stuffed with either 7 or 41 herbs (we were never sure which), to protect me from poisoning. (I think Pippa felt a little insulted

A fetish priest's showroom in the voodoo market of Akodessewa, Togo.

when she saw just how many of us had bought these things in Togo.) If anyone placed poisoned food before me while I was wearing it, I would (theoretically) see smoke and steam billow out of the food in strange colors, and I'd therefore know not to touch it. I also got a couple of gifts for folks back home.

The fetish priest put my chosen items in a little wooden bowl on the dirt floor, then shook four cowrie shells, threw them on the floor, and studied them intently. The cowries, he informed me, said I should pay 5,000 francs (about $20) for my purchases. I said that the cowries were wrong; I would pay 2,500.

He threw the cowries again. They still said 5,000.

I said, "Sorry, no," and rose to leave.

The priest urged me to wait and consulted the cowries one last time. "The shells," the interpreter informed me, "say show him your money, you can pay 2,500."

The bandits at the beach had been pointed out to me, but the campsite guards had not. Consequently, I screamed when I bumped into one of them just outside my tent one night. He had a sly, oily manner that was not remotely reassuring, and I thought it quite likely he was a bandit *pretending* to be a guard. Everyone else was in the bar, and I was alone out on the dark, windy hill with him. Not too surprisingly, I had nightmares that night.

The next day, the beach was eerily quiet. We learned that President Eyadéma had brought down a bunch of soldiers from the north the day before, and they had apparently spent the pre-curfew hours of the evening beating up civilians. It seemed a good time to leave Togo.

Believe it or not, tourist visas for Benin last an even shorter time than those for Togo. Unless you've got a good reason to stay, the Beninese make you leave after 48 hours. Of course, since Benin has one of the highest incidents of policital coups in all of Africa, most people probably don't want to stay all that long, anyhow.

Benin was, among other things, the home of the Dahomey kingdom, established in the 17th century. They were great warriors and wealthy slavers, selling their prisoners of war to the Portuguese in exchange for luxury goods and guns – which they used to conquer more territory and take more prisoners of war. Benin is also the birthplace of voodoo, and the people of this region who survived the journey to the Americas took their religion with them. Back home in Benin, only about one third of the population has ever converted to Islam or Christianity; the rest still practice traditional religions.

Dahomey cities were wealthy; a Dutch visitor to the city of Edo in the 17th century compared it to Amsterdam. The king's palace in Abomey, which is now a museum, was once the largest in West Africa. Interestingly, the Dahomey kings were guarded by women warriors. I was horrified to learn from our excellent guide at the palace that a busty woman like myself would have had one breast cut off to improve my spear throwing ability. The king's throne, by the way, was set upon a mound of human skulls. Get the picture?

I spent most of that Beninese 48 hours ankle-to-knee-deep in mud and water. Ever since reaching the Ivory Coast, we'd been in a region of daily torrential downpours, with very few paved roads and no such thing as sidewalks. I pitched my tent in a six-inch mire outside of Abomey and prayed I wouldn't drown in my sleep.

The coast was a bit more comfortable, with a cool breezy evening and a tidy campsite with flush toilets (with *seats!*) and real showers. A rough afternoon swim in the sea, with big waves and heavy undertow, scrubbed out my festering sores; I'd found that saltwater was almost as good for them as Listerine. Unfortunately, I stepped into a hole in the dark and picked up an abrasion that would turn into my worst sore yet, making me limp by the time we reached Lagos. Having fallen out of the truck the other day (during a "toilet stop;" i.e. everyone wanders off into the bushes for a couple of minutes), I was developing a reputation for suicidal clumsiness.

A British radio journalist joined us around the campfire that night. Having done an overland trip like ours some ten years ago, he had always wondered what it would be like to cross Africa on a bicycle – and was doing so now. Ironically, he told me he'd never been a keen cyclist; but now he rode about 100 kilometers every day, usually in the very early morning. He had just dashed straight through Togo, only stopping once for something to drink. He had attempted to cross the Sahara in Algeria during the winter. Like everyone else, he was permitted no further south than Tamanrasset; he eventually had to go back north to Algiers and fly over the desert.

The simple act of money-changing became, as usual, an hours-long, complex, traumatic process in Cotonou, Benin's capital city. Squeezing all we could out of our 48 hours there, we visited Ganvié, a place that even Africans visit as a tourist attraction. Ganvié's 12,000 inhabitants all live in bamboo huts built on stilts out in the middle of swampy Lake Nokoué. The people live strictly by fishing, and every-one gets around in tiny pirogues. Like the founders of Venice, these people moved to the middle of a lagoon to escape warfare two centuries ago. The location had the added advantage of protecting them from slavery, since Dahomey religion prohibited their warriors from venturing across water.

The greenish, yellowish, brownish water of Ganvié smelled over-whelmingly of sewage. Evelyn guessed that it might be different there if one arrived alone, but a group of a dozen or more whites is usually quite an announcement in Africa. We were followed by begging children everywhere we went. The guide did no justice at all to the village, just puttered us around in his boat for an hour in silence, then took us to a café and a shop.

He disappeared for about twenty minutes then, and the chil-dren became so aggressive that the whole experience became almost surreal; I was alternately annoyed, scared, and almost hysterically amused. Especially when the children were joined by an albino woman who seemed deranged and was covered in festering sores that looked a whole lot worse than any of ours. She started grabbing insistently at Becki of the mohawk hairdo. (By the way, having never met an albino in my entire life, I encountered at least a dozen in West and Central Africa – where I imagine life is very painful under that tropical sun.) All in all, I found Ganvié depressing and was eager to leave.

We picked up our passports, which we'd left at the Nigerian Embassy for visas, and headed for the border.

Entering Nigeria was a lengthy process, as Nigeria was an incredibly corrupt country. You couldn't go three feet in Nigeria, it seemed to me, without somebody wanting a bribe – at least not if you were white. On the road leading into Lagos, surely the most hellish city in the world, we were stopped every half hour or so (traffic is so bad in Lagos it takes *hours* to get anywhere), and had a choice between paying a "fine" or being "arrested".

We might have avoided Lagos altogether, except that we needed visas for Cameroon and the Central African Republic. Moreover, we still weren't entirely sure what to do about Zaïre, and we needed more information. The largest country in Africa, Zaïre is dense jungle with very few roads. It takes about a month to cross Zaïre overland, and it is so remote and lawless that you're virtually on your own once you cross the border. They were still experiencing considerable civil unrest in Zaïre – some uncharitable souls might even call it a civil war. We had to decide soon whether we would push ahead or give up and fly over Zaïre; a capitulation none of us wanted to make.

For three days we camped at a coconut plantation on the beach near Badagri, outside of Lagos. That first night, alone in my tent on a lonely African beach after dark, I heard chanting, many deep voices intoning some dark song. I peaked out and saw the Ku Klux Klan, torches, white robes, white hoods and all, approaching my lone tent. They had a goat with them. I ducked beneath my sleeping sheet and prayed they'd disappear, prayed that I was dreaming this.

They passed my tent and went down to the shore, where they stayed for what seemed like hours, singing most of the time. The goat wasn't with them when they passed me again.

Half-convinced I'd dreamed the whole thing, I got up early the next day and tended to my usual business: scrubbing out my festering sores, hauling up water from the local well to scrub my now-gray underwear, writing home, and repairing my tent. Then this well-spoken Nigerian man came along and started chatting with some of the overlanders, asking if we'd noticed the praise singers on the beach the night before – the KKK look-alikes who'd scared me out of my wits.

It turns out that those people are a religious group, a pagan cult that worships a sea goddess. Every night they bring a goat down to the beach, wearing their robes and carrying their torches, and they sing, dance, sacrifice the goat, sing and dance some more, then go home.

"How do they sacrifice the goat?" someone asked.

They can't kill it themselves, the man explained, because according to their faith, they have to give the goat to the goddess while it's still alive and let *her* take its life. But that presented a problem, as Nigerian goats are sturdier than you might suppose. They used to chuck the goat into the sea, and it would simply swim back to shore. They'd throw it back into the waves, and it would swim back to safety again. Well, they'd just lose too much sleep, spending all night chucking these goats into the ocean. They finally thought of a solution to this problem, and now they hit the goats very hard over the head; not enough to kill them, mind you – just enough to prevent them from swimming back to shore before the goddess has a chance to claim the sacrifice.

I have a mental image of dazed goats washing up by the dozen onto the shores of Bioko Island, Equitorial Guinea, far out to sea.

The man went on to explain that these pagans were refugees from Togo, which got tired of them and threw them out of the country. And how, someone finally asked, did this Nigerian man know so much about them? Well, he was a Nigerian Christian minister who'd been sent by his superiors to convert these pagans to Christianity.

"Oh? How's it going?"

Not so well, he admitted sadly. You see, French is the *lingua franca* of Togo; other than that, the pagans only spoke Ewé. English is the official language of Nigeria; other than that, the minister only spoke Ibo. He'd been here a year and a half trying to convert them, and although they were nice people and seemed to like him, they clearly didn't have the faintest idea what he was talking about or why he kept hanging around.

My diary refers to Lagos as "the worst city in the world." (But then, I was feeling negative when I wrote that, since I had just seen a nude corpse along the road.) Leaving the beach at 5:30am, it took us four hours to drive less than 50 miles into the city. This was due not only to the mind-boggling density of traffic around Lagos, but also to the proclivity of Nigerian police and soldiers to "arrest" us at regular intervals.

In this and future chapters (when things start getting *really* weird), I use the term "arrested" pretty often. For the purposes of accuracy, I should say now that none of us were ever handcuffed or thrown into a jail cell. However, according to *Webster's Ninth New Collegiate Dictionary*, we were "arrested" more times than I can count: brought to a stop; seized; made inactive; kept in custody by authority of law; detained. Sometimes the threat implied in the word "arrest" is more accurate than others; and sometimes the threats were very arresting indeed. In Nigeria, however, an arrest was always a brief stop requiring a little money or a bic to grease the wheels.

Alison, Grace, and I took our lives into our hands and hired a Nigerian cab to take us to the museum downtown. My heart still hurts when I think of that ride, and *I've* driven in Palermo and New York City. My leg was by now throbbing with pain, making me limp slightly. I wore light cotton trousers I'd bought somewhere in the Ivory Coast, childishly keeping the worst sore hidden from view; I was afraid that if anyone saw it, they'd make me cut it open and scrub it out, and the very thought was enough to bring tears to my eyes. Sure, I'd gotten casual about doing it to my other sores, but this one made my whole leg ache.

The museum was excellent. It was also air-conditioned, so I'd have spent the day there even if there'd been nothing but a couple of empty soda cans on display. Someone in the museum, well- dressed and well-spoken, approached me and, after a few friendly comments, asked me to be his "sponsor." I felt like I'd been slapped and reflected that I was becoming unappealingly defensive in Africa. I found it hard not to, when 9 out of 10 people who spoke to me only did so because they wanted money, clothing, a bic, or help getting to Europe or America. And my judgement was lousy; it seemed like I always relaxed my guard on the wrong occasions, and meanwhile rebuffed a number of people who later proved to be just genuinely friendly. Sure, I could have kept my guard lowered all of the time and waited for that one-in-ten person, but, frankly, I didn't *want* to. A number of people thought I should, and a few were openly critical of me and my sharp tongue. It took me a long time to come to terms with not being what other people thought I "should" be. Indeed, I only stopped fighting with myself when I realized that I had to stop worrying about how I "should" feel and just try to apply some intelligent behavior to how I *did* feel.

And one of the things I decided I *did* feel, as politically incorrect as this may be, is that we "Europeans" don't do any Africans any favors by thinking it's okay for them to constantly ask us, as total strangers in the street or around a campfire, for whatever they want, see in our hands, or imagine we have. I wasn't in a famine zone today; tourists aren't *allowed* in famine zones. I was in Lagos, where several men with nicer clothes than I had took one look at me, grinned, and asked me for money (or "sponsorship"). Months later, I would meet someone who advised, "Don't ever *give* a bic away. Trade it for something, exchange it for a service. Show more respect than just flinging it out there as charity, from white man to African beggar." That's what I really came to believe after several months out there.

On the other hand, sometimes I was just plain testy.

After we collected our visas for Cameroon (the embassy said that my expired visa for Cameroon was unacceptable, and the new one cost me $60), we spent the rest of the week heading east toward the border. As we stopped to make camp in the bush one memorable evening, a man walked out of the jungle with a huge snake he had just killed there. I was so scared I wouldn't come down off the truck's roof for a good hour, and I pitched my tent practically *inside* the truck. Between the heat and the humidity, I went to sleep wet, woke up wet, and put on wet clothes, living in a maddening mixture of sweat and mist. My slowly healing sores all got re-infected and had to be scrubbed and bled again.

As Alison, a woman of great sayings, put it: "This trip is a personal freshness challenge."

FEVER DREAMS

Considering that they had riots shortly after we left, a military coup later in the year, and a little border war with Cameroon the following year, you could say our departure from Nigeria was rather timely. Like the Ghanaians, the Nigerians seemed to have been blessed by particularly glib missionaries; The Will of God Bus Company, The Young Shall Grow Bus Company, and The Jesus Wept Garage will long live in my memory. A bumper sticker advised, "Take Care – Mary Has Come." However, there's always a rebel in the crowd; another bumper sticker said, "Mind your own business."

I loved Cameroon instantly, a lush, green, mountainous land of magical vistas and exotic flora. We were higher up here, so the air in this extravagantly beautiful country was fresher, sweeter, and *cooler* than anywhere in West Africa. Nights were deliciously breezy, and I slept like a baby. The people were friendly and honest, and children would rush out of their houses and huts when we passed, screaming, "White man! White man!" (Alison found this rather irritating, being neither white nor male; however, born to a black mother and white father, she looks more Jewish or Italian than black, with her green eyes, olive skin, and long, curly hair.) I just kept wondering what greeting I should shout in return; "Black child! Black child!" just didn't seem appropriate.

We began our visit by camping in the garden of the district prefect's house and swimming in a volcanic lake of crystal clear water surrounded by fabulous scenery. While I paddled around the lake, an African adolescent who had joined us and started chatting with me. After a few brief comments, he said, "When I saw you, I hoped you would give me money." He smiled. I said "no" and swam away.

When the kid tried the same line on Mark, Mark patiently talked him out of it, explaining that we didn't have tons of extra money; we slept in tents, cooked over a fire, and had carefully budgeted our money. Mark had a way of suggesting this alternative response to me without implying that I was a ruthless bitch, which made me listen to him. On the other hand, I was starting to call a truce with myself. I recognized that I didn't have the patience to explain this to every African who asked me for money (which could be anywhere from 1 per week to 40 per day, depending upon where we were); it's not my nature. I'd have to save the detailed explanations for those situations where I was personally interested enough to make the effort – especially since I wasn't convinced any of them would believe me or care. Some Africans equate *all* Europeans with fabulous wealth. Others might not, but they would look at our dirty, battered truck, our slowly deteriorating tents, our ragged clothes, and our fire-scarred pots and pans – and they'd see wealth which exceeded their wildest expectations for their own lives.

According to the 1990 World Bank annual development report, 27 of the world's 40 poorest countries are in Africa. (If you can't count that high, then how about this one: nine of the world's ten poorest countries are in Africa.) In the 1980s, the per capita African gross national product declined by 25%. African farmers produce 20% less food now than they did in 1970, yet there are twice as many mouths to feed. Twelve thousand African children die every day of hunger and malnutrition, and the United Nations estimates that 20 to 60 million people are at risk of starvation throughout the eastern and southern part of the continent (in other words, those figures don't even include Ethiopia, Somalia, or the Sahel). Meanwhile, the World Health Organization estimates that AIDS will kill 20% of Africa's working adults by 1996.

In her book *On Foot Through Africa*, Fyona Campbell blames overlanders for the spread of discontent in Africa, for "making people realize for the first time that they are poor." Call me crazy, but I suspect a lot of them already knew it. Anyhow, since a land rover travelled across Africa with Miss Campbell, stocked with the same supplies any overland truck carries and manned by two Europeans who were there for her sole benefit, I'm not entirely clear on how she represented a more benign influence than I did.

It rained that night, really *stormed*. We all ran around in it, washing our hair and bodies, thrilled to be cool after so many weeks of stifling heat. We then listened to an hour of *Lord of the Rings*, a BBC 12-part radio production which Fearless had thoughtfully brought from England to help us while-away those long jungle nights after the dishes were flapped and put away.

We split up a few days later, some of the group ascending Mount Cameroon, some going off to Yaoundé to conduct business, and some (including me) going to spend a few days lying on the lava sand beaches where part of the French movie *Chocolat* was filmed. I never did say good-bye to the overlanders we dropped off at the base of Mount Cameroon, since I was busy extracting myself from a deep vat of cow manure at the time (it's amazing what you can stumble into while looking for a place to whizz in the bush). While the lush, green mountain rising through the mist was truly glorious to look at, I had no intention whatsoever of spending the next few days walking straight up its side.

Nine of us spent a few peaceful days camped at a quiet little beach spot, with a café that never seemed to have any other customers, a huge lawn, and a fresh spring with the clearest, coldest water I'd ever seen. I'd take a dip in the sea each morning, then wash off the salt in the spring, then do a little laundry, then read, then eat lunch in the shade, and then do pretty much the same things with my afternoon. The occasional game of cards or Scrabble enlivened my evenings; we played by flashlight if the electricity went out. If the water in the café was working (which was about half the time), I might even hedonistically round off the day with a tepid shower.

From the shore of Cameroon, where the water was gentle enough for a real swim (instead of a life-and-death struggle against the undertow of West Africa), we looked out across the sea to Equatorial Guinea's Bioko Island, rising out of the ocean like Bali Hai, surrounded by lacy clouds. The guidebook, however, insisted that the place is a living hell on earth, with nothing but mosquitoes, poverty, and disease to recommend it. We also read that our glorious beach was the number one spot in the world for a type of malaria which is rare and instantaneously fatal. I took an extra dose of my anti-malarials and endured the strange dreams they routinely caused.

These few days gave me the time, privacy, and relaxation I really needed to pull myself together, get a handle on my increasingly volatile emotions, and make some choices.

Since not many people have the time or funds to make an overland journey all the way across Africa, my trip from Morocco to Harare was actually *two* trips: Morocco to Nairobi, and Nairobi to Harare. Only Fearless and six of the overlanders (including me) were continuing onward after a week's break in Nairobi, where we'd be joined by all new people. (Pippa was leaving for a new job in Zambia; Chris eventually decided to resign and go off on a round-the-world trip; perhaps he felt his life lacked adventure...)

I had recently learned that a second truck would make the Nairobi-Harare run at the same time as this one, though the two trucks would each go their own way. In addition, I'd learned that due to the political changes in South Africa, Guerba was about to run a truck through there for the first time in about six years. A second Cape Town-bound truck would leave Harare and head for South Africa just a day or two after I was due to arrive in Harare.

I took out my notebook and tried to coordinate all this information. I'd always been disappointed with the concept of my Morocco to *Harare* trans-African journey. I'd always wanted to go from one end of Africa to the other, not stop halfway across Zimbabwe. I worked out how much more going to Cape Town would cost me, considered the practical details of extending my trip, then muttered a few platitudes about "in for a penny, in for a pound," and committed myself to at least an additional month on the road in Africa.

Having made my decision, I learned that Sue had come to the same decision for herself. So we approached Fearless about it. Having grown used to everything being so difficult out here, I was pleasantly relieved to find it quite easy to reserve two places on the Cape Town-bound truck leaving Harare months from now. Fearless sent our requests and our credit card numbers to Guerba's head office in his next couple of telexes to them, and matters were settled fairly quickly.

The other decision I made was to request a transfer to the other Harare-bound truck leaving Nairobi the same day this one was. Fearless was excellent at his job in a number of ways and had an outstanding professional reputation. I, however, thought I might get along better with someone else, and so I asked him to tell the company I'd like a change of pace after reaching Nairobi. This, too, was accomplished with no fuss. There are times when you really have to appreciate the English.

I got mail in Douala, one of Cameroon's two major cities. Although the dusty red roads in Cameroon were unpaved and extremely bumpy, some of the city's streets were tarmac-covered, and it seemed a more orderly place than most African cities I had so far seen. After the hot, frenetic days in Nigeria, there was an apparent tranquility in bilingual (French and English) Cameroon that appealed to me, and I longed to stay longer.

The letters from home included one from my mother, one from my grandfather, and three from my father. Everyone wished me good luck in getting into Mauritania (the letters were rather old by the time I got them). My father also strongly advised against going to Zaïre. Having long-since learned how to deal with my parents, I decided that if we remained on course instead of flying over Zaïre, I wouldn't telephone or anything foolish like that; just a postcard before I entered the country and another once I was safely out would do the trick without opening a noisy discussion. Phone calls could wait until Nairobi, when the thing was done and they were over the shock.

As much as I liked Cameroon, we couldn't linger there. We had no idea what we would do about Zaïre or how long it would take to cross it if we got in. Having also lost time in Morocco, Cameroon turned out to be the country in which, for once, we had to hurry.

The days now passed in a whirl of beautiful scenery, friendly waves, broad smiles, a hundred villages, bumpy roads which tossed us around like salad, red dust which coated everything, and heavy rain which turned the red dust to gelatinous muck. Mangoes dripped down from the trees like heavy golden teardrops. Up in the roof seat, we would stand in awkward crouches, trying to capture them as the truck ambled beneath fruit-laden branches. The ripe mangoes we collected were eaten at meals, and the green ones were used in Pippa's mango chutney.

Travelling at a furious pace and living in the bush again, I gave up washing anything but my underwear and my sores. My hair looked like it belonged to someone else, someone I wouldn't care to know socially. Some people apparently just got too tired of their dirty, sticky, greasy, snarled hair one day, particularly as we all contemplated Zaïre and how difficult conditions would be there. With sudden resolve, six of the overlanders shaved their heads, including Becki of the mohawk hairdo, and Jenny, who shaved off every single strand of the thick, beautiful hair which grew halfway to her waist.

The six bald heads looked strange to me. I was nonetheless sorely tempted to shave my own head as I contemplated living with it in this filthy, tangled condition any longer. Indeed, I started feeling peer *pressure* to shave my head. I began to fear that if I didn't, someone would slip into my fever dreams and shave it for me. My dreams got increasingly strange as, to pass nights in the bush, we listened more regularly to the BBC's radio adaptation of *The Lord of the Rings* around the fire after dinner. Have you any idea how *real* Orcs seem when you have to leave your tent alone in the middle of the night to find a spot in the African jungle?

Another misty day dawns in tropical Africa. We finally cross the border into the Central African Republic (CAR). This, more than any other place we have been, is the beginning of the Africa our mothers have nightmares about. This is where Bokassa declared himself emperor, tortured thousands of his people, massacred school children, and ate his victims. This is a country of lawless roads, dishonest authorities, and terrible poverty. This is where, for the first time, I see skinny people wearing rags everywhere I go – despite the poverty in West Africa, most of the women there were beautiful and colorfully dressed. Not here. This is where few people have running water, and most villages rely on a single pump which operates by someone (*me*, on too many occasions) pedaling it like a bicycle to get water.

However, it seems that we may not get into CAR. Our fearless leader disappears into the customs house (a shack) at the border. Soldiers come to the truck and tell us to get out. I do the interpreting, since they are speaking French. They single out the six newly bald people among us and tell them to stand apart from the group. I translate the instructions, growing nervous. This is a border notorious for corruption and trouble. The guard in charge is fierce, unsmiling, and armed.

I wait for the soldiers to search the truck. They do, but their search is surprisingly brief. They have something else on their minds. They explain to me that our bald companions cannot come with us.

"In order to enter the CAR," one of the guards tells me, "it is necessary to have hair."

I laugh.

He doesn't.

I stop laughing. I have already witnessed stranger things than this and have finally learned to expect almost anything. I translate his comment to my companions. They laugh. The guards don't. My companions stop laughing. I'm thinking, *Oh, shit.*

"But what can we do?" I ask the guard.

"They must wait here until their hair grows," he says. "In a couple of months, they can join you."

I stare helplessly at his stony face.

Then I look across the way and see Fearless doubled up with laughter. I'm tempted to keep the joke going, but everyone else notices him by now, too.

We piled back into the truck, relieved to only spend an hour at such a notorious border, and started heading across CAR. People seemed truly *un*friendly here, for the first time. If one can generalize about a whole continent (and one really can't), I would have to say that Africans are generally very friendly. But people here threw things at the truck – usually mangoes that were as hard as rocks. They hissed and glared and looked menacing.

We decided to camp far from any villages and well away from the road. My tentmate and I pitched our tent in a glade deep in the bush, spread out our sleeping bags, hung up some laundry to dry, then went to sit by the campfire. I realized I'd left something I needed in the tent and went back to it. Whereupon I discovered we'd been robbed.

Not much was taken. We never put much in the tents, since one always expects something like this to happen. Our tent mallet was stolen, our tent bag, the sack in which I kept my sleeping bag, and a couple of scraps of cloth with which my nubile tentmate "clothed" herself on hot days. Even such items as these are valuable among most people in CAR.

We announced the theft to the camp, investigated the rest of the tents for trouble (found nothing unusual), listened to another terrifying episode of *Lord of the Rings* after dinner, and went to bed. At that point, the local bandits started circling our camp. They robbed the truck – but with considerable difficulty, since (as always) several people were sleeping on board; they got away with a frying pan. They tried twice more to break into our tent, which we now felt foolish for having pitched in such an isolated spot. They even punched their way through the fabric of someone else's tent. I heard Mark storming past our tent, shouting at them, and I screamed something like, "Kill them!"

We were all, of course, wide awake and vigilant by then, and we set up an all-night guard rota. This made it impossible for the bandits to steal anything, which made them really mad. So they spent the rest of the night purposely harassing us so that no one could relax, stalking the tents, screaming in the bushes, and running around the camp area. We were strangers there, and they knew the thick bush and its hundred of footpaths like the palms of their hands. They also knew – as we did – that there wasn't any help available to us. Even if there *were* police in the area (which there weren't), police are usually the last thing you want in a country like CAR. Hoodlums you can at least beat in a fair (or unfair) fight. Police and soldiers in certain countries differ from hoodlums only in that they also have the authority to lock you up and throw away the key.

When my tentmate had to leave the tent for a whizz, I insisted no one was going anywhere alone and, with my gut cramping, I followed her outside, brandishing my flashlight like a weapon. No one got much sleep for the rest of the night, and I had nightmares about someone entering the tent every time I started to doze in the long hours before dawn. As soon as the sun rose, I went out and searched for our tent bag, hoping the thieves might have dropped it somewhere; but the bush was thick and full of dozens of crisscrossing paths that I couldn't keep straight or follow for long.

I had the trots really bad by then. I thought it was due to nerves at first, but body-doubling cramps by midday made it clear that I had eaten or drunk something nasty. This is probably the occasion where I lost the last feeble shreds of my modesty. At one point, as I was engaged in a very private and uncomfortable act behind a bush, about fifteen Africans carrying loads of wood walked right past me. They all took a good look, laughed with sympathy, wished me a good day, and walked on.

Why, I decided thereafter, even bother with modesty?

That night, still nervous about bandits, I pitched my tent practically *underneath* the truck and crawled into bed, dosed to the gills with anti-diarrhea drugs.

Ever wonder what to take on a seven-and-a-half month overland trip through climates which vary from winter in the snowy Atlas Mountains to the extreme heat of West Africa, from the parching dryness of the Sahara to the rain forests of Zaïre, from the urban hellhole of Lagos on a hot day to the windy emptiness of the Botswanan bush?

Well, I learned a lot about what to pack. Here's a few tips. First and foremost on your list: DRUGS! You will need *GOOD DRUGS!*

I'm lucky. My doctor specializes in travelers' medicine, and he's spent time in Africa, so he knew what I'd be facing. Hint: many doctors, however good they may be at treating the common cold and checking your cholesterol levels, aren't really prepared to teach you how to stay alive and well on the Dark Continent. Indeed, now that he was practicing in Ohio, I felt like I had become a bit of a hobby for my doctor. The challenge of preparing someone to face all the diseases, bacteria, and injuries likely to threaten me out there, added to the fact that I would usually be days away from any decent medical help, really seemed to appeal to Doctor MacGowan. In addition to vaccinating me so thoroughly that I figured my blood could be used to sterilize surgical instruments, he also made it a point to teach me how to take care of myself out there.

My vaccinations included shots for yellow fever, cholera, typhoid, meningitis, measles, polio, tetanus, and several types of hepatitis – all of which made me feel awful and gave me strange dreams for a day or two. The typhoid vaccination was a series of pills taken over 8 days, during which I had a dull bellyache and was unbearably morose.

The drugs I took with me included larium, a strong anti-malarial. You take one a week, and I read that you're not advised to take it for more than 3 months (I took mine for 8 months). The side effects can be riveting, but malaria is worse. I met a lot of people out there who had malaria (lots of overland drivers get it), and I'd rather take the larium, despite what it must have done to my system. I only experienced a few of the minor side effects: bizarre dreams, a little nausea on the day I took it, a failure to tan, and a little hair loss toward the end. Sue, however, developed some illness from it whereby huge blisters starting coming up spontaneously on her skin. They'd break within a couple of hours and become painful, infected welts. These welts covered her whole body. A doctor in Zimbabwe told her this was a life-threatening condition and she must get off the anti-malarials, as well as anything else she was taking, immediately.

I brought immodium for cramps (from diarrhea) and cipro (to clear up intestinal infections). My doctor prescribed Vicodin for pain, in case I got badly hurt. (Fortunately, I wound up only using them for migraines a couple of times.) I also brought an ampule of adrenaline, which you pump into someone's thigh in the event of an allergic reaction which causes them to swell up. A biochemist from Oxford University told me that, when preparing for his Nairobi to Cape Town journey, his friends in the medical community told them that adrenaline was the single most important thing to take to Africa. Most other illnesses, or even fractures and burns, give you a leeway of a day or two to get help; but when someone's throat starts closing up from an allergic reaction, they can be dead within 15 minutes without help. Indeed, I heard of a campmaster who died that way.

I picked up antibiotics in Morocco to treat my two chest infections (one in Morocco, the other in Botswana). In addition, I had a heartening supply of syringes and needles (rather than risk getting stuck with a dirty one), gauze, bandages, ointments, calamine lotion (I should have brought a *big* bottle), and assorted first aid stuff.

Lots of insect repellant and sunscreen would be a good idea for your overland luggage. And don't forget the Listerine!

Bring dark underwear, nothing white. The white stuff looks horrible and gray after a few weeks of hand-washing in rivers, while red and black and purple underwear still look okay. Bring mostly dark clothes (same reason), and remember that patterned clothes don't show the dirt as easily. Leggings are as warm as pants and take up less room; they can also be worn under pants or inside a sleeping bag. This makes them perfect, since ideally everything in your wardrobe should have a dual purpose.

A good headscarf is useful to cover up your filthy hair and keep the bugs out of it. A couple of sweatbands come in handy in the hotter regions. And *don't* bring a towel! Towels never have a chance to dry (except in the desert), so they get moldy and disgusting really fast. Christine brought a little spongy shammy towel, bought at a camping store, which seemed to work well. I wound up using a cotton sarong as my towel, since I could dry it quickly by putting it in the sun for a half hour at lunch, or holding it above my head as I rode on the roof.

You'll need a good scrub brush for your clothes; also one for your hands and body (after a while, only a scrub brush will get the ingrained dirt off places even as soft as your upper arms); and those tropical sores, remember, will have to be scrubbed out. Put everything in sturdy plastic – not those ziplock bags, which disintegrate in a week, but sturdy, waterproof, zippered pouches. This helps prevent sand from getting into your toothpaste, and keeps your clothes from rotting any sooner than they have to.

Bring two flashlights: a little one you can hold between your teeth when you're putting up your tent alone in the dark or searching for your toilet paper at a particularly delicate moment in the bushes; and a big one for those nights when you want the hyenas to see you coming and get out of your way.

You'll want a lighter, since matches get wet. I recommend a walkman, too; for one thing, it's a good way of drowning out your companions when you're feeling irritable. Bring plenty of batteries for said flashlights and walkman – batteries are hard to find and very expensive in much of Africa.

Bring lots of cash (as opposed to travelers' checks), and a considerable sum in singles and fivers. Cash is easier to change than travellers checks, and a lot of people will deal with you for American dollars when you don't have local currency. However, they won't make *change* for dollars during these transactions, which is one good reason to have small denominations with you.

What else? A scissors to trim your hair. A couple of fans, because I never encountered any air-conditioning or electric fans, and there was seldom even a good breeze for three months. Plenty of bics! A 12-band radio isn't a bad idea, since the outside world gets news about Africa much more frequently and clearly than anyone actually *in* Africa does.

A good camera is obviously nice to have, depending upon your needs. I took a Pentax Zoom 1000 and loved it. It's an automatic with a few manual functions and a built-in lens that zooms out. I bought it for its sturdiness. You can drop it, smash it, roll it in dust, get mud on it, and it keeps on ticking. Moreover, the way you clean this camera is to dunk it in a lake, a river, or a bucket of water, then wipe it off. This was its key appeal to me, as I had no interest in fiddling with little brushes and chemically-treated pads. Some overlanders brought much fancier cameras with them, but I personally didn't have the patience to spend time maintaining one. I also brought little lightweight Nikon Travelite binoculars (Pentax

makes some good travel binoculars, too). A serious birdwatcher
might want bigger ones, but I found these good enough for me.

I kind of gave up on shoes after a while, but I would recommend
rafting sandals and some kind of sturdy walking boot. I brought a soft pair
of Reeboks which were halfway between a hiking boot and a sneaker.

Definitely bring a sleep sheet, for inside your sleeping bag. I
lost mine in Zaïre, and I can't begin to describe the color of the
interior of my sleeping bag now, even after half a dozen machine
washings. A good look at it will give you a notion of how utterly
filthy I was most nights.

> *May 9th:*
>
> Alison has apprenticed to the firemaker. I'm im-
> pressed. I may even follow in her footsteps, since I feel
> it would be quite an achievement for me – especially as
> I am afraid of fire and all the fire tools. Pippa objects to
> this notion, since I'm so senseless in the mornings. No
> one wants to see me wielding an ax and playing with
> matches when I'm barely capable of simple conversa-
> tion or menial tasks.
>
> Anyhow, Alison, our Buddhist-mode vegetarian
> who won't even kill ants, is showing a carnivorous
> nature toward bandits since that dreadful night: "Let's
> use an ax! Let's kill them! Let's get someone else to kill
> them!" Grace has bought a slingshot and has been
> practicing with it. If one of us stumbles into their tent by
> mistake one night on our way back from the bushes, I
> fear we'll have one less belly to feed by morning.
>
> However, they seem to have the right idea, at least
> according to the locals. While I sat under a tree drinking
> my morning tea today, I noticed a man near me with a
> bow and arrow.
>
> "Are you going hunting?" I asked in French.
>
> "No," he replied. "This is for thieves."

I was annoyed about the loss of my tent mallet. Not only would
it have been the handiest weapon against future nighttime raids, but its
theft made putting up the tent rather problematic. We were now always
obliged to wait for someone else to finish putting up their tent and then
loan us their mallet. We could have used a mallet from one of the spare
tents the truck carried, but all the spare tents were now in use. I wasn't
the only one who found communality a big adjustment; people kept
moving out of their two-man tents and claiming a spare as their own
until we simply ran out of spares. Alison and Grace (who had each

given up the fight and moved out of their respective tentmates' tents) didn't even *have* a tent; together, they made rotating use of the various tents which became available when people took turns sleeping aboard the truck.

My big problem in communal living these days was chiefly in the area of my regular truck cleaning duty. When it my turn to clean the interior of the truck (an increasingly dreary task as the dirt, dust, mud, and damage accumulated over the months), I'd loudly announce that everyone had 10 (or 20, or 30) minutes to put their stuff away before I started cleaning. It annoyed the hell out of me that people left cameras, boots, clothing, diaries, mud-caked trousers, and really disgusting things like used bandages and dirty hankies, all the hell over the place when I was supposed to be cleaning. I didn't want to move their crap back and forth, and I *especially* didn't want to touch their diseased leavings. It was at times like this that my mother's influence dominated me, and I would get really obsessed about this cleaning business, making enemies in the process. Not only did I shout, bitch, and publicly embarrass people who I thought were treating me like a maid, but I also got angry enough on quite a few occasions to simply toss unclaimed possessions out the back of the truck and into the dirt – even when it was pouring down rain.

May 10th:

We got stopped in Bossembélé yesterday. The guard told Fearless he wanted to see the truck's papers in the guardhouse. So Fearless turned off the engine and brought the papers to the guardhouse.

The guard then announced that he was fining Fearless 8,000 francs for "parking illegally." Same old bullshit.

Fearless usually handles these situations very calmly, much moreso than I can. After the attack on our camp the other night, though, Fearless was in no mood for this. He got into an argument which took forever, and which Chris claims nearly escalated into a fistfight. However, he got away without paying.

Alison and I rode in the cab with Chris all the way to Bouar. The guards at every police post looked into the cab and all asked the same questions: "Where are you coming from, where are you going?" (To which I am always tempted to reply, "Ohio, and Cape Town.") Another favorite question, as they study our truck, is, "What's a Guerba?" Someone helpfully pointed out to us that it's not a British word and therefore can't be the name of a British company. (Actually, *guerba* is an Arabic word for a goatskin waterbag; which is generally what my water tastes like, these days.

The guards usually also demand *cadeaux*. So if we actually *need* our pen, we hide it before we stop the truck.

In Bangui, I was immediately struck by the extreme contrast between the poverty of the countryside and the wealth on display here in CAR's capital city. Enormous old French colonial buildings sat slowly crumbling on vast lawns along tree-lined streets, while snazzily-dressed Africans drove flashy cars past sky-high modern apartment buildings and government palaces. Prices were high, and bank commissions were steep. Paying extortionate prices for flashlight batteries while someone drove past me in a Mercedes, I found it hard to remember I was in a country where the per capita income was less than $200 per year, a country where I hadn't seen running water or shoes until today.

We bit the bullet and committed ourselves to finally paying for visas for Zaïre. Visa costs were something you just couldn't figure into your budget, since they varied so tremendously. The price of any country's visa was based upon your own nationality *and* upon which country you were purchasing it in; moreover, these prices fluctuated so often that two-month-old information was too old. My single-entry visa for Zaïre, purchased in CAR, cost me about $80, payable in Central African francs; and we still weren't 100% sure we'd get across the border.

Our remaining doubts were finally – after months! – put to rest at the campsite outside of Bangui, where we came across a couple of overland trucks coming north from Zaïre. Like us, no one was using the route they had originally intended to follow, but travel was apparently all right (in terms of avoiding the violence) as long as you stayed well off the beaten path. Whereas we had originally expected to cross the great Oubangui River, which divides CAR and Zaïre, right there in Bangui, we were now going to drive further east through CAR for almost a week in order to cross into Zaïre at a less populous spot.

The campsite was a crowded, squalid place, surrounded by high, thick walls topped with broken glass (to discourage thieves). There were a couple of guards roaming around with bows and arrows (for thieves who hadn't been suitably discouraged), a bar, and a shower block. While impressed by such luxuries, I was so revolted by the toilets that I wouldn't use them; I dug little holes outside the toilet house with my trowel and tried to time my visits carefully in this densely populated camp.

It was always interesting to meet other overlanders, especially if they were coming from where I was headed. Many of these people coming from Zaïre, however, seemed ill, dazed, crazed, or just so focused on getting a strong drink that their conversation lacked a certain *je ne sais quoi.* One of the trucks looked like a garbage scow, and the passengers were riddled with malaria and something rather like dysentery. I calmed down after I learned that they didn't treat their water; my father would call that natural selection in action.

As was invariably the case, seeing the trucks and crew members of other overland companies made me really, really glad I had chosen Guerba. In Nairobi and Harare I wrote out long lists of suggested improvements for Guerba (hey, they *asked*), but I think very highly of their operation, their thoroughness, and their expertise, and I would recommend them enthusiastically to anyone who wants to make a trip like this.

I picked up more mail from home in Bangui, knowing these would be my last letters until Nairobi. My 81-year-old grandfather stopped partying and playing tennis long enough to write: "I'm glad that it's *you* there experiencing the winds, the uncharted desert, and all the delightful discomforts that go along with that, while I raptly relive your experiences in the pleasant comfort of my apartment with a chilled martini at my side."

I sent a note home saying I was going to Zaïre and they shouldn't worry. The day after we left Bangui, teachers went on strike after 8 months of working without pay. Riots broke out before long and public services halted.

Timing is everything in life.

Alison and I were sitting in the cab with Chris when we were hit by a truck east of Bangui. Overloaded and unstable, it zigged when it should have zagged. It took out our rearview mirror on the passenger side, which shattered into a million pieces that flew straight at the three of us. Alison was the only one who got cuts, and luckily they were few and mild. We both shook like leaves for a good ten minutes afterwards, and I didn't understand a word of the fight that ensued with the driver of the other truck.

Iron nerve and an ability to improvise melodrama were essential for the road in CAR. There were soldiers and check points every-where, and they all wanted something from us. If a guard tried to fine Fearless for something, Fearless would turn around and blame the problem on Chris, who would fight back. They'd keep it up until the guard didn't know who to blame and was tired of these silly Europeans arguing with each other. What had started off as a fine might then be settled with a bic.

As horribly hot as it was, many of us liked to ride sitting with our legs dangling over the sides of the truck to catch the breeze on every possible portion of our bodies. Some guards saw that as a good excuse to fine us, so we tried to keep an eye out for them and draw our legs inside immediately. If we failed and the truck got stopped, Fearless would yell at us and complain about us to the guard, and we'd mumble apologetically and do our best to look empty-headed and sorry.

Meanwhile, young men in many communities had decided there was no reason they shouldn't get a piece of the action, too. So in addition to official check points along the dirt roads, we often ran across *un*official ones. A few enterprising guys would erect a simple roadblock – a big branch or a small tree trunk, propped up to waist level – and explain that we had to pay them to pass. We always said no. Sometimes they didn't want to take no for an answer.

"My chief says to remove your tree or he will break it down with this truck," I translated into French as I sat in the cab with Chris one day.

"The young man on the road glared at me and tightened his grip on the big stick in his hand. "No," he replied. "Give me money."

"He wants money," I told Chris.

Chris had an uncannily calm, good-natured manner which seldom deserted him. "No, tell him we won't do that," Chris instructed me as serenely as if he were refusing a second cup of tea at his mother's house.

"My chief says no. Take down your tree now," I said.

The young man looked at his companions who were in the road in front of the truck; they had sticks, too. "No! Give me money! Give me gifts!"

Chris started rolling the truck forward. "Tell him I'll knock it down, Laura," he said in the tones of one offering me the last cookie left on the plate.

The young man raised his stick and stepped closer to my open window. The guys in the road held their ground. The truck crept forward.

"My chief will break it down!"

"Give me money!"

"He won't give you money! Take down the tree!"

The guy came closer. "Give me gifts!"

"He's got a stick, Chris!" I said in English.

"I'll knock it down," Chris said with all the volatility of a sleepy cat.

I was about to tell the guy to hit my chief, not *me*, with that stick when he finally capitulated. I guess he figured letting us go was cheaper than building a new barrier.

Rain barriers were another hazard of road travel in CAR. Every time it started raining (which was often), every check point and village would close the road to prevent any vehicles from using it. This strategy kept their dirt roads in far better shape than those of Cameroon. They were especially concerned about the damage which could be done by big vehicles like our truck. We weren't the biggest thing on those roads, though, not by a long shot. Most of the other road traffic in CAR consisted of enormous trucks hauling trees for lumber out of the forests. The girth of these great trees was so vast that a huge truck could only carry three (one stacked atop the other two). When we got stopped at a rain barrier, there was nothing to do but wait. However, Fearless could occasionally reduce the normal required waiting period of six hours by offering the guards some money or *cadeaux*.

If I had trouble budgeting for visas, imagine the trouble Guerba must have had budgeting such expenses into their truck funds.

Everyone's luck runs out sooner or later, and we were finally arrested somewhere between Kembé and Bangassou. Five people (by sheer chance, I was not among them) were spotted sitting on the ledge with their legs dangling over the side of the truck as we rumbled down the road.

For the benefit of the stone-faced guard, Fearless went through the usual routine: "Did you put your legs *out*? Like I've told you *not* to? Stop *doing* that!"

The overlanders hung their heads and cried, "Sorry!"

However, the performance was not a hit this time. The captain (I'm guessing at his rank) made the five overlanders descend from the truck with their passports and sit on roadside wooden benches, in the equatorial sun, while he and Fearless bargained for their release. The captain wanted about $60 per person, which was not only ridiculous, but also impossible to accommodate. None of us had that many francs left, since we were on our way out of the country.

Seeing this would take a while, I started to read. I finished a whole Dick Francis novel I found in the library (and while we're on the subject, let me mention that no romance writer would ever write a hero who propositions a woman by asking if she'd care for a "bonk") and looked up to find that negotiations still looked very unpromising. Fearless had a real knack for getting "fines" reduced or eliminated, but he wasn't getting anywhere this time. Two hours went by with no progress. Some *cadeaux* changed hands; one by one, Fearless gave the captain a pocket calculator, some bics, a whole carton of cigarettes, and a French-English dictionary. But the stone-faced captain wouldn't budge.

The argument got really heated after that, and Fearless got so annoyed, he took all his gifts back! Meanwhile, an American Protestant missionary from Pennsylvania drove past and, upon seeing us, stopped to greet us. After Ghana and Nigeria, I was tempted to ask him for some pithy sayings, but I decided to stick to business and just asked his advice about this situation. He'd been in CAR for over twenty years and ought to know a thing or two. He said not to pay locally for the *infraction* (violation).

"Ask for a written citation and say you'll pay it in Bangassou," he advised. "The soldiers usually back down when they realize they're not going to get any cash out of the transaction."

Fearless was reluctant to use this strategy, however, telling me he considered it a last resort gamble that could get us into worse trouble if it backfired. He thought the captain could get really angry and file all kinds of trumped up charges against us, or the officials in Bangassou could throw the book at us for questioning the authority of one of their officers.

Fearless toyed with the idea of offering the captain hard currency. (In case you don't know this: hard currency, such as the US dollar, is backed by gold and can be traded and exchanged all over the world; soft currency, however, is only valid within the borders of the country where it's issued. You can't, for example, take Zimbabwean dollars with you to New York and exchange them there; soft currency is worthless paper outside of its country of origin.) The captain was obviously not supposed to accept foreign cash for an *infraction*, so if he took hard currency (and many people are eager to get their hands on hard currency), we'd have him over a barrel (theoretically, anyhow) and could threaten to report him to his superiors. That would give Fearless the leverage he needed to get the overlanders released.

I thought it sounded like an intriguing but risky plan. Fearless never had to test it; in the end, after more long, dull, hot hours of passionate bargaining, the captain finally agreed to let everyone go for a total of about $120 in Central African francs — and the same *cadeaux* Fearless had taken back earlier in the day. Fearless thought this was still too much, but there seemed no likelihood of the captain settling for less any time this century. He'd pocket most of the money, of course, but he'd have to send some to his superiors; if they didn't get cash from him now and then, they'd have no reason to keep him in this post.

We'd stocked up on everything imaginable, since there'd be no supplies once we reached Zaïre. The back of the truck was particularly crowded now, since we'd run out of places to put all the dry goods we'd bought. A hundred-pound bag of flour took up so much room I had trouble getting into my locker for the next couple of weeks, and it seemed like I was always stumbling across bags of beans and rice and chickpeas when I was looking for shoes or books or medicine. We carried extra diesel now, and Fearless bought wooden planks we'd need for crossing decaying bridges and getting out of slippery bogs.

Our final stop in CAR was the village of Bangassou, on the banks of the Oubangui. A quiet, sleepy town with broad dirt avenues and little dirt paths, it had many crumbling old French colonial buildings with vast gardens and lush, exotic blossoms. The people here were by far the nicest I had met in CAR – which is admittedly a tough country where daily life probably doesn't inspire many people to be nice to strangers.

Depopulated long ago by the slave trade (Arab slavers hit this region even harder than the Western slave trade did), CAR has never recovered and remains one of the most thinly populated countries in Africa; this is particularly so in the eastern portion of the country, where Arab raiders captured whole villages at a time, continuing the slave trade on a major scale well into the late 19th century. Under French rule, great numbers of the locals were drafted as forced labor for the vast plantations and wealthy mines which made this region so profitable to the colonial government. The Europeans frequently killed or tortured African workers who tried to refuse, resist, or run away, and forced labor continued to be a mainstay of colonial society here through the 1930s.

Within a few years of independence, Jean-Bédel Bokassa led a successful coup and took over the country. Once in power, he didn't just *order* the imprisonment, torture, and death of thousands of political prisoners; he personally participated in dealing out these punishments on numerous occasions. He also incarcerated (and even assaulted) foreign journalists. He declared himself Emperor in 1977 and celebrated the occasion with a ceremony estimated to cost around $20,000,000 – the French government paid for most of it. Even the French blanched, however, when Bokassa had some 100 school children beaten and tortured to death in 1979. He finally toppled from power after that. He lived in exile outside of Paris, with his wives and children, for several years before finally returning to CAR, where he was tried and convicted for treason, murder, and cannibalism.

Lots of the foreign aid sent to the Central African Republic wound up lining Bokassa's pockets and paying for his extravagant lifestyle. Such is the fate of foreign aid in much of Africa. Another reason I've so grown cynical about foreign aid is that some of it wound up in my belly. Relief food from Europe and America, rather than being distributed to Africa's poor, is frequently diverted and sold in shops and markets at prices that only Europeans and wealthy Africans can afford.

Since the foreign aid food was canned and wouldn't spoil, we bought it. Over the months, I ate relief chicken, relief beef, and relief fish among other foreign aid foods, and if this surprises you at all, then you must not have read many books about Africa. Most foreign journalists and travel writers at least wind up commenting on this, if not actually eating the stuff. (Frankly, you'd probably have to be an overlander – or hungry African – to be willing to eat this slop.) Relief fish is packed in so much peanut oil it slithers around the stew like it's still alive. Relief chicken is canned with the bones still in it, but pressure-cooked in such a way that they dissolve in your mouth. Weird. Relief beef has the flavor and consistency of rubber (I speak from experience, having wandered through rubber groves in West Africa). And relief flour would best be used to make library paste.

In Bangassou, I went with Pippa on the eternal quest for bread. Overlanders need a *lot* of bread. Toast for breakfast, sandwiches for lunch, lots of bellies to fill every day. A nice boy led us through a maze of back yards, little paths, and crumbling houses to the local bakery: a family operation in someone's back yard where they deep-fried loaves of dough in a huge, oil-filled cauldron over an open fire. It was disgusting stuff, but we bought every loaf they'd sell us; overlanders aren't choosy.

We camped that night at a beautiful red-brick Catholic mission which was abandoned except for a few remaining ancient nuns and priests who'd come out to CAR during colonial days. An old Dutch priest proudly showed a few of us around the church, where they'd made a real effort to integrate Western Christianity with African heritage. A large painting near the altar, painted by a Zaïrois, depicted Christ and the apostles as Africans. The Christ on the cross wore an African mask from the Ivory Coast; the mask represented a god who was elemental in an African animist Creation story. The entire design and arrangement of the altar combined Christian and African symbolism.

Things at the mission, however, were not good. The government of CAR had nationalized all the Catholic schools, and since the government hadn't paid its teachers in 8 months, the nuns were now working for free. Nuns don't go on strike, so they were working through the current national strike.

The Dutch priest had been here forty years. Sophie asked if life here was better before or after independence. He shook his head and said sadly that life had gone way downhill in this community since he first arrived here. "The local people here used to have more. Life used to be better, safer. The country used to be wealthier." He shook his head sadly again.

I shook my head sadly, too. Picture this: the standard of living was *better* under a foreign government that had tortured and killed people for resisting labor conscription. Life here seemed a thing without feathers.

> *May 18th:*
> The insects have become very annoying. I've gone through two whole bottles of repellant, but nevertheless have itchy, hard, little bites all over – even on my butt! I was continually dive-bombed by numerous moths and hungry flying ants while cooking the other night. And bugs the size of taxi cabs have taken to flying into the truck at all hours of the day and night.
> I don't recognize myself or my possessions. I never knew I could be so dirty! All my clothes are stained, smudged, ragged. My sleep sheet is covered in red dust, my sleeping bag is grimy, and even after I scrub them, my underpants are brownish-gray.
> We're waiting now to exit the CAR customs post. Then we'll take the ferry across the Oubangui and enter Zaïre. I've *seen* Zaïre on the other bank of the river! After all these months of wondering, we're finally about to enter! I can't wait – bugs, rain, heat, mud, and snakes notwithstanding. I'm so excited that we'll really do it at last!

Two hours later, I was (according to *Webster's Ninth*) arrested in Zaïre.

HEART OF DARKNESS

Zaïre is the country I think of if I watch Bogart and Hepburn in *The African Queen* or read Joseph Conrad's *Heart of Darkness.* Vast, violent, primitive, poor, thick with jungle, honeycombed with thousands of rivers and streams and swamps, it's a green, magical, desperate land of pygmies, gorillas, and deadly diseases. It's the only place on earth where okapi live. It's where snakes grow to be so long you can't see one end from the other. It's the country where overlanders find out what they're really made of.

The Portuguese were the first Europeans to venture into the Congo. After converting the king to Christianity, they demanded slaves. They shipped some 60,000 slaves out of here in the 16th century – and *then* they got greedy, demanding so many more slaves that the succeeding kings resisted and a war finally erupted in the mid-17th century. Guess who lost? Right.

Nonetheless, wealthy tribal kingdoms continued to reign in the Congo throughout the 18th century, and the major cities of the Luba and the Landa boasted many miles of tree-lined streets, fine African homes, and well-dressed citizens carrying engraved and inlaid weapons of iron and copper. A visit to any exhibition of Zaïrean art and artifacts is like a fragmented trip through time, taking you back to the pre-colonial era and belying the still-lingering myth that the Congo was peopled by ignorant savages awaiting guidance from the white man.

After Henry Morton Stanley "found" Dr. Livingstone (who wasn't lost), he took a much-publicized voyage down the Congo River in the 1870s. Although disease, starvation, crocodiles, and local tribes killed most of his men, he *did* prove the Congo was chock full of navigable waters. And the European scramble for Africa was on! The French set

Crossing a bridge, Licati, Zaïre.

up business in what is now, on your modern map, the Congo. Meanwhile, current day Zaïre became the Congo Free State; the entire ill-named colony was in reality the private estate of King Léopold II of Belgium.

The demand for rubber in the West led Léopold and the various private interests operating in his territory to develop vast rubber planations, for which they used slave labor. Not only did the Belgians, mercenaries, and Belgian-trained African troops kill anyone who resisted conscription into the slave labor force, they also killed any slaves who weren't working really, really fast. In order to prove to their superiors that they had used a bullet on an African, as opposed to wasting it on an animal or some other frivolity, the soldiers cut one hand off of every dead (or dying) African they shot, which they then took back to their superiors as proof that they were doing their jobs.

The hands had to be smoked in a little kiln to preserve them for the long trip back to the Commissary. The less rubber a soldier was hauling, the more hands he'd better bring; men, women, or children, it made no difference so long as the hands were black and there were plenty of them. Before long, the hands themselves, regardless of the rubber harvested, seemed to be almost as valuable as... bics. A Swedish missionary who kept a journal while stationed in the Congo Free State wrote of seeing official letters which boasted of hands being brought out of the jungle by the hundreds. He reported a state official paying for hands with standard trade goods. He cited soldiers' claims that they'd been promised their terms of service would be shortened if they brought in plenty of hands.

Word of these and other widespread atrocities leaked out and finally became an outright scandal in Europe. In 1908, the Belgian government took control of their king's colony. While doing almost nothing to develop it over the next fifty years, they did manage to find plenty of time to plunder its wealthy copper and diamond mines. Under Belgian rule, political parties were illegal here until the 1955, and there were less than a dozen African university graduates in the entire country several years later when the Belgians announced they were pulling out. The Africans had roughly six months to prepare the overwhelmingly illiterate population, consisting of more than 200 tribes, for independence and free elections. Guess what happened?

The first prime minister of the country was Patrice Lumumba, after whom one of my college roommates was named. When a Belgian-backed provincial leader tried to secede from the nation, taking his wealthy mining province with him, Lumumba sought outside help, first from the United Nations, then from the Soviet Union. With the reputed connivance of the American CIA, Lumumba was overthrown, handed over to his enemies, and murdered. Civil war raged in Zaïre, with considerable interference from the Americans, the Russians, and the Europeans.

The CIA backed Joseph-Désiré Mobutu, who became the president of Zaïre in 1965 as the civil war was ending. Mobutu repaid the favor by backing US policies and cooperating with US political agendas for nearly thirty years thereafter; he stopped in 1993, as I and my fellow overlanders were heading toward Zaïre.

Upon first seizing power, he took the name Mobutu Sese Seko Kuku Ngbendu wa za Banga, which officially translates as: "The all-powerful warrior who, because of his endurance and inflexible will to win, goes from conquest to conquest leaving fire in his wake." A less official translation is: "The cock that leaves no hen untouched." The latter name is apparently quite fitting; besides his various wives and mistresses, Mobutu also likes to exercise his *droit du seigneur* on the wives of his political associates. "You get money or a Mercedes-Benz, and he takes your wife and you work for him," one former Zaïrean Cabinet member told *Time Magazine*. In that same article (February 22, 1993), *Time* reported: "Until recently, Mobutu was considered a close strategic ally and personal friend by President Bush." (The article does not mention what *Mrs.* Bush thought of him.)

By the spring of 1993, Mobutu (whom President Reagan praised as "a voice of good sense and good will") had been running Zaïre for nearly 30 years, a tenure marked by absolute power, the torture and killing of his opponents, and the bankruptcy of his country. His personal fortune, pilfered from Zaïre's treasury, is estimated to be around five *billion* dollars, with bank accounts, mansions, and estates in at least half a dozen other countries, as well as 11 marble palaces in Zaïre. Some of this money came from his country's own resources and rich mines; lots of it, however, came from foreign aid. Your tax dollars at work again.

In comparison to Mobutu's personal wealth, the per capita annual income in Zaïre at the start of 1993 was less than $170 per year, and real wages had dropped to one-tenth of their 1960 levels. Zaïre should be one of the richest countries in Africa. Its natural resources include diamonds, gold, and oil. It has fertile soil, plentiful rainfall, and rivers so powerful that they could provide all of Africa with electricity. Yet in 1993, factories, stores, and businesses had closed down. Charity- sponsored feeding centers were opening up – and at least 100 children per week were dying after they reached the centers; no one knew how many were dying in the urban slums and in the bush. People were also dying of treatable diseases such as malaria; there were no medicines in the hospitals, not even quinine. AIDS was again spreading at an alarming rate; AIDS-testing kits and condoms had been looted. Sleeping sickness, a fatal malady spread by the tsetse fly, had previously been almost

eradicated; in 1993, the infection rate in some villages was now as high as 25%.

If only to facilitate their own operations here during the colonial era, the Belgians had built almost 50,000 kilometers of paved roads in this country; today, less than 2,000 kilometers remain.

The Road.
A "major" road,
Zaïre.

Zaïre is larger than the United States east of the Mississippi River, but there are now fewer paved roads in all of Zaïre than there are in the town of Toledo, Ohio.

By 1993, civil servants, soldiers, and road workers (among others) were no longer being paid. The zaïre, the national unit of currency, was so worthless that you needed an armful of the stuff to buy a beer. Inflation was estimated at 7,000%. With little left to lose, the Zaïrois decided they were mad as hell and were not going to take it anymore.

In January of that year, Mobutu's own parliament accused him of high treason for "having blocked the functioning of the country's institutions at every level." Mobutu was given until January 23rd to submit his defence. Meanwhile, ten thousand villagers fled to Uganda after soldiers put down a rebellion in the provinces. Mobutu tried to pay the army by printing up five-million-zaïre notes (worth about two dollars apiece). Mobutu's chief opponent, Prime Minister Etienne Tshisekedi wa Mulumba, ruled that the notes were not legal tender (and forty thousand people were forced to flee Zaïre as Mobutu's forces attacked the Kasai, Tshisekedi's tribe). As a result of Tshisekedi's declaration, shopkeepers in Kinshasa, the capital city, refused to accept the 5,000,000 zaïre notes.

The soldiers revolted and rioted, looted and stole, torched buildings, killed merchants, killed citizens, killed foreigners, and killed the French ambassador. The French sent in troops to evacuate 1,000 French nationals. Estimates of the total number of people killed range anyhwere from 300 to 1,000. Fighting remained thickest in Kinshasa, but started spreading through the already unstable country more rapidly now.

In February, Mobutu announced that anyone who refused to accept the 5,000,000 zaïre note would be guilty of treason. Soldiers shot three merchants who refused to accept the notes. Mobutu's chief supporters – the French, Belgian, and American governments – now sent stern messages forcefully insisting he surrrender his power to Mr. Tshisekedi. Guess what happened?

Mobutu ignored the demands of the Western powers and publicly fired Tshisekedi (who ignored *him*). The fighting continued and, according to hospital officials, corpses simply lay around the streets of Kinshasa until someone dumped them in the great Zaïre River. At one point, Mobutu's private troops even held Parliament members hostage inside their own meeting hall for two days, without food, water, or medical supplies.

In March, France, Belgium, and the US began plotting "a joint strategy for dislodging Mobutu." Mobutu was busy appointing a new prime minister, despite the fact that Tshisekedi refused to step down.

By April, Zaïre had two prime ministers, neither of whom accepted the legitimacy of the other. Tshisekedi started to rule by decree while Mobutu sent troops to search his house for proof of "sedition."

Chaos continued to reign in Zaïre as we crossed the Oubangui River and entered the country in May. Because of the fighting and civil unrest, we were taking "the hard route," a little-used trail cutting across northeastern Zaïre and heading toward the Mountains of the Moon. Fearless warned us as we entered Zaïre that from here until we got to the border on the other side of the country, almost a month later, we were on our own. The police here hadn't been paid in so long that they had nothing to lose and everything to gain in harassing us. Even if we could contact our embassies (which we couldn't, because of the fighting around Kinshasa and the lack of telecommunications everywhere in Zaïre), they couldn't help us here. We must be careful, look out for each other, and be resourceful.

I confess that after three months of cheek-by-jowl living with a group of people I hadn't chosen, there were a few overlanders I secretly longed to abandon in Zaïre. Considering my bad temper and sharp tongue, I'm quite sure that a few of my companions felt the same way about me. But I never thought I'd be the very first person to get in trouble there.

You will have gathered by now that the money is Zaïre was worthless. In May of 1993, one US dollar was worth roughly 3.5 million zaïres. The black market was flooded with the now-infamous and generally worthless 5 million zaïre notes. A few of the overlanders traded for them strictly as souvenirs, since almost no one would accept

A million-zaïre note (worht about 30 cents American).

them as currency. At the tiny border post of Ndu, they weren't accepting zaïres at all. Only US dollars and Central African francs. And what would one need to buy at a two-room border post in the jungle, you ask? Answer: freedom.

It was another one of those cases where they had guns and uniforms, and we had lots of belongings that they wanted. And Mark, Christine, and I unwittingly gave them the excuse they needed to detain us.

First they searched the truck. Then they searched our papers. Next they insisted we enter a small shack one-by-one where they counted our money. Then (pay attention, because this becomes important upon our next arrest) they wrote down this figure in each of our passports: so much in dollars, so much in travelers' checks, so much in sterling, etc.

They searched my papers and found, to my surprise, that my cholera vaccination expired that very day; and one must have a valid cholera shot to enter Zaïre. We were crossing the border a couple of weeks later than I had anticipated, which is why my shot had already expired.

The guards explained to me that I had now two choices. I could pay them US $100 in cash. I would, of course, get no receipt, and no guarantee that some guard five miles down the road wouldn't arrest me anyhow. Or I could turn around and go back to CAR without my truck or companions, get a cholera vaccination somewhere, wait eight days, and then return to this border.

Even if I had been willing to abandon the truck (forever, since I'd have no way of rejoining it in Zaïre) and return to CAR alone, it was impossible. I had left CAR and had no visa for re-entry, nor was I within a two-week journey of anyplace where I could *get* a visa for re-entry. Moreover, even if I were willing to give into this outrageous blackmail, I simply couldn't afford $100. I had plenty of money in travelers' checks but very little left in cash; I had vastly underestimated how much actual cash I'd need out here, and hugely overestimated how useful travelers' checks would be.

I explained that I couldn't go back to CAR, and I refused to pay the money. The border guards refused to let me go.

Willing myself to neither rage nor cry in the panic that suddenly seized me, I said quietly in French, "I must go speak to my chief and ask his advice."

Fearless said it was unfortunate that on this occasion, they were in the right: my shot *had* expired according to my vaccination certificate. Meanwhile, we now also learned that Mark's and Christine's shots would expire in two days. Fearless thought he could get our fines

Men coming north through Zaïre in a Land Cruiser. The road south of here was much worse, they told us.

reduced if we wanted him to intervene. Since my attempts to talk my way out of this situation had done no good whatsoever, I most definitely did want him to intervene; this was one of those times when Fearless's experience in these matters was invaluable.

It didn't take him long to discover a solution. We found out the guards had blatantly tried to steal cash from one of the overlanders while "counting" his money. Fearless used this "misunderstanding" as leverage to bargain down our fines, and we wound up only having to pay $15 apiece, which I was happily willing to settle for. Everyone on the truck, though, had to pay an additional $4 "photo license" fee for bringing cameras into the country.

Afterwards, to avoid another such incident, Fearless doctored my medical record with a rubber stamp which many drivers carried for such emergencies. Another overland driver updated my documents once more in Nairobi. Ironically, many medical centers consider the cholera vaccination so worthless that they stamp your documents without giving you the shot.

So we finally left the border and entered the heart of darkness. For the next few weeks, the road was no wider than the truck, and it was made up entirely of mud and water. Sometimes the water so out-proportioned the mud of Zaïrean roads that dozens of vehicles – cars, jeeps, trucks, transports, what-have-you – would literally disappear.

This is a rain forest, mind you, and under Mobutu's devastating rule, no one had been paid to repair the roads in.... well, a really, really, *really* long time. Of course, hardly anyone in Zaïre owned vehicles, anyhow – which was probably just as well for them, because virtually all the gas pumps (on those rare occasions when we saw them) were empty.

As you might guess, the roads were pretty overgrown in Zaïre. Branches hung low -- we occasionally had to cut them down before the truck could pass. On one memorable occasion, such a big tree was growing straight across the road that we couldn't even cut it away. We finally took our machetes into the bush and hacked a new road around it. Any wood we chopped down, we hauled away as firewood. You will gather that our social life was a little dull when I tell you that Alison, Sophie, and I took up woodchopping as a new hobby.

With all this foliage coming into the truck (indeed, sometimes we squeezed through so tightly that a branch would actually get stuck *inside* the truck, and we would be pinned to the spot until we sawed it off), a lot of insects came into the truck, too. Luckily, I don't mind insects all that much. I thought the praying mantises and leaf insects (which look exactly like two green leaves stuck together) were kind of cool. I wasn't fond of the spiders, though, and I rather loathed all the centipedes and millipedes.

However, I *hated* the ants! In succeeding months I would see gorillas, warthogs, lion, cheetah, leopard, black rhino, and all manner of fierce animals in the wild. But I say now and for all time that the single most frightening creature in all of Africa is the ant. They were everywhere! Several varieties of them. Fire ants would bite and hang on, even after you dismembered them and beat them with a shoe. They'd leave red marks that hurt for days. The smaller varieties of ants would creep secretly into your clothes and bite your armpits, your back, your thighs, and, yes, your private parts. I still remember seeing Sue suddenly leap up from her camp stool, spill her tea, and hop up and down wildly as she ripped off her underwear – ants in the pants.

Even with my cool skin temperature, I had to lather myself in repellant and fight off insects day and night. You see, they didn't just drop in now and then. No, we were plunging through a green tunnel, leaves and branches sticking into the truck and dropping their treasures on us every minute of the day, every single day, come rain or come shine. Instead of reading, napping, writing, and chatting, as we normally would while making mileage and riding all day, we raced up and down the truck, slaughtering small insects with the shoes we never wore anymore (our feet were encrusted with mud, and shoes would only get lost in the bogs we daily dug the truck out of) and throwing larger ones out of the truck as fast as they poured in.

Alison, a strict vegetarian who had once refused to kill ants on the grounds that they were living creatures, was now driven to say bitterly: "You know, deforestation isn't such a bad idea, after all." The circumstances were beginning to wear on her. One night, when Fearless suggested listening to another episode of *The Lord of the Rings*, she declined, saying, "The fight between Good and Evil is a bit heavy, isn't it, when you've spent all day being marauded by ants and foliage." Evelyn and I staked our tent in the middle of a murky bamboo forest and went to bed early.

By now, everyone had sorted out who they got along with, who bored them, and who they couldn't stand. Alison, Grace, and I stuck together, having found each other a compatible mix for the long months on the road. As conditions deteriorated and we relied more and more upon each other, I was sharply reminded of one of my favorite novels, *King Rat* by James Clavell, wherein the prisoners of a tropical Japanese POW camp in World War II find that the best way to survive is to form a 3-way buddy team.

Inspired by Alison, who had apprenticed to the firemaker and was now taking on the duty single-handedly a couple of times a week, I decided to learn firebuilding, too – precisely because I was afraid to. I'd stopped being afraid of being filthy, having no privacy, getting ill, whizzing in dark bushes at night, and many other things, mostly because I had done them and lived through them. So now it was time to face a new challenge (besides just the slog of getting through each day in deepest Zaïre).

As I've mentioned, I had always been terrified of fire. I think it's the main reason I never took up smoking; I couldn't light a match until I was in my twenties. (I'm not making that up.) And while I could light a match by now, I was nonetheless frightened of everything to do with the firemaster's chores: hot coals, searching for wood in snake-infested jungles, axes, saws, machetes, and knowing that twice a day, everyone in camp relied upon the firemaster to get a good fire going so they could have tea, coffee, and a cooked meal.

Alison had decided to take on firebuilding as a way of being more involved in our daily survival, and this way of looking at it inspired me to confront my fears. So, like her, I convinced John, a big Australian guy who was one of our two firemakers, to teach me. Luckily, he was a patient guy pleased to help me learn. Unfortunately, though, I couldn't have picked a worse time to start. Months later, when I was the full-time firemaster, I would build fires in the desert of Botswana by waving a match somewhere near a pile of sun-dried wood. But in Zaïre, where it rained every single day (and often all day), we had only wet, green wood, bad matches, and no breezes. We were running low on diesel (we had no kerosene, for some reason), and it had to be saved for the truck; so we had to build every fire without fuel. John and I would stand over the fire all morning and all evening, nursing it with the palm leaf fan I'd bought in the Ivory Coast, while the overlanders stared mournfully at the feeble wisps of smoke and tried not to look like they blamed us for this disaster.

No editor ever put so much pressure on me.

We were basically just crossing the country, heading for the mountains. There weren't exactly any "sights" along the way. In this part of Zaïre, at least, just being there and crossing a little of it each day was the big event. So we often measured our days by how many kilometers we killed. To give you some idea of how slow the muddy track was and how long we spent in bogs, we considered 76 kilometers (about 45.5 miles) in one 8-hour day average, even rather good; eight hours to push, dig, drag and haul that truck across 45 miles, killing ants and other beasties all day long. On our worst day, it took us the whole day to cover 30 kilometers (about 18 miles). It was all rather mind-boggling.

And yet, while I bitched about the discomforts of heat, insects, sores, and ingrained filth as much as (or more than) anyone, and while I found the boredom of days spent digging mud and killing insects positively mind-numbing, I didn't hate it. I found that I couldn't. Something else had taken hold of me.

> *May 19th:*
>
> We've camped tonight at an abandoned, shut-down school in the bush [I saw half a dozen schools in Zaïre, all abandoned and overgrown] near a little village, i.e. a few huts. The noise of the jungle is all around – it really *sounds* like we're in Africa now. The heat, filth, and burning sun, the jungle, the insects, and the inconveniences – these all wear on me, but I also feel enormous exhilaration. Although I don't enjoy these trials, although I'm sure I'll be glad to look back from the other side of this jungle and know I'm *out* – still, it's a thrill to be here.
>
> This feels like real adventure, like Darkest Africa. I'm seeing things which probably none of my family, friends, or acquaintances back home will ever see. This is the land of Stanley and Livingstone. These are experiences I couldn't have really imagined.

We continued to drive through the green tunnel all day, every day: extraordinary forests of green bamboo, sky-high trunks with hundreds of stalks, each formation as big around as a redwood.

As we got more accustomed to daily digging the truck out of the deep, water-and-mud pits which are the roads in tropical Zaïre, we discovered a handy but rather hazardous method of getting the truck out of bogs. First, we had to clear at least one wheel, which was a messy, sometimes waist-deep, business of digging, bailing water, and passing slop-filled wash basins along a firemen-like chain till the last person dumped the stuff in the bush and tossed back an empty basin. Then we'd put sandmats, rocks, or wood under the wheel, to provide traction and a hard surface. Some of us would then push the truck. The rest of us, preferably women with real hips (ahem!), would clamber up onto the truck where a wheel stuck up in the air, and we'd cling like fleas, hanging from the roof, the windscreen, the side mirrors, and the doors. There we would bounce in unison, using our weight to give the up-in-the-air wheel occasional contact with the ground, while the truck lurched wildly.

Yes, it was dangerous. Yes, I was always afraid I'd topple off the roof or the windshield and fall directly beneath the wheels of the truck just as one of its lurches finally propelled it forward. But I did it anyhow. I didn't want to grow old in a bog in Zaïre.

If you're wondering about hygiene, we'd given it up. For one thing, it was very hard to find wells or pumps of any kind. Often, whole villages would be using a spring deep in the bush as their only water supply, and we'd have to carry our 25-litre jerricans there, fill them up by hand (scooping water into cups and bowls, then pouring water into the mouths of the jerries), then haul them back to the truck and treat them. For this reason, all water was being used strictly for drinking and cooking. How you kept clean (or not) was your own problem. Caked with slimy mud, we often washed in those same vast mud puddles we had just pulled the truck out of. Yes, we smelled funny. No one washed clothes anymore; most of us stopped even changing clothes. With Zaïre being so wet, you couldn't wear those clothes forever, though, because the seams simply rotted away one day. When I did wash my body or any of my belongings, it was in rivers, streams, ponds, and swamps.

As you will perhaps have concluded from my mention of streams and rivers, we had many rivers to cross. Really big rivers in Zaïre still have ferry crossings (though you must revise your probable mental image of a ferry). The thousands of streams and creeks in Zaïre, however, have log bridges. This means that someone cut down four or five trees and simply laid them across the creek. Driving across them was yet another adventure I hadn't imagined before coming here. Someone had to get out at each bridge, test it for strength, figure out if it was wide enough for the truck, and decide where the wheels should go. This last part could be tricky, since the logs were round rather than flat, and the wheels might slide off one side or the other if the approach wasn't perfect. The logs were also often so unevenly spaced that there were rather alarming gaps into which the wheels might slip.

For these reasons, I often insisted on walking across bridges before the truck crossed them. It was here that I finally saw Chris nervous for the first time. He'd been on a truck that fell through a bridge once, and the experience was apparently not one to be forgotten. He'd sweat, grip the wheel till his knuckles turned white, and look like he wanted to throw up every time he had to drive the truck across one of these.

One day I felt too lazy to get out and walk. That, of course, was the day we finally broke through a bridge.

An Australian girl went on an overland trip (with a different company) about four years before I did. One day in the Congo, the truck crashed all the way through a rotting bridge and fell into a shallow riverbed. There were several serious injuries on board: a concussion, a couple of fractures. The truck had to be hauled out of the river in pieces by the diminished number of able bodies that remained – a process which took almost two weeks.

At some point during this process, the driver (who was the sole crew member on that truck) went insane and abandoned the overlanders in the bush. The Australian girl never completed her overland journey. It took her 7 more weeks just to reach a town from which she could leave Africa, which she had to do, as she was by then quite broke.

It didn't discourage her, though. She turned right back around and signed on to work for Guerba as a campmaster. By the time I met her, Deb had graduated from co-driver to driver and was leading Guerba expeditions all over Africa.

Some people are just made of the Right Stuff. (Or else they have a death wish.)

I have to disappoint you by admitting that we did not plummet to our deaths. For a moment, as the wheel beneath my butt took a sudden plunge, I was pretty sure that I was going to die without ever having written a best-seller. However, only one wheel went through the bridge. Nevertheless, since the truck was wider than the bridge, and

Chris directs a daily bridge crossing in many-streamed Zaïre.

the bridge was the main access route between a village and the market place, we caused a considerable disturbance.

Well, you know, African women are *amazing*. They carry that continent on their backs. Almost every place I went, the women were doing all the agricultural work, all the buying and selling in the market, all the domestic and household work, all the heavy lifting, and all the child-rearing. I mostly saw their menfolk sitting around not doing much of anything. So, with about three inches to spare on either side of the truck, on a row of rotting logs about 15 feet above a shallow river, dozens of women were squeezing past the truck, with babies strapped to their backs and carrying heavy loads of produce on their heads – and smiling about it! Those women are something else. Those women are *tough*.

The town, by the way, was Bondo, the first real village we saw in Zaïre. The people there surprised us by wanting to deal in money. Since zaïres were so worthless and so hard to obtain (I was in Zaïre for over two weeks before I saw a bank, and it was closed indefinitely), most people we met were trading for goods.

Anyhow, since they wanted money in Bondo, so someone offered us some black market money exchange. Officially, there was no legal currency exchange in Zaïre at the time, and money was apparently necessary if we were going to eat that day. Consequently, some unofficial money exchange took place with individual overlanders (not me; I was elsewhere at the time), and also with the truck funds.

It turned out to be a set-up. Once free of the bridge (working in close quarters, it took Fearless and Chris a few hours to dig the wheel out of the bridge, put something under it, weight the truck in our usual manner – i.e., with our lily white bodies – and get off the bridge), we were arrested.

Again.

Remember when I said the border guards had written the amount of all our cash and travelers' checks into our passports? Well, now that some people had just changed some cash, guess what? The figures in their passports no longer tallied with what they now actually had. And *right* after we traded for the only Zaïrean cash available, so that we could go marketing, we were picked up.

We were hauled off to some shack for questioning and "fines." Since I was clean in this instance, I was left alone after a preliminary search and questioning. The guard concluded by asking me if he could have my home address so we could become correspondents; I told him my husband would disapprove. After that, I stayed with the truck to guard it.

Many locals, as always, crowded around, watching and talking, both out of curiosity and also in the hope of acquiring something (either as a gift or by stealing; it varied). I met young Kanda, a polite student who wanted to try out his French and English. All the schools had been closed, but the local teacher continued to teach for free, and the students continued to study, especially since there was no work and nothing else to do.

Kanda asked me where I was from.

"America," I said.

He smiled. "Oh! But you speak English rather well!"

"Thank you," I said. (This was, after all, more than most English people would say about me.)

We chatted for a while, and Kanda asked for my address at some point. Africans who could read often did this, and I occasionally gave it, wondering if I'd ever hear from them. Kanda was the only one who ever wrote to me, months later. He offered me the once-in-a-lifetime opportunity of becoming his benefactress. He asked me to send him money for his schooling, as well as a pair of track shoes as soon as possible.

The Zaïrois who had changed money for several of the overlanders, as well as for the truck funds, now showed up "coincidentally" at the post where we were being detained – to give evidence against us, of course.

The soldiers accused one of the Boys of being a mercenary, a soldier of fortune; they accused Alison of being a terrorist; they searched Grace several times ("At *my* age!" she later said indignantly) and accused her of being a smuggler. I was as amused as I was scared; it was an absurd play in the theatre of the real. Once again, they had the guns and uniforms, and we had something they wanted.

After several hours of this sort of thing, I took my trowel and wandered off into the jungle to take care of business. Wouldn't you know it? The guards picked that moment to release us, and I was dragged back to the truck with extreme urgency. After fining us $100 – the final amount settled upon after all these hours of shouting – we were free to go. We hightailed it out of there, too.

SHEENA OF THE JUNGLE

We continued on in this fashion for quite some time. Thick rain forests, deep bogs, narrow tracks, utter wilderness broken up by the occasional encampment or small village. Despite our recent adventure, most people we met did not use money; they wanted to trade goods. Empty jars, empty bottles, even used tin cans, were extremely valuable there. An empty vegetable oil bottle or Coke bottle, traded for food, might stay in a family for over a decade. The people of this region once made all of their own storage vessels; later on, manufactured goods were available locally, though never in great abundance. In recent years, with the country going back to the bush and the major cities torn by war and corruption, articles such as clothing, utensils, storage containers, and tools (not to mention bics) had all become rare and valuable.

There was hardly any agriculture in this part of the country. Most people had gone back to living off the bush, picking pineapples, bananas, and other fruits. They hunted for meat; grubs and green monkeys were the two principle sources of protein in the region. I declined to eat either, and we pretty much relied on the beans, rice, and flour we had hauled across the border with us. We ate chapatis (sort of a flour and water frybread) every day, often 2-3 times a day, supplemented with other dry-goods – peanut butter, canned food, pasta, dehydrated mixes. For anyone with cash, there is food available in most of Africa, and often very good food, but not here. Even if people *had* crops and livestock to bring to a market town, the condition of the roads and the lack of transportation meant that most market villages we came across were nine-tenths empty. And people were so poor that the merchandise was heartbreaking; small onions, for example, were chopped up and sold in little pieces. I'd cooked and eaten a lot of meat (including camel) that I never would have thought myself capable of consuming, but the meat in Zaïre was beyond even my considerably reduced standards: green, with yellowish streaks, and covered with flies and other parasites.

Then one day, while we were bogged in the jungle (a twice- daily routine for the most part), an African wearing (I kid you not) tweeds and spectacles came *bicycling* past us. I saw the chicken baskets strapped to his bicycle and threw myself in his path. Within minutes, Pippa and I had bartered empty jars, bics, and an old T-shirt of mine for his chickens, which the Boys slaughtered. Zaïrean chickens are too skinny for a feast, especially for 20 overlanders, but at least the rice was chicken-flavored that night – and a day of de-bogging and then chopping and sawing wood really works up a girl's appetite.

The hunting they did out there, by the way, was mostly the bow-and-arrow type. One day we woke up somewhere in the bush to find a man with a hand-carved crossbow sneaking up on us. He was out hunting and had stumbled across us. Once he realized we were harmless overlanders, he greeted us and went about his business.

I had reached a mental point of no return. I had to learn to love this life, or else go crazy. I mean – the ants, the festering sores, the diet of flour-and-water frybread and beans, the lack of hygiene, wearing the same dirty clothes day-in-and-out until the seams rotted away, trekking into the jungle to find springs from which to get our drinking water, the isolation, the heat, the rain, the boredom which was only relieved by fear, frustration, rage, or hysterical amusement... I finally coped by simply changing; Sue called it my Sheena of the Jungle phase. Suddenly, when we bogged, I would disappear into the jungle with my machete and come back with interesting things. One day I harvested and cooked wild bamboo for our supper (which gave a little variety to those beans and rice). Another time, after we had lost all of our trowels in a bog, I chopped down green bamboo stalks and decided we should fashion trowels and shovels out of them with our knives and machetes. I gave up toilet paper and just used leaves. I bore the hair on my legs proudly, gave up brushing the hair on my head, and was generally a pretty scary person to be around. From this day forward, physical discomforts ceased to rule my life. Four months into the trip, I finally became tough.

We could have gone south to Kisangani at this point. The fighting had stopped (unlike the fighting in distant Kinshasa), and the area was reputedly safe for the time being. However, we decided not to go for two reasons. First, we met a Land Cruiser coming north. It had taken them two weeks to travel 300 kilometers from Kisangani to here. Their vehicle could have traversed the road faster, but it *couldn't* drive over or around the dozens of vehicles bogged in their path – some bogged so deep you could walk on their roofs. Second, we heard that there was banditry on the road going south, and that the police were in collusion with the bandits. We needed to find a real town, though, if one still existed outside of Kisangani and Kinshasa. With twenty people and limited storage space, we were starting to run out of food.

We had reached that point in the trip where even *I* started losing weight (though I quickly fattened up upon reaching Nairobi). Although the life-style wasn't aerobic, it was a pretty tough life at that point, what with all the bogging, wood chopping, and water carrying. Having encountered very few villages since entering Zaïre, and even fewer with food for sale or trade, we had been living off the dry goods we'd hauled all the way from CAR, supplemented with jungle fare (i.e. pineapples, mangoes, and bananas; no one but Alison was really willing to eat the bamboo I harvested). Flour and water pancakes and chapatis, beans, rice, dehydrated food, and pasta all got a little old, despite our and Pippa's best and most creative efforts to somehow make it palatable. And then we started running out.

The problem was, we had no idea how much time to plan on being in this situation. No one knew what lay directly ahead in terms of towns and agriculture, and no one knew how long it would take us to reach the mountains. Nor were we even quite sure what we'd find when we got there. Communications were completely, broken down, with little news passing between local villages and almost none passing between different districts. Consequently, we had to use the food sparingly. Don't get

Zaïrean handbags. The locals kill the monkeys, hollow out their backs, and turn their tails into shoulder straps. (Photo by Christine Watson.)

me wrong — we ate plenty, better than most people in Africa will *ever* eat. But it was less than we were used to. We started daydreaming about food.

For entertainment, I would read a cooking magazine we had found at the bottom of one of the storage lockers. Sometimes, just to keep busy, I would painstakingly write down some of the recipes in the back of my diary: Iced Coffee Mousse with Mocha Sauce, Pizza Loaf, Ricotta Buttermilk Cheesecake, Liqueur Fruits With Mango Cream, Creamy Chicken and Mushrooms... I've still got all the recipes. Right around tea time every day, about four o'clock, someone would break down and start talking about their favorite meal or favorite restaurant, planning where they'd eat when they went home. Some would join in for a bit, then others would snap at them to shut up, why make it worse? I admit, I was frequently the one who started these conversations.

It was all a good indication to me that I would never last long if anyone tried to torture me by starvation.

However, despite all the time I had to let my mind wander in Zaïre (where I thought up the fantasy trilogy I'm now writing), I never once fantasized about sex. I spent my days covered in bites and infected sores, dripping with sweat, caked in mud, fighting off ants and bugs, and then madly fanning damp, greenwood fires and trying to make a meal out of some flour and water and canned stuff. Jungle sex ranked just above malaria on the list of things I'd find slightly preferable to death.

People often ask me if there are many love affairs among overlanders. Answer: a few, though "love" would be a wildly euphemistic way to describe it. Discretion prevents me from being more specific (in print, anyhow), except to say that, while many overlanders forge lasting friendships somewhere between Morocco and Cape Town, I never personally knew (or even heard of) anyone whose affair lasted longer than their journey. (I did, however, once hear of a honeymooning couple who headed for divorce court right after their overland trip.)

In Zaïre, I started to hear the rumor that Bill Clinton was black. I'm not sure how the people in those remote areas heard about the US elections, but clearly they took an interest.

We stopped in Buta, a big town, but found only a bit of grimy meat and a few onions in the market. We hauled water through the bush outside one town only to later learn that there was a still-functional water tap not thirty feet from where we had parked the truck. At another village, far from the madding crowd, we again hauled water jerries to fill them up at some spot deep in the bush, then got lost on the way out. Children guided us back to the truck, and as we set up camp for the night, some adults came by with a special request. They were Christians and had a choir, but they had never been able to sing for anyone. Would we mind if they stopped by after dinner and sang for us? It was a great evening! We all wound up mingling, dancing, and whirling around the campfire with them by the end of the evening.

Unfortunately, things got a bit tense as we moved on. Isiro had a real market and the people were using real money, but we were encouraged to leave the area at first light by a local who warned us of fighting and killing around there. He didn't want to see us get caught in the middle by accident. The next night, a truckload of Zaïrois parked very near us in the bush. Fearless was worried about a nighttime raid (with theft as the goal, but someone could get hurt), so we set up an all-night guard rota. I was cooking breakfast at dawn, so I didn't have to take a shift. However, since Mark, Christine, and I were therefore sleeping aboard the truck that night, I didn't get any sleep anyhow. The truck, after all, would probably be the focus of any attack and was therefore the focus of our own guards. A wakeful night.

I admit, despite my Sheena of the Jungle phase, I was starting to feel terribly foul-tempered and petty. The result of too much time with too few people and too little real entertainment. I mean, boggings and battling the elements are interesting for only so long. I was terribly cranky and increasingly intolerant of my companions. Alison and Grace and I scarcely spoke to anyone else, and the same was true of the other little groups that had formed. There was not much "group feeling," despite having come through so much together.

Luckily, we finally reached Epulu before I decided to take a machete to anyone.

Epulu is where the okapi capture station is. Since okapi only live in the Ituri Forest in Zaïre, zoos and wildlife foundations fund the station, where okapi are captured, studied, and either shipped to zoos or eventually released back into the wild. After such a long period of...well...weirdness, this place seemed like an oasis. It was small and humble, but it looked like a kingdom to me the day we arrived.

The capture station is a group of small buildings on a riverbank. A crocodile had chewed off a woman's arm there less than a month ago, so I was very wary as I crouched at bankside and scrubbed my clothes against the rocks. There's a European in charge (he was away at the time), as well as several African rangers. They employ Mbuti pygmies to haul out of the jungle – and then wash – the 30 or so different kinds of leaves the okapi like to eat (this is for a number of okapi living in captivity at the station). And – *get this* – there was a

Mbuti pygmy smoking his pipe. Zaïre.

shower at the capture station! You can't imagine the sheer bliss I felt at soaping up and rinsing off under running water again!

If you don't know what an okapi is, go look it up. My description can't do it justice. It's *very* big, with round ears, an antelope head, a long neck, a cowlike body, and long striped legs. It looks like it was pieced together from bits of animals that didn't quite work out. It's very shy and seldom seen in the wilderness. The station employs elaborate dugout pit methods to capture them. The okapi living at the station each have a big forested pen to roam around in, and they're so shy that they're pretty hard to spot even in their pens. One of these okapi was particularly lucky – or perhaps he clung to life with particular tenacity; he bore a chewed-up ear from a leopard attack, and some wire in his leg from a poacher's snare, but he was still alive.

The station is involved in other wildlife and ecological projects, though the okapi are their main focus. Among other things, they take away from tourists (of which there are obviously very few) any wild animals which the tourists have "bought" or been "given." They raise them and eventually try to return them to the forest. While several of the captive monkeys affectionately groomed our guide's head, they backed off with obvious distaste when I presented mine for the same service.

We packed up whatever we could carry on our backs and set off into the forest (genuine rain forest now; no more bamboo) with two African guides who were taking us to a Mbuti pygmy encampment. (Pippa stayed behind and stocked up on food, since they grow beautiful vegetables at the station.) Our guides, Remo and Atamato, were great. Friendly, dignified, handsome, and knowledgeable, they were eager to share what they knew about the forest. Eager to improve their English, too, they asked us to correct their mistakes and caught on quickly whenever we did. They also carried serious-looking rifles to ward off predators. That gave me rather too much food for thought whenever I went into the bush alone for a whizz during the next few days.

> *June 2nd:*
> We saw primal rain forest and also secondary growth, which is the result of chopping, burning, and clearing. We saw fresh and old elephant spoor: dung, tracks, destroyed foliage. We leapt over columns of red ants, then exhausted ourselves killing the ones that crawled into our clothing or stubbornly clung to our socks, refusing to die. They're big, fast, painful, mean, and quite hard to kill. Even Remo and Atamato leapt around like girls whenever we came across another column.
>
> To my dismay, we also encountered a snake. One big enough (or poisonous enough?) to make Remo puff out his cheeks with worry a few times. It was hiding under a bush, and I walked quickly past, insisting (rather loudly) that I did *not* want to see it and thought we should stop dawdling here.

We crossed many creeks on narrow little single-log bridges. I, of course, fell into every single creek. As I picked my way through the tangled jungle, it was humiliating to see a Mbuti grandmother running past me, leaping over fallen trees and skittering across those slippery log-bridges fast as lightening. And, yes, she *did* look down on me because of it.

There's an awful lot to say about the pygmies, much more than I can say here. They peopled this whole region long before the Bantu peoples arrived. Living mostly in clans in the rainforests now, they have no say in government and have generally been best off when they've been ignored and left alone. Few of them remain unaffected by the changing world around them, and the nomadic jungle clan living an entirely self-sustaining existence is an increasing rarity. Nonetheless, the clans we saw personally seemed to be striking a balance between maintaining their independent lifestyle and cooperating with the encroaching world.

Pygmies live in small family groups without any hierarchy or division of labor. They live by hunting, have very few possessions, and move their camps fairly often. They have no form of punishment or law enforcement other than exclusion from the group, and banishment is usually temporary. Colin Turnbull's *The Forest People* remains one of the best books about pygmies, particularly if you're specifically interested in the Mbuti people. Whether my experience is representative of not, I must add that pygmies were among the very few groups of people in Africa whom I never saw begging.

There are two major types of roots in the forest: stilt roots, which look like the roots of a mangrove tree, and buttress roots, which act as doorbells in the Ituri Rain Forest. Remo announced our arrival to the Mbuti by thwacking a buttress root with a stick kept beside it for that purpose, a couple of hundred yards outside their encampment.

We entered a typical pygmy encampment in the middle of the forest: about 8 simple, squat, leaf- thatched huts circling a series of smouldering cook fires. This is a family grouping of (I gather) a father, his seven sons, and their wives and children.

Rather than short, I'd say that the Mbuti are tiny all over, with little faces, little features, little hands, etc. But with so many locals being small, I can't always tell around Epulu whether or not someone is a pygmy.

As soon as we arrived, the Mbuti brought out trade goods: bows and arrows, necklaces made of seeds, whistles decorated with beads and monkey or duiker fur, and other handmade items. Most of us had no money, but they were willing to trade for whatever we had brought. Unfortunately, I hadn't brought anything that anyone in the world could conceivably want, not even in deepest Zaïre, so I came away empty-handed. (Don't leave home without bics!)

While it was still light, we went on a hunt with the Mbuti. Turnbull explains their hunting methods in great detail (as well as everything else about them) in *The Forest People*. Briefly, they build a smoky fire, sing some prayers, and string nets across an area of jungle. The women beat the bushes to drive the prey (already disturbed by the smoke) toward the nets. When it becomes entangled, the men catch and kill it. We waited quietly near the nets (being marauded by ants the whole time). The Mbuti are good hunters, and they caught two duiker (a small antelope) during the next hour or two. They let the second one go, as it was still too small to eat.

Despite ruthlessly trading for the chickens and having them killed so I could have chicken-flavored rice one night, I was still horrified to hear the terrified bleating of the grey duiker as the Mbuti examined and then killed it. Alison's enthusiasm and curiosity about Africa warred with her beliefs. In the end, we stood nearby clutching hands while they killed it. (The Mbuti think no more of this than we do of opening a can of soup, chatting and laughing the whole while). I did make myself go back and watch the duiker's posthumous twitching, and later found I was able not to dwell on it when one of the Mbuti gave me a bite of its tender, juicy meat that night. Hunting Bambi had its place here, I found, as did killing chickens.

I went and sat by the river for a while, mindful of crocodiles. I took off my shoes and bathed my feet. A red ant seized upon my flesh. I tore it off and beat it to death with my shoe, then flung it in the river. Five minutes later, I kid you not, this same ant hauled itself out of the river and came staggering toward me for another round.

I made an effort with the women back at camp, having gotten the impression that my behavior so far (i.e. *not* making an effort) had confirmed a bad opinion they had already formed about Europeans and their manners. I had just felt awkward.

Anyhow, I now sat down and tried to exchange names, then I shared some truck food from my daypack with them; that went down okay. Mostly, though, they adored Becki and her harmonica. They made her play it again and again, and they enjoyed trying it, too. But they eventually seemed to grow tired of these big white women taking up space by their fires and asked us to move away. They had children and husbands to feed.

The visit with the Mbuti was not a *National Geographic* experience. How could it be? Twenty white people suddenly stomped into the daily life of a small clan. We weren't unexpected – the capture station has an agreement with them. Visitors pay a fee to the capture station for guides and so on, and the capture station pays an agreed-upon fee to the Mbuti. The Mbuti obviously don't care about money, since their fee was 8,000,000 Zaïres (less than $3) for the whole group.

Of course, between the roads and the political problems, there are very few visitors there. However, everyone in Zaïre assured me (and except some soldiers, I believed them) that no one wanted to see outsiders get hurt. It's just each other that they want to fight and kill. They've got a few things that they're just trying to work out, Remo told me, urging me to convince my friends to visit Zaïre, where they would be welcome and appreciated. Mannerly, well-spoken, literate, and intelligent, he was living in a country which held no opportunities for him. I met so many people like this and wondered what would happen to them. However, it was also the people like Remo who thought of their lives, their problems, and their countries' problems as something that *they* (and not

Me and some Mbuti pygmy women, Just.... hanging out.

we) must solve; and so they also provided the sparks of hope there.

Anyhow, as unnatural as the visit was, everyone relaxed after a while, and it became fun. Women can always communicate when it comes to food, children, or cosmetics, and men can pretty much do the same thing with trade goods and tobacco and muscles. At night, they played music and sang, and it was unlike anything I'd ever heard, a direct connection to the music of eons past (except for the jerrican one of them used as a drum).

Some of us slept in their huts, which turned out not to be an imposition, as they usually sleep round their fires outside. The fires, by the way, fascinated me as an avid student of fire- building. Six logs would fan out from a center point, like the spokes of a wheel; at the hollow center of these spokes would be a tiny glow, with an occasional hint of flame. As the glowing edges of the logs burned away, a woman (each woman had her own cookfire) would push each of them forward a bit to keep the fire going. Her little round cooking pot would fit just as perfectly over the glowing hole as if it were an electrical burner.

John, Alison, and I shared one of the tiny huts. The floor was very dirty, full of all kinds of strange little bits of refuse; I took off my glasses so I wouldn't be able to see any of it. In the morning, I woke up, sat up, looked down... and saw a six-inch-long millipede where my head had been. I think they heard my shrieks all the way to Nairobi.

Have I mentioned that I don't like slithery things?

Of course, I'm not the only overlander who ever hated snakes and other slithery creatures Chris (who wasn't fond of them himself) told us a story about some overland driver who was working on the engine of his truck in some African game park one day. To his astonishment, a snake crawled out of the engine and slitered away. I gather they couldn't get the guy to go near the truck again for a full day.

Stories like that heartened me, especially after everyone laughed at my shrieks over the millipede in the Mbuti camp.

Someone who overlanded a few years back told a story I was glad I didn't hear until after I came home. They had the misfortune, one night, to build their campfire right over some kind of snake nest. All night long, snakes kept crawling out and marauding the camp area. Don't ask me why they didn't just leave. *I* certainly would have.

Deb (the Australian girl who became a Guerba driver) told me about once dashing behind a tree for a quick whizz somewhere in Central Africa, just the way we did half a dozen times a day, every day. As she squatted, a hooded cobra rose up before her. They stared at each other for a moment, equally astonished, before the cobra slithered harmlessly away. Spitting cobras are particularly dangerous, by the way, since they don't have to bite you to ruin your day; the acid they spit can reputedly blind you from 15 feet away.

I only saw a few snakes during the seven and a half months I spent camping in Africa. Mostly I'd see them running away, slithering across the road or something. I tend to suspect that I didn't see many precisely because I tried very hard *not* to see them. Sure, I was getting rufty-tufty, but why push it?

Back at the capture station at Epulu, I saw the first (and only) six-wheel-drive vehicle I've ever seen. It looked like something out of *Star Wars*. It was developed by some wildlife film company as a means of getting through rough terrain. I gather a 6WD vehicle could practically drive up the side of a wall. This baby was crewed by cameramen who had come to film wildlife in the region.

I chatted with one of the Epulu rangers while Pippa and the cooks laid lunch out on our weathered table. Seeing the overlanders dive headfirst into the meal and recognizing that a late start would give me a competitive disadvantage, the ranger gestured toward the hungry crowd and said, "Oh, you need to participate in the feeding time."

How apt.

We saw armed soldiers as soon as we entered Kivu, a province divided by vicious ethnic conflict. Less than two months later, an article about the province of Kivu appeared in *The Economist:* "Whole villages have been massacred with spears, machetes, and bows and arrows. Each new atrocity provokes another in revenge. Villages are burned, people – the lucky ones – flee into the forest, cattle are looted."

In the town of Beni, we divided forces to stock up on supplies. Some of us went to fill up the jerricans at a Catholic mission which would later become a refuge for women and children during the violence to come. A 77-year-old Belgian nun ran the orderly school, orphanage, and hospital which comprised the dozen or so tidy brick buildings here.

I translated for the impromptu tour the tiny, sweet, and terrifyingly energetic Belgian nun gave us after the jerricans were full. In the midst of Zaïre's chaos, the mission was truly a place of peace and light. Dozens of active, healthy children played, sang songs, rehearsed a school play, studied their lessons, and greeted the old nun with enthusiastic affection. All of the rooms were bright, clean, and cheerfully decorated with pictures painted by the kids.

One of the greatest problems in Africa is the population explosion, to which missionaries contributed significantly. Traditional tribal life had customs which helped ensure against the birth of too many children. In many tribes, for example, a woman nursed a baby for several years, reducing her chances of conceiving; she might even refrain from sex during that period.

Missionaries discouraged such customs. Secular aid helped this missionary zeal by, among other things, introducing infant formula into Africa. The formula didn't necessarily meet Western health regulations. The Africans didn't have such regulations against these foreign products; nor did they always have clean water with which to mix these supplements.

Would you have thought – did *they?* – that a couple of "civilizing" adjustments would have such a profound effect? The birth rate exploded, and so did the need for more Western medical aid to keep up with all the babies getting sick on formula which wasn't necessarily regulated and water which was contaminated. No one had thought ahead about how to feed these rapidly multiplying mouths when they got too old for formula, and so the need for food aid also increased. And this is just *one* example of how the population started expanding beyond its ability to feed itself.

So I found this Catholic mission another confusing and contradictory thread in the tapestry of Africa. Looking at the first really bright-eyed, educated, well-fed, rambunctious children I'd seen in Zaïre, I couldn't deny that this mission was doing some of the only good I'd seen in this country.

I left Beni wishing the answer – or at least the question – could be simple for once.

MOUNTAINS OF THE MOON

June 4th:

We've crossed the Equator! There was a sign marking the spot, since (contrary to what I believed as a child) there's no dividing line on the earth when you get there. Locals stopped and watched as we took the obligatory photos. The experience wasn't quite what I expected of Equatorial Africa – it was so cold that we were standing around wrapped in blankets when not actually posing for photos. It's chilly this high up in the mountains.

We had reached the Ruwenzori Mountains at last, also known as the Mountains of the Moon. As we climbed up, up, up on terrible roads, the land started to look like something out of Tolkien's *Lord of the Rings* (which we were still listening to every few nights – that thing is *long*). After months of being hot and thirsty, we were suddenly in a chilly, misty land amidst the clouds. We started pulling out clothes we hadn't worn in months, shaking sand out of trousers and fleeces and piling them on in layers while the truck went higher and temperatures kept dropping.

Some say the Ruwenzoris are the most beautiful mountains in Africa, primarily because of the incredible variety of almost mythical-looking vegetation. Enormous flowers, plants bigger than men, thick clusters of many-colored orchids, vast trees, lush carpets of moss, and dense tangles of green, yellowish, and lavender vegetation all produce a fairytale effect in the shifting mist. Shattered tree trunks, heavy fallen limbs, and thick, gnarled roots squat in the fog, and you'd swear that elves and trolls live in every hollow and shadow. There's snow even higher up, a sheer white topping to a multicolored sundae.

Before independence, this region was the dairy country of the Belgian colonels. Big stone houses with steep slate roofs, vast enclosed cattle pastures, and little dairy farms covered the overgrown hills. Like everything else in Zaïre, these, too, had fallen into ruin. We camped at one farm, and though they still had plenty of cows, we bought their very last wheel of cheese – perhaps the last they would ever produce, since there was no market for cheese in Zaïre, no reliable way to get the cheese to market anyhow, and no foreign trade. In a food-poor country, these dairy farms were all going bankrupt and shutting down.

We bought cheese everywhere we could find it (often using hard currency and damning the consequences if we were caught again). Eating cheese sandwiches, macaroni-and-cheese, and what- have-you with cheese sauce, I began regaining what precious little weight I had lost. Now wet and cold every night, I had *finally* learned to be indifferent to the climate. Being cold was now like being hot – best to ignore them both, something I had never thought I would learn to do.

We were supposed to go on a mountain gorilla safari, the logistics of which had seemed nightmarish for months. Zaïre, Rwanda, and Burundi are the countries with stations from which you set out with guides in search of habituated mountain gorillas. Due to civil conflict (an estimated one million people, for example, had already been displaced due to civil war in Rwanda), all three locations presented a whole series of problems–not the least of which was simple communications. Finally, Fearless was able to confirm that Djomba, a gorilla station in Zaïre, was operational. However, no one was sure if the road from here to there, which ran through Virunga National Park, was open. Some people said it was; some said it wasn't; some said it was only open on certain days; and some said that the European (i.e. Brazilian) road crew might let us through regardless, because we were Europeans, too. We encountered a series of delays when attempting the route, so it was nearly sunset by the time we drove down the Kabasha Escarpment and reached the vast plains of Virunga National Park.

We'd heard that the Virunga National Park wasn't operating anymore, that it was all poached out, that things were so bad here that the rangers had shot what little game was left to feed their families. We expected to see nothing. So perhaps you can imagine our surprise when we stumbled across a herd of Uganda kob (antelope), some topi (antelope), a pod of hippopotami, a herd of Cape buffalo, and a herd of at least forty *elephants!* We were so shocked, so stunned, and so inexperienced that we whooped, hollered, cheered, and scared quite a few of them away. (Later on, this same behavior in other newcomers would thoroughly annoy me; but I know how hard it is to control yourself the first time you see big game in the wild.)

I was overwhelmed! I'd been raised on television wildlife programs and went to the zoo almost as often as the playground in my early years. More than anything else in Africa, I wanted to see big game; but I'd never expected to see it today! Enormous black Cape buffalo sniffed the air with fat noses as the truck paused near them, their thick, curled horns paler than their fur. Elephants sauntered slowly past, swaying gracefully from side to side, ears flapping and bellies rumbling. Round portions of hippos protruded from murky ponds, their muddy gray bodies showing hints of pink here and there. The purple-brown topi and the golden kob gleamed with healthy muscles and twitching senses. The park, though not abandoned, was virtually empty, enhancing the feeling of being alone in the wilderness. Nothing but the waning light could convince me to turn my back on all this, go to the campsite (a spot of beaten earth in the bush), and set up camp.

We slept amidst the sounds of wildlife – and amidst its dangers. Fearless warned us not to go anywhere without a flashlight. Surrounded by the noises of night-feeding hippos and a coughing lion, I didn't need the reminder. Unfortunately, however, my flashlight had broken the day before.

We left the park the next morning after another game run and drove to the town of Rutshuru – where we were promptly arrested. The guards said the truck's insurance documents weren't satisfactory. They were stubborn about it, and Fearless wound up paying something like $250 just so we wouldn't have to spend the rest of our lives there. We camped that night near Rutshuru Falls, a lovely little spot. Months later, I was told that, unbeknownst to us, an overland truck had recently been attacked by gunfire there (no injuries, fortunately); bandits or revolutionaries had apparently thought they were someone else.

As the crow flies, the distance from Rutshuru to Djomba is negligible. We, however, spent most of the next day pushing the truck up a muddy road that turned into an uphill swamp as the day wore on. We were also obliged to push a couple of bogged local vehicles out of our way if we ever hoped to reach our base camp.

The population pressures in this little corner of the world are enormous. People have cleared the forest for agricultural purposes nearly right up to the very top of the Virungas. The only reason they haven't cleared *everything*, leaving nothing for the gorillas, is because of the money that tourism, wildlife organizations, and universities bring to the area because of the gorillas. The people here don't give a flying fuck about some big, furry primates that fascinate well-fed

Westerners. They want that land. Foreign money (and, hence, government interest in conservation) is the *only* reason they have not (yet) taken that remaining land and destroyed the last of the mountain gorilla habitats. While poaching has done irrevocable damage to the gorilla population, habitat destruction is now the biggest threat to their continued existence.

We set up camp at the bottom of the path leading up to the ranger station at Djomba. Within a few minutes, as was so often the case, locals started appearing out of nowhere. Very soon, as usual, fifty or so people were standing around watching our every move, gesture, and breath. We were better than television (which they didn't have, anyhow). The people there were so poor that someone actually tried to prevent me from throwing out my dirty dishwater (I was on washing up duty that night), certain that she could use it for something. I was afraid she'd try to use it for cooking (or for her own washing up), and so I insisted on throwing it out. A basin of dishwater was utterly polluted by the time we'd finished washing the utensils, dinner plates, and fire-blackened pots and pans it took to feed the whole truck; I used to be afraid that stuff would kill the vegetation when I threw it away.

The war in Rwanda and subsequent stream of refugees into Zaïre have added more tragedy to an already disastrous situation, in terms of people, natural resources, and wildlife. The damage done to the gorilla population by the fighting and population displacement in 1994 and 1995 is still being assessed, so I can only address the situation as it was in 1993.

Dian Fossey, of course, devoted her life to the study and protection of mountain gorillas, and it's probable that she was murdered by poachers. A complex and controversial figure, there's a good, brief account of her life and work in Alex Shoumatoff's *African Madness* (which also has a good chapter on Bokassa, CAR's former "emperor"). Fossey's own book, *Gorillas In The Mist*, will tell you everything you ever wanted to know, and then some, about mountain gorillas – which live only in the Virungas, the extinct- volcano mountains in this little corner of the world.

A typical gorilla family is dominated by a silverback (mature male) and will usually consist of anywhere from 6 to 20 individuals. A full grown silverback weighs over 400 pounds, and even a female or young adolescent gorilla could easily kill a full grown man. They're gentle creatures, however, who are (generally speaking) only moved to violence when protecting their young or defending their territory. Gorillas live a nomadic existence over an extended territory, travelling by day and sleeping in temporary nests at night. Their movement is directed by the silverback and dictated by their varied seasonal diet;

they seem to instinctively know not to overgraze any particular area.

Have I mentioned that I don't like walking uphill? Just hiking from our base camp up to the ranger station nearly killed me. However, I forced myself to get there, then collapsed in a sweaty heap while we waited for the guide (who theoretically knew lots about the gorillas; ours, however, seemed pretty under-informed whenever anyone posed a question) and the trackers (who were in charge of finding the gorillas and hacking away bush so we could follow their trail).

Rules for visiting the gorillas are pretty strict. Only eight people at a time can go up. If you find the gorillas (which is *not* guaranteed, though you are allowed two or three trips into the bush if your first isn't successful), then the visit lasts *exactly* one hour. You may photograph the gorillas, but you may not touch them or allow them to touch you; this is to prevent the spread of disease, and also to prevent any situation which the silverback could interpret as aggression against his family. No one who is at all ill is allowed to go (again, to minimize the risk of infection). The one hour begins from the very first moment you see your first gorilla: if you see the hind end of one as it runs away from you, that *begins* the hour, and one hour later you must leave.

It has been determined by scientists studying the gorillas that one hour seems to be a key time period for them, particularly the silverbacks. For one hour, they are comfortable with your presence. Any longer than that, and they start to feel restless, threatened, intruded upon, and upset.

Those mountains are wet, chilly, and very steep, and I'd heard stories of innocent blondes like me hiking straight up and down the slippery hills for 7, 8, or 9 hours at a time, in terrible rain and cold and mist, through thick brambles and nettles and bush, without ever seeing anything more than a couple of glimpses of gorilla fur. Indeed, I was expecting the worst. I was expecting to die of exhaustion and misery on some lonely, wet, prickly mountain in Zaïre. This expectation was firmly rooted in my consciousness as my little group left the station with the guide and trackers and headed into thick, heavy, thorn-ridden bush, walking steadily uphill. But if there was any chance of seeing gorillas in the wild, then I was willing to die trying.

The hiking was a little hard, but nowhere near what I had feared. There were two main gorilla families at Djomba, and we were tracking the larger family. People studying the gorillas have "habituated" certain families – accustomed them to the presence of humans. Although Fossey (and probably other observers) interacted with the gorillas just as physically as in the Sigourney Weaver film, habituation generally means that you're simply able to be among them without causing stress or an interruption of their normal activities. Once a

Young Female gorilla. Djomba, Zaïre.

group is judged to be completely habituated, then tourists can go up to visit them. The gorillas are *wild,* however. At any given time, they may decide they don't *want* to be visited, or they may feel threatened and respond accordingly. (One or two overland drivers I met had been present when the guides or trackers were attacked).

Trackers and guides visit habituated groups every single day, even if weeks go by with no tourists showing up, in order to *keep* them habituated – and also to track their movements. Gorillas are highly mobile, often crossing national boundaries, and can disappear if not contacted regularly.

Beginning our search where our gorilla family had last been seen yesterday, our trackers found them within two hours – which is considered very good time to make when tracking them through dense bush. As you can imagine, not too many people get to this part of the world, and the gorillas (though I'm anthropomorphizing wildly), seemed really pleased to have guests.

Out of all the incredible, wonderful, shocking, stupendous things I did and saw in Africa, if I had to single out one hour or experience as the best, this would be it. It began so amazingly. We were hiking along, our guide assuring us that we were very near to finding the gorillas. Since it's good manners among most Africans to say what you think people want to hear, I didn't believe him. Then suddenly, someone exclaimed and pointed overhead: there were two great, huge, enormous, dark, furry gorillas, clinging to tree trunks high

Alison and some gorillas, just... hanging out.

overhead, and looking down at us somewhat curiously!

My first reaction was absolutely awed wonder. My second reaction was sheer terror. I mean, they're *big*. We're talking major huge! And there was basically nothing in the whole world between me and them. The guide seemed very pleased and immediately changed his direction so that we were suddenly scrambling up a steeply sloping hill, heading straight for them.

What the hell. In for a penny, in for both arms and legs. I followed, as did my companions.

One of the gorillas stayed up there, casually returning our stares. The other came down, looked at us, and playfully tumbled downhill. Seeing another gorilla on a more level patch of land, our guide led us that way.

The rest of the hour was sort of like a *bar mitzvah* or a really good Italian wedding. Either they all started noticing us, or else they were communicating our presence bit by bit to the entire family, which consisted of over twenty individuals. They were highly sociable and seemed very welcoming, ambling right up us, making lots of eye contact, sitting down, lying down, rolling over, clearly asking to be admired, trying to be companionable. The youngsters showed off, just like children. One baby did all sorts of swinging stunts on a little branch right above my head, stopping every ten or twenty seconds to make sure I was still watching. Other youngsters started wrestling violently, till an adult female cuffed them all.

Based on my reading, I had expected the visit to be very tense and formal. I thought we'd have to sit or stand rigidly in a circle, avoid eye contact, speak in whispers, and move very slowly. Nothing could have been further from the truth. Over the space of about a quarter acre of dense jungle, we milled around, wandered back and forth, sat down, stood up, and talked, while they milled around, too. Some of them got bored and decided to eat, but others were so sociable they followed us around the whole time. The group of wrestling youngsters moved *en masse* along with us, at times rolling around so violently they bumped into one of us (at which point the guide would caution us against being touched). They were remarkably gentle, too. You could see that they had no desire to harm anyone by accident and were aware of the possibility. A couple of gorillas shoved people out of the way v-e-r-y gently when they were standing in the way of a particularly tasty bush. One gorilla kept trying to find a way to get around someone without pushing her, until I said, as casually as possible, "There's a gorilla behind you, trying to get past."

The guide clearly felt that no one would be satisfied with the visit unless we could get photos of the dominant silverback. This wasn't the case, but he resolutely kept trying to get us into a good position for it. Our first glimpse of the silverback was startling. He sat inside a bush, and all I saw was this huge, *enormous*, GIGANTIC, *REALLLLLLLLLY BIG* hand reaching out, grabbing leaves, and pulling them inside this sheltering bush to eat them.

The trackers started following him as he withdrew deeper into the bush, not wanting to be bothered by us. I watched uneasily as they started chopping down the bush with their machetes. This does not, by the way, contribute to the habitat-destruction problem. A couple of trackers hacking a small trail does so little damage in bush like that, it will grow back within a week; and a gorilla will undoubtedly soon eat whatever they cut down, anyhow.

Getting nervous about the trackers' zeal, I suggested that maybe we should leave the silverback alone. I mean, why make him mad? They persisted, though. I had to credit the silverback's patience. He finally realized we simply weren't going to leave until we'd had a good look at him, so he resignedly came out into a tiny clearing, played with one of his babies for a couple of minutes, then clearly dismissed us and ambled off.

We stayed at our base camp for a couple of days so that everyone had time to go up for a visit. I used the slow days to repair my tent, write letters, and do some laundry. Several of us carried our clothes to a little rocky stream someone had found in a valley about a 15-minute walk

Me and a gorilla (one I didn't date).

from our camp. I washed my clothes against the rocks, bathed in the stream and washed my hair. Then I laid myself and my laundry out on the rocks to dry, and told my friends to go back to camp without me while I took a little nap.

Wouldn't you know it? I hadn't paid attention to how we got there and couldn't find my way back.

We were getting into the Swahili-speaking lands now, and I had at least learned how to say "hello" (*Jambo!*) and "How are you?" (*Habari?*), but my vocabulary so far ended there. I later learned a lot of useful phrases, like "Where's the tea?" and "Are there any lions around here?", but at the time, I was pretty helpless. I bumped into a couple of men, shepherds I suppose, but they had no French or English, and I didn't yet know how to say, "Where are the white people?" in Swahili (I later learned that it's "*Wapi wazungu?*"). So I gestured, acting out being lost and searching for my camp. They clearly thought I was insane – and quite possibly dangerous – and waved me off with nervous smiles.

Now, there was no chance of encountering gorillas. They lived at least an hour's walk straight uphill from where I was wandering, and I had a feeling they'd be friendly anyhow; but I really wanted to find my tent, my truck, and my dinner before it got dark. I finally solved the problem by (*very* reluctantly) climbing up to a peak until I was so high I could spot the camp in the distance and figure out how to get there.

(And, no, no one had realized I was missing. Or if they did, they decided to be quietly grateful for it.)

We finally packed up camp, slid back down the hill up which we had pushed the truck a few days earlier, and headed for the border. Fearless had been doing all the driving recently, since Chris was extremely ill with some strange malady that started attacking the overlanders one by one. He lay stretched out on the seats, under a dirty Moroccan blanket, looking pale, feverish, and so sick that I felt terribly guilty every time I had to ask him to get up so I could get into my locker. Now equally unwell, Sophie could often be found lying comatose on the opposite seat. Half of the truck was taken up by this sick bay. It was only as we approached Uganda that Chris started improving.

The border – that often longed-for destination of my fever dreams in Zaïre – turned out to be remarkably anticlimactic. We sat there for four long, very *dull* hours, then left Zaïre without a single *infraction* or fine, and entered Uganda. I'd come all the way through the inferno, and I was alive and well – unlike millions of people who would remain there forever. The internal situation would worsen after my departure, and the fighting in Rwanda would spread this way. As I write this, overland journeys now fly over Zaïre rather than going through it; even overlanders aren't that crazy.

More than a year after I left Zaïre, I saw the following headline in an American paper: *Zaïreans Go Hungry As U.S. Props Up Mobutu.*

Will some things never change?

MZUNGU!

U pon crossing the border into Uganda, we immediately got stuck in the mud. I found this so depressing that I refused to get out of the truck. Since there seemed to be nothing we could do for the time being, no one objected very loudly. A couple of the overlanders were so opposed to the concept of another bogging now that we'd left Zaïre, they wouldn't even interrupt their card game. I lay prostrate on the cushioned bench, staring out at the rain which pelted through the open sides and drenched me. A couple of people lay near me in our sick bay, struck down by this mysterious illness that was attacking the group one-by-one; they were virtually unconscious.

I never got sick anymore. I hadn't felt ill since CAR. Even my sores had finally healed, leaving only angry-looking scars which have almost completely disappeared now. But as the wheels of the truck slipped sideways and, accompanied by the shouts of our companions outside the truck, we started careening down a muddy slope, out of control, I confess that I did feel my own mortality looming large in the scheme of things.

June 10th:

Most of us had no current-day mental picture of Uganda before coming here. We've only heard of it as a war-torn hellhole where 9-year-old boys carry machine guns.

We've seen nothing like that, however. The country is now peaceful and slowly trying to get on its feet after two decades of civil war. It's an extremely beautiful land of lush hills, dramatic views, deep valleys, rolling rivers, and a great climate – warm and sunny by day, cool and breezy by night.

Uganda's notorious Idi Amin staged his coup in 1971, when the country was already festering with corruption, tribal animosity, and political murders. During his rule, an estimated 300,000 Ugandans lost their lives – shot, beaten to death, and tortured, their screams could be heard day and night in Kampala. Whole villages were wiped out, as were nearly all professionals, academics, lawyers, doctors, and business people. The Asians (which generally means Indians in East Africa) were forced into exile, having been given 90 days to leave the country; they had to leave behind their homes, businesses, money, and possessions. Roads fell into ruin, the economy collapsed, the cities became charnel houses, and the countryside became a wasteland. Wildlife was gunned down, first by poachers, then for sport, and finally for food. Once known as the Pearl of Africa, Uganda became Hell.

In order to occupy his dangerously restless army and destroy his most outspoken opponent, President Julius Nyerere, Amin launched an invasion of Tanzania in 1978. One of the poorest countries in the world, Tanzania stood alone against Amin. Nyerere managed to mobilize an army, consisting mainly of rural youngsters, which drove the Ugandans all the way back to Kampala. Amin fled the country and went into permanent exile. Despite the horrified outrage I remember Western politicians expressing over Amin throughout my youth, no Western country ever contributed a penny to help Tanzania pay for the war which brought him down – a war from which the Tanzanian treasury has never recovered.

Unfortunately, Amin's departure didn't actually improve life in Uganda – nor were the Tanzanians blameless in the violence and chaos which ruled Uganda after the war. After a confusing period with several different presidents who all barely lasted long enough to make an inauguration speech, Dr. Milton Obote – Uganda's first president, overthrown by Amin – now returned from exile and took power. Guess what happened then? Martial law, mass murders, atrocities on a national scale, and the expulsion of Western journalists. Obote was overthrown again, by one of his own military leaders – again. Then there were more killings and more... Well, you get the picture.

This was all finally brought to an end by Yoweri Museveni, who had served very briefly as a government minister after Amin's downfall. Educated, principled, and ruthless when needed (which is often in Africa), Museveni began with a guerilla band of 27 men and expanded it into a rebel army of over 20,000, many of them children (since so many adults were already dead). His army fought until their opponents were finally driven out of Uganda, and he took power in 1986. Unlike his predecessors, Museveni focused on stamping out corruption rather than human life, and he taught his army to be servants of the people rather than their oppressors. The soldiers in Uganda are astonishingly courteous these days, whether you're white or black.

President Museveni's biggest challenge is repairing Uganda's ruined economy. Progress in this area has, of course, been badly hurt by the hundreds of thousands of refugees that have flooded Uganda as a result of the violence in Zaïre and the war in Rwanda (to say nothing of the tens of thousands of Rwandan corpses which were dumped into Lake Victoria in 1994 and then washed onto shore in Uganda). Nevertheless, the Ugandans hope tourism, which virtually disappeared after Amin came to power, will again flourish someday. To that end, they have begun slowly trying to repair the devastation in their once bountiful game parks.

We pulled into Ruwenzori National Park (formerly Queen Elizabeth II National Park), east of the Ruwenzori Mountains and bordered by Lake George and Lake Rutanzige (possibly Lake Edward on your map), which are connected by a long, wide channel.

The park still showed the ravages of war. The game was nowhere near as plentiful as it would be further south, in the famous parks of Tanzania, Zimbabwe, Botswana, and South Africa. However, there *was* game, and lots of exotic birdlife due to the vast lakes here. Also, there were virtually no Europeans. During the two and a half days we were there, I saw one small car with tourists, and one wildlife cameraman. That was it. Riding around the vast savannah, with the mountains in the distance, spotting leopard (yes!), hyena (yes!), elephant, war hog, Cape buffalo, hippo, Uganda kob, bushbuck, waterbuck, and monitor lizard, I felt like Meryl Streep in *Out of Africa*.

An interesting feature of the park was that the animals were totally unaccustomed to having people there, so sparse is the tourism. We camped out in what was once (and is now again) an official camping area. You could recognize it because there was a hut with a pipe from which ice cold water sporadically emerged. I say sporadically, because it usually stopped emerging any time anyone stood beneath it covered in soap and shampoo. Anyhow, for two nights, the game totally disrupted our lives and our camp.

A lion and some warthogs made quite a fuss one night. Hyenas kept digging up our pit of buried garbage, then the baboons would play with it. I woke up one morning to find a Cape buffalo munching grass right outside my tent. Cape buffalo are relatively placid when in large herds. They are only seriously vulnerable to predators when they are alone; hence, it is *then* that they are aggressive and dangerous.

After months of stalking around the bush at night with our hand trowels, we now all adopted a policy of having a whizz just six inches from the tent flap, lest we be mistaken for something really tasty out there in the dark. I would eventually become quite accustomed to hearing big animals cough, grumble, sigh, snort, growl, and search for food in the night, but it was rather frightening and incredibly exciting the first few times.

There was a lodge at the park, and we were so thrilled to have something to do at night – a bar, a small restaurant, a television showing old wildlife documentaries, a little shop, and strangers to talk to – that we wanted to spruce up (a cold water wash and some wrinkled but nicely rock-beaten clothes) and head for the lodge in the evenings. Getting there in the fading light wasn't bad. Coming home was a real adventure, a thing only to be undertaken in large groups. The hippos, you see, had come up on land to feed by then; to get back to camp, we had to walk right past them. There were a number of mothers with babies, and the wildlife cameraman had already warned us that a mama hippo with her baby is extremely dangerous.

Indeed, just generally speaking, did you know that hippos are the most dangerous animals in Africa? I was most terrified of the ants, followed closely by baboons, as these were the creatures that often made my life a misery, but *hippos* kill more tourists than any other animal. By day, hippos stay in the water, where they feel safe. They are nocturnal feeders, though, and by night they come up on land to consume vast quantities of vegetation. As big as they are, they nonetheless feel threatened if you get between them and the water, and they trample anyone who does.

My father once had to use the ablution block in the middle of the night in some safari camp in the Okavango Delta. While inside, he heard something scraping along the flimsy wall. He looked out and saw a hippo right there. He knew he was probably only in danger if he got between the hippo and the water. However, on this tiny island in that vast swamp, he would be between the hippo and water no matter *where* he stood. So he was stranded inside the latrine until the hippo got bored (or full?) and finally went away. (I used the incident in one of my pseudonymic Silhouette novels several years ago, only the character got trampled and spent six months in a body cast; poetic license.)

I guess it tells you how badly we wanted a little social life after so long in the bush, that we were willing to go back to the lodge a second time after looking at those mama hippos staring at us as we walked past. Just staring, and staring, and *staring*.

If you're like me, you think of big game when you think of Africa. Most Africans, however, have never – and probably will never – see big game. After decades of the white man's trophy hunting, followed by poaching, followed by the growing need for agricultural land, most surviving big game in Africa (with a few exceptions) now lives in protected, guarded parks and reserves.

These parks are often vast; Serengeti, for example, is the size of Connecticut. And they *are* wild; everywhere I went, some idiot had recently been killed because he (or she) thought he was in a zoo, and he'd behaved as if the animals were tame and contained. The parks have definite boundaries, and you have to pay to go in (or else risk arrest and huge fines). Very few Africans in any country can afford to travel all the way to a park, and even those that can, can't afford to pay the entrance fees and camping or lodge fees. So most Africans who see big game are those who work in the wildlife or tourist industries.

Realizing that the support of locals is needed to maintain conservation efforts and end poaching, some governments have now instituted programs to bring locals into the parks for free, to let them appreciate the birthright which some of us travel halfway around the world to admire. Such an effort was being made with the villagers living near the mountain gorillas (before the war, anyhow). In addition, a number of conservationists now concentrate part of their efforts on ensuring the locals get something to make up for the park lands they cannot develop for their own use; funneling tourist dollars directly into the local economy to establish schools and medical facilities, for example. Moreover, some educational institutions sponsor wildlife field trips, though this is still beyond the means of most. In Zaïre's largely deserted Virunga National Park, we met a group of college students on a school-sponsored visit to the park. None of them had ever seen big game before, and they were even more thrilled than I was.

I found myself getting irritable, *really* irritable, as we left Ruwenzori National Park and headed deeper into Uganda. Irritability, and a general difficulty tolerating some of my companions, certainly wasn't a new development, but I suddenly found myself biting people's heads off, absently scratching myself (almost non-stop) by the fire morning and night while I thought about killing them, then going to bed early to fall into deep, nightmare-ridden slumber. Then I'd oversleep the next morning and bite the head off anyone who tried to help me pack up for the day. I was not pleasant company. I even wanted to kill the prostrate bodies in sick bay, longing to lie down in their place.

However, there were positive things, even in my worst moments. I *loved* Uganda. I hope to go back there. You can't imagine how beautiful it is. Green, lush, rolling, verdant, with a heartbreakingly gorgeous view every time you turn around. And there are no nicer people anywhere on earth. It was so hard to imagine these lovely people engaged in so many years of brutal civil war – but the bullet-ridden road signs and burned-out buildings were a constant reminder. Nonetheless, everywhere I went, Ugandans were all unabashedly thrilled to see a foreigner, a stranger, a tourist. Shouts of "*Mzungu!*" (the Swahili word for a white person) followed me everywhere, and everyone wanted to talk to me. How did I like Uganda? Where was I from? Why was I here? Wasn't Uganda beautiful? They were going to make something of this country, they were going to rebuild it, just wait and see! What did I think of President Museveni? Where had I visited so far? Did I want help? Did I need anything?

On one occasion, I walked away from the truck at lunchtime and set out on the road alone. I walked through a little hillside village where I don't suppose they'd seen a white person in years. It was like being John Lennon returned from the dead. The whole village shouted and screamed and laughed with joy. People came running out of their homes to see me, even crippled old men and little toddlers, all shouting, "Welcome!" Several women literally started dancing in celebration. I'd been through places where people stared, where they weren't used to seeing whites, or where they were very friendly, but I'd never been anywhere where people leaped, danced, shouted, and laughed with joy just because I walked by.

The markets had more food than we'd seen since Nigeria, and the merchants were all too happy to see us to be hard bargainers. I even found a fax machine in some little shop in Mbarara, so I tried to fax my parents to let them know I'd come safely out of Zaïre. It took almost all day to accomplish, and I wasn't wildly confident about the printed confirmation we finally got that the message had been successfully sent. However, the young man running the office was so cheerful, mannerly, and eager to help, I felt it would be abominably rude of me to say so.

We'd been camping on unusually hard ground for several nights, so hard that it took a long time just to get the tents up, and going to the bathroom with our bamboo trowels was increasingly problematical. As I scratched my skin and moped one evening, I saw Chris come out of the bush with his bamboo trowel, put it away, pick up the pick ax, and go back into the bushes.

My increasingly bad temper was highlighted that night when some of the overlanders got rowdy and started tearing down each other's tents. Someone tore down mine by mistake, and I was utterly vicious about it. I finally examined my moods and behavior, my itchy mottled skin, my hot flushed brow, my chills, my nausea, my nightmares – and realized I now had the malady that was felling our group one by one.

The next day, I was denied entry at the Tanzanian border.

This illness, whatever it was, had a number of symptoms: nausea, fatigue, achiness, fever, chills, and a rash. I hadn't recognized it coming upon me because the nausea, which was the primary symptom in some people, scarcely touched me. On the other hand, I developed the mother of all rashes, which was a symptom that looked more like a flush in others.

By the time we reached the Tanzanian border, a place called Mutukula according to my passport, I was dizzy and not quite in touch with reality. I remember seeing an adult beating a weeping child with a stick, while everyone else walked by and went about their business. (Many borders in Africa have vast quantities of people wandering around with trade goods or huge baskets of food on their heads). I remember watching this beating with an absolutely blank brain. I had seen many children beaten during my months in Africa. It seemed that every dog I saw in Africa was being beaten at the time. I'd seen one man chained by the foot and anchored to a post in Zaïre. No African can afford a weak constitution; and now, it seemed, neither could I. Bewildered and devoid of emotion, I just watched the beating and wondered who they were and why they were doing this thing right *here*.

The trouble at the Tanzanian border was related to my nationality, not my condition. The Tanzanians had stopped issuing visas at the border. Four of us were nationals who could not be admitted to Tanzania without a visa. We had to get out of the truck and stand in the sun while negotiations commenced. I remember I was so exhausted that I sat down in the road and wouldn't get up. The deal finally agreed upon was that we could each pay the "standard" visa fee in cash – twenty U.S. dollars. We would get no visas or receipts or letters of guarantee, only an entry stamp. The drawback was, of course, that we could get caught in the police checks in the trading town of Mwanza. However, this being Tanzania, old British East Africa, things were a lot straighter here than what we'd been used to; we'd have to pay the visa fee again, but we probably wouldn't be arrested or fined.

In order to avoid the frequent police checks in and around Mwanza, Fearless suggested that those of us without the necessary visas in our passports remain hidden inside the truck, without breathing, moving, or talking, and try to disguise ourselves as furniture. Since I was too blonde to pass for furniture, I tried (unsuccessfully) to think of a better plan. I also didn't see how we could expect not to get caught when we left Tanzania for Kenya, but I had at last learned not to anticipate.

I finally got up off the road at the border and returned to the truck, where I gave up and lay down in the sick bay. I was to remain there in a semiconscious stupor for the next few days, remembering little of anything that happened. Six people left the truck for a couple of days to take the ferry across Lake Victoria. I never saw them pack up and go, not even when they rolled me off the seat for a while to get to their lockers underneath me; it took me over a day to realize they were missing. I was so weak that I had to be helped out of the truck when I wanted to have a whizz. The rash drove me mad with itching, and the fever made me see things. Nothing we tried – various medicines from my personal stash and from the truck's medical kit – seemed to help. My only consolation was that anyone else who'd had this had survived, though that seemed like scant comfort at the moment.

Happily, I started to get better when we reached Mwanza. I sat up and looked around when we parked in the town, and what did I see? Another Guerba truck! This one was fresh out of Nairobi, heading to collect its overlanders in Burundi; they were flying into the capital city. Seeing that truck really gave me a sense of how much we had put ours through. Theirs was still white – ours was the color of the road. Our sandmats were scarred, mud-caked, and twisted with use, our side mirror was missing from that road accident in CAR, we'd repaired or replaced all our shovels and trowels with bamboo, a cloud of dust rose from the seats every time someone sat down, and we were missing things that had been stolen. We looked like we'd been through the wars. The three *people* on that truck also looked awfully strange to me. I puzzled over it for a bit before I finally realized what bothered me about them: they were clean.

Someone else took a pick ax into the bush that night, due to the hard ground. He should have practiced by firelight first, since he wound up hitting himself in the head with it. Luckily, I was feeling well enough by then to relinquish my place in the sick bay.

BREAD COMES FROM ARUSHA ON THURSDAYS

We drove to the westernmost edge of Serengeti National Park and made camp just beyond its boundaries, in full view of munching zebra and wildebeest. Since we had left the regions of nightly downpours behind us at last, I was sleeping outside, lying beneath my mosquito net, looking at the stars, and listening to the final episode of *Lord of the Rings* – when someone in a nearby tent screamed at the top of her lungs.

Apparently a thief had tripped over a tent pole. We could find no trace of anyone, but set up an all-night guard rota just the same. I hauled my sleeping bag into the truck so I wouldn't be murdered in my sleep. Big mistake, as I was then forced to sit up and guard the truck. Anyhow, I never did hear the end of *Lord of the Rings*, though I gather the good guys win.

Almost eight months later to the day, another Guerba truck also camped up for the night somewhere between Mwanza and Serengeti. They were awoken around midnight by men beating against a tent with machetes and demanding money. An overlander coming out of his tent was hit across the back with the flat side of a panga blade. Although the overlanders began packing up camp as soon as the attackers ran away, the men returned within ten minutes and began firing poison-dipped arrows at them. The Waissenye, a hunting tribe of this region, have made poison for their arrows for centuries from the sap and bark of a local tree; I gather the stuff is even available in local markets. According to an article in London's *Daily Telegraph*, rangers in anti-poaching patrols have been killed with such poison-dipped arrows.

One of the arrows fired that night hit Robert Collier, a thirty-year-old Canadian, in the leg while the unarmed overlanders were attemptingto abandon camp and flee in the truck. He died a few hours later at a local mission school where the overlanders sought shelter.

The Kenyan Guerba driver, several overlanders, and a police escort later returned to the abandoned bush camp. The tents had been ransacked, several of them slashed open with machetes; sleeping bags, clothing, and small personal items had been stolen. Villagers near the camp gathered for a meeting and denounced several men to the police. The Tanzanian officials acted quickly, and suspects were taken to the local police station for questioning. According to the vague report of another London paper, three men who confessed to being involved in the incident are now dead, and two others escaped.

Back at the mission school, students made a coffin for Robert Collier and filled it with frangipani blossoms. Hundreds of students and villagers reportedly came to pay their respects and sing hymns in Swahili. Then the truck took Collier's body to Seronera lodge in the heart of Serengeti to establish communications with Guerba, who notified Collier's parents. From there, the body was taken to Arusha, one of the main towns in Tanzania, where it was cremated in a ceremony performed by Arusha's Hindu community; the ashes were flown back home.

The overlanders decided to continue their journey; all accounts suggest that Collier would have agreed with their decision. Guerba, inundated with calls from journalists while trying to deal with this tragedy and also ensure that their crew had acted appropriately (they had), announced that their trucks would no longer bush camp in the area, but would instead make camp at the mission school.

According to all reports and statements, Tanzanian locals and authorities were shocked and horrified by the incident. Guerba, the Tanzanian government, and the international press have all stressed that it was extraordinary for locals to attack tourists like this and emphasized that Collier's death was the result of a criminal element, such as exist all over the world. Following the spontaneous memorial service held by locals, Guerba's managing director issued a statement concluding: "Tanzania and the peoples of Tanzania should not be judged by this isolated event. It was without doubt absolutely dreadful and cannot be justified in any way, but Tanzania as a whole deserves better than to be categorized by this."

Considering the potential dangers of an overland journey, a number of Americans have asked me why on earth we weren't carrying guns for protection. Leaving aside all the complex moral issues, I'll focus on the simple answer. Most countries (including mine) don't *like* foreigners bringing guns into their sovereign territory. In fact, you could go so far as to say they really *frown* upon the whole idea.

Indeed, they've passed *laws* against it, laws which carry serious penalties if violated. Wealthy hunters paying huge sums of money for guided safaris into African hunting concessions may bring in carefully monitored weapons (probably for a pretty steep fee), but African governments don't let ordinary tourists bring in weapons for the purpose of shooting Africans.

Call them crazy, but that's the law.

The subject of the great Serengeti Plains has filled many, many books, films, documentaries, and T-shirts. Serengeti, an area of 14,763 square kilometers, is the site of the largest migration of big land mammals on earth. I've watched many of those films and documentaries, read a dozen of those books, and worn a couple of those T-shirts, so I was incredibly excited to *be* here at last. Coming here was the dangling carrot which had kept me on my feet during some of those really rocky days in long-ago Morroco. When I die, I hope they can scatter my bones in Serengeti, the way elephants scatter the bones of their deceased, one by one, strewn over the miles.

Over two million animals follow the rains and the grasses in an elliptical circle, back and forth across the Mara River, in an endless year-round cycle. They come south in November or December, at the start of the long rains, grazing the nutritious new grass. By June, the plains begin drying out, and the great herds begin the long migration back to their dry-season range in northern Serengeti and the Maasai Mara in Kenya, where they eat the grass that has grown up in their absence. The greatest herds here, of course, are the wildebeest (or gnu) of whom there are roughly one and a half million. Coexisting with them are a million Thomson's gazelles, several hundred thousand zebra, and tens of thousands of impala, buffalo, topi, and eland. With all of this meat on the hoof, there are also plenty of carnivores in Serengeti: lion, leopard, cheetah, hyena, a few remaining wild dogs, and many varieties of scavengers. While rhino and elephant are still listed as part of Serengeti's population, poaching has so drastically reduced their numbers that I never saw any there.

We arrived in Serengeti as the great herds were pushing north, which is the very best time to be there. Once they're gone, you could conceivably spend three days driving around Serengeti without seeing a thing. But while the herds surround you, so does every other living, eating, breathing creature in the vast park.

Zebra and wildebeest like to travel together because they compliment each other's survival skills. Zebra are good at sensing danger, wildebeest at finding water. They also compliment each other's eating habits, rather than competing for the same types of grasses. I can't tell

A lioness perused the menu from cover. Serengeti National Park, Tanzania.

you how many wildebeest and zebra we saw: tens of thousands, perhaps even hundreds of thousands. Everywhere we looked, there were zebra and wildebeest, some eating, some drinking, some strolling. Many were dashing north in a mad rush, as if desperate to reach Kenya (across the Mara River) by the weekend. We saw them fording rivers and streams (where many drown), blocking the truck for long dusty road crossings, running in vast herds or single-file in long strung-out lines. And where they were, so was everything else. During the days we spent in Serengeti, we saw lion, leopard, cheetah, Thompson's gazelle, Grant's gazelle, impala, wart hog, baboon, vervet monkeys, black- backed jackals, hyena, topi, Maasai giraffe, ostrich, hartebeest, eland, and a whole helluva lot of birds.

At night we camped in an official campsite (notable for its drop toilet) and were harassed by nature's creatures non-stop.

> *June 17th:*
> We spotted a hyena lurking in the bushes around camp last night (and Alison and Grace found pawprints right outside their tent this morning). The sound of wildebeest bawling and stomping around continues non-stop; sometimes I think they're going to plunge straight through camp. I heard lions coughing in the

dark, so when it was time for a whizz, I sang *High Hopes* the whole time – loud enough to wake everyone in camp, I was later informed. The drop toilet is not only rather far from the tents, but also the last place I saw the hyena, so I've decided to stick to whizzing right outside my tent.

We arose before dawn, collected our Tanzanian guide George from Seronera, and set off on a game run. It was a chilly and dry morning, so on the roof, we were bundled up and huddled together.

We saw *eight* cheetah – phenomenally lucky! One was a family, a mother and four cubs that were almost as big as she was, though obviously less experienced. They stalked an amazingly plucky (or stupid) Thomson gazelle for a while, but eventually lost it after a brief, abortive attack-run. That alone made my day, but then we later spotted three more cheetah. They may have been mother and cubs, or perhaps grown brothers. They were just kind of wandering around, pausing to play now and then. There is nothing on earth like this.

Our camp was constantly menaced by baboons, too, who strutted around the perimeters like leather-coated hoodlums. The moment we left to go game-viewing, they'd tear open our tents, haul out our belongings, unstring our drying laundry and drag it through the dirt, turn over our table, and throw our firewood and campstools around. Twice a day we came home to a camp that looked like North Hollywood after the big L.A. earthquake. Then the baboons would strut near me and try to scare me. They always succeeded.

I hated baboons. From here to Cape Town they would bully and torment me. The thing about them that's so frightening is that they're very like people. Most animals behave logically. They want to avoid trouble and are only dangerous if you threaten them or their young – or, in some cases, if they're terribly hungry. But a baboon, like a person, will do something just for the hell of it, just to see what will happen, just because it's curious or bored or feeling its oats. They're intelligent and aggressive, and they learn fast. There was always the danger of them trying to climb into the truck while we were in it. I've even heard that down on Table Mountain in Cape Town, baboons have taken to mugging trail hikers. If you come across a troop of baboons, you're supposed to take off your daypack, open up all the zippers, and let them take what they want.

Otherwise, they apparently just beat the shit out of you and take what they want, anyhow.

We came upon a number of hyenas running madly down a dirt trail, straight at the truck! As they got closer, we realized that each was carrying an antelope's body part in its mouth. They would run around the truck, then get back on the road and keep going, clear into the distance. For about twenty minutes, we just kept seeing them approach, one or two at a time, in this way. It must have been a mighty big antelope.

With its heavy forequarters, sloping back, big head, and unearthly whoops, screams, and cackles, the spotted hyena is not the most attractive animal in Africa. Nonetheless, it was greatly underrated for a number of years. Far from being the cowardly scavenger which it was once believed to be, the hyena is, in fact, a very efficient hunter, as well as a territorial enemy of the lion. When you see lions feeding on a kill while panting hyenas watch from a distance, it's entirely possible that the lions chased the hyenas off their kill and moved in to scavenge. Hyenas, by the way, are also perfectly capable of chasing lions off a kill if the numbers are right. These two species compete for the same food supply, and they coexist with enormous enmity and frequent inter-species attacks.

George, our dapper Tanzanian guide, was like a good luck charm. Above and beyond his skill as a guide, you were virtually guaranteed of stumbling across something wonderful and unexpected if George was on the truck. He also had a flowery way of speaking, as if he had learned his English from a Victorian lessons book, that delighted me.

Overlander: "Hey, George, what are you looking at?"

George: "I am trying to ascertain if there are lions concealed in that thicket."

Overlander: "George, do you think I can leave my laundry out, or will the baboons get it?"

George: "Ahhh. Those baboons are of a cunning disposition."

Overlander: "These lions sure look fat and lazy, don't they, George?"

George: "These lions are resting after having eaten profusely of their kill."

For reasons which ought to be obvious, we never stopped the truck for a quick whizz in lion country (tall yellow grass), but only where there was little or no grass whatsoever, so we could clearly see everything around us. Even this had its dangers, though. I crouched by the wheel one day in the middle of Serengeti (you never wander behind trees and rocks in a game park, even if you're dumb enough to stop near them; you see how impractical modesty is on an overland truck?), only to keep hopping around just before the, uh, moment of truth, because every time I relaxed, I'd look up and discover another jeep appearing out of the dust and bearing down on me. The final time, it was no jeep, but rather a hyena. I think he was more surprised than I was.

Self-preservation, however, is sadly lacking in some members of our species. At Seronera, the site of our camp, some tourists had apparently been *feeding the lions at night.*

The mind boggles, doesn't it? They were baiting lions at night, with raw meat, in order to get good photos! I'm still amazed when I think of this.

Those lunatics escaped unscathed. According to the story I heard, however, an overland truck camped there a few nights later, and a hungry lioness came looking for the expected raw meat. Not finding it, she tore open a tent with her claws, cornered a screaming overlander, and demanded her meat.

The commotion woke everyone up. People started running around making noise, hoping to scare the lioness away. A driver climbed into the cab of the truck; when this sort of thing happens, you're supposed to turn on your headlights and drive your vehicle straight at the animal to scare it away. The lioness only left when she finally realized that no one was going to give her any meat. She was rather put out about it, too, I gather.

The park management (i.e. the Tanzanian government) insisted they were too poor and understaffed to provide armed guards for the campsite. Well, in a way, you can hardly blame them. They *do* make it quite clear that you're not supposed to feed the animals.

We left Serengeti and drove through vast, hot lowlands, barren and scrubby, until we reached the Olduvai Gorge. You know: Birthplace of Man, the famous workplace of the Drs. Leakey, etc. There's a really *big* gorge you can't go into, a tiny museum that apparently hasn't been updated in years, and a resentful guide who has memorized a spiel which he delivers at a very rapid rate. From all this, you may gather it's something of an anticlimax. The best entertainment at Olduvai are the well-dressed Maasai who appear out of nowhere to sell jewelry and get their photos taken for a fee. This land, and Ngorongoro, are on Maasai tribal lands, so although it's a national reserve, they may freely roam, gather firewood, graze some cattle, and so on. They're not supposed to hunt, but they occasionally still do. (Then again, we weren't supposed to collect firewood, but we did.)

June 19th:

There are fossil remains here of *enormous* animals, mostly the ancestors of Africa's modern big game. I imagine early man, much smaller than me, coming face to face with those creatures. His world must have been a perilous place.

There's also some kind of plaster reproduction of the famous footprints Mary Leakey found here, the footprints of three individuals walking north over 3 million years ago: two larger individuals and a smaller one. Two adults and a child? A family? The largest one walks ahead, like a protective father, while the other two walk side by side. A suggestive portrait of our distant ancestors. A pilgrimage to the birthplace of my species. Wild, barren, and bleak, the gorge seems like a sacred site.

By evening we arrived at our campsite above the Ngorongoro Crater. Way, way, w-a-y above the crater. So high up that I slept in five layers of clothes and dug my old blanket out of the back of the truck. There were real showers, but only ice-cold water, so I couldn't be bothered to wash. A hyena snuffled around my tent all night. You might wonder what an animal was doing way up there when they all live on the Crater floor, but I was later to see an elephant that high up, too.

The Ngorongoro Crater, as famous as Serengeti, is actually a caldera – a collapsed volcano. The animals living on the Crater floor are among the few that don't follow any kind of migration route, since there's no convenient way out of the Crater, unless you're a hungry elephant or very nosy hyena. The Crater has plenty of water and lots of grass, and it's a very lazy way of life. We couldn't take the truck down, as the Tanzanians have strict regulations about what vehicles can descend into the Crater. We went in Land Cruisers with Tanzanian guides who were very knowledgeable – not only about animals, but about where they were likely to be found on any given day.

The Crater, I have to admit, was a bit crowded. It's a contained site and chock full of animals, so they're very easy to see. It's the only reserve I ever visited where you could simply say, "I want to see jackals (or lions, or zebra, or hippo, or rhino)," and simply be taken to them. This makes it very popular with tourists, since most parks are so vast and wild that you always run the risk of seeing nothing all day. I liked

Mama and baby rhino. Ngorongoro Crater, Tanzania.

the Crater, but it seemed awfully tame to me. However, it was a good opportunity to observe many kinds of animals close up. I have a three-page list of all the animals I saw there, including rhino, elephant, golden jackal, lion, silver-backed jackal, and over thirty varieties of birds. I was getting to be quite an enthusiastic birdwatcher; it's a lot more interesting when you've got dozens of exotic species to look at and learn about.

The fattest animals in the world (except for my mom's cats) live in the Crater. The zebras, with their enormous thighs, looked like those old Toulouse-Lautrec paintings of fat French dancehall girls. I saw lions and hyenas so full they couldn't get up, and wildebeest that virtually waddled. Hippos, of course, always look fat. There was one hippo, though, who broke my heart. An old male who had lost dominance, he was now reviled by the others and driven away whenever he came near. Covered with sores (which look particularly gruesome on a hippo because of the reddish antibiotic ooze their body fabricates around a sore), he lay quietly in muck, alone and apart. Call it anthropomorphic, but I saw a tear rolling down his cheek.

A few hours from the Crater, Mto-Wa-Mbu (Mosquito Creek) was the most awful place I'd been since Marrakech. It apparently used to be a pleasant little village. Then safari vehicles started coming through to stock up on their way back and forth between Tanzania's vast game parks, and someone got the bright idea of selling souvenirs. He made

A Maasia boy. Ngorongoro Crater, Tanzania.

money, and everyone for miles around decided to try the same thing. There soon grew to be too many of them. At the same time, tourism in Tanzania slowed way down for a variety of reasons. Now, any time safari vehicles drive into town, they're immediately surrounded by an aggressive crowd of souvenir hawkers and self-appointed guides whose persistence turns into abuse in a very short space of time. I was to wind up visiting this garden spot four times; it never changed.

My first visit, however, was my most memorable. I was accompanying Pippa on yet another quest for bread. We chose a guide, whose main job was to keep away all the other guides. Since it's often considered bad manners to disappoint someone (until you absolutely have to) in Africa, our guide didn't tell us how hopeless our quest was. Instead, he took us to every shop, café, and inn in Mosquito Creek, asking for bread. No one had any. There was no bread, absolutely none, in the entire overpopulated village of Mto-Wa-Mbu. We asked if the bread was baked in the mornings, and in such small quantities that there was none left by midday?

"No," our guide said. "Bread comes from Arusha on Thursdays." It was Monday. There was no bread in town, and there would be none till Thursday. We considered this, and our guide used this lull in the conversation to ask us for money.

Pippa, who was born in Tanzania, made a suggestion to him. "Instead of begging from the tourist vehicles that come through here, why don't you go home, build an oven in your back yard, bake bread, and become the richest man in town?"

Now, I thought he might say something about logistical problems: where would he get the materials, how would he build even a small oven, what would he use for fuel, and where would he get his initial baking ingredients? These were real, if solvable, problems.

Instead, he claimed there was no need for a local bakery, because bread came from Arusha on Thursdays.

"But there's *plenty* of need," I said. "Your entire town is without bread, since yesterday they say, and more won't arrive till Thursday. Think how many people would buy bread if it was available right now!"

He clearly thought I was crazy. "No one wants bread. Who would buy it?"

"*We're* looking for a dozen loaves right now," Pippa pointed out, "and would pay well for them. Every truck or jeep that comes to this town comes here to stock up on provisions; they'd all buy bread. And there must be someone in this town – surely lots of people – who would buy bread today if it were available."

"But bread comes from Arusha on Thursdays."

We talked with him for about ten minutes, but – irregardless of the practical aspects of building an oven and baking bread – the notion that things might be different, that he could do something new, seemed insane to him. He clearly thought we were crazy. If you know the bread comes from Arusha in four days, why not just wait for it? Why should it be any different? So what if there is no bread? That's the way it is.

And I knew, sure as night follows day, that sooner or later an Asian (which is how Africans refer to Indians) would see Mto-Wa-Mbu, recognize the business opportunity, build an oven, and make lots of money selling bread every day instead of waiting for it to come from Arusha on Thursdays. He'd soon get rich enough to build a real bakery, and he'd become the richest man in town. The locals would all hate him for being a sneaky, cheating Asian merchant who was getting rich while they remained poor. If he was lucky, though, they wouldn't kill him, threaten him, or vandalize his property. *If* he was lucky.

So much of what I had seen in Africa suddenly seemed distilled into this single argument in a dusty Tanzanian town: *bread comes from Arusha on Thursdays.*

We pressed on to Tarangire National Park, a starkly beautiful place in Maasailand, where we were very lucky. We saw many lions and elephants, our *fourth* leopard (some people go to Africa half a dozen times without ever seeing a single leopard), my first dik dik, and, most amazing of all perhaps, we saw a civet (a nocturnal animal) by day. All animals are beautiful in the wild, even the ridiculous wildebeest which are reportedly every bit as stupid as they look. Leopards, however, were the *most* beautiful, I thought; sleek and enormous, gorgeous and deadly, their spotted coats almost seemed to glow in the slanting light of the dying sun as they stalked through the bush.

Generally speaking, leopards are more dangerous to man than the other carnivores in Africa. Any animal is dangerous when it's hungry or threatened, and (as with the notorious man-eaters of Tsavo) some even develop a taste for human flesh. Usually, though, an animal prefers to stick to its natural prey, or to things that *resemble* its natural prey. Even after eating lots of Pippa's macaroni and cheese, I didn't remotely resemble a Cape buffalo, let alone a zebra, wildebeest, Thomson gazelle, or any other four-legged herbivore of the savannah. Leopards, however, include baboons among their standard prey. Not only do we all faintly resemble baboons (some of us more than others, but this isn't the time to reminisce about dating), but the leopard's method of killing a baboon is also a *very* effective way to kill a man. The leopard wraps his powerful forepaws around the baboon's torso to trap its arms, then takes a big bite of its jugular. I started singing *High Hopes* rather loudly again after I learned that.

Everything in the wild has a place, every event has a logical balance quite foreign to the world we've built apart from nature. A wounded animal or limping zebra was a sad sight out there, since we knew it wouldn't last the night; on the other hand, it also meant the predators would eat that night and continue to survive another day. Even the vultures are divided into varieties whose feeding hierarchy ensures that no part of a carcass goes to waste. It was the only time I've ever wondered if there might have once been a Great Plan to the world, after all – before someone lost the blueprint.

We camped just outside Tarangire one night, after obtaining permission from the locals. Later that night, a few Maasai we hadn't met before, but who had obviously heard about us, came along. Though they weren't physically threatening, they kept everyone awake very late (I was already in my sleeping bag). First, they wanted money to buy their silence, because (they said) bush camping was illegal in Tanzania. Since this isn't true, Fearless was unphased and refused. Then they came up with other reasons why we should pay them, lowering their price each time. Fearless kept refusing them; then another round of arguing would take another half hour. Sometime after midnight (which is late when you're used to getting up before dawn), they finally said, "Okay, no money. But you must give us a drink." Fearless said he would have, but he'd drunk all the beer while they were arguing. They made threats about coming in the morning with more demands, but never showed up again; I think Fearless had exhausted them. An old Maasai woman with beautiful jewelry and rotting teeth did show up, though. She flirted outrageously with Mark and seemed to find me terribly funny for some reason. She didn't get along at all with Pippa, who didn't take kindly to the woman trying to correct her cooking methods.

Arusha and Moshi are two more towns on the safari route in Tanzania. They're bigger and less frantic than Mto-Wa-Mbu, though I wouldn't actually say there's a whole lot more to do there. During the next few weeks I went to both towns four or five times. I always saw other Europeans there: ex-pats, whites born in Africa, aid workers, naturalists, or tourists. All sorts of people wandered through, and some simply stopped wandering and planted themselves there. Ex-overland drivers would set up in business: safaris, tours, supplies, small hotels. One ex-driver was even running camel safaris out of a little office there. Many of the shops are owned by Asians, and there's even a Chinese restaurant in Arusha. I somehow always felt like I was in the fictional frontier towns of old movies and pulp novels, and I liked those places, even though they could be dreary.

Winding down on the way to Nairobi, we camped for a couple of days in the gardens of the Hotel Marangu, an old colonial hotel owned by two old European ladies who traveled out here on donkey wagons with their families before World War I. The hotel is at the base of Mount Kilimanjaro, and most of its clients are people who are about to go up or who have just come back down. The ladies who own the hotel have some great stories. One of them has climbed Kili half a dozen times. The first time, she ascended with her father, wearing a wool dress knitted by her mother, back sometime before 1920. I waited eagerly for a sight of Africa's highest mountain, but it was shrouded in mist and fog, and I didn't see it. After two days of colonial teas and great stories, we pushed north toward Nairobi.

There was a real end-of-term feeling as we made bush camp the night before crossing the border into Kenya. Though I was little more than halfway done with my journey, most of the group were leaving in Nairobi, going back to work at jobs, to *look* for jobs, to go to school, etc. Alison and Grace would be leaving Africa in just a few days, going back to their respective homes, and I was fidgety about their departure; I would miss them very much.

I still had almost half of Africa to cross. While I no longer had any doubts that I could do it, I nonetheless felt like a little kid wondering who I'd sit next to on my first day back at school when my new truck pulled out of Nairobi a week later.

LIONS BY NIGHT

I was seized by a migraine the day we crossed the Kenyan border. I only started getting migraines after I began writing books. Before then, I used to sneer at people who complained of them, thinking they should stop whining about a simple headache. This is my punishment, no doubt. I don't get them often, but when I do, the pain is so severe I genuinely feel (at the time) that I'd prefer to be shot. This was a full-blown vomit-inducing, staggering, pale-as-death, blurry-speech, please-kill-me-it-would- be-kinder attack. So I took some Vicodin and slept most of the way to Nairobi, only waking up long enough to exit Tanzania without incident (despite having entered the country illegally). All I really remember about the border is plowing my way through a thick horde of Maasai women selling trinkets at "good price."

When the medication finally wore off, I decided I was eager for news from home, and so made a trip to Nairobi's central post office just before closing time. A vast, cavernous building with several floors and many different windows, offices, and departments, it was nonetheless the best-organized place I'd seen in almost all of Africa. A huge pile of mail awaited me, as well as a notice informing me to go to the second floor to collect a package from America (from my mother).

I went upstairs and spent the next hour working my way through a series of lines ("queues"), getting various papers and receipts stamped so I could collect my package. To my intense frustration, I then learned I had to pay 23 Kenyan shillings to claim my package from customs. Having only just arrived in the country, I had no shillings, and all the banks had already closed for the day. Seeing my distress, Mr. Osir, who ran the desk where my package was being held, gave me 23 shillings

out of his own pocket so that I could take my package away. This was
my first taste of kindness in Kenya, a quality which I soon learned
characterized so many Kenyans. (Mr. Osir gruffly brushed aside my
thanks when I returned two days later to pay him back.)

I had become increasingly confused about my career as I travelled
across Africa. Although it would be pleasingly dramatic to say I had
burned all my bridges, I hadn't. Some people envied me for making
this journey, but some people in publishing clearly thought I was
insane for abandoning my career for nearly a year. I had at least
partially covered my bets by leaving some book proposals in submis-
sion with my two category romance publishers before leaving home.
I expected to receive their responses in Nairobi. But as I retrieved those
envelopes from the post office, I really didn't know what I wanted their
responses to be. While I didn't have an alternate career plan in
mind, I had nonetheless started asking myself on a daily basis,
"Can I really go back to writing those books?" The answer was
always *no*; unfortunately, this silent voice didn't tell me how I
would support myself instead. So I couldn't decide if I wanted
those book proposals to have sold or not.

Well, I got precisely the reward that such ambivalence usually
reaps: a totally confusing message from the universe. A letter from my
father notified me that at about the same time I'd been scrubbing out
my festering sores on a beach in Nigeria while Togolese religious
refugees flung a dazed goat into the ocean every night, one of my
Silhouette books had won an award (at the annual *Romantic Times*
awards banquet) as the best book published under its particular
imprint that year. There was also a letter from my Silhouette editor,
dated three weeks after this event. She notified me that after ten novels
(and an eleventh which would be released the following winter), they
had finally decided that Laura Leone's (my) books were not selling well
enough for them to keep publishing them (which perhaps tells me what
awards are worth).

I had worked with my editor for almost five years, I respected her,
and we got along well (indeed, we've stayed in touch and she's done
me a couple of favors since then). She spent some time softening the
blow, but the bottom line was the same. Considering that my earn-out
(the eventual sum a book has earned for the writer once the royalties
are all paid) more than doubled my advance on every single book, I
was a little surprised.

However, I would have expected myself to be more upset. I mean,
the mainstay of my career for the last five years had just kicked me out
the door and told me not to knock again. Surely I should be... I don't

know... *crying* or something? Maybe the fact that, while reading this letter by flashlight, I had to stop every so often to chase a wart hog away from my tent somehow reduced the letter to its proper proportions. (We were camped at the edge of Nairobi National park, a wildlife reserve just outside the city.) Something about tonight, something about the past nineteen weeks, all made the issues in this letter seem really distant and unimportant. So I was no longer a Silhouette writer; so what?

And, just to make sure I was *really* confused, a competitor of Silhouette (same market, same type of book) to whom I had sold one book before leaving for Africa wrote that they were interested in buying another one from me. I stared at the letter and wondered what the universe was playing at. Since I expected to need the money upon returning home, I thought I should probably be grateful. However, my diary is full of really indelicate comments about how I suddenly felt about my career in this field.

We had our farewell dinner the next night in the beautiful Norfolk Hotel in Nairobi, a hotel famous for decades for all the well-known figures who have stayed there. The Norfolk and the New Stanley were the two major hotels in pre-Independence Nairobi, so any movies, books, and stories you've seen about those days may well have a scene or two taking place there. Grace and Alison and I parted tearfully, and I went back to the very nice room I had rented at the Hotel Boulevard. Since I wouldn't be leaving Nairobi for a week, I was looking forward to the prospect of actually being in one place for more than a couple of nights for the first time in almost five months.

Do you want to know what happened to everyone "afterward?"

Sophie and a few others went on to Harare with Fearless, so I saw them all occasionally over the next couple of months; Sue, as I've mentioned, went all the way to Cape Town on the same truck I took out of Harare. John, who had taught me and Alison to build fires, jumped ship (so to speak) for reasons of his own, so we were on the same truck to Harare.

Sophie eventually went home to a good job. Last I heard, Fearless had finally quit overlanding and gone home to get his degree. Jenny worked in Europe for a while and had gone back home last I heard; so had Evelyn. Chris went travelling round the world. Pippa left Guerba to work at a lodge in Zambia; I recently heard that she was still in Africa, working in a refugee camp.

Grace went home to England, retired to Scotland, got bored, and, as I write this, is overlanding somewhere again. Mark and Christine, instead of going straight home to New Zealand, took jobs in London, which they've been using as a travel base ever since. I've visited them once and often receive letters from them.

Alison, who probably won't know a dull moment even in her grave, took a job in West Africa, lived through a revolution, got engaged to a Nigerian airline manager, embarked upon a (at this date) disastrous attempt to raise chickens, and just recently sent me a wedding photo from Sierra Leone. If I finish my next book on time, I may scrape together enough money to go visit her.

I spent part of the week in Nairobi just shopping, replacing torn, stained, and rotted clothing, and stocking up on Listerine, band-aids, shampoo, shoe laces, and other staples. Nairobi is a big city, a sophisticated tourist center, with many shops, cafés, restaurants, and hotels. Despite its reputation for violence, I liked both the city and its citizens. A number of the overlanders were there all week, too, and we often went to restaurants or the movies (*movies!*) together.

Whether you enjoy mountains, desert, savannah, or beaches, whether you're interested in wildlife, nature, history, music, or literature, whether you want to meet traditional tribal people, urbanized Africans trying to balance their heritage with Westernization, or whites trying to maintain a colonial life-style in post-colonial Africa, Kenya has something to enthrall you. My greatest regret is that during nearly eight months in Africa, I only spent one week in Kenya; and I stayed planted in Nairobi, enjoying the sensation of not having wheels under my butt.

Kenya was the home of most of the famous white adventurers, explorers, hunters, colonials, farmers, cads, and bounders you've read about. The notoriously bloody anticolonial Mau Mau uprising took place in Kenya, at a time when the white population had reached 80,000. The country's first president was Jomo Kenyatta, one of the most famous figures of the African independence movement, whose cry of "*Harambee!*" ("let's pull together") united this country of such diverse races and tribes. More than fifteen years after Kenyatta's death, Kenya now faces the same problems of most other African countries: a nose-diving economy, disastrous overpopulation, unemployment, violence, civil unrest, and environmental destruction (which includes catastrophic levels of wildlife poaching).

Since I was in Nairobi for a week, I looked up a friend of my father's. Perry went out to Kenya as a nineteen-year-old to fight the Mau Mau uprising as part of the British armed forces. He then spent twenty years working as a white hunter; when hunting was outlawed, he became a photo safari guide. He's also a champion steeplechase jockey, a horse breeder, and chief steward at the Ngong Race Track outside Nairobi. He represented Kenya in the All-Africa pistol-shooting contest three different times, and was a bodyguard to the late Jomo Kenyatta. He doesn't ever talk about any of this, by the way; I had to pump my father. If I've gotten anything wrong, then it's Perry's fault for not bragging as most men would.

Perry and Vivien, another horse enthusiast, invited me to stay at their lovely home in Karen (a suburb named after Karen Blixen) for a couple of days. This was a life not only outside my experience, but, after the past few months, outside my imagination. Servants, cocktails, a spare bathroom, a beautiful garden, a television... I felt like Alice slipping into Wonderland. Perry and Vivien showed me far more hospitality and kindness than was required by their acquaintance with my parents, and they made me feel welcome in a world quite different from my own. They threw a luncheon party one day, then took me to the races at Ngong the next, the sort of horse track where people dress up and get served tea. As I wandered around Ngong, I ignored how people's gazes flickered over me in astonishment and just hoped that my appearance didn't embarrass my hosts too much.

The first three times I took a bath in my Nairobi hotel room, the water turned a murky brown as I soaked. Although clean and even tidily dressed now, I still didn't resemble many of the whites I encountered in Nairobi. Mindful that I was going back on the road soon, I decided I didn't want to deal with brushing my hair, so I'd paid a local woman to secure it in a few dozen tight, tiny braids that made me look sort of like a blonde, pink-cheeked Rastafarian. I had only two pairs of shoes: my shabby hiking boots and the car-tire sandals (generally worn by poor people) I'd picked up somewhere in Tanzania. I'd go unnoticed at a youth hostel, but not many other places.

Having mostly encountered missionaries, aid workers, naturalists, and travelers among the few whites I'd met in Africa, I was to start learning in East Africa that the Afrikaners of South Africa are not the only white tribe. The whites of Eastern and Southern Africa may hold British or European passports, they may even have been born back there; but despite the resemblance, I don't think they're really British or European anymore. After a few encounters that bewildered (or appalled) me, I decided I was a foreigner among African whites, too, in the strongest sense of the word. They, too, are part of Africa now, and I really can't pretend to understand them any better than I understood Africans I saw stabbing themselves in the belly, covering their hair with cow dung, or fasting for Ramadan.

I did, however, think some of the unconcealed bigotry I

encountered was amazingly myopic; who did these people think their nations, and this continent, belonged to? It's a new world, and whites are only there now because the Africans (for their own reasons – which are usually economic) allow it.

Anyhow, the bright lights, intriguing people, exciting pace, and unaccustomed luxuries of Nairobi held me in thrall for a few days, but after a week I was tired of town and chairs and pavement and beds. I was ready for the bush again.

In a nice, clean, well-lighted conference room at the Hotel Boulevard in Nairobi (so different from the abandoned disco at a frozen Spanish campsite in February), I met my new companions and we went over the route and our plans.

Our driver, Deb, was a 26-year-old Australian woman who had already crisscrossed Africa several times. The co-driver and campmaster, Joseph and Richard, were both Kenyans; Guerba employs quite a few Africans. These guys were both trainees, and this trip would be Richard's first time out of Kenya.

You pay the bulk of the money for your overland journey directly to the company upon booking the trip. The price varies depending upon the company and the trip. While Guerba is not the cheapest company (indeed, there are some one-truck operations that are *really* cheap), I thought it was the best deal, since almost everything was included in the onetime fee I had paid them. Quite apart from the quality of the company, which can suddenly seem terribly important when you're staring at a land mine in Western Sahara or under arrest in Zaïre, I suspect that expenses can *really* mount up when they're not included. For example imagine going to Djomba but not hiking up to see the gorillas because, after four months on the road, you haven't got $125 left.

Next, your food money gets collected for the kitty at the start of the trip: a sum of which you are advised well in advance, and which you can pay in hard currency or travelers' checks. The kitty pays for groceries, fee-charging campsites, firewood, and similar purchases. Any money leftover at the end of the trip is evenly redistributed among the group. There was always money left over in my experience, and my contribution over the months rounded out to about $100 per month – certainly less than I spend on groceries at home!

Other than that, you bring along however much money you estimate you'll need (or however much you're able to scrape together) for all the extras in life: visas, tips for guides, personal supplies, souvenirs, fines, special side trips, etc.

The trucks are supplied with a fairly amazing array of travelers' checks and hard and soft currency to pay for fuel, supplies, emergencies, crew wages, customs fees, fines and *infractions*, game parks, guide fees, and so on.

One of the reasons I was able to make this long journey is that I had worked out that I'd spend about the same amount for this trip as I would spend in nearly eight months of my normal life in the US. Overlanding isn't expensive.

I still didn't have a visa when we crossed the border back into Tanzania. The Tanzanians were a little annoyed, since I had come straight from Nairobi, where I easily could have gotten one from their embassy. (I confess, it just slipped my mind.) But then, while idly flicking through my passport, one of them finally noticed that I had been to Tanzania before with no visa, that I had exited Tanzania at *this very border post*, and that no one had noticed I was coming and going with *no* visa.

Naturally, I played dumb ("A visa? You mean I needed a visa? No one ever told me that!"), but that didn't do me much good. No one was upset with *me*, no indeed. The supervisor was just upset with every civil servant within shouting distance. How, he demanded of his subordinates, had they let this American girl slip across *two* borders without a visa? His shouting caused everyone else to shout, and the little office was soon filled with Tanzanian bureaucrats in a communal uproar. They all ignored me completely, as well as my repeated suggestions that they let me get my visa now and *then* sort out their own problems.

After the shouting died down, there was the visa fee to pay – for real this time. I didn't have Tanzanian cash, and the border bank was closed. Things got very confusing after that, but we sorted it out eventually. It was one of the few times that I was sorry that East Africa is so much straighter than West, Central, and North, and you can't count on smoothing things over with a bribe every single time.

I was mulling this over on the roof of the truck as we rolled through Maasailand around sunset. I smelled something burning. Distracted, I glanced down. I saw smoke – waves and waves of it billowing out from under the truck. I hit the emergency stop signal and was climbing down the side of the truck before we came to a halt. No one in the cab had been able to see the smoke, and the brand new overlanders in the back weren't sure if something was *really* wrong or if this truck always smelled that way. (In their defense, Deb *did* have one of the company's oldest trucks.) So they all felt rather shy about stopping the truck. I think they lost some of that shyness as I jumped up and down screaming something like, "Why didn't any of you idiots press the goddamned buzzer? What the fuck is wrong with you?"

Deb and Joseph crawled under the truck and started fixing it. Knowing nothing about trucks, I haven't the slightest idea what went wrong, but things would *always* go wrong with this truck, and usually at the worst possible moment. Some Maasai came along and hung around watching us, since it was undoubtedly good entertainment watching the *wazungu* struggling with their toys and machines. They are splendid looking people, especially if you've only recently stepped off a plane from Europe or North America. The Maasai generally remain aloof from mainstream life in Kenya and Tanzania, though modern encroachment has limited their territory and destroyed some of their customs. A herding tribe, reliant on their cattle and usually contemptuous of farming, they're often depicted on postcards, tourist posters, and the covers of guidebooks because of their impressive tribal dress – dangling earlobes, elaborate beaded necklaces, manured hair, spears, and robes of purple, orange, or rust. At Ngorongoro, pre-pubescent Maasai boys wear the elaborate feathered headdresses of a Maasai warrior and charge for photos (so I guess they're not *that* far outside the mainstream).

We camped up for the night right there. Deb explained to the new overlanders how life on the road would work for the next few months. I taught a couple of the women how to whizz in the bush without hitting their shoes and ankles (the secret is to face downhill on a slope). When jobs were being assigned, I decided it was time to test my mettle, so I volunteered to be a fire-builder and took over the axes, saws, matches, deadly fluids, and other implements of my apprenticeship in the jungles of Zaïre. I can't tell you the difference I noticed here! Building a fire with dry wood on windy plateaus was easier than rolling off a log.

The Maasai hung around our camp all night, and I think some more came to have a look at us, too. I heard lots of squealing and gasping and general alarm from the other women, but I was too worn out from my new tentmate's already ceaseless chatter to care. I doubted the Maasai were there to steal anything, and except for vaguely wishing they'd kill my tentmate while I slept, I didn't give them another thought.

However, the way everyone else jumped every time one of the Maasai would take a step or tilt his head, and the way people were reacting to the bush in general finally brought a realization to the forefront with stunning clarity: *I had really changed.* As my new companions daily changed their clothes (to, you know, put on *clean* ones), asked for someone to accompany them into the bushes, worried about washing, and screwed up their noses at any mention of tropical sores, jiggers, parasites, or diarrhea, I finally noticed that I was not the same woman who had struggled desperately with this life-style, and this continent, for so many months. All the overlanders asked my opinion, asked me to show them how to do things, and sought my help. I found it unnerving. *I* was the woman who everyone on Fearless's truck had thought should never have come here. I had spent so long in the same company, I'd had no yardstick against which to measure my growth.

One evening I built a fire *and* set up the portable gas cooker (which ran off a small tank, and which Pippa had taught me should only be used in emergencies) for Richard who, I was discovering, could spend four hours, burn all my firewood, and use up all the gas preparing what, night after night, turned out to be noodles and tomato sauce. Anyhow, when I was done with my work for the time being, I absently mumbled "I'm dirty," as I looked at my grime-blackened hands.

One of the Girls (as we had dubbed the nubile young blonde women in the group) said to me, "Oh, people like you don't notice being dirty."

I decided she meant it in a nice way, and I said, "Oh, no, that's people like the drivers and the campmasters. No, I'm a clean, fastidious type." Admittedly, my tire sandals, old torn clothes, Maasai hairdo, scarred legs, and already dirt-stained skin probably didn't look very convincing.

She looked at me speculatively. "I know you *say* that, but it's awfully hard to picture. You seem so normal and comfortable here, like this."

As proof of my claims, I showed her my passport photo. She found it so funny that everyone insisted on passing it around. No one could believe it was me. Who was that well-dressed woman with normal hair, a clean face, and eye make-up?

I realized that I had indeed changed. My "real" life back home seemed like a distant memory, no more real than the publishing gossip I'd received in the mail in Nairobi. And I loved the life I was living now.

Wow. Turn around one day and find that somewhere, somehow, you became someone else. And while this person still had a dreadful temper, at least she didn't whine as much.

The great herds had moved far north by the time we reached Serengeti (the trip to Harare meant there was some backtracking for me, but I was certainly content to pay two visits to some of the greatest game parks in the world), so game wasn't as plentiful here as it had been a couple of weeks earlier. Among the zebra and wildebeest, we mostly saw stragglers now – the sick, the lame, the old, the lost – who would be eaten by territorial predators who remained behind rather than following the herds north. Lions, for example, tend to stake out a territory, staying there year around as the game comes and goes. We saw some wildebeest carcasses already. One was very fresh, a wildebeest which had keeled over from disease. Apparently no predators had seen or smelled it, for the vultures were breaking into a whole carcass, not just picking at unidentifiable remains.

They are nasty creatures, and they make the most disgusting noises. There's a natural hierarchy among the different varieties of vultures, and hence an important order in their attack upon a carcass: some pierce skin, some devour intestines, some eat one part, some another. Normally they would just eat what was left behind by lions and hyenas, followed by jackals, so this untouched carcass was quite an opportunity for them. They were just doing their job, but watching them stick their long necks deep into the bowels of the carcass and then pull back, their heads dripping with blood and internal body parts hanging from their beaks, was pretty eerie.

As a result of the recent lion attacks (thanks to those tourists baiting lions with raw meat) Seronera Lodge had posted this useful advice: "If you are attacked by a lion, sound the alarm."

I would certainly write that down and try to remember it in times of crisis.

We pushed north and camped at Lobo, since Seronera was still supposed to be risky. So I spent the next day and a half being menaced by baboons and hyenas at Lobo; I would have preferred lions. I heard that soon after I was there, a hyena looking for food broke into a tent while someone was sleeping in it. No one had been feeding them at Lobo; apparently the hyenas simply decided the campers just hadn't thrown enough refuse into the garbage pit near their camp that night.

We normally dug holes for our garbage and buried it. This could be easy (in the desert) or a major challenge on hard land requiring a pick axe. There were actual garbage pits at Lobo, probably intended to work like compost heaps. They never got the chance, since the hyenas and baboons hung out and played with anything they couldn't eat – meaning we had to be very careful about what we threw away there, since you don't want them seizing upon tin cans, glass, or anything toxic.

Added to this interesting problem, the garbage heap was next to the little tree-lined path leading to the drop toilets (outhouses). One would like to use the national park's outhouses, since they are provided for a reason, but one risked considerable harassment (or worse) by doing so at Lobo. After all, you don't want to trip over a hyena, or startle one, or make one feel cornered. Even supposing you survived an attack by those powerful jaws (quite capable of crunching a hefty thigh to splinters), they're probably carrying enough diseases in their teeth to fell an elephant. However, hyenas are relatively logical animals, like most animals, and will usually try to avoid a confrontation with something that isn't their usual prey (like me, for instance).

Baboons, as I have had occasion to mention before, are another matter entirely. Indeed, I would entertain a debate that they're even more terrifying than safari ants. An ordinary female baboon can kill a strong grown man. They have twice as many hands as we do, their jaws are extremely powerful, and their teeth are appallingly sharp. Moreover, a baboon will tease you, challenge you, test you. It will get angry, insulted, pissed off. And they're extremely clever. Anything *I* can open up, close down, get into, or unfasten, so can *they*.

There were baboons *everywhere* at Lobo. Since Deb told me she had even once seen baboons open the sliding glass doors at Seronera Lodge, come into the restaurant, pick up plates of jam, lick off the jam, and drop the plates and run away as the waiters started shrieking, I didn't really anticipate being able to keep them out of our supplies.

Having been bullied by baboons all night and all morning, we decided that we'd spend the next night far to the south, at Serengeti's Naabi Hill. Unconfirmed rumors of a black mamba in the drop toilets only increased my desire to try someplace new. (Have I mentioned that I *hate* snakes?)

There was also one other menace I had decided I couldn't live with any longer: my new tentmate. I'd never had much in common with my former tentmate, Evelyn, but she was easy to get along with. After only a few days, however, I was ready to kill my new tentmate. I dubbed her Imelda in the privacy of my diary, since she had brought enough shoes with her for a whole *army* of overlanders. She talked nonstop, an incessant chatter from the moment she woke up to the moment she fell asleep. Actually, I don't mind a talker, being one myself, but I'd never met anyone so *nasty*. The few times she stopped talking about herself, it was only to bitch about our companions, the crew, the truck, the wildlife, the tent, the campsite, the locals, the food, Africa, the sunset, and the world in general. After three days of living with her, I thought death by slow poisoning would be preferable. So I told her she'd be sleeping alone from now one.

As we pulled into Naabi Hill at sunset, an empty campsite overlooking a vast plain, I looked forward to a peaceful night. I sat in the cab and admired the scene until Deb suddenly said, "Oh, no! We have to tell them, don't we? I wish we didn't. The Girls have had all they can take for now."

I followed the direction of Deb's gaze. Three male lions and one very large female lay about one hundred yards away. All of them were looking rather intently at us. "I don't think we've been invited," I said.

We couldn't leave, however. The law in Serengeti – and every African park I ever visited – was that you must be safely camped up, or in a lodge, or gone by sunset. No driving whatsoever after dark. Mostly for the protection of the animals, but I imagine the rule protects people, too. Other than a few special nocturnal safaris, I know of no exceptions (though I assume you'd be excused for driving after dark if you were wounded or seriously ill), and the penalties are very stiff. Certainly the situation before us wouldn't be enough to convince the Tanzanians we had a good reason to break the law. Besides, where else could we go? The nearest campsite was two hours away, and *that* was Seronera – with its hungry lions.

Generally, lions are unlikely to attack people. There are exceptions, of course, but barring real stupidity (feeding lions, threatening them, pissing them off), the greatest danger is surprising one (on the way to the drop toilet after dark, for example). There are occasional man-eaters, but most lions who attack people are quickly hunted and killed these days. Or else they're captured and taken off to private safari reserves, where they're considered a real tourist attraction.

Sitting in the cab, John, Deb, and I thought that it seemed extremely unlikely that that these lions would cause us any trouble as long as we weren't stupid (stupid as in sauntering closer to get a good photo, or wandering alone to the drop toilets after dark). They looked peaceful, lazy, a little timid, and quite fat. No trouble there, we figured. However, everyone else, including the Girls, would have to be told.

The Girls didn't take it too well. They'd only been in Africa a few days. They were already stressed by the lack of washing facilities (no plumbing on the Serengeti plains), the dust, the long days, the menacing baboons, the apparent black mamba, and the glowing-eyed hyenas; and *now* they were surrounded by lions. Lions which were, I must admit, getting rather noisy as the sun went down. Deb was at the end of her rope, too, since the truck had broken a spring (what did I tell you?), and we were not only stuck here for the night, but would be stuck here until she could fix it. Since she had big enough problems to wrestle with, she asked me to talk to the Girls, who were inside the truck, crying, and reluctant to come out.

I sat down with the Girls, sympathized with their fear, assured them that the lions would not trouble us, told them that we just happened to be in their territory but it was nothing to worry about, promised there would be water at Ngorongoro in a couple of days (I wisely neglected to mention it would be ice cold water at the top of a misty mountain), and generally assured them this would all get better.

They threw me off the truck.

They told me to stop making fun of them! To go away! I assured them that I had found this trip and this life just as hard in the beginning as they now did. I had thought about quitting every single day for nearly the whole first month. I had obsessed about washing, going to the bathroom, privacy, safety. I had slept badly in the bush, hated campfires, hated the cold, the heat, the inconveniences. I had been afraid the first time I heard lions near my tent.

They didn't believe me, and they threw me off the truck before I could make them feel even more wimpy with my pathetic efforts to cheer them up. Go figure.

Then Imelda got on my nerves, whining all evening about how I had "abandoned" her, and what a "shit" I was for leaving her to put up her own tent by herself (this delivered *while* I was helping her put the damn thing up, in the vain hope that she'd shut up), and how she wasn't at all pleased about being alone. Having failed in my attempt to comfort the Girls, I snarled at Imelda that if she couldn't cope with being alone tonight, then she'd never survive, because there was *lots* worse in store. On that note, I stomped away.

I didn't get much sleep that night. Wouldn't you know it? These were the *noisiest* lions in the whole wide world. They spent all night circling camp, calling to each other, coughing, growling, moaning. And loud, *LOUD*, let me tell you: a voice that deep carries for a long way. There were moments when they sounded like they were five feet from my tent flap (though no one ever saw any of them closer than thirty yards). None of this activity seemed to involve us in any way, though it did make having a middle-of-the-night whizz somewhat problematical. Judith, a very game Englishwoman about my age, got fed up with them at one point and shouted, "Oh, for God's sake, I'll come out and help you find whatever you're looking for if you'll just *SHUT UP!*" In the brief lulls, I heard voices chatting nervously most of the night. Normally two people slept on board the truck to guard it; that night, *nine* people slept on board.

It was an interesting beginning for my new companions.

After Serengeti, we went to Olduvai Gorge and the Ngorongoro Crater, which I had the great good fortune to see for a second time. Then back to Marangu, and the old colonial hotel at the base of

Kilimanjaro. Sadly, despite spending a total of at least eight days camped in the vicinity of Mount Kilimanjaro, I only saw it once very briefly in the distance. The mist was just too damn thick the rest of the time, at least at that season. I'd sit on the lawn at Marangu and say, "Where is Kilimanjaro?" And a local would sketch an outline filling most of the cloudy sky, and say, "There."

The truck would be based at Marangu for a little over a week now while we all struck out on our own. Half a dozen people decided to hire some local bearers and guides and climb Kilimanjaro. You already know my feelings about walking uphill unless it's absolutely necessary, so you won't be surprised to learn that I decided to go to Zanzibar instead.

MR. HAJI AND ME

few of us caught the train in Moshi and headed for the coast, a ride of about sixteen hours. We brought our own food, water, flashlights, and books, so we were set for the night. The scenery was pretty great while the sun stayed up. By night, we bounced and flailed and rolled around as the train jerked along the ancient track, but after more than five months of snatching naps as I bounced over the back wheel of the truck, I had learned to sleep anywhere anytime.

It got nippy at night on the train, but the smell of urine from the loo was so overpowering, even from several compartments away, that I was afraid of being overcome by the fumes if I closed my window. I desperately needed a whizz, but if there was one thing about which I was still squeamish, it was public toilets in Africa. I was particularly reluctant to attempt it there, in a train that rocked and jerked and kept throwing me against walls, doors, and seats. Besides, the prospect of climbing down off the top bunk (no ladders or steps) in the dark, unbarricading the door (there were no locks, so we'd used a little ingenuity), waking my cranky companions, and wandering around the train with a flashlight just didn't appeal. I didn't give in until we reached Dar Es Salaam, by which time we were all fighting to be first.

From Dar we took the ferry to Zanzibar, an island just off the coast in the Indian Ocean. Although Zanzibar joined with the former Tanganyika to form Tanzania at independence, they nonetheless have a strong separatist movement; consequently, we needed our passports to get there.

I had wanted to go to Zanzibar ever since reading M.M. Kaye's *Trade Wind* when I was a teenager. Also known as the Spice Island, Zanzibar has been ruled by many foreign conquerors. The clove tree,

Zanzibar, from the sea.

for which the island is now well-known, was first introduced here in the 19th century, when the Omani sultans ruled Zanzibar. Within a few decades, the island became the world's largest producer of cloves – and also the biggest slave trading center in East Africa, with almost 50,000 slaves passing through its market every year. The Omani Arabs continued to rule Zanzibar under a British Protectorate until independence in 1963. A year later, they were overthrown in a bloody revolution and Zanzibar united with the mainland.

Some say the purest Swahili is spoken in Zanzibar. Indeed, there's a famous Swahili language institute here; I met a couple of Americans studying there. Now the lingua franca of East Africa, the Swahili language developed out of interaction which began centuries ago between Arab traders and the many different tribes of East Africa. The actual Swahili people are not a tribe, but rather an ethnic group, descended from an amalgam of Africans and Arab immigrants going back a thousand years or more. There are an estimated half million Swahili people, mostly along the coast of East Africa, and mostly Muslims. Millions of East Africans, however, speak Swahili.

I'd met some travelers who had highly recommended the Malindi Guest House. Some overlanders were put off by the neighborhood and wouldn't stay there, but I liked it: bustling markets, winding streets, crumbling buildings. John, Jo (an Australian woman who was a hard worker and great company), and I got a lovely, vast room with three real beds, hanging mosquito nets, carpets, wall hangings, floor-to-ceiling windows, a simple but scrupulously clean private bathroom, and a huge breakfast every morning – for about $12 per person. The inn had many different levels, strange dark corridors, and a couple of little courtyards. Everything was very clean, it was always quiet, and the staff were very nice. I could have moved in permanently.

The old stone town is rundown and crumbling, but it still looked very much like what I'd expected (or hoped for, I should say): Arabic buildings, elaborately carved doors and windows, narrow twisting streets and alleys, shaded courtyards, spectacular seaviews, colorful bazaars, ancient mosques, dusty cafes, dark little shops, former colonial mansions, and fading cathedrals.

The people of Zanzibar are extremely friendly and hospitable, making it a pleasure to idly pass the blue-skied days and starry nights there. Unlike most of food-poor Tanzania, there are many wonderful little restaurants in Zanzibar Town, all of them very reasonably priced. We ate several times at a place called Kiponda, on a terrace overlooking the neighborhood, where the waiter actually ran out to buy mineral water the first time we ordered it, rather than disappoint a customer. An old man sold pre-independence coins in the alley below.

There's a strong Eastern influence in Zanzibar, obvious not only in the architecture, but also in the strong Arab and Persian influences one sees in the people, their dress, their religion, their food, and their customs. All these months after leaving North Africa, I was again awakened daily at dawn by the Muslim call to prayer and had to be careful not to dress immodestly, despite the heat.

After a couple of days in town, we decided to take a bus across the island to the East Coast, which was supposedly less populated, less "commercial", and more "real." Such pompous claims always make me nervous. Invariably, the worst places I've ever been were reputed to be "less commercial and more *real.*"

We decided to spend the next few days in a small hotel next to a Swahili fishing village. A simple place with a dozen rooms opening onto a central courtyard (full of all the guests' laundry, including ours). There was one bathroom; strictly cold water (when there *was* water), but clean. There was no electricity, but we got kerosine lanterns at night. The ocean was lovely – turquoise-colored and clear as crystal – and the sand was soft and white. The tides were really weird; the water seemed to come and go several times a day, and when the tide went out, you couldn't even *see* the ocean. Yet when it came back in, you could practically leap off the porch of the inn and straight into the ocean. At night, when the tide was out, we could hear the ocean roaring in the distance, as if it were always struggling to reach us.

It all would have been idyllic except for three things. One, Imelda was there, too; and since she had decided to stay for awhile, I wanted to leave as soon as possible. Two, the food was awful. We tried every eatery in walking distance (there were only two), and they were dreadful. It was some of the worst food I've ever had, and – oddly for Africa – there was no fresh food except the fish; the rest was rice, canned milk, canned vegetables, and powdered coffee, all of it remarkably bad. Yet just an hour or so away, in Zanzibar Town, were all those great little cafés and restaurants. Three, there wasn't much to do.

Some people like doing nothing, especially at the beach, but I was already relaxed and living a life which (except for Imelda) I found pretty stress-free by now. I didn't need a rest. Even when I vacation at the beach to really get away from it all, I like to eat out at night, hear music, go on a day-trip, go snorkeling, learn to water ski, go out in a glass bottom boat, and so on. And what with not being able to read at night (the kerosine lamps weren't very bright), I was pretty bored. I don't tan and even *I* can only nap for so long.

So it was during my stay in Zanzibar, east and west coasts, that I really started confronting a serious character flaw: my notorious lack of patience. I have always been an impatient person. Long before I went to Africa, I was known for my impatience among my friends, family, and colleagues. It had really caused some problems for me in Africa, and I had embarrassed my companions more than a few times with my behavior. Once I got used to life on the road, the physical inconveniences, and living cheek-by-jowl day-and-night with all the other overlanders, one big problem remained: getting emotionally adjusted to Africa. I needed to accept that I was an alien there, that they do things really differently, and that I wasn't ever going to get anywhere by quarreling with their ways.

In Moshi, getting ready for the train journey to Dar, I realized that no matter how many months I had spent daily dealing with these things, I had still not gotten used to the fact that, in Africa, whatever you need is almost always not available, and that whatever you want to do is impossible or complicated or terribly time-consuming. We had trouble finding food to take on our journey, yet we *had* to take food, since the train, though it had a kitchen and a restaurant car, couldn't be counted on to have food (and it didn't). Finding water for the journey was an ordeal. Buying an ordinary ferry ticket to get to Zanzibar took over an hour. Most things are impossible and make no sense, and I just couldn't seem to learn to lie back and go with the flow.

After settling into our simple rooms at the beach, I see a sign at the front desk that urges me not to carry around my passport, money, and valuables, but to deposit them in the safe of the hotel with the "relevant authorities." So I go up to Mr. Haji, who runs the front desk, and say, "Do you have a safe?"

"Yes," says Mr. Haji.

"I'd like to leave my wallet in it," I say.

"No, you leave your wallet in your room."

"But my room has a big, open window and is not secure."

"Yes," Mr. Haji agrees.

"So I'd like to leave my wallet in your safe."

"But we have no safe."

"But you just said you did," I say.

"Yes." Mr. Haji nods.

"Yes, you have a safe?" I snap. "Or yes, you said that, but you didn't mean it?"

"No..."

Confused, I say, "*Is* there or *isn't* there a safe?" Surely *this* will get me a clear answer. Mr. Haji giggles and looks helplessly at one of the Swahili men hanging out in the lobby. I decide to try a new tack. "Sir, that sign – that sign *right there* – says to deposit my valuables with the relevant authorities. Who *are* the relevant authorities?"

"Yes..."

"*Who?*" I demand.

"Yes..."

"WHO?"

"Yes..."

"Where *are* these relevant authorities?" I hear my voice growing shrill.

"Here," Mr. Haji volunteers. "Me. I am."

"Ah!" I see a glimmer of hope. "Is there somewhere I can keep my wallet safe?"

"Yes. Here." He pats a draw near his elbow. I write my name on my wallet and my friends' wallets and deposit them.

The next day I return, needing to get some money out of my wallet.

"Not here," Mr. Haji says.

"What?" My heart seems to stop. I'm stuck in eastern Zanzibar with no money. *I've been robbed!*

"Your wallet is not here."

Feeling faint, I wait for an explanation. Mr. Haji offers none. I wonder if he is trying to ruin what's left of my pathetic excuse of a life. "Where is it?" I cry.

"My friend has it."

I frown. "Where is your friend?"

"I don't know."

This sounds very bad. "Why did you let him have my wallet?" I ask desperately.

"So he can put it in the safe."

"Ah!" I consider the dubious safety of my wallet, which I learn has been carried out of the inn by a friend of Mr. Haji's to be put in some safe across town – a safe which I now suspect doesn't actually exist. I ask Mr. Haji to send for it so I can pay him the money I owe him. When it arrives, I decide it will be safest in my room.

Why did I begin this? Everyone else is out lying in the sun, having a relaxing day. Only *I* ever seem to work myself up this way. Why do I still want logic, after all this time out here?

Another sign over the desk says they have boats here, for fishing, sailing, and snorkeling. Like a fool, I ask Mr. Haji:

"What can you tell me about this snorkeling you offer?"

"Yes, there is snorkeling..."

"Yes?" I try to look pert, interested, encouraging.

"You want to go snorkeling?"

"I don't know," I say. "I need to know more about it before I can decide if I want to go. That sign there says I should ask here for more information. So I'm asking you for more information." Surely I have made myself clear now.

Mr. Haji looks at a Swahili man hanging out in the lobby and giggles.

I sigh, realizing I was a fool to begin this, but now I feel stubborn. "How much does the snorkeling cost?"

"Free. First time is free for guests of the hotel."

"Free?" I'm easy. "Okay. I'd like to go. When is it?"

"When you want."

"Can I go now?"

"No."

"Okay. Then when can I go?"

"When you want."

I frown. "But I want to go now, and you said I can't."

"Yes..." He clearly means to ruin my miserable excuse of a life again today.

Feeling very stupid, I say, "Yes, I can go now, or yes, you just said I can't?"

"Yes..."

Silly question, I realize. Bag that. "Can I go later this afternoon?"

"I don't know."

"Oh. When will you know?"

"It depends."

"On what?"

Mr. Haji looks at another Swahili man hanging out in the lobby and giggles. Finally, he says, "Maybe you can go this afternoon."

"And it's free?" I say, to confirm.

"No."

"No? But you just said the first snorkeling trip is free for guests of the hotel."

"Yes..."

"So, if I go this afternoon, it's free. Right?"

"No."

"Why not?"

"Only free in the morning."

"Ah! The snorkeling is usually in the morning?" I am pleased; I have cleverly tricked him into releasing this information to me.

"Yes."

"When in the morning?"

"After breakfast."

"When is breakfast?"

Mr. Haji shrugs. Then he points to the wall. There are two signs on the wall. One sign says that breakfast is from 7:45 AM to 8:45 AM. The other sign says that breakfast is from 8:30 AM to 9:30 AM.

I am not willing to get involved in that discussion. So I say, "So snorkeling is after breakfast tomorrow and it's free?"

"Yes."

"Do I need to book ahead? To reserve my place?" I ask, covering all contingencies, though I doubt anyone else on Zanzibar has had enough spare time to get this information out of Mr. Haji.

"Yes. Book ahead."

"Okay," I say, "let's do that."

"Yes..."

I wait. Nothing happens. Finally, I say, "So do you need to write this down or take my name or something?"

Mr. Haji looks at a Swahili hanging out in the lobby and giggles.

"Look," I say (like a fool), "you just told me I need to book ahead for the snorkeling."

"Yes..."

"So let's do that."

"You want to go snorkeling?"

"Yes! What do I have to do to book it?"

"You just tell me how many people you are."

"We are five people."

He stares at me.

"Do you need anything else?" I ask.

"No, you just have to say me when you want to go."

"And tell you how many people we are, right?" I don't feel well.

"Yes."

"I'm telling you now: we are 5 people and we want to go tomorrow after breakfast."

Exhausted, I go outside. On the beach, John has met a fisherman and offered him 4,000 Tanzanian shillings (about $8) to take us all out in his boat. In two minutes, we're on the water.

So how do *I* manage to make everything so complicated?

I scoured the local village for food, hoping I wouldn't have to keep patronizing our two local eateries. However, as experienced as I was at locating food by now, I never found any. I still don't know what the locals around there eat besides fish, rice, and glucose biscuits, which was all *we* ate for three days.

I thought that the East Coast, besides having bad food and an ocean that was often missing, was awfully crowded for an Unspoiled Paradise. There were white people *everywhere*. Moreover, I kept bumping into people I knew. Somebody we'd met on the train showed up. Then overlanders I'd met in Arusha showed up. Then some Danes who we met on another part of the island appeared. Then a few people from Fearless's truck turned up. Then some people from *our* truck turned up. We left the coast, and not a moment too soon, as far as I was concerned.

To this day, one of my strongest memories of Zanzibar is the song "Careless Whispers," recorded by George Michael around the time Wham! broke up. The driver played it over and over again on the van going out to the beach, and also on the van going back to town. The song also seemed to be playing almost everywhere I went in Zanzibar Town. At the oddest moments, I'd hear George Michael wailing: "Never gonna dance again! Guilty feet ain't got no rhythm!"

It was pretty grim.

By now my "Maasai braids" were filthy and coming undone, and I looked like the Wild Woman of Borneo. I finally decided to unwrap my hair. It was so dirty my hands got filthy brushing it, and I pulled out enough hair to stuff a pillow. This is just a warning, in case you ever want to put your hair in corn rows.

Well, Zanzibar Town was also filling up with people we knew, so we all decided it would be a good idea to get away for a day and go on a Spice Tour. The 3M Company (owned by Mohammed, Muhedin, and Moussa) has only one vehicle, so they hire cabs to accommodate extra clients. Then this string of 6 or 7 cabs goes zipping around the island, through rural areas, showing off the historic and agricultural sites of Zanzibar, ending at a quiet beach with waves pounding on the rocks and clear, azure water for swimming. It was pretty neat. However, upon taking out my pen to write down the names of some plants, I was attacked by children all grabbing for my priceless bic. Did I mention my problem with patience? I slapped several of them rather hard, and though they just laughed, my friends were very embarrassed. Sadly, I embarrassed my friends the next night, too.

The fearless mountaineers had finally come down from Kilimanjaro, and some of them had decided to join us for our last couple of days on the spice island before we all had to rendezvous with the truck in Dar Es Salaam. I was pleased to see them, since I had already become quite fond of Sally and Lionel, a Canadian couple who kept me laughing when I was fed up and calm when I wanted to kill someone, and David and Jane, a really nice English couple from Oxford. David and Jane were fanatic rock climbers who had an alarming habit of scrambling up the side of any perpendicular obstacle they saw. They both had PhDs in biochemistry and were always trying to explain the composition of things to me, a useless exercise.

We dined that night at Africa House, a hotel with a veranda overlooking the Indian Ocean. Dinner was a long time coming. Indeed, as David said, we'd be better off if we simply started thinking of dinner in terms of geological time.

The food was okay when it arrived, but they kept running out of things. We asked for an order of French fries the waiters had apparently forgotten to bring. "Chips finish," we were told. (We hadn't been told this when we ordered them, since it would be thoughtless to disappoint us before it became absolutely unavoidable.) Also "finish" were fruit salad, yogurt, cake, and anything else that could be remotely described as dessert. Yet there was only one other small table of clients in the restaurant all evening; it's always that way in Africa.

We decided we wanted a nice finish to the meal, and someone came up with the notion of going to the Spice Inn, which we'd grown to like very much, for coffee and cake. Well, the café was closed when we got there at 9:30. So we went upstairs to the restaurant, where we were told that we could have dinner, but that if we didn't want dinner then we couldn't have dessert.

I was suddenly, desperately, horribly, unappealingly tired of nearly six months on a continent where nothing is available or ready or possible or answerable. All I wanted was dessert − even a glucose biscuit would do − and this was already my *third* attempt at it in a half hour in a touristed town brimming with restaurants. Surely there was a way around this waiter's repeated insistence that I could have chicken or beef? I questioned and prodded and nagged the waiter, until the two of us were going around and around in circles. He was always polite, but increasingly frustrated. I was increasingly frustrated, and increasingly shrill. Finally someone just snapped, "They don't have any, Laura!"

I looked at the embarrassed faces around me and realized I was making a terrible scene. I was so ashamed. I'd been here for months, and I knew damn well that the waiter's prevarication meant that they didn't have any, and he was just trying to be polite; saying "no" is often considered bad manners. I also knew that he was probably embarrassed to admit to these *wazungu* that his restaurant didn't have any fruit or cake or biscuits. Moreover, I realized that I wasn't really pushing him for cake or coffee. What I *really* wanted, what I was *really* trying to get, was for him to answer me in the way I wanted: "We have no cake tonight. We've run out. It's all gone." And that was inexcusable of me. Imagine a Tanzanian coming to the US and making a terrible scene because someone said "no" directly, rather than saying, "Well, wouldn't you like some chicken instead?"

I walked back to the Malindi House feeling like I should never have been let out of my room.

However, sometimes there *was* a hidden purpose to these circular, seemingly meaningless conversations, and sometimes (about half the time) being obnoxious was exactly what was required. I got used to being obnoxious a lot sooner than I got used to the inconsistency of it all. For example:

David and Jane wanted to buy some hard currency; travelers' checks were reasonably easy to change in Zanzibar, and this was not so of the rest of Tanzania, where hard currency was the thing you needed. I took them to an exchange place where I had been told by one of the clerks that buying US cash with travelers' checks was possible. Well, there was someone else there today, and she insisted it couldn't be done. David and Jane turned around, prepared to leave and forget about it. I said, "Wait a minute." I could see by their expressions that they were afraid I'd make another scene. However, *this* time, saying, "Now wait a minute" actually worked. David and Jane walked out with a wad of US dollars ten minutes later. Go figure.

One of the Girls had a birthday, so we arranged a birthday party our final night there. I talked to the restaurant, explained that there would be a lot of us, and asked if a cake was possible. They, of course, said yes, though I knew better than to count on it. Our arrival at the restaurant that evening was clearly a total surprise to them, even though I'd confirmed the arrangements that afternoon. They were quite unprepared for us.

As we all ate our way through a slow but tasty and pleasant meal, I occasionally asked the woman in charge about the cake. Would there be a cake? It was all right if there wasn't, I said; I was just curious. She kept saying yes, and I kept waiting for her to tell me that there wasn't one, after all.

Then, to my utter astonishment, she finally brought out an *enormous* cake, topped with buttercream frosting, lavishly decorated, and bearing the words "Happy Birthday!" I hadn't seen a tub of butter the whole time I'd been on Zanzibar, yet they must have needed two pounds of the stuff to make this exquisite cake, which was so big it took us several days to finish it off.

You should never expect anything in Africa except surprises.

As fond as I became of Zanzibar, I didn't think it was working out very well. It's flooded with tourists, drowning in booking agencies, and swarming with seedy fellows trying to sell you a trip to Prison Island, or a ride to the East Coast, a room, or a cab ride. Yet there is not a single tour of the old stone town, which dates back for centuries. There are no organized, reliable watersports, despite the beautiful location. There are no bookstores, where cash-rich tourists could buy guidebooks, histories, maps, and biographies. There are only a couple of gift shops, and we had to scour the city to find even one nicely- packaged spice set, despite this being the Spice Island.

The island's poverty is reflected in the spice trade. Basically, it doesn't exist. Zanzibar still ships out cloves, but its trade has been heavily diminished by competition. Moreover, many spices and herbs grow on the island – often in the wild, too – but none of them are sold. There is no trade set up, and (I was told) no money to set up trade. So pepper, sassafras, cinnamon, chocolate, anise, and at least a dozen other valuable commodities rot in the jungle, or get partially used by local families, but nothing more.

With reflections such as these, I gave in to a bad case of seasickness on the ferry back to Dar.

A LIFE OF DANGER

We headed south, killing kilometers in some long, uneventful days of driving across Tanzania toward the Malawi border. Our route took us straight through Mikumi National Park, and then directly between Ruaha National Park and the famous Selous Game Reserve, the world's biggest wildlife park, and one which remains largely unexplored (due to sheer inaccessibility).

Tanzania's history is rich with tales of Arab traders and slavers (Bagamoyo, the town from which slaves were shipped to Zanzibar, gets it name from a word meaning "lay down your heart"), warrior tribes like the Maasai (who were so fierce even slavers wouldn't mess with them), and white explorers (this is where Henry Morton Stanley finally "found" Livingstone, and where Burton and Speke wandered around looking for the source of the Nile). Julius Nyerere, known as Mwalimu (teacher) by his people, led the nation to independence in 1961. One of the most influential leaders in all of Africa, he experimented with radical socialism, educational programs, and agricultural schemes. He could not, however, make a poor country rich. The West's ambivalence about Nyerere's leftist politics, his refusal to trade with the apartheid regime in South Africa (despite, in 1979, having more political prisoners that *they* did), and the Ugandan war which Tanzania fought without help all contributed to a formula for failure in each of Mwalimu's national programs. Tanzania is one of the ten poorest countries in the world today, as can be plainly seen by driving through the impoverished countryside, or stopping long enough for beggars to accost you anywhere you go. Nonetheless, I loved Tanzania, with its beautiful scenery, fabulous wildlife, and kind and varied people. It's always food for thought when the poorest people in the world can still be kind to a stranger.

Much to my surprise, I came down with a *bad* case of the trots our last day on the road in Tanzania. While everyone else packed up camp one morning, I spent an hour crouched by two huge, unlikely, anonymous stone tombs deep in the bush. Sick with cramps and sweat, I finally crawled into the roofseat, where I stretched out and napped most of the day, except for those moments when I would hit the buzzer. Then the truck would come screeching to a halt for me, I would tumble out of the roofseat, someone would throw me a trowel and a roll of toilet paper, and I'd dash off to the bushes again. Whatever I had, a few other people started coming down with it, too.

By late afternoon, though, I was feeling well enough to come down and sit in the cab. The countryside was spectacularly beautiful – steep hills, fabulous vistas, old tea plantations. Unfortunately, the area wasn't so good for finding a bush camp: no flat spots. Happily, around sunset, we finally found a good spot outside of a town called Tukuyu. It was a large patch of flat ground, surrounded by bush, set back from the road, down a narrow track which was sheltered by thick trees on either side.

We pulled in, settled the truck in a good spot, and started setting up camp. I had recovered enough to build the fire, though I felt kind of shaky – queasy now. About twenty young men, as well as a few women and children, appeared out of nowhere to watch us. I was used to this by now, as I had been the nightly show in almost every bush camp I made from Morocco all the way down to this spot in southern Tanzania. However, since the group was still new to this sort of thing, some of them were uncomfortable with the audience. I accompanied two of the Girls into the bushes for a whizz, assuring them there was nothing to worry about. Then I doubled over and started vomiting.

Just another happy day in the life of an overlander.

Feeling a little better, I ate some dinner. I even ate some dessert (banana custard). Ignoring the Girls' assertion that it might not be safe to wander into the bushes alone with so many men still around, I went back into the dark and threw up all my dessert. To this day, I cannot face custard *or* bananas. I stayed there for awhile, feeling like hell. It never occurred to me to be afraid, though I know now that I probably wasn't alone out there.

After I seemed to have exhausted all my bodily functions for the day, I crawled into the back of the truck and sat around feeling sorry for myself. As usual, everyone was chatting around the fire, or reading, writing, or playing cards in the truck, or milling around somewhere nearby.

Imelda was the first to stretch and announce she was going to bed. Normally, at Deb's behest, people put up their tents close to the truck, often in a semi-circle around the well-lit side where we built the fire and did all the work. Tonight, however, feeling tired, cranky, and ill, and having found a nice isolated bush camp, most people had pitched their tents far away from the truck, deep in the dark. (I hadn't put one up, intending to sleep in the roofseat.) So Imelda disappeared into the dark. She returned a minute later in a panic, claiming the tents had been slashed open!

Well, if it had been *anyone* else, we'd have all dashed out to investigate. However, since Imelda saw lions behind every tree, we ignored her. I think I said, "Oh, really?" and went back to my book. Deb, however, suggested that it would probably be sensible to investigate. So Lionel went out into the dark to take a look. Guess what happened? He came back a moment later to say yes, it was true! Several tents had been slashed open with machetes!

Thieves, obviously, looking for the quickest way into the tents. We never put anything in the tents before going to bed, just in case of something like this, so the thieves had only made off with some tent bags, tent mallets, and a roll mat or two. This meager haul had apparently angered them – a couple of the tents were slashed to bits.

I immediately thought of the Girls. If lions in Serengeti had frightened them, what would *this* do to them? But lo and behold, they started really coming into their own on this night! They were calm and matter-of-fact. Young Jo (as opposed to Jo the Australian) announced she was on security duty that night (making sure everything was locked up and put away) and then laughed, realizing that that might not be an announcement designed to make us all feel Really Safe.

Then we heard a lot of men (probably our watchers from earlier in the evening) in the bushes – crashing around, whooping, hollering, laughing, shouting. It really pissed me off. I was too sick for this shit. Deb called us around the campfire to set up a rota for all-night guard duty. We were volunteering for shifts when one of the women suddenly howled. She had been hit by a rock. Suddenly rocks – *big* rocks – started flying through the air, coming fast, propelled by slingshots! Deb pointed out that this would make guard duty dangerous and guards ineffectual. She suggested that perhaps we should leave.

Leave! What a concept! We started scurrying around, determined to get out of there before we wound up collecting on all that insurance we'd been advised to buy.

Things got very chaotic after that. We normally had a very set, organized routine for packing up camp, but it was thrown to the wind tonight. It was dark, we were under attack, and everything went to hell, including our nerves and tempers.

While putting something away on the far side of the truck, David and I stumbled across Dick, an Englishman in his fifties. I never knew what inspired him to come to Africa, though I had the vague impression it had something to do with keeping himself out a higher tax bracket. Don't ask; I didn't. Anyhow, Dick was either hard of hearing or hopelessly distracted. Not only did he not know we were leaving, he didn't even know we were under attack. He'd been sitting in the dark having a shave and a wash while a riot ensued on the other side of the truck.

It always paid to be simple, direct, and clear when speaking to Dick. David said, "Dick, we're under attack. Pack up your tent *now*, or we'll leave without you."

Dick said "Oh," and asked us to watch his shaving gear so he could go pack up. We left it to fend for itself and went back to packing up. As rocks continued flying in, and those hooligans kept whooping and hollering in the bush, the situation in camp was sheer pandemonium. People were getting hurt by rocks as they tried to take down their tents. Jane's headlamp was shattered by a flying rock. Someone else got it on the arm, someone else on the leg. People began to fear getting hit in the eye or some other irreplaceable part. Upon taking down the tents, people realized that their tent bags were missing, whch made packing them rather problematic. With normal duties abandoned, we were trying to do everything at once – break down the fire, put away the table and stool, pack up the water and food and firewood.

The chorus of "Ow! Ouch! Dammit!" got louder and more frequent, and it became apparent that the most distant tents couldn't be taken down until the bandits were beaten back a little. So I sacrificed some of my precious firewood to the fight, giving long, heavy sticks to four of our biggest guys, who raced out into the night to confront our attackers. I distinctly remember watching them scurry away. I distinctly remember feeling glad that I was a girl and didn't have to go out there in the dark with them.

Well, you know... adrenaline's a funny thing.

The next thing I remember is stalking through the dark out there, a stick in my hand, screaming and shouting as I beat the bushes. I swear I have no idea how I got there. It certainly wasn't what I *intended* to do, but there I was. Joseph said something like, "Go back, you crazy woman!" Then he and Richard disappeared into the bushes. I stared at my stick and wondered with sheer horror what I was doing there. Then a rock flew past me, just inches from my head. Bursting with fury, I started hitting the bushes with my stick, running around in a blind rage, screaming things. Crazy, insane things! *Bizarre* things. Things like: "Come here you fucking lily-livered sissy-asses!" And even more improbably: "Where are you hiding, you cowardly uncircumcized bastards?" (They undoubtedly *were* circumcized; I was just trying to be really cutting.)

I swear to you I have no idea where this purple prose came from. None of my novels reads that badly. Really.

Anyhow, I stopped shouting for a moment and stood there panting in confusion. Then I heard footsteps crunching into the earth behind me. Terrified, I whirled around and snarled (rather convincingly, I thought), "Who's there?" Well, it was just Craig, a Canadian from the truck, come to help the others. He told me to go back to the truck.

"Where is it?" I cried. "I don't have my glasses on!"

He pointed it out and then disappeared into the bushes. I stared at the stick in my hand and realized that if I bumped into someone with a machete in *his* hand, I was dead meat. Perhaps I should go back to the truck, I thought, rather than shouting arcane insults into the bush and waiting to get killed.

So I did. Camp was in even more disarray than it had been when I'd had my adrenaline blackout. The rock-hurling had escalated to the point where Deb (speaking as if she'd been tranquilized; she goes into a state of preternatural calm in a crisis) told everyone to stop worrying about packing correctly.

"Just throw everything in the truck and let's get the hell out of here," she intoned. "We'll worry about it later."

We started dumping whole tents, roll mats, sleeping bags, pots, pans, blankets, mallets, and tools into the truck willy-nilly. I had the wits to lock away my saws, chains, axes, and machetes. Mostly so no stranger could get ahold of them, but also so no one on our truck could go nuts and try to kill one of those hooligans out there; a white man who kills a black man in Tanzania, whatever the circumstances, is in big trouble. I was throwing hot kettles of boiling water, chunks of firewood, work gloves, loaves of bread, and everything you can imagine into the truck, making a mountainous mess of stuff.

Then we heard a loud, roaring, primeval scream from the bushes. I thought they were torturing Joseph out there. Well, you know... adrenaline's a *really* funny thing.

The next thing I remember is someone holding me and telling me to get a grip on myself. I had apparently gone tearing around in circles, crying, "Where's a stick? I need a stick! Give me a stick!" God only knows what I thought I could do out there. Luckily, however, Joseph's scream just turned out to be a scare tactic while he was chasing some men. He and the others came back to the truck just as we finished throwing everything inside.

We formed a plan of action for our escape. The truck was vulnerable to attack due to its open sides and easy access, so we would ride with all lights off, and we'd arm ourselves with shovels, rolling pins, and firewood in case anyone tried to climb on board. Joseph, Richard, John, and Craig would go ahead of the truck as we drove down the narrow track through the trees. This was to protect the windshield. If someone hit the windshield with a rock, it could hurt Deb, who was driving. Besides, replacing the windshield wouldn't exactly be a piece of cake out there.

Everything was set, and everyone knew what they were supposed to do – except Dick, who kept sticking his head out the back of the truck and saying, "*Now* what's going on?"

We took our places. I grabbed the rolling pin and crouched in the dark. Up in the cab, Deb turned the key to start the engine.

And nothing happened.

The starter motor wouldn't engage. I couldn't believe it. *I absolutely could not believe it!* It was like some awful, sensationalistic, wildly improbable action movie. The goddamned engine wouldn't start!

We piled quickly back out of the truck and milled around in the moonlight, confused and scared. From their hiding places in the dark, our attackers saw us, and a wild war whoop, a cheer of victory, arose all around us.

They got to the engine, I thought wildly, *somehow they got to the engine!* I experienced the single greatest moment of fear I had known during the entire time I'd been in Africa. I was going to be murdered here in the bush, outside of some little village in Tanzania. We'd never escape them; they knew this place in the dark a lot better than we did. No one else even knew where we were. There probably wouldn't even be any remains. My poor mom. She'd get a letter... "Dear Mrs. Resnick ....sorry about the non-refundable deposit..."

Then a lot of things happened at once. Lionel came back and passed around word that we hadn't been sabotaged. This was merely an astonishing coincidence; the starter motor had chosen that particular moment to stop working (*what* did I tell you about this truck?). So we'd have to push the truck.

I looked up at the moonlit sky and wondered, *Why me?* It was past my bedtime. I had alternated all day between diarrhea and vomiting. People had ruined my evening, thrown rocks at me, and scared me into fits. And now I would have to *push* that bloody twelve-ton truck to make it start. As if things weren't bad enough, we also seemed to have parked in a gully that I was *sure* hadn't been there before. So we would have to *rock* the goddamned truck back and forth to get it going. I'd done it before, and it was a dangerous enterprise even at the best of times – a phrase which did not encompass being under attack in the dark with a lot of people who'd never had to push an overland truck before.

However, everyone was glad to now have a focus for all that adrenaline. We pushed the truck forward, jumped out of the way as it rocked back on us, then jumped in again to push it forward. We finally got it going, and the engine kicked in. We all piled back in and took our positions. As we drove through the dark corridor of trees, our guys routed the bandits and chased them off. Four overlanders against anywhere from twelve to twenty of them – and they ran away. Well, what kind of men would throw rocks at women in the dark anyhow, I figured? Bullies and cowards, whatever the country. In fact, our guys got so excited chasing them away that they *kept* chasing them; we wound up having to stop and wait for them to come back. When they finally did, we proceeded on down the road, wondering where we'd find another place to sleep tonight.

Squashed together with our kettles, tents, weapons, pots, and pans, we found a strange place just about a half hour further down the road. It would have looked reasonably normal in Europe, but it looked incredibly weird in the middle of rural Tanzania. It was a modern housing compound: European homes with satellite dishes, tennis courts, and a swimming pool, all lit up, surrounded by high fences, with guards at the gate. It was a complex built to house EEC workers and adminstrators who were here to build roads in Tanzania as part of some European aid project.

We camped the rest of the night on their floodlit tennis courts. The Belgian in charge said that this happened all the time here, that many people asked for shelter in the compound after bad experiences. He said that the rate of theft and vandalism was terrible in this part of Tanzania – hatred of foreigners, of whites, of rich people. Considering how extraordinarily wealthy this compound, or even our scrubby truck, was in comparison to the hundreds of tiny dirt villages I'd been to, the hatred didn't really surprise me. But ordinary thieving in Africa seldom assumed such a violent and sinister turn.

I went to bed on the roof then. It rained. I didn't wake up till just before dawn. I was soaked and cold and felt terrible. I had to build my fire with kerosine, which smoked incessantly and turned my stomach. All the breakfast toast was charred and soggy, and everyone's eyes were streaming from the smoke.

Ah, well, just another day in the life of an overlander. Anyhow, I was far too glad to be alive to quibble about details. Indeed, everyone was cheerful that morning as we set off for Malawi. The memory of that night added gusto to a ditty I learned over a few drinks one evening:

> *"I want to be an overlander,*
> *I want to live a life of danger!*
> *Overlander: life of danger!*
> *Life of danger: overlander!"*

Such good cheer was not always the case, though. Deb was once in a stoning in Zaïre which had bad consequences. They had crashed through part of a bridge, as we once did, and were stuck outside a village all night. They *couldn't* leave when the rocks started flying. No one was seriously injured, but it was a terrifying experience, and the group never recovered psychologically. People couldn't sleep at night and wouldn't go into the bushes alone for firewood or a whizz or anything else, and one or two of the crew quit the business when they reached Nairobi.

We were a happy group, though. We had won, after all.

The next day, just as we entered Malawi, I discovered that someone had stolen over $200 from me.

THE GOATBUSTERS

H is Excellency, Lifetime President Hastings Banda, was still in charge of Malawi at that time, and it was a punishable offense to refer to him without using his whole title. He ruled the nation according to his numerous personal quirks – which meant that we had to make some preparations before crossing the border.

Women were required to wear skirts at the border and, indeed, the whole time they were in Malawi; and the skirts must cover their knees. Men must wear trousers. No one wearing shorts would be permitted across the border. Anyone wearing shorts after entering the country risked arrest. I believe jeans were officially verboten, too. Dr. Banda, Malawi's octogenarian dictator who spent forty years in the US and the UK before returning to lead Malawi to independence in the early 1960s, disapproved of immodest dress.

We're not done with the regulations yet. Men had to have short hair. If a man came to the border with long hair, the guards would cut if off. If he refused, he couldn't enter the country. Some men had been known to try stuffing their long hair under a hat; I gather they usually got caught and shorn.

We also had to hide all our *Lonely Planet* guidebooks, which were forbidden in Malawi because of what a previous edition had said about Banda. The new edition, in fact, contained a paragraph warning you that this book would probably be confiscated from you at the Malawi border if you didn't hide it.

We also hummed the old Simon and Garfunkel song *Cecilia* for the last time and hid our tape of it. Playing or humming it meant you risked arrest in Malawi. Banda felt the song was disrespectful of his mistress, Cecilia.

There were currency controls at the border, as there frequently are in a soft-currency economy. It was while counting my travelers' checks for currency exchange that I discovered $220 was missing, all in denominations of $20; missing from the *middle* of two separate packets. I knew immediately it had been stolen, since I was religious about keeping records of my expenditures and cashing my TCs in numerical order (specifically to help me keep an eye out for something like this). Stealing from the middle of a thick pack is a common trick, since it usually takes days for the owner to realize the checks are missing. Except for my week in Nairobi, my TCs lived beneath my dirty laundry, at the very bottom of my locked locker, in the back of the always- guarded truck, so it seemed evident that I'd been robbed in Nairobi – more than three weeks ago. Since I had no need to leaf through my entire collection of TCs on a regular basis, I hadn't noticed the theft until today.

Guess what? That handy American Express theft-report service doesn't work so well in Africa. The next day we reached a town, Mzuzu, and I went to the telecommunications building. Collect calls (as advised by Amex) are not possible in most of Africa. I willingly paid for the call, figuring I'd just try to get reimbursed by Amex when I returned to England. I spent over an hour trying to get through to the UK, but the polite man in charge of the telecommunications bureau kept informing me that the telephone lines out of Malawi were all congested.

I then tried to fax my father in the US, writing out all the information for him and asking him to contact Amex on my behalf. However, all lines to America were congested.

Bored, I started reading the national phone book. Lo and behold, there was an Amex office in the capital city of Lilongwe. I canceled all calls, figuring I'd go there and deal with this in person.

We got to Lilongwe about a week later. I paid a taxi $20 for a round-trip ride out to the Amex representative's office. There was only one man at this office who could help me with my problem. He was gone and no one knew when he would be back. After an hour and a half, he finally showed up. He was very polite, but he couldn't get new checks for me right away. Perhaps I could come back in three days?

I explained that I couldn't; we were crossing the border into Zambia the next day. I suggested that we telex the Amex people in the UK, give them all the relevant information, and ask them to have new checks waiting for me at the Harare office, which I would be able to pick up the following month. He agreed to this plan, and we telexed England.

About ten days later, at my request, Deb sent a telex ahead to the

Harare Amex office, reiterating all the information, quoting the reference numbers of the telex sent to London, and indicating that I expected my Amex replacement checks to be waiting in Harare when I arrived.

When I finally arrived at the Amex office in Harare with copies of both telexes, they said they had never heard of me. They had no record of ever having received this telex. They put me on the phone to the UK office. While two Zimbabwean Amex employees and an apparent acquaintance shouted at the tops of their lungs about five feet away from me, I explained the situation to some woman in England. The UK office had no record of any of this and had never heard of me. Since a considerable amount of time had elapsed between the time I claimed the checks were stolen and the time I was reporting the theft (now, officially), my request for replacements would now have to go into some kind of arbitration, and I would be informed of the results in 6 weeks.

When I returned home to the USA in October, there was *still* no word from Amex in the UK. I wrote them a detailed letter and enclosed photocopies of all my telexes and receipts.

Amex/UK wrote back, denying my request for refunds because I had "waited" so long to report the theft.

I wrote a letter to Amex in the USA, explaining why I hadn't noticed the theft sooner, how many times I reported (or tried to report) the theft to no avail, and also pointed out that there was no time-limit mentioned in any of the papers I had signed. I also swore never to deal with Amex again.

Fortunately, Amex USA wanted to keep a customer, and someone was appointed to investigate and appeal my claim. I received an apology and a full refund several weeks later. (I also received photocopies of all the stolen checks. They were forged quite skillfully and cashed on the black market in Nairobi.)

Heading south through Malawi, we also had to find a clinic to test Richard and Aussie Jo for malaria. They tested negative, but this apparently means nothing. I gather you can have it but *test* negative if you're not actually in the middle of an attack. Since this area was experiencing an epidemic of malaria, Deb dosed them both up with Fansidar just to be on the safe side. This standard treatment can produce symptoms almost as nasty as the illness, and we all watched them turning green with morbid fascination.

We drove south through Malawi, camping on the shores of Lake Malawi every night, washing clothes in basins full of lake water and stringing them out to dry between palm trees. Malawians are very friendly, and locals were always waving to us and smiling at us as we rumbled past. Many locals also gave a hand salute reflecting their recent political victory. After almost thirty years of dictatorship, Hastings Banda, whose rule had been characterized by the imprisonment, torture, and murder of thousands of Malawians, had finally been forced (by external economic pressures and growing internal unrest) to accept a national referendum legalizing opposing political parties. (A year later, in the first multi-party election ever held in Malawi, Banda was voted out of office, and a year after that he was on trial for various political murders.)

We finally stopped for several days at Salima Bay, a resort on Lake Malawi. There were so many recreational options, I hardly knew what to do with myself. Swim, suntan, ride the "big banana," or stroll into town to shop for wood carvings. Malawi is one of the best places to buy wood carvings in Africa – they are especially famous for their chiefs' chairs, and also for wonderful little three-legged tables they make that can be taken apart and folded up for easy transportation. After months of wondering what to get my parents (who were dealing with all my paperwork and mail at home while I was out here) I finally found something in the wood-carvers' market – a huge ebony bowl (some 2 feet in diameter) with the story of a fisherman's successful day carved around its sides.

There was nearly a riot in the marketplace to see who would wrap it. Small boys and cocky adolescents (some of them carrying big sticks which I eyed warily) choose you for a mark as you walk toward the village. They charge a small fee to wrap your package for you, and you have no say in the matter (kind of like having no say about having a guide in many towns). Well, wrapping my bowl represented quite a few kwacha (Malawian money) due to its size, so it was seized from me and became the center of a vicious tug-of-war in the middle of the market. I was actually afraid for a moment and regretted buying the damned thing.

In the end two biggest guys with the biggest sticks won the fight and wrapped the bowl, demanding a fee of 12 kwacha. Everyone else – more than a dozen boys and teenagers – was angry with *me*. Everyone felt *I* had cheated them: the white woman should have paid everyone for wrapping it several times over. It was a miserable experience. I suggested they try to cooperate with each other in future: two guys to a tourist, and everyone else leaves her alone, regardless of what she buys. Well, this well-meaning advice just pissed them off, and they became even more convinced that I owed them something. The wood-carvers found the whole brouhaha either worrying or amusing, depending on their point of view. Then there was another battle over who would carry another overlander's purchase back to the lake. White people don't carry their own belongings; white people pay someone else to do it unless they want to make the locals really angry.

Despite all that, I went back to the market again before leaving Salima Bay. Happily, it was a much quieter day. Some of the carvers had expressed interest in trading for clothes, so I traded my crazed-lepidopterist hat and my tattered shorts (which apparently *someone* in Malawi wears) for a nice bowl.

We then experienced some miscommunication with Richard. When we had crossed into Malawi, we crossed a time zone: 9:00 AM in Tanzania is 8:00 AM in Malawi. Deb said she wanted the truck packed up by 6:00 AM the following morning. When we groaned, she jokingly pointed out that, on our Tanzanian-adjusted body clocks, it would really be 7:00 AM. Well, for Richard, who had never been out of Kenya until now, the time-change was bizarre enough, but this new information threw him for a loop. I originally thought it was shyness that kept him from asking for an explanation. I eventually learned it was the language barrier. Keep in mind that although English is one of the two official languages of Kenya (Swahili being the other), far less than half the population can speak it, let alone read or write it.

Richard, we were to learn, could speak very little English and could understand even less. However, since he insisted he understood everything that was said to him (partially because this is good manners, and partially, I suppose, because he knew that the job *required* him to speak and read English), it was several weeks before it finally dawned on me that Richard's frequently inexplicable behavior was due to the fact that he couldn't communicate.

He understood just enough of Deb's joke that day to get confused. For the next week, every meal was served at a bizarre time. I'd get up as planned, only to find that Richard had already built my fire, cooked breakfast, and was cleaning up – or else I'd build a fire and wind up waiting for him to cook the meal an hour late. Deb spoke to him about it a couple of times, since now everyone was missing meals, not just Imelda (who was always late for everything). By the third conversation, Deb finally found out that (based on her joke) Richard thought that, now that we were in Malawi, whenever she said she wanted breakfast ready at 7:00 AM (for example), she really *meant* 6:00 AM. Or maybe 8:00 AM. But not 7:00 AM.

Despite the recent national referendum and the imminent political changes in Malawi, Banda was still the biggest figure in Malawian life; bigger, it seemed, than any god. His face was everywhere, all of the time: on television, on banners, on the sides of buildings, on billboards in the capital, and on people's shirts and skirts, even woven into the cloth of women's kangas. (In January of 1995, however, Banda was arrested by the new government and tried in connection with several murders.)

There's precious little wildlife left in Malawi. Although lovely, the country didn't have the spectacular beauty of some African countries, or the wild mystery of others. The people didn't have the cultural diversity of the Tanzanians, or the robust energy of the Ugandans. I liked the Malawians, but I didn't long to stay longer, as I had (and would) in so many other places. I felt ready to push on as we headed west. After Lilongwe (of which I saw nothing, since I was ensconced at the American Express office), we turned our thoughts toward Zambia.

We bush-camped one night just this side of the border, stocking up on everything we'd need before entering Zambia. We traded biscuits, chocolate, needles, thread, and, of course, bics for bundles of firewood, then collected more on our own. We filled up on water, food, toilet paper and fuel. Zambia was undergoing a cholera epidemic. Although we had to go through Zambia to get to Zimbabwe, we mustn't buy, eat, or drink anything there, and we must keep our contact with locals minimal. Cholera, though more likely to take you if you're poor, undernourished, and have no access to good treatment, is highly contagious and dangerous to everyone. My shot had expired, of course, but the shots are of dubious value anyhow.

The border crossing into Zambia was dull and uneventful, exactly what one hopes for when crossing a border in Africa. We didn't learn much about the cholera epidemic there. Indeed, people in London probably knew more about it than we did. There was a roadblock near a bridge, but it had nothing to do with the cholera epidemic. Two Zambians, fully armed with nets and looking rather like over-worked lepidopterists, searched every vehicle from top to bottom. They were – I'm not making this up – the local Tsetse Fly Patrol.

Formerly Northern Rhodesia, Zambia became independent in 1964. Kenneth Kaunda came to power then and would remain the country's president until 1991. Throughout this period, he remained fiercely committed to African independence struggles. He also, unfortunately, ran a regime which impoverished the country and which, under the infamous Emergency Powers Act, regularly had dissenters beaten, jailed, or sent into exile. Riots and unrest finally forced him to allow elections in 1991, when he was defeated by his opponent, Frederick Chiluba. As a legacy of Kaunda's rule, Zambia was the eighteenth poorest country in the world and had a 500% inflation rate when I visited it in 1993. That spring, President Chiluba claimed there was a coup plot against him and reinstated the emergency powers that Kaunda had imposed during his rule. All things considered, we thought it best to just keep driving and minding our own business.

Somewhere outside the village of Katete, we came rumbling up to a hedge alongside the road; it was the only hedge I saw in all of Zambia. I turned away from the view, got up, and walked to the back of the truck to get my water bottle. Suddenly I – and everyone else – was thrown wildly around. The truck skidded and lurched and bounced hard, then chugged forward uncertainly for a moment. Then, up in the cab, Deb hit the gas *hard,* and we all tumbled around again as the truck heaved forward.

"We've hit something!" someone cried.

This was a first for me. I'd been on the truck when it had crashed through log bridges, foundered in sand, and disappeared in bogs. We'd been hit in CAR, but *we'd* never hit anything before, and Deb was a very good driver. Confused, I lurched to the back door and looked out. Sure enough, we were barreling away from a goat herd which had appeared out of nowhere – or rather, out of the hedge – quite suddenly. Four goats lay dead in the road. The rest were milling around in confusion. A couple of shepherds waved sticks violently at us. We sped away. I don't think that old truck had ever gone so fast before (indeed, going uphill, I could usually *walk* faster than that truck.)

Commendations to Deb, who could have killed us all if she hadn't been using her head. By the time the goats appeared, it was too late to avoid them without overturning the truck. (Dr. MacGowan, by the way, had warned me that the greatest danger to my health would be road accidents.)

We hadn't stopped for a very good reason. If this was truly an accident, then there was a very real danger of violence. One typical way of dealing with a situation like this (and not only in Africa) is to kill the person who hit your livestock. And if it *wasn't* an accident, the situation would have been little better. Considering that the goats had been driven into the road suddenly from behind the only hedge for miles, it was possible that this had been done on purpose as we approached, with the intention of extorting money from us. Either way, Deb's responsibility was clearly to protect her passengers and the truck. But I thought it would be a long time before anyone invited us back to this neck of the woods.

Well, frankly, I *like* goats. My family very nearly got one as a pet when I was growing up. So I felt bad about slaughtering four of them. So did everyone else. Deb was understandably shaken up, not only for having killed four goats in a single blow, but also for having nearly lost

The Goatbusters Truck in Zambia — where we'll never be invited back.

all her passengers. Such things look bad on an overland driver's record, you know.

Most of us dealt with this in true overlander fashion: really sick, dark humor. (Imelda disapproved, which convinced me it must to be the right way to cope.) We wound up slinging a banner over the front of the truck: GOATBUSTERS. We added a little sign next to it – a picture of a goat, surrounded by a red circle with a diagonal line running across it. On the driver's door, we painted a scorecard and drew in four little goats.

We were thereafter known as the Goatbusters throughout Southern Africa, easily identifiable and notorious in our own way. South Africans traveling in Zimbabwe were always particularly curious about the sobriquet and quite impressed with our record: *four goats at a go*, they would murmur, eyes wide with awe.

One night a couple of weeks later in Victoria Falls, we vandalized a Dutch overland truck in much the same way. They had pulled into the Vic Falls campground while we were cooking dinner. First they knocked down a tent. Then they disrupted our meal. *Then* they knocked down a tree – all while trying to maneuver their truck into a good position. The next night (rather intoxicated, I confess) we took large magic markers, crept into their camp, and drew the appropriate TREEBUSTERS sign and cartoons all over their pretty yellow truck. I blame Jane.

A couple of weeks later, we bumped into them in Botswana. None of them had gotten the joke.

Either the Zambians have a terrible rate of accidental fires, or they do a *lot* of slash and burn agriculture. There were fields on fire everywhere we went. Since no one but us seemed to be even a little alarmed about these fires, we figured they must be intentional. However, one nearly overtook us during a lunch break one day, which I found rather unnerving.

Still racking up points as the most villainous white people to visit Zambia since Cecil Rhodes himself, we then started our own bushfire. Dick was on fire duty that evening. We were camped in a bushy spot with high grass. Having neglected to chop down the grass around the fire, well – it caught fire. We beat it to death with blankets, then took out our machetes, and chopped down anything within twenty yards of Dick. Just to be on the safe side, we camped in gravel pits for the next couple of nights.

I wish I could tell you more about Zambia, but between dead goats, bushfires, 500% inflation, a state of emergency, and cholera, it just didn't seem prudent to hang around, so we headed for Zimbabwe just as fast as our tires would carry us.

Back in the 1950s, the colonial government decided to build a dam on the Zambezi River to harness hydroelectric power to feed industry in (what became) Zambia and Zimbabwe. A valley of 5,200 square kilometres was flooded, thus forming Lake Kariba. Of course, no one warned the animals living there that this was going to happen, and those that didn't perish immediately kept moving to higher and higher ground as water levels rose. High ground soon turned into isolated islands. Starvation Island (as it came to be known) had one of the highest concentrations of stranded animals. Many thousands died before they could be saved by Operation Noah, mounted by conservationist Rupert Fothergill in 1959; the operation was able to save about 5,000 animals.

The valley was the tribal land of the Batonga people. They were warned about the apocalypse to come, and they were forced off the land. Apparently not all of them cooperated, though. People say there were those who didn't believe or understand what the white government told them would happen, and so they died there. Devastated by the seizure and flooding of their homeland, the Batonga believed that their wrathful river god, Nyaminyami, would destroy the dam project. Storms, floods, intense heat, and a few freak accidents seemed to favor their predictions for several years. Even today, there are nervous

An elephant strolls in the Matusadona National Park, Zimbawe.

reports of cracks in the dam, and drought in the 1980s reduced water levels to below the amount necessary to meet Zimbabwe's hydroelectric power needs.

The lake is as strange as it is beautiful. The tops of tall trees stick up through the water almost everywhere you go. The water is murky and churned up all the time, so you can't see how far down the bottom is, or if any hint remains of the huts, dens, mounds, and burrows that once existed there. You can't even see the tree trunks below the surface; just these tree tops poking out of the lake in abundance. At sunset, the lake seems full of ghosts, as if the spirits of terrified animals and bewildered Batonga are rising from the water to float through the air.

Matusadona National Park is a vast wildlife reserve on the lake's shores now, absolutely full of hippo, crocs, birds, and big game, many of them descendants of the animals rescued in Operation Noah. The flora and fauna have slowly adapted to this new environment and now thrive here. Tourism has developed into the mainstay of the local economy, and houseboating safaris on the lake are a particularly popular pastime; Africans are ever-resilient. We rented two houseboats, waved goodbye to Deb and the truck, and set out for a few days of pleasure cruising.

The houseboat had sleeping cabins, though I chose to sleep up on deck, being accustomed to fresh air and the open sky at night. We spent most of our time on the upper deck, but took our meals in a covered porch on the lower deck. George and Doreen were a pleasant, white, middle-aged Zimbabwean couple who ran the boat with a small crew of black Zimbabwean employees. George had a huge wooden staff carved with symbolic figures that have become a common theme in the artwork of the region: angry spirits, lost souls, a vengeful river god, and stolen memories.

It was a pretty incredible few days. For one thing, there was no work involved. I never had to lift a finger on the houseboat; indeed, I was very strongly urged not to. I think the most strenuous thing I did for three days was to put ice in my glass. We ate fabulous meals: dinners of roast chicken and potatoes, cauliflower, cheese sauce, snowpeas, fresh rolls, vinegar pudding with fresh cream, Kenyan coffee with liqueur; breakfasts of grapefruit, porridge, toast, eggs, bacon, sausage, fried onions, potato cakes, and broiled tomatoes; luncheons of fresh bread, cold meats and cheeses, and various salads. Cocktails started around 11:00 AM (not being British, I tended to wait until later in the day) and continued until bedtime. The "official" cocktail hour around 5 o'clock, accompanied by snacks or bits of fresh roasted fish which some of the gang had caught while out fishing in one of the little speedboats.

We did nothing but enjoy and indulge ourselves. I lounged on the deck as the boat cruised along, mooring here and there, and watched the abundant game and glorious scenery. The weather was perfect. The only cloud in my pure blue sky was the presence of Imelda, who, even in Paradise, bitched constantly about everything. Otherwise, the company was wonderful: David and Jane, Sally and Lionel, John, Joseph, and Jo.

Although the weather was perfect for swimming, none of us dared to try it. When we went out cruising in the smaller boats, hippos were constantly popping up around us, emerging from the murky depths of the water. And the crocs! While we were moored along the shore our first night there, George took out a huge high-powered flashlight and swung it around in a wide arc. I saw dozens of tiny, glinting lights: the reflection of crocodile eyes.

At night on the lake, I liked to watch hippos and their babies, silhouetted in the moonlight, go up on land to feed. Once, I rolled over restlessly on deck in the middle of the night, waking to hear something splashing only a few feet away; I looked down to see some Cape buffalo walking straight past me in the shallows. George had said elephants might come down to shore in the morning to drink. I didn't want to get my hopes up, but as I drank my morning coffee, four bull elephants appeared in the distance, slowly munched their way down to the water's edge, and drank and lolled around for an hour.

Among our companions was Fudge, Doreen's Chihuahua. I generally like big dogs that you can thump on the sides, but Fudge was very sweet. She worried us with her impetuosity, though. She apparently didn't know she was just the perfect size for a quick crocodile snack. We hiked around a little atoll one afternoon, and Fudge nearly gave me a heart attack, constantly dashing off to investigate logs and big rocks and strange little dugouts, all of which could be hiding (or which could even *be*) a croc.

Floating around out there on Kariba, watching elephants walk up to the boat as people brought me food and drinks, basking in perfect days and nights, I finally understood what had always made the colonels hang on so brutally to a land that was never theirs. I'd often heard British friends back in England talking about white Africans who'd never been able to adjust to life in the West, people who refused to leave Africa despite the economic and political chaos, people who tried to live in Europe and wound up going back to Africa. As someone who has lived abroad, I thought I understood what makes a person keep going back home. But I had never seen or known a life of such privilege as this; it hasn't existed in Europe and North America for anyone but the very, very richest people since long before I was born. Most of us just hope we can someday afford a cleaning woman to come in two hours a week; the thought of 4-5 full-time servants has never occurred to us. Of course, there was a lot more to the appeal of Zimbabwe and Kariba than servants – but living in the lap of luxury in this utterly splendid setting for a few days shed some light on lives that had always baffled me.

Well, all good things must come to an end. We had to be virtually dragged off the houseboats when it was time to return to shore, and Deb

Dinner on Lake Kariba, Zimbabwe.

had to order us back on board the truck. As if returning to the life of an overlander wasn't enough of a shock, we then had to go back to Zambia. The road to Victoria Falls was washed out or something, so we'd have to travel overland on the Zambian side of Lake Kariba and the Zambezi River, then cross back into Zimbabwe at the Falls. Grumbling all the way, we felt bored and confined in the truck, and we got as rambunctious as children on a driving trip. Then the starter motor malfunctioned (again) in Zambia, so we had to push the truck to start her up.

"We never needed to push the houseboat," I told Deb with a definite sneer.

I'd like to blame what happened next on the tedium of those Zambian days, but it was really my own damn fault. Remember that character flaw I had promised to work on? Well, when we reached the border, I was thrown out of the immigration office for my behavior... which included slapping a local citizen, arguing with a Zimbabwean immigration official, and failing to present proper documents.

THE SMOKE THAT THUNDERS

Crossing the Zimbabwe border overland is more complex than you might suppose. I say this with some authority, since I more or less crisscrossed it for over a month, going in and out of Zambia, Botswana, and South Africa. The two reasons it's confusing are that (1) Zimbabwean dollars are soft currency and the Zimbabweans have very strict currency controls, and (2) the Zimbabweans demand proof that you're going to leave Zimbabwe and not hang around dragging on their economy. There is, of course, a third factor: this is Africa, and hence the procedure is always inconsistent and unpredictable.

The strict currency controls meant the Zims insisted on our filling out paperwork every time we entered or exited the country, detailing our currencies and the amount of each. Any Zim official could demand to count our money at any time, as often as he wanted, to make sure we were telling the truth. If suspicious, they could search the truck for money. There is no recourse; this is their country, their border, and they're entitled to uphold their currency laws.

However, we felt compelled to break their currency laws. You see, one of their strict rules is that you can only export about US $20 worth of Zim currency. That would be fine if you weren't coming back for a year, but not so good if you're coming back in a few days or a week. Zim banks are like most other banks in Africa; it takes *hours* to change money. Hence, you tend to want to change all the money you'll need for next week, too, and not just this week; particularly if you know you're crossing the border back into Zim in a place that doesn't even *have* banks.

Consequently, we wound up hiding a lot of Zim currency in our underwear every time we crossed the border. The delicacy of the hiding place reduces the risk of getting caught, but when you're traveling with a mixed bag of overlanders, it still has its risks. Since one person's indiscretion can get everyone arrested, I was always nervous. On one occasion, a guard said, "Declare all your money." An overlander of less-than-stellar intelligence looked blank and replied, "What, even the money hidden in our knickers?" (By the grace of Nyamimyami, the guard didn't hear her.) At another border, this same woman got through customs and immigration, came back to the truck while I was guarding it, and pulled a huge wad of undeclared Zim dollars out of her locker *while* a guard was inspecting the truck! Miraculously, her behavior again went unnoticed – perhaps because there were so many of us milling around.

Today we approach the Zim border at Victoria Falls, having done our best to demolish the nation of Zambia. I'm feeling hot, cranky, and (stretch your imagination to picture it) decidedly short-tempered. It's unseasonably hot today, and the immigration office is amazingly crowded. The notion of personal space is largely peculiar to Westerners. In Africa, it's frequently disregarded, often unknown, sometimes considered rather strange, and even occasionally perceived as rude. Now I am crowded from behind by a man whose hand keeps brushing my butt every time he shifts his weight. To my shame, I lose my temper and wind up swatting him. Everyone around us either glares at me with distaste or laughs uproariously over my neuroses.

I finally reach the head of the line. As I did the last time I entered Zim, I show my passport, all my money, and my money declaration forms to the woman behind the counter.

She isn't interested. "Where is your air ticket to prove you are leaving Zimbabwe?"

Shit! I've left my ticket back to London locked up in the truck, even though I knew there was a possibility I'd be asked for it. "It's locked up somewhere," I say, "but I've brought all my money. See? And it's enough to *buy* an air ticket. Anyhow, I can tell you all the details of my air ticket. Isn't that enough?"

She sternly ignores my pleading, ignores my money, and sends me back to the truck, saying she only needs to see my air ticket.

I return a few minutes later with my air ticket, having put my money safely away, and get back in line. After another long hot wait, I get to the counter again. There is a man there this time.

"Show me your money," he says.

"What money?" I ask blankly. Is he asking for a bribe, I wonder?

"All your money. All the money that you have declared on this form here."

"My money?" I repeat stupidly, distressed. "Why?"

"*Why?* Because I need to see what money you have. Where is your money?"

I decide to brazen it out. I can't face going to the back of the line *again* in this hot, stuffy building redolent of rancid sweat. "My money is safely locked away."

"Why is it there? Why didn't you bring it with you?"

"Because it's safe there. It's not safe if I carry it around with me." I later learn that this exact same response worked perfectly well for David, with the very same official. But David is a *man*, and I am a mere woman, so the guard shakes his head.

"Go get your money," he says.

"You mean you want me to go all the way back and start over?" I whine.

"Yes. You should have brought your money."

"Now *wait* a minute." I get decidedly stroppy. "I was just here with my money, and your colleague sent me back for my air ticket. She had no interest in seeing my money."

"What colleague?"

"That lady over there."

He laughs at me. "What are you talking about? She didn't say that!"

"Yes, she did."

"No."

"Yes, she did. Just *ask* her!"

"I don't need to ask her. She didn't say that."

I am mentally transported back to the bank in Bamako, where I underwent this exact same conversation with the bank manager. I nearly started a riot there. I want to start one here.

"Yes, she *did* say it!" I insist, getting really nasty now. "Look, here's my onward air ticket. You don't need to see my money."

"You always have to show your money."

Now I get downright ugly. "I have been to nineteen countries in Africa, and I have *never* had to show my money!" It's an outright lie, and a very stupid one. Moreover, I say it pompously enough to really piss him off.

"Oh, you are getting impatient with me, are you? Fine! Go away. I don't need this. I don't have to pass you. Go."

I stare at him. "You're telling me to *go*?"

"Yes, go get your money and start over," he orders, really angry at me.

"Fine!" I snarl. "Give me my papers!" I reach for the forms I have laboriously filled out.

"No!" He takes my papers and tears them up. I stare in disbelief.

"Fill out another," he snaps.

I return to the truck, fuming over his pettiness. I am also angry at myself. How could I be so *stupid?* Not only does a harassed, bored, overworked, underpaid civil servant not need to deal with a stroppy foreign bitch, but I should know by now that this is just how things are in Africa – slow, inconsistent, frequently illogical. I should know better than to show up at immigration without *all* the papers I'll need for *any* contingency. I should also know that I'll have to pay for getting pompous, arrogant, and pushy. Not to mention rude.

Hoping *someone* will let me into Zimbabwe, I get back into line again. I've got everything but my birth certificate with me this time. When I get to the counter, the woman is there again.

She asks to see my air ticket. She refuses to even glance at my money when I try to show it to her.

Victoria Falls is Paradise. It's where I want to go when I die. It's like some movie-maker's fantasy version of Africa. It was another place I had to be dragged forcibly away from when it was finally time to pack up camp and move on.

Dr. Livingstone was reputedly the first white man to see these falls, which are the longest in the world, stretching out some 1,700 metres. The water falls for over 100 metres and sends up clouds of spray as high as 500 metres which sustain the surrounding tropical forest. Livingstone named the falls after his queen, but the local Makololo people had a much better name for it: *Mosi oa Tunya,* "The Smoke That Thunders." A fitting sobriquet; from a distance, you can hear the thundering water and see the mist rising from it like smoke long before you can see the actual waterfalls.

The national park there is absolutely beautiful, full of little paths and lookouts, and lush with tropical foliage. The Zambezi River floats wide and lazy above the Falls. Below the Falls, heading toward Mozambique, it's one of the premier whitewater rafting rivers in the world. The town of Victoria Falls is small and quite pretty: nice shops; restaurants and cafés; clean streets; trees and flowers; nice homes and beautiful hotels scattered out from the town centre.

There were many well-off, educated Africans there. I was in a boutique there one day when two Zim women, probably in their mid-twenties, came bursting into the shop. One was saying something to the other about a great dress she'd seen here. She wanted her friend's opinion about whether or not to buy it. The other woman fell in love with another dress in the shop. They were in a hurry because they were on their lunch hour, but they wanted to try on about half a dozen dresses they saw there. They laughed a lot, checked themselves out in the mirror, checked each other out, and checked out what I was thinking of buying.

It was a scene so *normal,* and yet so tragically abnormal: two women having fun shopping for a pretty dress. It's seldom normal out there unless you're talking about the tiny rich minority. Seeing two working girls doing it now suddenly made me happy and optimistic. I'd seen so many people in Africa struggling just to get from day to day, wearing rags, begging from every European they saw, and aging fast under an enormous burden of hard work and poverty. It was so good to see two African women whose cares seemed so manageable and so familiar to me: Can I afford this beautiful dress? Do I have time to try on another one before I have to get back to work? If I leave it and come back tomorrow, will the dress still be here?

We camped at the municipal campsite, conveniently located right in the center of town. It was full of overland trucks from companies both big and small: Guerba, Dragoman, Exodus, Encounter Overland, Acacia, Which Way Adventures, Kumuka, Hobo, and others. (This was where we vandalized a Dutch overland truck.) It seemed like a gathering of my herd. Wildebeest in Serengeti; overlanders in Vic Falls. As firebuilder, I went on strike. With so many fabulous and famous restaurants within walking distance, I had no intention of hacking wood, coaxing a fire, and eating Richard's noodles and tomato sauce here.

By necessity, and also by custom, many African families eat a much less varied diet than we do in North America and Europe. Most Africans cooking for tourists know this and compensate accordingly; unfortunately, Richard had trouble with the concept. No matter how often Deb discussed it with him (eventually resorting to asking Joseph, whose English was excellent, to act as interpreter), he kept dishing up the same food every night. Deb would say, "Richard, you can't feed the *wazungu* tomato sauce 21 days in a row. You must cook something different tonight." He would agree politely, then prepare tomato sauce for dinner. We'd poke at it morosely and think longingly of all the wonderful food we'd seen in the local markets.

There were other conflicts, too. Richard was a *very* hard worker, but he either didn't like or didn't understand the notion that *everyone* is supposed to participate in the work on an overland truck. (Come to think of it, there were a few overlanders who also didn't seem to understand the concept, so I guess Richard's confusion wasn't unique in this respect.) He generally ignored his cooking crews. He never revealed to them what he was making (though tomato sauce seemed a safe guess most nights), and he was so rude and curt to any *females* on duty that a number of them, understandably, simply stopped working their cooking shifts (so dinner got even slower). I began to appreciate how truly excellent Pippa had been at her job. Whereas, working under her supervision, we had prepared delicious meals (including campfire- baked *desserts*) within 90 minutes of camping up for the night, we now routinely waited three and a half hours after making camp for a dinner of noodles in canned tomato sauce. I started developing a fixation about garam masala, a sort of curry powder I'd never liked all that much to begin with; it seemed to be the only seasoning Richard ever used.

Richard had told me early on, in one of our rare attempts at conversation, that he'd never worked a trip like this before. He did "high class" safaris, where he started preparing the evening meal around one o'clock in the afternoon and served it some seven hours later. I suspected he cooked very good meals when working under those circumstances and shopping in markets where he knew the language and felt comfortable. Now hopelessly out of his element and out of his depth, living on the road in countries where no one spoke Swahili, he was not coping well. Guerba asked us for written comments when we reached Harare, and I was not the only overlander to suggest they'd used poor judgement in sending him out on the road without more thorough preparation. Although I could never ask him (since just asking "What's for dinner?" produced so much confusion), I had the impression that Richard was as frustrated as we were by his problems with the job. (Upon returning home, by the way, I got a very courteous response from Guerba, which included the good news that Richard wound up back in Kenya, again cooking for a "high class" operation that Guerba ran there.)

I, meanwhile, had running battles with Richard over the fire. He would, for example, tell me he didn't need a fire for breakfast because he intended to use the portable gas stove that morning. Then someone would come find me a half hour later, saying Richard was frantic and everyone else was furious because he needed a fire and I hadn't built it yet. I think those occasions were language barrier problems; I don't think he knew what I was saying when I asked him if he wanted a fire. At other times, his contempt for my gender was the problem (the feminist movement isn't precisely an overwhelming force in Africa). Moreover, I can be very rigid about how I want things done. For example, I preferred to take care of the fire grate and tools myself, not liking the way Richard treated them. He often ignored me (or perhaps didn't understand me) when I told him that *I* would take care of them, proceeding as if I weren't even speaking to him. Then I would be snappish with him, and he wouldn't know why. Our disgruntlement would be mutual and would last for hours.

So I preferred, while in Vic Falls, to go to high-ceilinged restaurants with napkins (napkins, I tell you!) and ceiling fans and tables, where we ate crocodile thermadore, impala steaks, ostrich *en papillote*, and warthog stir-fry (though, as Lionel said, it's so hard to know what wine to order with your warthog). Fabulous meals, including wine, coffee, dessert, and tip, would come to about US $15 per head, thanks to the exchange rate.

The town and the hotels were full of bars, and the bars were full of all manner of people. It always felt like some kind of modern-day Rider Haggard novel to me. There were overlanders, of course; where there is a bar in Africa, there will always be overlanders. There were wealthy people on safari who stayed in hotels (you know: places with beds and ceilings and plumbing). White Zimbabweans would come into town from the farm or the big city. Many ex-patriates, adventurers, journalists, documentarists, sportsmen, gamblers, smugglers, and wanderers showed up. Vic Falls is one of the few places in the world where I really enjoyed going to bars, because you were always sure to meet someone interesting or see something astonishing. One night at the Explorers Bar, I actually saw a white man stick his head through the ceiling. (Imagine my alarm when, the next day, it turned out he was leading our rafts down the Zambezi River).

Feeling troubled and reflective, I went to see the Falls alone, after most of the gang had already trekked all over the place. I hadn't made many resolutions out there, but I had kept the ones I'd made: to stick it out; to get good at it; to forgive myself my many, many mistakes; to become indifferent to physical discomfort; even to become a good firemaster. The only resolution I never kept, in fact, was the one about coming home as thin as a wraith (I came home as chubby as ever).

I was now distressed by this bullheaded, insistent, ethnocentric impatience of mine that was getting increasingly out of hand. I was ashamed of my behavior in Zanzibar, at the Zim border, with a Malawian communications clerk, with a Malawian banker, and with the manager of a Vic Falls tea shop. (And those were just the examples off the top of my head.) This behavior wasn't doing anyone any good, least of all me. Something inside me coiled tighter and tighter each time I lost my temper over something that was never meant to be insulting or deliberately difficult, and which was never dangerous or hostile. If I wanted things to be exactly the way I expected them to be, then why had I come halfway around the world?

I knew all of this intellectually, but I kept jumping the gun and getting riled anyhow. Wandering around the Falls alone for several hours finally gave me some perspective. It gave me a feeling of peace and contentment. I was so lucky to be here! I once had an acting teacher who used to say: "Deal with what you *get*, not with what you think you *should* be getting!" It was time for me to do that here, or I would have wasted being here. I resolved to be calmer, more patient, and more flexible. Believe it or not, I was different after that day. Not with my companions – I saw no reason to be more patient with Imelda or more flexible with someone who damned well ought to do their share of the work. But that coiling, twisting tension and explosive frustration started fading and diffusing after that day.

Feeling lighthearted and almost giddily calm, I went with the gang to one of the Vic Falls shows that night. There was a performance of "traditional" African songs and dances: celebrations of circumcision rites, victory dances, courting songs, etc. It was quite touristy, but I *am* a tourist, and I enjoy anything that's well-done, which this was. I reflected, however, how lucky I was to have attended the Festival of Dipri (the belly-stabbing, demon-chasing rituals in the Ivory Coast) – unself-conscious, genuine religious rites and festivities in a continent where traditions have been ravaged and torn apart and are disappearing every year.

My friends, by the way, went to see the local bone-thrower that same afternoon, while I was rebirthing at the Falls. These were the friends with whom I would share my white-water raft the next day. They were all told that they would live a long time. I never got around to visiting the bone-thrower.

The next day I fell into the whitewater rapids of the Zambezi River.

BLADDERS OF STEEL

The Zambezi River is one of the best and most famous whitewater rivers anywhere. It's also one of the few rivers whose rapids get *more* – rather than less – exciting as the water gets lower (in the dry season). I've arrived in Vic Falls right in the heart of the dry season, and the river is *wild*.

We show up at one of Vic Falls' big hotels, along with many other people. It's a huge crowd – rafting is a big business here. I now see why there are so many hotels around town – all these white folks have to sleep *somewhere* after all, not all of us being the type to sleep under an overland truck when it's raining.

We're going rafting today with Sheerwater, a company which runs all kinds of stuff around here: rafting, canoeing, flights over the falls, etc. I'm told that they put 3-20 rafts on the river most days, depending on weather and crowds. We appear to have pretty near the maximum number today, this being prime time for Zambezi rafting. We sign in at the hotel, get tea and biscuits, and acquire wetsuits. Mine is so tight across the chest (I'm rather *zaftig*) that I can't breathe. Someone helps me out of it before I pass out, and I find one that doesn't constrain my, uh, lungs quite so much.

Then a black Zim guy welcomes us all and gives gave an introductory talk. Somewhat nervous to begin with, I am absolutely *terrified* by the time he's done. We have to sign a disclaimer absolving the company of anything that might happen to us, even in the event of their negligence. We are warned that the walk down the gorge to the river is notoriously steep, slippery, and strenuous, and that anyone of questionable fitness had better drop out now (Jo restrains me as I try to get up and leave). We are warned that the climb *out* of the gorge (750 meters almost straight up) at the end of the day is twice as brutal (David restrains me as I try to get up and leave). We are asked to give our address on one of the disclaimers.

"Not your local address, but your permanent address, so we'll know where to send the remains," the guy adds. (Sally and Lionel restrain me as I try very hard indeed to get up and *leave*).

We are told to choose whether we want to go in a highside or a paddle raft. I don't know the difference. I've never been rafting before. I scarcely know what a raft looks like. Jo and I shrug, and the others (David, Jane, Sally, Lionel, and a Dutch guy we call Deet) assure me that a paddle boat is the best choice. Well, yes, I vaguely think that paddling on a river sounds better than *not* paddling. Indeed, I wonder why someone would go down the river in a raft that (if I understand correctly) *has* no paddles. Sounds crazy to me! So I (foolishly) entrust the decision to my friends, who have done this before.

We drive out of town on an air-conditioned bus (yet another moment of luxury in the life of an overlander!), then switch to a vehicle which makes even this hardy overlander blanch. It's an enormous sort of flatbed truck, where we are squashed in like sardines. Some total stranger's elbows get awfully friendly with my wetsuit-wrapped chest, and the girl next to me nearly eats her own knees. We drive over bumpy bush terrain in this thing for a while, traveling from the road to the top of the gorge. Once disgorged from the vehicle, some of us are given paddles and all of us are given lifejackets. Then we're sent down the gorge with one final warning about its treacherousness.

It's just as bad as promised, so steep that I descend parts of it on my bum. Not everyone does this, but I'm not going to let a little pride stand between me and old age. There are also portions so steep that we descend via ladders, or holding onto knotted ropes as we ease ourselves down. I keep dropping my paddle – sometimes on people's heads. I'm now drenched with sweat beneath my wetsuit, and my sweatproof sun screen is running into my eyes. Between fear, anticipated fear, and exhaustion, my legs are shaking, my knees ache, and my stomach is churning by the time I near the bottom of the gorge.

A good-natured Aussie girl right behind me chats with me once the worst of the descent seems to be over. Like me, she's cursing her friends the whole way (I have by now convinced myself that this was all *their* idea).

She says to me, "I gather you've been rafting before."

"No, never," I say. "What makes you think that?"

"You've got a paddle. Didn't you read the brochure? It says only experienced rafters should paddle on this river."

"It *does*?"

"Uh-huh."

My stomach does a full flip-flop with a jackknife twist. I now curse my friends in earnest. Slipping, sliding, sweating, shaking, and in desperate need of a whizz, I scramble the rest of the way down to the docking point. The water is reassuringly calm, not yet foaming and frothing like a rabid dog, not yet ready to drag me down with its icy tentacles. *But*, I think morosely, *just wait.*

I march forward, brandish my paddle at Jane and Sally, and shriek, "That girl says only experienced rafters are supposed to paddle on this river!"

"Uh-huh. That's nice," they murmur absently, looking around with excitement. *They've* done this before. *They* don't have unwritten best-sellers to worry about. *They* have been told by the local witchdoctor that they'll live to be old.

"You didn't tell me that!" I cry accusingly.

"Mmmm...."

"You people will be the death of me," I snarl.

Jane smiles and squeezes my shoulder in good fellowship. I try to kick her, but I miss because my legs are still shaking. I realize with horror, with a dawning sense of revulsion, that I have fallen among... THRILLSEEKERS!

We collect our helmets, flimsy, plastic affairs that will never keep my precious skull from becoming pulverized. And the helmets are *yellow*! One of my *worst* colors! We are then given a rousing safety talk by the head guide. I am unimpressed, since I saw him stick his head through the ceiling of the Explorers Bar last night.

If we find ourselves inadvertently swimming through the rapids, he advises us to put our feet forward to brace against the rocks, keep our heads up, and keep our arms out for balance. We probably won't die in the rapids, we are assured, but if we spend much time in the water once we've reached the calm... Well, be warned; that's where the crocs hang out. We should try to get back into the boat *fast*.

In a highsider boat, I finally learn, only the guide (sitting in the middle) has paddles. The passengers hang on for dear life and throw their weight around to help direct and stabilize the raft. In a paddle boat, however, all the passengers (as well as the guide) have paddles. The guide calls out instructions, but the paddlers bear a lot of responsibility for getting the raft through the rapids. If everyone does their job, it should go well. If people freak out (as our guide later tells me often happens), things go rather badly. I'm told that many guides prefer a highsider because it's less mental work and they don't have to count on frightened strangers.

I calm down a bit, living now at merely a mild pitch of terror instead of an outraged frenzy. While part of me wants to just hang

Whitewater rafting on the Zambezi River. I'm the one who's white-faced with terror.

on for dear life for the next few hours, I have confidence in my friends and their good sense (well, usually), and I figure I'd rather play a part in my own fate than entrust it completely to a stranger who, for all I know, has *also* recently stuck his head through the ceiling of the Explorers Bar.

We find our raft and pile in. Our guide, it turns out, is an American. *From Ohio!* He put himself through college as a whitewater guide back home and then got a special six-month visa to come out here and guide trips. He's been here for a few weeks and loves it, can hardly imagine ever leaving (I'm starting to feel that way myself). If I'm meant to face my destiny today, then I'm glad my guide is American; Americans take their leisure sports *very* seriously, so I have a feeling he'll be very capable. His name is Todd, and his instructions are very clear, concise, and sensible. Once we have rehearsed the basic procedures, we set off for death or glory.

I thought a rubber raft seemed like a pretty flimsy thing to protect me from rocks, crocs, and rapids, especially when I was sitting on its rounded sides with nothing holding me in place except my feet wedged into its folds. Nevertheless, I found the splashing rush through Rapid 11 (they number these things) pretty exhilarating, despite the bouncing-around disorientation.

Rapid 13 was the first real test of my grit, however: big waves, fast water. A lot of rafts tip over there; it's a Grade 5 rapid, which may mean something to you if you've ever rafted. All I know is that it's *big.* Todd was very thorough, explaining what the water would be doing – left currents, right sweeps, waves, and holes – and what we would do to maximize our ride through it without losing anyone or flipping over. That was the key to rafting, I gathered – not to just get through a rapid, but to do it in the most thrilling way possible, hitting every wave.

An enormous wall of water rose up in front of us. The raft shuddered, dipped, and soared off into space. Water poured down on me in vast sheets. I tumbled into the center of the raft, clutching my paddle and feebly trying to follow Todd's shouted instructions. We hit every wave head-on, smack in the middle, flying, soaring, bouncing. Terrifying! And wet – we were *wet*.

After Rapid 13, when we finished cheering and whacking our paddles together in celebration, Todd stood up and called through the gorge to some of the other rafts, "Who's got the repair kit?"

Ha-ha! I thought. *What a kidder!*

Receiving no answer, he repeated, "Who's got the repair kit?" His voice echoed around the gorge, bounced off the towering cliffs overhead, and died away in the endless blue sky. No answer.

"Who's got the pump?" he bellowed. No answer.

He *wasn't* kidding.

We paddled around in the calm. Some interrogation of his fellow guides revealed that no one had remembered to bring the pump or repair kit. Meanwhile, the left rear section of our raft was losing air.

Unable to repair the leak, Todd thereafter cheerfully referred to it as our "extra challenge." As the day progressed, our raft got more and more flaccid (the forbidden "f" word that makes most men wince), and therefore less and less capable of withstanding the rigors of the rapids. It kept folding up like a card table at the *most* inopportune moments. Todd and Deet were sitting on that part of the raft, and Nature got closer and closer to them as the hours passed. Indeed, by the end of the day, it wouldn't have been at all difficult for Nature to crawl into the raft with us, had Nature been hungry enough. By the time we docked late that afternoon, that portion of our raft was sort of a puddle of shapeless rubber.

We saw wildlife, despite all the noise we made: lots of birds, some klipspringers (small antelope), a couple of crocs. The crocs were so well-camouflaged in the rocks that, had they not been pointed out to me, I'd never have seen them. (I am not notoriously sharp-eyed).

Sheerwater sends a photographer downriver alongside the rafts, so there are actually lots of photos of us that day; I purchased a dozen of them. The gang all look exhilarated (indeed, Jane looks half-mad with glee). I look white-faced with terror. However, despite my overactive imagination (which is a disadvantage when you're not actually using it to make a living), I *loved* rafting after the first few terrifying rapids. It was perhaps the first time in my life where I felt an exhilaration that was actually more powerful than the fear I felt at the very same time. I'm no adrenaline junkie, not by a longshot. Indeed, I associate adrenaline with some of the worst and most horrifying moments of my life. That day on the river, however, adrenaline acted on me like a love potion.

For his part, Todd claimed we were the best group he'd ever taken out on the river (and I cheerfully decided to believe him), keeping him vastly amused and doing such a good job of teamwork that he had us paddle back and take some of the best rapids a second time. He was also dead impressed by what he called our "bladders of steel," since we didn't require a single riverside stop, despite drinking water and orange-aid all day. Hey – we're *overlanders*, man.

Everything was going so well that I felt wonderfully confident, even cocky, when we finally reached Rapid 23, the last big rapid of the day. And that's where I fell in.

To be honest, I don't even remember falling into the water. It hit me hard from the side. Everything went black. I apparently catapulted out of the boat and was gone before anyone could grab me. The first thing I knew, I was bobbing and felt my helmet hit the underside of the raft. I pushed against it, holding my breath, and thought, "Shit! I'm in the water! What am I doing *here*?"

Still clinging to my paddle, upon which I had a death grip, I hauled myself out to the side of the whirling raft, kicked, came up to the surface, took a big gulp of air – and coughed as rushing foam filled my mouth and throat. I couldn't see. Couldn't breathe. Reached for the rope on the side of the raft, couldn't find it. Felt a hand on mine. Clung to it. The water pulled me away.

That's when I started to feel afraid. It's also when I let go of my damn paddle and concentrated on not drowning. Oddly enough, I had never really thought about the possibility of drowning, not even though I lost a dear friend to drowning several years ago. *Now* I thought about it.

I'd never been in such strong currents before. I wasn't prepared for the force of the water, the lack of control over my own body, the water churning up over my head again and again, the lack of air.

The boat and I whirled around each other in the water. Somehow I was on the other side now. I saw paddles being extended to me. I reached up for them and was dragged away. My chest started to burn. I saw Jane, Sally, and Lionel reaching down for me. The current pulled me away from them. I swiped at the rope again, then went under water. Having no rafting sandals, I was wearing shoes. They were like lead

Having survived falling into the rapids, I enjoy some hightcaps on the Zambezi River, Zimbabwe. From left to right: Me, Judith, Jane, David, and Jo.

weights now. My arms felt heavy and weak. My chest was on fire. Another attempt to pull me on board failed, and I felt too weak to help effectively. I tried to remember the proper position for swimming through the rapids, but only swallowed more water. I thought, "Shit! I'm going to drown! I never thought I'd go out this way!"

Raw, mindless, desperate *fear*. I have never been more scared in my life. I've never felt more sure that I was about to die.

Coming up again, I saw Todd shove my friends out of his way. He practically came out of the boat himself to reach me. He grabbed the lapels of my lifejackets, then heaved and threw himself bodily backwards, taking me with him – and I am not light. The two of us flew up and back and down. I landed on my face in the middle of the raft. I discovered my face was in his crotch, and I flopped around like a wet fish. And we were *still* in the rapids, swirling around madly in our loss of control. I thought I'd vomit. I choked it down, not wanting to disgrace myself.

We reached the calm at last and everyone started checking me for injuries and panic and death. The fear was still horrible, and my heart was pounding so loud I couldn't hear they said. In truth, I was in the water for much less than half a minute; it just *seemed* like half an hour. Naturally, I'd also had a few minutes before I'd actually drown, by which time the water would have carried me to the calm (where the crocs could get me). Anyhow, Lionel assured me that there was never any chance of my drowning, since it was quite clearly a matter of pride for Todd: he *wasn't* going to lose a client.

There was only one more rapid after that, and it wasn't a particularly big one, so my jangled nerves suffered no more. Then, legs shaking and stomach now churning with reaction, I climbed out of the raft, picked up all my wet gear, and began the long climb out of the gorge.

It was brutal. Again, many parts of it were so steep that we hauled ourselves up by ropes and ladders. After a thrilling and terrifying day on an empty stomach, I now hauled my lifejacket, wetsuit, and paddle up that gorge in the heat. Having survived the river, I thought the climb would kill me. Todd found me resting on a rock about two-thirds of the way up and offered to carry my stuff for me. I refused, since he was already carrying his own stuff, the raft's spare gear, and two enormous jugs with our leftover drinks in them. He insisted that he did this climb every day and could easily handle my stuff, too. Feeling old and chubby and pathetic, I let him. When we reached a section where we had to lean against a rock and edge along, pulling ourselves upwards with a rope, I was damn glad he'd taken my gear. If he hadn't, I'd have thrown it off the side of the cliff at that point.

Back at camp, we barely had time to hop into dry clothes before heading back to the Zambezi (above the falls this time). We had previously decided to go on a sunset cruise that evening, and we were back later than expected. There was no time to eat in our rush to get to the appointed place on time.

There weren't enough riverboats that night, so our little group piled into a speedboat stocked with goodies and set off. Our pilot was an older Zim named Ellie, the magician of the Zambezi – he was the only good diesel mechanic on the river, and since all the boats kept breaking down that evening, he kept being called into service. In exchange for taking up our leisure time this way, the pilot of every boat Ellie fixed gave us a bottle or two of champagne.

Mostly we were hungry. Desperately hungry! There was only one little plate of munchies on board, and we devoured it like hungry lions. After that, we just kept downing more and more wine and bubbly, our supply constantly being refurbished by the boats we stopped to help out. I'm not precisely abstemious, but neither am I a heavy drinker. Tonight, however, I was a *guzzler*. On an empty stomach, with my nerves shot to hell, and just feeling glad to be alive, I kept holding up my plastic glass and saying, "Pour me another. I nearly died today. My *God*, I nearly died today. It was *great*, wasn't it? Except for the part where I nearly *died*. Jesus, I'm hungry, why won't anyone give us any *food*? I'm so hungry! Pour me another!"

It was glorious out there: a warm day turning to cool evening, the sun setting over the Zambezi, hippos geysering out of the water, elephants browsing on the shore. Ellie eyed the elephants on the Zambian side, who were carrying heavy ivory, with a connoisseur's eye and idly estimated how much those tusks were worth on the black market. He seemed a little embarrassed when he realized he'd spoken aloud and we were listening intently. I rather suspected Ellie had done some poaching in his day.

By the time the bubbly was gone and we were working on the wine and beer, I was feeling very convivial. I told Ellie that all that engine-fixing was thirsty work, and I started pouring him drinks, too. Just to ensure that we weren't being irresponsible by giving booze to the driver, we occasionally hit him with really tough questions to test his sobriety: Which way are the Falls? Which bank is the Zambian side? Is that a croc or an elephant you see before you?

Humming a little ditty ("*I want to be an overlander! I want to live a life of danger!*"), we finally returned to shore. I noticed the ground was undulating wildly when I stepped on it. Needing a quick whizz, I found a bush and answered nature's call. Pulling up my trousers, I noticed white people staring at me with disapproving frowns – which was when I realized I was skirting the gardens of a hotel. That's when I began to suspect I might be drunk.

I was still singing as I blindly followed Jo and Deb into a beautiful marbled bathroom in some hotel 10 minutes later, needing another whizz; I was *perfectly* willing to do it in a toilet if people were going to *stare*, after all. I nearly knocked over some white lady. She didn't even smile at my apology. No sense of proportion! Then I was seized by a brilliant inspiration.

"Deb!" I cried. "Say, Deb! Let's go to the Ilala Hotel so we can see the video showing of today's raft trip!"

Deb took me firmly by the shoulders. She stared into my eyes and said, "Where do you think we are, Laura?"

The truth dawned. I took a wild shot in the dark: "The Ilala?"

She nodded.

I thought about this, then asked: "I'm very drunk, aren't I?"

She nodded.

I burst out laughing and sat down on the floor, disturbing even more of the hotel's patrons. My friends hauled me up and away while I explained loudly, to anyone passing by, "I nearly *died* today!" We got another round of drinks and went to watch the video screening.

I was so impressed! All of those rafts flipping over! All that whitewater! What daring, thrilling, rufty-tufty stuff! We looked like we were really challenging death! I was *there!* I bumped into Todd and tipped him now that I had cash on my person. I later learned that

Lionel had tipped Todd on my behalf, figuring I was way too far gone to think of it. (Americans are never too far gone to tip, not if they've been raised right). Anyhow, old Todd did all right that day.

By now I was *so* hungry! We still hadn't eaten, so we called Eatza Pizza and ordered 10 pizzas. You can *do* that in Victoria Falls! I was so impressed! I'd been to towns that didn't even *have* food, and suddenly I could order a carry-out pizza! We went back to the truck and found out the pizzas hadn't been delivered yet. Unable to wait, we went in search of them. We bumped into the delivery man on a public street in Vic Falls and assaulted him. Joseph saw us and was shocked. He was doubly appalled when we sat down on a curb in the street and started tearing into the pizzas with our bare hands, eating like hungry hyenas, occasionally tossing pieces back and forth, mumbling, "Try some of this one, it's really good." Deb, who had gone ahead to the Explorers Bar, claimed she wasn't hungry. We took her at her word and devoured her pizza, too. (All the names she called us later indicated that she wasn't pleased about this, as she rifled through the truck in the middle of the night searching for something edible).

I was slowing down by the time we reached the Explorers Bar. I was unable to drink anything but water now. For some reason, the bartender wouldn't bring me water — but he *would* bring it to any *man* who ordered it for me. I didn't stay long, anyhow. The bar was crowded enough to begin with, but when I started seeing double, it became positively claustrophobic.

SUFFERIN' SWAMP SAFARI

B otswana gained independence from the British in 1966. Soon thereafter, some of the richest diamond formations in the world were discovered in Botswana, ensuring the country's economic well-being. Ruled by the Tswana tribe, which accounts for 60% of the population, Botswana never suffered the civil wars, internal unrest, and inter-tribal conflict which so many African nations endured after independence. It's rumbled along in a politically moderate way, combining Western and African structures into its governmental system, cultivating high-cost low-volume tourism, and resolutely staying out of its neighbors' wars. Although English is the official language, 90% of the people speak Setswana (which is also the language of instruction in the primary schools). The great Kalahari Desert, home of the San people (or Bushmen), covers 85% of Botswana. Rain is so valuable in this desert country that they've named their money after it; "pula," the Botswanan unit of currency, means "rain." And prices were so high in Botswana that even a humble overlander needed a lot of rain there.

Although diamonds and gold are now enriching Botswana, the Tswana are traditionally a cattle culture. Cattle are a symbol of wealth and an extremely important commodity. The well-being of cattle is an all-important concern in Botswana. Hence, the government has installed some challenging border regulations.

For example, it is illegal to carry any milk or meat products across the border into Botswana. This is to protect their cattle against foot-and-mouth disease. For reasons too obscure to contemplate, this ban applies not only to fresh meat, milk, and yogurt, but also to things like canned lunch meat, milk chocolate, and milk

Squatting baglike over my work at dawn as I make the morning fire. Botswana. (Photo by Jane Garnett)

powder. Such foods are staples of an overlander's diet (particularly in places like Botswana, where you can drive for two days without encountering a town). We had such staples aboard the truck. Not only did we not want to waste them, we also didn't want to replace our entire stock in Botswana, where things are three times as expensive as they are in the surrounding countries. Nor did we want our supplies confiscated at the border. The typical solution is to smuggle them across the border.

Deb explained the situation to Richard who, as campmaster, was in charge of the food supplies. She explained the situation several times to him, sometimes in English, sometimes with Joseph translating into Swahili.

I came back from the Vic Falls post office one morning to find Richard tearing the truck apart. I assumed he was doing as instructed and hiding milk and meat products under the engine parts stored beneath the floorboards.

I found him hiding bags of tea, packets of biscuits, and canned fruit. Deb stopped him and explained again: milk and meat products only. He said he understood now. *Milk and meat.*

We found him hiding grapefruit, breakfast cereal, and orange drink mix. Deb stopped him. She explained: milk and meat. Joseph translated into Swahili. Richard said he understood now.

We found him hiding flour, canned beans, and coffee.

Judith took this opportunity to point out to me that Richard's cooking lacked nutritional balance. We often went more than a day with no protein source, she said, despite the high caloric content of the food. Didn't I think we should discuss this with Richard?

I pointed to Richard, who was shoving bags of tea under the floorboards while Deb held her head in her hands and said, "No, Richard, no. Just milk and meat products. *Milk and meat.*"

"Protein sources?" I said to Judith. "Is that a discussion you really want to begin?"

Deb gave up and hid the milk and meat products herself. By popular consent, we all began to take over planning (and preparing) meals from that day forward.

With our milk and meat products safely hidden away, we headed for the border, passing roaming elephant, giraffe, and sable antelope along the way; I *love* Zimbabwe. Despite the usual money controls, as well as the milk-meat thing, the border was easy, if bizarre. As part of Botswana's protection against foot-and-mouth disease, the truck had to drive across a medicated sterilization pad set in the road. Then we all had to get out and walk across a disinfectant pad one by one, in case our shoes carried any disease. I wondered what would happen when I *changed* my shoes.

Our first stop in Botswana was Chobe National Park, with the Chobe River flowing through it. Chobe is famous for its elephants. It has too many of them for its fragile ecosystem, in fact, and there is considerable concern about the elephants (who are destructive feeders) turning the park into a wasteland.

This is the reason for the practice, particularly in Zimbabwe and Botswana, of culling elephants. Elephants travel in family groups of females, babies, juveniles, and very young males; a bull or two may tag along for a while, but bulls generally live alone or in tiny bachelor groups of 3-4 individuals. The modern method of culling is to quickly kill a whole herd at once, leaving no survivors; they disappear, leaving no trace of what occurred, and no opportunity for traumatized stragglers to contact other elephant groups. Elephants are highly intelligent, and it is not yet known just how much they can communicate to each other. The general theory is that a surviving elephant – or one who witnesses a culling operation – may well communicate terrible panic and terror to other elephant groups; perhaps even more than that, for all we know. Also, their family ties are so strong that it's considered more humane to kill them all rather than leave behind orphaned survivors who have witnessed the death of their families. I gather that babies may sometimes be spared and turned over to orphanages, but not often. Most elephant orphans you hear about are the survivors of poaching expeditions which didn't bother to kill them.

The reason the herds are culled is due to overpopulation. It's a terrible irony. If they're not protected well enough, they're slaughtered by poachers. If they *are* protected well enough, their numbers outgrow the reserves to which they are now confined, and they are culled. If they're not culled, then they destroy the environment and exhaust the food supplies. Then *all* of them in the reserve suffer – and eventually die – and so do the many species of animals living alongside them.

In southern Africa, elephant bodies are stripped of their ivory after culling. Ivory trinkets, elephant-hide products, and even elephant biltong are available down there. However, international trade bans prevent most tourists from buying these things, since they can't take them home. This infuriates the southern Africans, since they're trying to use the profits made from selling ivory and elephant-hide to improve park conditions, train more rangers, buy more ranger vehicles, and thus keep their elephants alive and safe from poachers – who are still trading illegal ivory while *they* can't trade it legally.

The Zimbabweans say that if the bans were lifted and they could flood the world market with their stockpiles of ivory, they could bring the price down so low that it would cripple the illicit ivory trade overnight; it simply wouldn't be profitable anymore. However, ethical considerations aside (i.e. ivory is now politically incorrect; and I confess that, as much as I loathe political correctness, I think I'd rather touch a snake than wear ivory around my wrist), there is no certainty that flooding the market would stop the poaching. The poachers who actually go out and kill the elephants are not highly-paid professionals in well-mounted expeditions. They're hungry men who will kill an elephant and carry that ivory overland for several days, often on foot, all for the price of a few meals or a new shirt. The big profits exist in the arena of illegal international trade, not in the African bush where men gun down the greatest land mammals on earth.

When buying me a birthday present in Zimbabwe, David and Jane said the gang encountered the ultimate yuppy dilemma. Since I'm a writer, they wanted to get me a spiffy-looking leather folder that I could flash at editors during my important meetings (okay, I never really told them much about what a writer's life is *really* like). However, of all the folders they saw, the elephant-hide was far and away the most beautiful and supple. They argued about it back and forth: Should we or shouldn't we? Is it right or wrong? What will Laura think about it? It *is* absolutely the most beautiful one here.

They finally realized that, as an American, I'd never be able to take it home. So they bought me another folder instead. And very beautiful it is, too.

When we settled in at Chobe, Deb warned me that I was not even to *think* about sleeping out in the open. Too many hippos were known to wander into the camping area by mistake. I was a lot less likely to get hurt in a tent than if I was simply lying out there amidst nature. Since Botswana was where my dad was stranded in a latrine one night because of a hippo, I decided discretion was called for and unrolled my tent.

The Chobe River has a lot of crocs, and the camping area is on the banks of the river. I was told they lose about one tourist per year here due to croc attacks. Jo and I considered this as we sat on a log and watched the sun set over the Chobe one evening.

"Should we be here?" Jo wondered.

"Do you suppose they come up to the tents?" I wondered.

We were pondering this when a German camper came down to the shore, leaned over the shadowed riverbank, stuck his arm in the river, and scooped water into the plastic basin in his hand – rather than walk uphill to the water pump.

"Aha!" I said.

"So that's how they're taken," Jo said.

"Only one a year?" I said. "Perhaps not that many lazy people come here." We watched the sunset in perfect tranquility.

We drove out in big open-air Land Rovers with local guides the next day. There are so many elephants at Chobe that the guides have forgotten that the rest of us still think they're pretty exciting. The guides spent their time pointing at some faraway bird or antelope that "you'd be able to see if only all these damned elephants would get out of the way." Literally. A herd of them was crossing the dirt road as we drove toward the gates of the park, and we had to stop for about twenty minutes to let them pass. Our guide reacted the way I do when rabbits get in my way – exasperated. Elephants don't cross the road swiftly. They don't do much of anything swiftly. They don't really have to; I mean, who's going to make them move faster, after all? They munched, browsed, swayed, sighed, rumbled, and flapped their ears. They stepped forward, then back, then sideways. They surrounded the Land Rover on all sides. Two of them came so close I could have touched them, if I'd been that silly.

The rest of the day was pretty good: lots more elephants, lots of antelope, zebra, buffalo, birds. We heard a gunshot at one point, but it seemed to be coming from across the border. We also took a riverboat ride and got close to crocs – yes, they're really there. We saw predatory birds swooping down into the water, carrying away squirming things, and we saw lots of hippos. I became particularly fascinated by hippos and read quite a lot about them.

We never saw any lions, though. Our guide was so depressed by this that he refused all tips and insisted on our coming to the bar after dinner so he could buy drinks all round to make up for such a dreadfully disappointing day. Well content with my life, I stayed by my fire that night and watched the moon. Living outdoors like that, I followed its cycles in a way I never had before. I could tell you any given day what shape the moon would be that night, and I often regulated my bedtime by it, staying up later if a full moon lit up the syrupy dark of nighttime in the bush.

Deb was feeling ill that night and asked if she could share my tent. She normally slept in the cab of the truck, but she thought her malaria was coming on, and she needed someone to keep an eye on her. I said, sure, no problem.

At 3:00 AM she started coughing. It woke me. She coughed all over me and my tent repeatedly for the next three hours. I started to suspect that maybe she just had the flu, and that letting her sleep in my tent had been a mistake. Sure enough, by that afternoon, I started feeling feverish, achy, and dizzy. By nighttime, I, too, was coughing up my lungs. If I'd had the strength, I would have killed her for this.

Skirting the northern edge of the Kalahari as we headed for the frontier town of Maun, Deb and I took up the whole back of the truck, lying prostrate on the dusty, cushioned seats, coughing horrible green stuff into our hankies, weakly sipping tea and soup that the gang brought in to us, and occasionally limping out into the sunshine for brief stretches. At night, someone put up a quarantine tent and sent us into it; cups of tea would be left outside the flap for us until the fire died down and everyone went to bed.

The weather was deeply weird. I don't think I'm much of a desert woman. It was too much like that old folksong; the sun was so hot I froze to death. The sun would burn my skin to a crisp after just a half hour, yet the air was so cold (it being winter in August) that I was constantly freezing. My face chapped in that bone-dry climate, my lips bled, and the flesh of my fingers cracked and split. I'd suffered from dehydration before, in Mauritania and Mali, but I'd never before had to drink so much water when it was so damn cold out!

Of course, my fever and sweats and chills made everything seem worse than it was. Nights were miserable, since sand loses heat the moment the sun goes down. Lying on my roll mat, I couldn't stay warm, and Deb gave off no body heat. All she did was cough all the time. I'd wear layers and layers to bed, wrap myself up in my sleeping bag with the hood up, and shiver till I fell asleep. I'd usually wake up an hour later drenched in sweat. Then I'd get chilled again.

Then Deb started hallucinating, which was *all* I needed.

"What's this for?" she asked me.

"What?" I snapped. (She swears I handed her a baby and said, "This is your son.")

"I don't remember having a baby!" she cried.

"What baby?" I snapped. (She swears I said, "Well, it was a painless birth.") My tent became the Twilight Zone.

With Deb laid up, Joseph was doing all the driving. Being a trainee, Joseph was still getting used to driving the truck in different terrains. Somewhere, in some vast sandy wasteland, the truck got stuck. It was late, and I'd been crankily wondering when the hell we'd stop and make camp as I stared at sand and scrub for hundreds of miles in every direction. Then, for some reason, Joseph tried to turn the truck around. Maybe we were lost. I was too sick to care. When the truck got stuck, he started rocking it. We just dug in deeper. We'd have to get out, put down the sandmats, and push. Joseph didn't stop, though; he just kept rocking the truck. Deb sat up and started shouting instructions, but he apparently couldn't hear her. Other people hung over the sides, suggesting he stop. We kept rocking. I finally sat up and announced I was going to be sick. Suiting action to words, I started vomiting. Someone had the sense to direct my head over the side of the truck, while someone else screamed at Joseph to stop. Whether it was the increased volume of the shouting, or the sight of me tossing my cookies right behind him, he finally stopped. I tumbled out the back of the truck and refused to get back in. We unstuck the truck and made camp for the night.

The dusty frontier town of Maun was growing like a weed. Overland drivers who'd seen it a year ago scarcely recognized it, there'd been so much construction. Parts of it looked like some suburb in the southwestern USA. There was lots of diamond-mine wealth here, and some tourist money, too, thanks to the Okavango Delta. There were lots of Europeans living here, many of them ex-pats: hunters, missionaries, safari operators, guides, pilots, whatever. There were dozens of shops and businesses in Maun, even a big bookstore with a few copies of my latest romance novel; I carefully hid them, lest anyone be tempted to buy one and read it aloud during one of our long days on the road.

I saw Herero women in the streets. You can identify them immediately by their clothing: ankle-length hoop skirts and broad, flat hats. They adopted this clothing from German missionaries more than a century ago and look grand parading down the streets of modern Maun.

Since my lungs were still rattling and gurgling, Judith, who's a physical therapist in real life, decided to pummel me before dinner that night. I was so congested that even walking to the ablution block exhausted me, and she thought a pulminary rubdown might help loosen the gunk in my lungs. All that hitting had to be tiring for her, and everyone who entered the truck thought she was torturing me, but it perked me up enough to eat supper and pack a satchel for the following day's journey into the Okavango Delta.

The Okavango River flows inland from Angola across more than a thousand kilometers of sand, where it finally becomes trapped between deep fault-lines and forms one of the largest inland deltas in the world. The Okavango Delta sits in the middle of the desert, an extraordinary oasis of swamps, lagoons, islets, and secret waterways. The game is abundant and world-famous here, and I had wanted to come to the Delta ever since seeing *Animals Are Beautiful People*, a fabulous documentary film.

We packed up provisions for a few days, then loaded them (and ourselves) into boats going downriver. Deb stayed behind to guard the truck. She was not unhappy to do so, since a Tracks truck had just arrived; Deb was − "dating" is a good euphemism − the driver. (They're now married.)

We started out in motor boats which careened wildly along the swampy waterways like some dizzying carnival ride. After thirty minutes of this, we arrived at a tiny island village. The villagers there are among the many people who participate in the local tourist industry; they take tourists deeper into the Delta on little mekoro (pole-pushed pirogues). With two passengers and one poler per mokoro, we set off into the swamps. The balance of a mokoro seemed rather precarious − which worried me, in view of all the documentaries I'd seen about crocs, snakes, and other critters in the Delta. However, none of us capsized. We all leaked, though. I didn't much care. The journey had already so exhausted my feeble resources that I was happy to just lie there in the sun, using my umbrella to shade my face, and let my chest soak up the rays while we coasted along the channels of that vast swamp, listening only to birds, insects, the soft chatter of the polemen, and the glide of the boats through the water.

After a couple of hours of this, we reached the little island where we would be based for the few days. I was apprehensive as we unloaded the mekoro; I'd once heard a story about a snake dropping out of the trees on top of an overlander carrying supplies from a mokoro to a base camp on one of these little islands. And while the snake may have been more scared than the overlander, *I* would be more scared than any creature in history.

Since mekoro are tiny, we'd brought minimal supplies into the Delta – including a minimal number of tents. So I had agreed to let Imelda share mine. Go figure.

I had briefly kidded myself that since I had been horribly sick for days, she would make some effort to help me put up the tent, perhaps even offer to put it up alone so I could sit down before I *fell* down.

Wrong again, Watson.

I put up the tent alone and then, light-headed and gasping for air, crawled inside. I unrolled my sleeping bag and lay face down, coughing and spewing vile stuff into my hanky. Imelda finally turned up and crawled into the tent, complaining about something-or-other. I kept coughing. She finally noticed.

"Why are you coughing like that?" she asked.

"Because I'm sick," I rasped irritably.

"What?"

"I'm sick."

"You're *sick*? Are you *sure*? You're *SICK*?"

I squinted at her. "I've been sick for days. Didn't you notice that I've been lying in the truck coughing for four solid days?" Cough, cough. "Didn't you notice that I haven't done my work or been at any meals?" Cough, cough. "Didn't you notice that Judith gave me a pulminary rundown in the middle of the truck before dinner last night to try to clear my lungs?"

"You're *sick*?" Imelda repeated.

"Yes." I sighed, and lay face down again. "I'm sick." Surely now she would leave me to die in peace.

There was a brief silence, followed by an angry outburst: "I can't believe you agreed to share this tent with me! I can't believe you didn't tell me!"

"I thought you knew."

"Don't you realize *I* could get sick? Did you never even think of *that*? I get sick very easily! That's so irresponsible of you! I can't believe you didn't tell me!"

I threw her out of the tent. I don't remember the exact words I used, but I essentially told her to get out of my tent before I killed her.

"Where am I supposed to sleep?" she cried. "Oh, my God, this is too much!"

I told her I didn't care if she slept on the pile of elephant dung I'd found behind the tent. She just wasn't allowed to sleep *here*. I'd kill her if she tried to.

Too weak to really kill her, I simply lay alone in my now blissfully quiet tent and fantasized about it.

I'm not the only overlander who ever fantasized about killing a companion, but I did hear of a case where someone actually acted on this fantasy. I doubt Guerba will appreciate me dragging this up after all this time, especially as it got so blown up in the press, but it *is* pretty interesting.

I may have mentioned that we carried potassium permanganate, and that we occasionally even remembered to use it to wash our fruits and vegetables. Deb found the vegetables floating in dark purple water one night and pointed out that a pinch is all that's needed; too much of the stuff can poison you.

A few years back, someone got sick enough of a fellow overlander to put a fair amount of potassium permangante in his water bottle, which, of course, an overlander drinks out of all day long. Every Guerba driver who tells this story refers to it as a murder attempt, though the head office considers this an exaggeration. In any event, the polluted water was discovered before the intended victim drank it. The person who confessed to putting the stuff in the water, as well as two apparent accomplices, were kicked off the truck by the driver; three more people left the truck "in sympathy" (which perhaps gives some indication of how generally disliked the intended victim was).

Although the remaining overlanders supported the driver's actions and confirmed this in writing to the company, there was an amazing brouhaha over the whole thing back in England. Eventually, a British politician got involved, flying off half-cocked in public defense of the overlander who'd put the potassium permangante into the water bottle, and Guerba was drawn into a legal squabble. Fortunately, things died down after the overland company filed their defense.

In America, of course, Guerba would probably wind up paying hundreds of thousands of dollars to everyone who felt they'd suffered emotional trauma as a result of the incident.

Coughing and waking intermittently, I dozed feverishly through dinner, the night, breakfast, and the morning boat ride. I slept through the afternoon's nature walk, too. That was just as well, since they saw a black mamba. In case you don't already know, it's an exceptionally deadly snake. The legends of its aggressive viciousness, while too improbable to be believed, nonetheless terrify me.

I *did* pull myself together for the next morning's walk, and nearly three hours of brisk walking in the cold tired me out but helped clear my lungs a bit more. As a game run, however, it was a dead loss. While lots of animals in game parks, even many shy ones, don't run away when they see a vehicle, they *all* run away as soon as they hear people walking or scent their presence. We did come across a bull elephant, but we couldn't get close to him on foot. Our guides spoke very little English and so couldn't answer my questions. I also began to strongly suspect after a bit that these particular men didn't know much more about game than I did. Deb had already warned us that they were local villagers rather than "guides," but I was disappointed anyhow.

I was less than enthralled with the whole experience, although my health obviously limited me and colored my impressions. I was used to being cold and dirty, and I was certainly used to Richard's cooking by now (although we did have a dreadful fight about garam masala at the only meal I attended), so that wasn't a problem. The island, however, was *way* too crowded. I was convinced that even Lagos hadn't been this crowded! There were twenty of us and twelve of our non-guides in camp, which certainly eliminated any "close to nature" feelings I might have had. The overlanders from Fearless's truck were in the Delta, too, camped so near that a few of them were always dropping by for a visit. Moreover, the Treebusters were camped so close I could see their fire at night. And while the photos of us in the mekoro look terribly picturesque, we scarcely saw any game – in one of the most famous game reserves in all of Africa! So I wasn't sorry when it was time to pack up and leave.

After loading up, I got into a mokoro and made myself comfortable. A poler came over and said to me, "Out."

I was tired of the non-guide polers, who had been pretty unfriendly. I coughed hard, then sighed. "Look," I said wearily, "if you expect to get tipped today, then the word is 'please.'"

I forgot he had no English. "Out," he repeated.

"Oh."

I got out. He put Dick in my place. With his usual tact, Dick (who was a small man) said, "Well, he probably took a good look at you and took a good look at me, and then decided I'd be much easier to carry. You're twice my size!"

I refrained from clobbering him. I didn't have the strength. An overlander named Caroline and I got in another mokoro. It was low, unstable, and soaking wet. Our poler was clearly not as experienced as the others. He kept rearranging us, but never got us arranged to his satisfaction. He finally told Caroline (who weighed considerably less than me) that*she*was too heavy for this boat. She'd have to trade places, he said.

"With whom?" we asked.

He pointed to Craig, a tall Canadian guy who outweighed Caroline by a good fifty pounds.

That settled it. We didn't tip the poler.

The motor boats we later transferred to finally dropped us off at a meeting point in the middle of nowhere. Deb had trouble with the truck (imagine that) and was late. Stray children and feral dogs hung around while we sought the increasingly scant shade of a few trees and longed for lunch.

I had a confrontation there that really shook me. One of the little girls hanging around got bored. So she walked over to a dog that I had befriended and, as it lay napping in the shade, started beating it with a stick. Its shrieks and whimpers were horrible. I told her to stop. She grinned at me and beat the dog again, laughing at its cries. I told her to *stop.* She paused and then, as if testing me, laughed at me and beat the dog again.

I snapped like a guitar string. It wasn't another problem with my lack of patience or anything like that. It was an instinctive response to the dog's cries and the girl's grinning glee. I went after her. I took her stick away and waved it threateningly at her, swearing I would beat her. I wasn't just pretending; I *meant* it. The girl ran away. I broke her stick into little pieces and threw them on the ground. Then I turned around. Some of my fellow overlanders were already looking away, embarrassed; a few were staring at me in shock.

I was too shocked myself to feel defensive or embarrassed. I sat down under a tree and tried to hold myself together, feeling like I was splitting apart at the seams. I knew that kid was beating the dog out of boredom *exactly* as she'd seen her elders do; for months, I'd seen adults beating animals and throwing stones at them as a matter of course. I'd seen children beaten without any fanfare, either. This was not a soft world here, not a place for the fainthearted.

I felt sick when I realized that if that child had persisted tormenting the dog after I took her stick away, I would have hit her with it. And that would finally be something I couldn't forgive myself for.

My cough was finally starting to get better. Having been so disappointed with how little game I'd seen in the Okavango Delta so far, I decided to book a flight over it; five of us went on a six-seater plane. There was some confusion when we got to town. I'd never bothered to ask Island Safari Lodge for the name of the charter company. I guess I thought there was only one. I probably got that impression from Deb, because last time she'd been in Maun, there *had* been only one. Now there were over half a dozen, and it took us nearly an hour to find the right one (since none of them knew who they had booked for that day, or *if* they had booked passengers for that day, or where any of their pilots were, or what the hell was going on). I felt it was a sign of genuine progress that I simply felt discouraged, instead of furious and impatient and demanding.

I was really excited, since I'd never been in a little plane before. I'd already been motion sick on a ferry and the truck, and I still wasn't at my best, so Judith stuffed me full of dramamine before I went.

Our pilot was Jan, a Norwegian daredevil who should be *LOCKED UP*. I wished I hadn't taken the dramamine, since it didn't stop me from feeling sick, it just stopped me from spewing up all over Jan's little plane, which was exactly what he deserved. Deb had warned me that pilots wind up out there because they're nuts. At first, Jan only worried me a *little* when he spun the plane around and around on the wing tips; I figured he was trying to give us the best views of the game. He worried me a little more when he dived down and flew *among* the game. But when he soared *straight up*, vertical, nose-to-heaven and tail-to-earth, and laughed as I reached for the airsick bag, I knew he was one sick puppy.

However, apart from Jan, it was a great way to see the Delta. I saw more game in that hour than I'd seen since arriving here. Giraffe, elephant, zebra, wildebeest, Cape buffalo, reedbuck, and impala. I even saw sitatunga, an antelope which lives strictly in semiaquatic environments. Now *this* was what I'd come here for! Flying overhead also gave me a better sense of the landscape. It's hard to get perspective on the ground, where it's so flat and you're is usually surrounded by reeds. From up there, though, you can see the network of streams, channels, rivers, puddles, and the thousands of atolls and islands.

We left the Delta the next day. Feeling better, I regained control of the fire that night, and David and Jane cooked up a fabulous pot of curry. We voted it Most Versatile Meal, since they recycled and disguised the leftovers at breakfast *and* lunch the next day.

At night, I spread my sleeping bag out under a clear, star-filled sky and fell asleep gazing at the southern constellations. I awoke before dawn, gathered up some scrub, barely touched it with a match, and was already enjoying my coffee by the time the others emerged from their tents.

On my thirty-first birthday, we crossed the border back into Zimbabwe.

GREAT ZIMBABWE

It's not an original observation, but it *is* a true one: considering that the Zimbabweans were locked in a brutal civil war less than fifteen years before I arrived, I found the country amazingly cohesive and the people remarkably open and friendly.

During its days as a self-governing British colony, Rhodesia passed legislation in the 1930s which excluded black Africans from ownership of the best farmland and which excluded them from skilled trades and professions. When Ian Smith became the president of Rhodesia in 1964 and started lobbying for independence, the British government insisted he must first guarantee racial equality here and progress toward majority rule. Smith had other ideas, so he declared independence without British permission. The British declared his actions illegal and imposed economic sanctions; the UN followed suit in 1968.

Guess what happened? Rhodesia actually prospered, because this gave them the incentive to expand and diversify domestic economy production. However, two African groups in the country, ZANU and ZAPU, launched a ferocious guerilla war against the white population, and whites began fleeing the country. The next few years were pretty confusing, as peace talks broke down, promises were broken, rebel groups squabbled with each other, the economy started collapsing, white emigration increased, and various political deals fell apart. As the bitter and violent conflict continued unabated, Ian Smith was finally forced to concede. A new constitution was written in 1979, then ratified by carefully-monitored elections in 1980. Robert Mugabe, a former school teacher and former political prisoner in white Rhodesia, was elected prime minister

Although armed conflict continued to erupt over the next few years (mostly as a result of rivalry between Zimbabwe's two great

Celebrating my 31st birthday in a Bulawayo nightclub in my Nairobi-bought finery, in Zimbabwe.

tribes, the Shona and the Ndebele), the economy finally started recovering, and the government established basic social programs in health and education. The next decade saw government corruption, political opposition, potentially disastrous land reform measures, 35% inflation, and a severe drought which caused widespread crop failure. Despite all of this, the Zimbabweans remain a friendly and welcoming people, and their country boasts an abundance of paved roads, buildings with electricity and running water, and fabulous wildlife.

The film *A World Apart,* which takes place in Johannesburg in the early 1960s, was filmed in Bulawayo (which means the Killing Place), which apparently looks just like Johannesburg did 30 years ago. It's a big town, with broad, clean streets, characterless modern buildings, banks, fast food shops, clothing stores, and booking agencies. Judith and I went with Jo to confirm her flight out of Harare, then we stopped at the Creamy Inn for a milk shake – my first since leaving home. The Girls went to the Beefy Hut. I didn't dare ask what one got there.

The campsite in Bulawayo is practically smack in the middle of the town, and it's nicer than half the hotels I've ever been in. Zimbabwe is like that. We washed off the sand of Botswana, put on our duds, and went in search of a restaurant for my birthday dinner. We wound up at a place called La Gondola where, instead of Italian food, they served garlic steak, chateaubriand, filet mignon, steak with mushroom sauce, etc. Beef is very big in Zimbabwe, and very good.

August 17th:

I have finally learned to expect and accept the screw-ups that occur. No matter where you are, there are bound to be problems dining out with fifteen people, and I counted on chaos in this small African restaurant (with the Italian name) which wasn't expecting us. Someone explained to the waiters that this was a birthday party. All the staff were immediately determined that whatever else happened, they'd give Perfect Service to the birthday girl. Every single waiter in the place, as well as the owner, asked Jane to point out the Birthday Girl at least once.

Ironically, I was the one person in our group who didn't get good service. My wine glass never arrived until after the first bottle of wine was finished. I asked for water three times, but it only came after someone else requested it for me. My entree was forgotten and had to be cooked after everyone else had eaten. The waiters were clearly so mortified about all of this that I felt really sorry to have to mention it and ask for my glass, my water, my dinner, my dessert, etc.

However, they brought out two bottles of champagne, complete with sparklers at the end of the meal, and the gang gave me a birthday card and a beautiful buffalo hide writing folder. I coveted just such a thing in the shops of Victoria Falls, but felt I couldn't justify spending the money on it, so I am especially touched by the gift.

The rest of the restaurant's clientele were a couple of white locals, and a number of black prostitutes and their clients. Since there was a dance floor, we stayed the rest of the evening. One of the employees doubled as a DJ, playing lots of really bad old disco music. Deb insisted that such a putrid selection of music always made for the best night out, because even the most self-conscious snob can't get "serious" about the music, and so everyone's free to just have fun. Which we did.

Some got tipsy, some got drunk, some got absolutely plowed. We danced in ones, twos, threes, and by the dozen. We were loud, silly, and cheerful. The Zimbabweans – black and white – kept coming up to ask who we were and couldn't we stay in town a few extra days? It was a great evening.

Staying out till 1:00 AM was a pretty big deal for people who had come to consider 10:00 PM a really late night. The next morning, we paid dearly for all that fun.

We had hired a guide and chartered a vehicle to take us into Matopos National Park, a nature reserve about an hour outside of Bulawayo. Facing the brilliant African sun with a merciless hang-over, I couldn't imagine why I had agreed to this scheme. Some were even worse off than me. There'd been an altercation – well, a small fistfight, followed by some intensive late-night verbal fighting – at my birthday party. I insisted that apologies to *me* weren't necessary, since I had not been involved or disturbed in the slightest, and these sorts of things occur among people who not only live cheek-by-jowl day-and-night, but who have also left behind many of the niceties of polite living.

Our cheerful Zimbabwean guide spoke so quickly and with such a strong accent that I couldn't understand a single word he said. Neither could anyone else. I gave up trying, and ignored anyone who thrust a guidebook under my nose. I dozed in my seat, drank any liquids offered to me, and never removed my sun-glasses. I was a year older, and feeling it. We stopped at the thrilling site where Cecil Rhodes' body had rested on the way to its grave. After that, I refused to get out of the truck again for a while.

We later drove to a park and climbed up a rocky hill to see Rhodes's grave. And some of his friends' graves. And the grave of a British military party that was massacred 80 years ago. There were some rock formations and a whole bunch of lizards. Admittedly, the views were good up there, but I squinted disinterestedly into the distance and then searched for shade, wishing I'd stayed in my sleeping bag that morning.

Still, one does have to admire the Zimbabwean government. They acknowledge their country's past and leave the monuments standing. They fought a long bitter war against the white government, but when it was over, they looked toward the business of living (and tourism, of course) rather than vengeance and retribution. I would later stand before similar monuments in South Africa and wonder how things would eventually unfold there.

I do have to admit that we did see some interesting stuff that day. For one thing, we saw a lot of Bushman cave paintings, 2,000–10,000 years old. Unfortunately, the cave paintings were all at the end of long, steep, rocky paths, which somewhat colored my appreciation of them, but they were nonetheless extraordinary. There is, by the way, a Zimbabwean company called Zimbabaluba that has taken these paintings and worked them into the design of colorful cotton fabrics.

They've developed a whole range of shirts, jackets, trousers, shorts, dresses, hats, and bags. We raided one of their shops in Harare, and I now own quite a bit of their beautiful, practical clothing.

We also saw black rhinos in the wildlife park at Matopos. Rhinos are in even more danger from poachers than elephants. In an attempt to protect their rhinos, the Zimbabweans tried cutting the horns off of some of them. It didn't work. Poachers still killed them just to get the quarter-inch of horn that remains on the face after such an operation. White rhinos, being far more placid than black rhinos, are in the most danger of all. Black and white, by the way, doesn't refer to their color; they're pretty much the same color, actually. Rhino species are differentiated by the shape of their mouths. "White" is a bastardization of the Dutch word for "wide;" the white rhino has a wide or square-lipped mouth for grazing, whereas the black rhino has hook-shaped lips for browsing.

After returning to camp that night, I restored myself with some solid food and about four pints of water. We stayed up talking around the campfire. It was one of those nights when Deb's love of and enthusiasm for Africa was contagious, when its problems seemed specific instead of insurmountable, when its attributes were both funny and magical. It was one of those nights when I could scarcely imagine leaving.

I rolled out of my sleeping bag in even worse shape the next morning. I was annoyed with my health. My cough still wasn't completely gone. I had a migraine. I had the start of a yeast infection. I was suffering from nausea, dehydration, and diarrhea. I was vomiting again (I'd vomited so many times from Mauritania to Bulawayo that people never even blinked anymore). My lips were bleeding. My fingers were cracked and still splitting. My feet were blistered. It seemed like my body was just falling apart. In little, insignificant ways, to be sure – but the sum total was depressing. Was I really older? Or had I just been living on the road for too long? I took some vicodin, washed it down with some lariam, downed a couple of remaining moxicillin capsules just to see what would happen, and went about my business. All this, I add, in a woman who is usually reluctant to take aspirin; but I had no more time or patience for little illnesses. If I wasn't dead, then I needed to be functional.

We spent a night camped near the Great Zimbabwe ruins, which we scrambled all over in daylight. The word *zimbabwe* is derived from a Shona phrase meaning "stone houses," of which there are several hundred scattered from Mozambique to Botswana as a result of the influence wielded by the rulers of Great Zimbabwe. Building in stone has always been rare in sub-Saharan Africa, and has always evinced the wealth and power of the people who did so.

The great stone city of palaces, towers, stairs, twisting passageways, dwellings, and enclosures once housed some 10,000 people. It wasn't a fortress, since the rulers of this Shona-speaking civilization controlled a vast territory beyond these walls, in a kingdom made wealthy by cattle, gold, and trade. Archaeological finds at the site include beads and crockery from India and China which would have been brought to Great Zimbabwe by Swahili traders from the coast.

Built around 1,000 AD, Great Zimbabwe's power collapsed some five hundred years later. It is believed that around the mid-fifteenth century, they exhausted the land and could no longer feed the ever-growing population. People began to migrate, spreading their culture and building techniques across the savannah, and the kingdom slowly dissolved. The city continued to be inhabited by other tribal groups who entered the region, though it was more or less abandoned and overgrown by the time it became the focus of European interest in the 1890s. A few European adventurers had heard of it before then, often in wildly romanticized accounts which suggested that it was the fabled city of Ophir, the site of King Solomon's mines.

Cecil Rhodes and the other colonial entrepreneurs and politicians of the time realized that the Great Zimbabwe ruins couldn't be ignored, not while they were justifying their subjugation of black Africans under the guise of civilizing a barbaric race of people. Great Zimbabwe had boasted as much wealth, sophistication, and comfort as any European city of the same era, not to mention a complex social system. Rhodes employed an amateur antiquarian who decided that, although all materials and artifacts in the ruins were of African origin, the city obviously couldn't have possibly been built by black people. The city must have been built by a lost Roman legion, the lost tribe of Israel, Phoenicians, Arabs, or the mythical Pelasgi of Greece.

Professional archaeologists investigated the ruins and insisted that, regardless of how inconvenient to the colonial government's policies the truth was, Great Zimbabwe was unquestionably built and ruled by Africans. (The locals knew this, too, although the government wasn't interested in their opinion.) When the black liberation struggle arose in the 1960s, Great Zimbabwe became a positively explosive topic. During the final decade of white rule, the Rhodesian government banned all publications – guidebooks, museum displays, school textbooks, newspapers, magazines, radio programs – which suggested that Great Zimbabwe was an African creation.

Upon achieving majority rule, the new government named their country in honor of the site, which had become a rallying point and symbol of black nationalist pride.

The place is enormous, by the way. You may have seen some of its more famous features in photographs and films: the mythological birds carved in soapstone, the mysterious conical tower, the Great Enclosure, the Valley Enclosure, the Hill Enclosure, the massive walls, bizarrely twisting passages, and extensive curved stairways.

Have I mentioned that I *hate* walking uphill? I nonetheless climbed a million stairs all the way to the top of the Hill Enclosure, the oldest and highest portion of the city, from which you can see for miles around. We roamed around for hours, getting lost, bumping into each other unexpectedly, and getting lost again. On the road leaving Great Zimbabwe, women sell some of the stone sculptures and the hand-crocheted vests and tablecloths for which the Shona are well known.

We were all sad and nostalgic as we headed for Harare, knowing that in just a couple of days we'd be separating, most of us forever. Eight of us – me, David and Jane, Imelda, Dick, and the Girls – were continuing on to the Cape, along with Sue, in a truck which would leave Harare Sunday morning, along with five new people fresh off the plane from Europe. Deb was scheduled to do some repairs on her truck for three weeks in Zimbabwe before heading out to Namibia.

Unloading the truck in Harare seemed like moving or leaving home. I piled all my stuff into my duffle and wandered into the inn we were staying at for a couple of nights. With everyone running around town attending to business, we arranged to meet at a restaurant that night for a farewell dinner. We met at Remambo's, a fun, touristy place serving lots of game, with a floor show, and galleries featuring Shona stone sculpture. Between courses, we met a bunch of Italian soldiers attached to UN forces in Mozambique. This was their last night of leave, before being sent back there at dawn; they were depressed about it.

Like Nairobi, Harare is a jumping-off point for lots of overlanders, and half a dozen overland drivers stopped by our table to greet Deb and catch her up on trail gossip. We wrestled with our warthog stir fry, ostrich *en papillote*, and kudu steaks. I wouldn't touch the crocodile thermadore this time, though. There's something awfully gamey about croc, if you ask me; it *tastes* like it eats rotten food. (Crocs usually pull their kill down in the water, drown it, and stow it somewhere safe until it's so rotten they can pull off huge chunks and swallow them whole; they're not able to chew, you see).

I collected my *poste restante* from the general post office the next day. There was a lot of letters from home, full of good news and good wishes. As for my career... My secondary publisher, the one who was still interested in a book from me, had just gone out of business. The deal was off, and I was out of work. I took the news well. As in Nairobi, there were too many important and distracting things going on for me to give much attention to publishing events halfway around the world, and my life in the US now seemed surreal and hard-to-remember. While there were still one or two markets I could probably try with the proposals I'd submitted to Silhouette and this other publisher before leaving the US, I had been waiting for A Sign about my career, and I felt certain this was it. In big red letters, it seemed to say: *Change your work.*

Having read in the British papers about the floods in Midwestern America that summer, and considering all the wars, riots, and famine in Africa, being out of work just didn't seem all that important. I felt like just one more person wandering out there into the fray in a muddled daze and saying, "What do I do next?" No big deal, I figured.

Also, I had rethought my position on writing. I'd been really proud of being able to actually make a living from my writing, but that pride had vanished. I finally realized in Africa that writing is so hard, so uncertain, and (usually) pays so badly, that there is only one good reason for me to do it: the work itself. Now don't get me wrong. I definitely want to be paid, and I want to be paid lots and *lots* for it, but if the work itself doesn't satisfy me, then I might as well go get a job I don't like, since at least it would be easier and more reliable. While many people write books for my former publisher for love of the work, I had been doing it solely for the money; and they found me out.

As I walked the streets of Harare with my mail, I figured that losing two publishers in one season confirmed what I'd been suspecting – that I had to stop writing for the money if I was ever going to enjoy it again, take pride in it, or get any better at it.

Harare had become a very dangerous city. Hotels urged guests not to even go outside to hail a cab; the staff would do it for you, to prevent your getting mugged. Even people with money belts or heavy backpacks were urged to lock them up and carry nothing with them. I had heard this kind of thing about Nairobi – and many other cities – and thought it was probably alarmist.

I was proved wrong. Our group experienced three robberies in one day, and I realized that things were as bad as we'd been told. Someone was attacked on the street – knocked down and hurt when someone tried to steal a pack attached to his wrist – someone else was pickpocketed, and David and Jane's room was robbed. More than $1,000 in travelers' checks were stolen. (They had only just taken them out of the hotel safe for a moment, then decided they'd probably be all right, hidden in the room while we were at dinner). They spent half the night on the phone to UK American Express, while I spent half the night wondering why my parents didn't phone as they said they would. When they finally got through, they explained that the hotel's international line had been busy all that time.

Piling into our new truck with our new crew the next day, we had a very emotional leave-taking as Deb and the whole gang, most of whom would be flying back to Europe the following day, hugged us repeatedly and waved us off. There were a lot of tears, including mine, and I don't cry very readily.

Deb left Guerba that same year, and went to work alongside her fiancé in Africa, where they eventually hope to make a permanent home. Married now, they were in New Zealand last time Deb wrote me. The others returned to the ups and downs of their lives in the four-corners of the earth, and the ones I don't hear from, I usually at least hear *about* when I hear from the others.

Stuart, our new driver was a quiet English guy. Peter, the campmaster, was a Kenyan who'd been doing this job for several years and was very good at it. When we were on the road, he usually sat wrapped in a sleeping bag reading books by the great Kikuyu writer, Ngugi wa Thiong'o. Darren, the trainee co-driver, was a remarkably good-natured fellow who'd been out here a couple of months. In fact, he was *so* nice and easygoing, I wasn't at first sure I'd be able to live on the same truck with him. In the end, though, I managed to cope with his amiability.

The Eastern Highlands of Zimbabwe look a lot like parts of Scotland (I'm afraid that's not an original observation): high, misty green hills, perpetually cloudy skies, and lots of rain. I couldn't imagine what we were doing here. As I put up a tent in pouring rain high up in the mountains, I thought of all the sunny, crisp days and nights down below and felt very depressed. I thought the five new people, three of whom had never been to Africa before, were probably also depressed, but I was struggling with too many things − missing the friends we'd left behind, wondering what to do for a new career, keeping water out of my tent − to go out of my way to be kind to them.

We all bought blankets in Mutare, since it was only going to get colder as we headed south. I couldn't wait to get to a lower elevation, as the weather remained drearily British.

I had intended to volunteer for fire duty when new camp jobs were assigned, but I got interested in managing the kitty instead. It was an opportunity to see where funds go on a trip. Sue, who had known me long enough to recognize that I have no left brain, thought it was a big mistake for me to volunteer, and an even bigger mistake for Stuart to agree, but the next day he turned over the cash box and about $5,000 to me, all in American and English cash, Zim dollars, and TCs. I counted it all as we headed on to Chimanimani National Park, where people (oh, boy!) hike uphill all day long for fun. I felt rufty-tufty enough that, when we got there, I didn't think I needed to prove myself anymore. I told everyone *they* could walk uphill all day to spend the night in some grubby hut in the mist. *I* was staying with the truck. And so I did, along with Stuart (who had to stay with the truck, he *claimed*), Sue (who was still covered with the painful sores that were part of her body's life-threatening reaction to the anti-malarials after so many months), and two or three others who had good excuses for not going up.

Dressed in eight layers of clothing (you can get by with a jacket if you're living indoors and just *stepping* outdoors, but it's cold up there when you eat, sleep, wash, and whizz outside day and night), I'm repairing torn parts of my ramshackle tent at Chimanimani while the other non-hikers nap and Stuart does something or other to his engine.

A very flashy Land Rover-type vehicle (that's as specific as I get about cars) pulls up. Two white Zim guys drop off two Dutch girls they found hitchhiking down the road. One of the guys flirts with the girls while helping them put up their tent. I look at the thing and know it won't last the night in this wind; neither will those girls, if you ask me. I try to remember being that soft. It seems like another person.

The other guy sees me. I take an instant dislike to him – just one of those instinctual things. So I glare and turn my back. This usually works. He clearly has a learning disability, though, for he bounds over to me. Besides his flashy car, he's got flashy clothes, a flashy pony tail, flashy sunglasses, and a really smug, supercilious smile that makes my hackles rise. He's probably younger than me. I *am* 31 now, you know. He just stares. My mother raised me right, despite my evil temper, so I finally speak. I even use a reasonably friendly tone, since it's painfully obvious that he's not going to go away.

I nod at the looming mountain. "Have you been up?"

"No." He just keeps grinning at me. Grin, grin, grin.

I am not impressed by his dental work. (I am American, after all). I hope he'll go away if I get the chatting over with, so I say, "Going up today?"

"No." Grin, grin, grin.

Evidently, *his* mother didn't raise him right. "Just hanging out?" I ask in a dry tone.

Grin, grin, grin. No answer. Grin, grin, grin.

Ignoring him was obviously the right thing to do in the first place, so I now go back to ignoring him. He comes closer and examines my tent.

He admits, in the way Mick Jagger might admit to being Mick Jagger, that he *lives* in Chimanimani. He LIVES THERE!!!

Well, whoopee-cush, can I lick your boots, Mr. I-Am-A-Godlike-White-African?

"What do you do in Chimanimani?" I ask, because he won't go away. I blow on my numb fingers and keep stitching.

"As little as possible." Smirk, smirk, smirk.

I do not find this tired old joke funny, so I keep ignoring him. Stitch, stitch, squint against blowing dust.

After my unresponsive silence, he does not go away. No. He talks some more. Why, I ask you, are some people encouraged by total disinterest? He says he's trying to set up a little company, camping and guided hikes at the other end of Chimanimani. The camping is better there, he tells me. The mountains are better there. Doubtless the air you *breathe* is better there, I reflect sourly. And, need I even add, the guides are handsome, modest, *manly* men there.

I ignore him, wishing he'd go away, because I was actually enjoying the lonesome afternoon till he showed up. Living on an overland truck in Africa, I am almost never alone, and I enjoy this rare solitude.

He asks, "Aren't you going up?"

"No." Perhaps he'll go pester my companions. But, damn them, they're all out of sight, tucked away somewhere.

He smirks at the truck and reads the name, Guerba, in scathing tones. I am offended, as some Guerba truck or other has been my home for over six months, but I ignore him. Stitch, stitch.

He stares inquisitively at me and asks again, "Not going up?"

"Not me," I say, confirming his quick grasp of the situation.

He continues to stare inquisitively at me. I feel obliged to say more. God knows why. Probably because my mother taught me better than his taught him.

"I don't climb unless there's something at the top I really, really want to see," I volunteer. Remembering one of the best days of my life, I add, "Like mountain gorillas."

"You're different from me, then," he says. "*I* wouldn't go to see the gorillas."

I shrug and keep sewing, quite glad to be different from this flashily dressed, smirking cretin who does "as little as possible" and doesn't seem to know when he's being ignored.

He starts talking again. A scathing, critical challenge against me and anybody else who climbs into the Virungas to see the remaining mountain gorillas. You surely don't think it can be *good* for them, he sneers, you can't pretend there's anything *natural* about so-called habituation, sitting *this* close to a wild animal.

(I frankly don't think there's anything natural for me about sitting this close to *him*).

I agree with him that it's not natural, but tourism is the only incentive for people in those overpopulated, overfarmed, desperately poor (and hence, totally unsentimental) countries to let the gorillas go on living, to refrain from more habitat destruction. Only money pouring in from tourists coming to see them will convince the locals to let them go on existing. For people that poor, there is no other argument.

He ignores that and gives me a really rude, sneering lecture about how bad tourism is for the gorillas, ending by snarling, "But *you* got patted on the head by a baby gorilla! Wow! So what if you gave it some contagious disease!"

This idiot obviously doesn't know that you're not allowed to touch them or to let them touch you, and that you're not allowed to go up if you're suspected of having anything contagious. The African rangers take better care of their gorillas than this jerk supposes. Nor does he know (as I have recently been told by a scientist) that gorillas pass diseases on to humans at least as frequently as humans pass them to gorillas, although that is hardly the point. He adds snidely, "But they don't care up there, so long as they get their lousy $100!"

Yup. That's absolutely right, genius. Pretty easy to sneer about it while you sit on your ass and "do as little as possible," in your flashy car, expensive glasses, and trendy clothes.

I'd forgotten how utterly wealthy you have to be to be so knee-jerk righteous. I don't want to waste my time on such an important topic (because, actually, both sides of the argument have merit – it's not as clear-cut as all that, I agree) with such a jerk. I tell him to fuck off and turn my back, hoping someone will rescue me if he pulls out a gun. But, of course, we aren't back home in America, so he has no gun.

After a few more days in Zimbabwe, we headed south for the famous Beitbridge border. South Africa. The final country of my journey, and, for many people, the most famous – or infamous – country in Africa.

SOUTH OF THE BORDER

Most overland trucks gave up going to South Africa a decade ago. Not because of civil unrest (not hardy overlanders!), and certainly not because it was a long drive from Nairobi.

No, various drivers told me that the reason most companies had stopped going was because, due to the various trade sanctions and bans African nations established as a response to apartheid, having South African stamps on any travel documents made it hard to get in and out of a number of other African countries, in much the same way that no one with a South African passport could visit most African nations. Even getting separate documents from the South Africans didn't necessarily help. If the Tanzanian border officials saw stamps in your documents for border towns in Namibia, Botswana, and Zimbabwe which were transit points into and out of South Africa, they knew you'd been to South Africa and were consequently likely to refuse to let you into Tanzania (just as there are still Islamic states which won't let you cross their borders if your passport bears an Israeli stamp). This was a problem for overlanders, since it's pretty hard to get anywhere in East Africa without going through Tanzania.

Everything was changing now, however. In March of 1992, white South Africans voted in favor of a mandate to establish a non-racial democracy in South Africa. Even President FW de Klerk was reportedly surprised at the nation's 2-to-1 vote in favor of reform. "A population widely perceived as the most stubbornly racist in the world," *Time* reported, "was effectively agreeing to give up its monopoly on power and share it with a black majority that whites have traditionally feared, persecuted, and patronized." Nelson Mandela's long walk to freedom was nearly at an end, and President de Klerk announced to the world, "Today we have closed the book on apartheid."

The biggest change I had so far personally seen was the availability of South African wine in Tanzania the following year. Hey, if Tanzania, the most ideologically propelled nation in Africa, was now trading with South Africa, then it *must* be politically correct. I felt really excited about going to South Africa now, in this time of change, challenge, and transition.

The first thing I noticed upon crossing the border was that there were an awful lot of white people in South Africa. (*Nothing* slips by me.) There were whites at the immigrations and customs desks, whites in the banks, in the shops, in the cars, on the streets. So many white people, I thought! And look at how white – really *white* – they are! Gosh! How interesting! Moreover, I had to keep pinching myself to remind myself I was still in Africa. The towns, roads, and roadsigns all looked so different from what I'd grown used to. People sounded different.

Black Africans down here were noticeably less enthused to see us, a bunch of white people, passing through. Most places we went, from one end of the continent to the other, people grinned and waved. Not nearly so much in South Africa. Maybe they figured they already had enough white people there.

This far south in August, it was cold, especially when we camped high up. In one place, there was frost on the ground! Temperatures improved in the lowveld, where days were warm and nights were merely cool. Our campmaster, Peter, was a pleasure to work with – friendly, polite, clear, organized, capable – and the food was always very good and ready to eat within 90 minutes of our camping up for the night.

We stopped one afternoon at Swadini Reptile Park, a privately owned snake reserve and educational center. Donald, a tall, dark, strikingly handsome South African, greeted us and said, "Follow me." Sue blurted something like, "To the ends of the earth."

Donald told us he'd been fascinated by snakes since infancy. Sad. In other ways he seemed like quite a nice man. A dozen years ago he turned his lifelong interest into a professional enterprise and developed this completely self-supporting reptile conservation center. The place was extensive and interesting, a testimony to his business acumen, as well as his, uh, commitment to reptiles.

He's got some crocs, tortoises, lizards and scorpions, but most of his animals are snakes. They live in glass cages in a beautiful maze-like stone building. Education is his primary purpose – to get people to understand, appreciate, and stop fearing and killing snakes – and he eschews the sensationalism often associated with snake exhibits. We had a lecture and an extensive slide show, then a guided tour of the zoo, and then a snake-pit demonstration. During the demonstration, he handles and explains ten different species, nine of them terribly poisonous. No questions allowed during the demo, as he has been distracted and bitten in the past.

Well, it was interesting, but I remain frankly phobic, and only Donald's rippling muscles and soulful eyes kept me from racing out of his reptile park in a panic. I actually touched the rock python when he encouraged us to. It was absolutely *disgusting*. All this information merely provided fodder for my nightmares as well as fodder for a deeply sick short story I later wrote which was published in an anthology called *South From Midnight* (ed. Richard Gilliam). The sight of the mating green mambas put me off my feed for the rest of the day.

We continued south to meet a guy I dubbed Afrikaner Pete in my diary. He was helping us sort out the problems with our visit to Kruger National Park, an enormous wildlife park (surrounded by lots of private wildlife reserves) in northeastern South Africa. The truck, of course, was open-sided, and the South Africans have strict rules about vehicles needing to be closed in Kruger. They were pretty strict about a lot of things in Kruger, actually. All game parks have official campsites, but Kruger's were walled and fenced and plumbed and lighted. When I admitted to South Africans that I'd camped in Tanzanian parks, where the only thing distinguishing a campsite was a drop toilet somewhere in the bush, they thought I was insane.

Guerba was busy designing some kind of cage which could be fitted over the sides of the truck for visits to Kruger, but it wasn't finished yet. We couldn't take our truck into the park. So Afrikaner Pete had arranged for us to rent something called the Biz Bus. It was a horrible, hot, cramped little vehicle with a noisy engine and terrible visibility. I was used to the truck, where there was nothing between me and nature, where I could see everything with no obstructions. I glared at the Biz Bus and started packing. We had to transfer supplies for all of us (except Stuart, who had to stay with the truck) for three days aboard the Biz Bus in Kruger.

August 30th:
    Afrikaner Pete stood around in the sun and heckled us. He's typical, in appearance, of lots of Tough White Men I've seen up and down East and Southern Africa: khaki shorts too short, a khaki vest with a million pockets, a snazzy hat, sunglasses. Stuart likes

Afrikaner Pete and says he's much nicer than I give him credit for... but Stuart's a man, so what can you expect? I wasn't in the mood to deal with this guy, especially not when we had so much work to do.

As I hauled gear from the truck to the Biz Bus, Afrikaner Pete gave me a load of crap about how much stuff we were taking, and why did we think we needed this and that, and what was wrong with us, and surely we didn't need *all* this. Well, six months ago, I'd have felt uncertain, even intimidated by this rufty-tufty bush fashion-plate who was giving me shit. However, my reaction *now* was to shrug and snap, "Buzz off, buddy. I've crossed all of Africa without your advice, and I know exactly what I need for three days in a game park. And stop blocking traffic, we're very busy here."

Well, I don't think Afrikaner Pete liked me much either. Anyhow, the biggest mistake anyone on the truck made was taking his advice and leaving behind some cooking and camping gear he insisted we wouldn't need in Kruger. Turns out we *did* need it, and we missed it.

So much for know-it-all Great White Hunter types.

Kruger National Park is enormous, and rich with game. We saw elephant, hippo, impala, kudu, giraffe, wildebeest, zebra, and dozens of species of birds. We even saw two lions flirting and mating. As David said, it's rather nice to know they have fun doing it. Hyenas prowled the fence around one of our campsites one night, stealthy shadowy shapes trying to find a way to get closer to the food they could smell. At one of the watering holes, a hyena watched a carcass floating in the water; it looked like a small mammal or large bird. He was afraid to go in after it, since there was a croc on the bank, also watching it. Yet the hyena wasn't willing to go away either. He just kept prowling around, trying to figure out some way to get the carcass without *becoming* a carcass. I don't think he ever found a way.

Kruger is extraordinarily organized. Maps and roads and signs. Encampments with huts, cottages, shower blocks, and shops. Cafeterias, doctor's offices, reception desks. There's even an elephant museum where you can learn about Kruger's seven famous "tuskers" (elephants carrying heavy ivory), all dead now.

Kruger is also full of Afrikaners. Most of South Africa is very well set up for tourism, having long had a wealthy white population that likes to travel and vacation, and that hasn't been allowed to go many places. They've all seen a lot of their own country and have ensured that it can be seen in considerable comfort. Much of South Africa is as easy to visit as Britain or France. Indeed, with such fast, well-paved roads and sophisticated campsites, the overland truck was – for the first time ever – not the ideal vehicle for travel. David suggested that a BMW would have been more practical.

The Afrikaners founds us fascinating. We found them pretty interesting, too. Up in the north part of the country, one feels one has stepped back in time to 1960. Hairdos, shoes, buildings, food, music – it all seemed vaguely reminiscent of old movies. Everyone else visiting Kruger seemed to be elderly and traveling in a caravan. It was like waking up and finding oneself somehow transported to Florida in February. I came into the ablution block one evening to find Sue helping two ladies find a set of false teeth which had skittered across the floor. And they all thought we'd *die*, sleeping in mere *tents!* They were all very curious about us. Explaining why most of us weren't married and why the women were putting up their own tents instead of making the fellows do it for them required exhaustive cross-cultural translation. I nearly doubled over laughing when one well-meaning gentleman insisted that any man in my group would be more than happy to haul water for me, if I would just ask rather than doing it myself. I imagined the obscene comments that would result in the event of my making such a suggestion would get us thrown out of the rather starchy campsites of Kruger. It was funny, too, considering everywhere else in Africa, among all other peoples, the women do the heavy hauling.

Most of all, everyone asked the question I would hear over and over again during the weeks I was there: What do you think of South Africa?

Wendy, the other American in the group had come all the way from Nairobi with us. She phoned home while we were at Kruger. Her family was in a panic; they wanted her to leave South Africa immediately. Amy Biehl, a blonde American Fulbright scholar, had just been murdered in Cape Town. She drove some fellow students home, taking them into the black township of Guguletu. Her car was attacked by "a group of teenagers." She got out of the car and tried to run away. Her assailants caught her, beat her, and knifed her repeatedly in the head. They had never seen her before; her skin color had marked her for death.

Wendy and I talked about it for a while, somehow feeling kinship to another blonde American who had died so violently while we were in the same country with her. I rather bleakly considered that, as Americans, we live in the single most violent country in the industrialized world (so logged for the third decade in a row). I had recently read in some news journal that you were more likely to be shot if you lived anywhere in the USA than you would be if you lived in Belfast. One of my closest friend's brothers had been wounded twice in a drive-by shooting in Kansas City the year before, and another good friend was threatened at gunpoint in an attempted car-jacking just south of Cincinnati.

Somehow, I had a feeling I was actually safer in South Africa.

As I traveled south, I heard more about Amy Biehl's death. South Africans had a day of mourning for her. They were desolate that it had happened. Yet they were also angry at the international press. They felt that the way the story had been depicted in the media around the world, it seemed as if Amy Biehl had driven a few friends home one day and been attacked by surprise and killed. This is certainly how it reads in the mainstream press articles that I dug up after returning to the US. Black and white South Africans, however, told me that the township where Amy (they all refer to her as Amy) was killed was so volatile the day she went there that normal activities were already disrupted when she chose to drive in. She was taking a risk by entering Guguletu that day. When she panicked and left her car, she had no chance of survival. South Africans insisted again and again that Amy's horrible murder wasn't the sort of thing that might suddenly happen to anyone anywhere at any time in South Africa, yet they felt the foreign press portrayed it that way.

We spent three days in Kruger, tempers flaring as the hot, cramped, stuffy confines of the Biz Bus made us increasingly irritable. It had a flat tire our final day there, and we stood around in the road amidst "Do Not get Out Of Your Vehicle" signs. It was with considerable relief that we finally moved back into the truck and waved good-bye to the Biz Bus forever.

Our route took us through Swaziland, which is an independent kingdom, not a South African homeland. The Swazis are a relentlessly cheerful, friendly people, and their country is mountainous, green, misty, and very beautiful. Most Swazis dress in a Western fashion now, but every so often you simply stumble across someone dressed traditionally. I bumped into one such man at the vegetable market. He wore a cross-draped gown, a feathered headdress, carried a spear, and was walking around with a basket, buying fruit. Traditional dress there is just a choice, not considered showy or outlandish. I seemed to be the

only person who even bothered to glance at this man in the market. We
shopped for a bit in the capital of Mbabane, restocking all the food
we'd eaten in Kruger, exploring the crafts market, wandering amidst
Swazis who kept crying, "Hi! How are you?"

While in Swaziland, we camped at Malotje Nature Reserve, which
is full of blesbok, a kind of large antelope that I had never seen before.
They were all over the place. You couldn't hike for two minutes in any
direction without stumbling across half a dozen of them.

We relaxed for a bit and recovered tempers badly frayed by our
sojourn in the Biz Bus and our arguments about our route. Having
nearly come to blows with another overlander one night in Kruger, I
welcomed the respite.

Before I knew it, we were back on our way across the border into
South Africa. We reached Pretoria by night, in pouring rain and chill
winds, and we put up tents in the dark and the downpour. Eight people
decided to sleep on the truck that night, too demoralized by the
weather to deal with it. I was getting used to it by now. I can't say I *liked*
it or wouldn't have preferred those clear breezy nights of Zimbabwe,
but I was pretty used to it.

Happily, I awoke to a beautiful, sunny day. I was also immediately
befriended by a dog who was the spitting image of Jock of the Bushveld,
a dog in a famous South African turn-of-the- century book of the same
name. He's famous as Lassie or Black Beauty or Johnny Appleseed are
in America, and as innately South African. I'd bought a copy of *Jock of
the Bushveld* in Kruger and had been reading it. It's all about the
bushveld adventures of Jock and his owner as they wandered around
the Transvaal a hundred years ago. I kind of liked it, despite not only
the obvious racist stuff in there, but also the even *more* obvious modern
rewriting of these passages (quite bizarre). Stuart read it, too, and
pointed out that they seemed to go around killing an awful lot of things.
Anyhow, our campsite dog, also named Jock, liked me so much he
grabbed my right ankle and wouldn't let go, not even as I climbed into
and out of the truck. Some people found it rather alarming, but I
respect a strong herding instinct.

The campsite was right next to the Jan Smuts Museum, home of the
late great South African statesman. I confess, I hadn't heard of him
until I started reading up on South Africa as we approached the border,
but he was a fascinating man – lawyer, botanist, philosopher, author,
statesman, military general, devoted husband, father, and grandfather.
One of his grandchildren recently told the curator one of the children's
games with Smuts: They'd make him sit in a chair in the library with
his eyes closed, with his back to the vast wall of his books. They'd pick

The Voortrekker Monument, Pretoria, South Africa.

out a book at random, open it, read a few lines, then he had to tell them which book the lines came from. Apparently he usually guessed right.

It was kind of an Afrikaner day for us, since we then stopped by the Voortrekker Monument. This enormous, elaborate structure commemorates the Voortrekkers, the Boers who trekked north from the Cape into the heart of the African veld. The monument's bas-relief interior tells the story of the Battle of Blood River in 1838, when 470 Boers under the command of Andries Pretorius defeated some 12,000 Zulus. This was the occasion of the Covenant: the Voortrekkers promised that they and their descendants would worship God forever in their particular tradition if He let them win the battle; they believed that His divine intervention assured their victory against such overwhelming odds and proved they were a chosen people.

One wonders what monuments will arise in years to come in South Africa, for there are no monuments to commemorate the Zulu, Xhosa, Ndebele, Swazi, Venda, and other peoples who have shared in South Africa's history. One also wonders if the new South African government will choose to leave white monuments in place, as the Zimbabweans did. It must be awfully tempting to tear them down, but they are part of the long story.

Spending a few days in the Pretoria-Johannesburg megalopolis was really weird. I had to constantly remind myself we were still in Africa. I kept thinking we must have made a wrong turn and wound up in Australia or something.

Though separate cities, Pretoria and Jo'burg are very close together, and the urban-suburban sprawl between them links them like Dallas-Fort Worth or Minneapolis-St. Paul. There's a Paul Kruger monument in a vast, elegant square in central Pretoria which looks like it should be in Europe. The office buildings could have been in London. Many of the streets seemed like they could have been almost anywhere. Even in Harare and Nairobi, the most most sophisticated cities I'd been in since leaving London, even in the vast, endless, crowded sprawl of Lagos or Abidjan, you always knew you were in Africa. Here, I felt disoriented.

The proportionate mix of blacks and whites on the business streets of the two cities was similar to that of many cities in America, though that wouldn't be true of their domestic neighborhoods. Until recently, a person's skin color legally dictated where he could live in South Africa. The economic reality was such that most of people were still living where laws had once forced them to live.

There was also a huge variety of people on the streets who were (I thought) not easily classified by race. Until the early '90s, every South African, by law, had to be racially classified from birth. There was an entire government service devoted to ensuring that everyone was classified correctly. Yet I saw lots of people who sure didn't look to me like they could be clearly and certainly classified as black, white, Indian, or Coloured. *After Apartheid* by Sebastian Mallaby talks about the confusion resulting from this practice: many people had to be reclassified, some people never fit the official classifications, and other people sought to change their classification so they could marry someone of a different classification.

Deeply weird. It had always seemed very strange anyway, but you wonder how they could have looked at their incredibly polyglot population (probably more varied than any other country in Africa) and supposed for a moment that they could apply a realistic and workable system of racial classification.

Jo'burg represented a considerable challenge to an overland truck. As absurd as this sounds, we couldn't find a place to park. I had read up on the city, looked at a map, and suggested a central location for our visit – a big complex in the heart of the city, with a multilevel indoor shopping arcade, a hotel, a restaurant, and a business tower with a viewing gallery overlooking the whole city. I suggested it because everyone was very nervous about Jo'burg, which has a well-earned reputation for violence. I assumed there would be a parking garage in such a complex, and that we could keep the truck out of sight.

I was right about the garage, but our truck was too tall to drive into it. It was also too tall for the one or two other garages we approached. Not having foreseen this, I couldn't think of a contingency plan. We finally parked on a side street and hoped for the best. As always, two people guarded the truck at all times. A lot of people were nervous about it now. The truck always attracted a lot of attention, as did we, and guarding it (though often very boring) could become quite challenging – people trying to get inside, trying to steal something, etc. However, Jo'burg was the first place we'd ever been where it seemed that serious trouble was a real possibility by day. An open-air truck, with only two people at a time guarding it, parked in a quiet street all day. This was a city where troublemakers often *did* have guns. A couple of people were so nervous, they wanted to simply forget the whole thing and clear out of Jo'burg. We settled on shortening our day there. I was extremely frustrated, as I like big cities and was interested in seeing this one, but I was a minority voice. In any event, absolutely nothing happened to the truck all day.

I went into the arcade with some of the gang. I had to go off on my own to see about changing the date of my airline ticket, and I was surprised by a couple of overlanders asking if I'd be all right on my own. I'd been wandering alone into the bush in the middle of the night on my own for nearly seven months, and no one had *ever* asked if I'd be all right. Then again, I don't think anyone in this group had ever seen New York City, whereas I have lived there. Not many urban places can frighten one after that.

September 3rd:

It puts me in the minority, but I like Jo'burg. There is an electricity here, the electricity that makes me love some big cities. There's also a tension, as there is in New York. Walking around here, one must be sensible, guarded, aware –whites are targets here, and the danger is real. However, there is a charge, a vibrancy in the air– thoughts, words, deeds, ideas are born here. Despite all the warnings, I don't feel hatred spilling out at me here. It seems like blacks and whites here are used to each other and know they are locked together forever here in South Africa. When I open my mouth and speak, I feel a lot of sudden interest and goodwill directed toward me, from both blacks and whites, curious about a foreigner, a tourist coming here.

The Africana Museum in the public library had an interesting, eclectic exhibit, a bit of everything thrown in and scattered around. I saw the first photos ever taken at the Great Zimbabwe ruins, when it was covered by bush and scrub and looked deeply mysterious. An entire wall was covered with photostats of the pages of a black man's passbook, covering a period of nearly 40 years. There was a miniature of the battle at Rorke's Drift, Swazi costumes, a selection of diamonds, opal, garnets, rubies, gold, and glowing fluorescent rocks, and tribal crafts.

I stumbled across a dusty, unobtrusive souvenir case at the back of the museum. An older black man, wearing a dark blue uniform, worked there. His name was Joseph. I bought a beaded Zulu bag, and we started chatting. He took a long time making out my receipt, writing very carefully, and I recalled that something like only 1 in 5 blacks has any access to education in this wealthy country full of gold, diamonds, arcades, and highways.

Like everyone else in South Africa at the time, Joseph was worried about the future. Everyone there was worried about something different, depending upon their politics, their social group, their income, and their color. Joseph was worried that Buthelezi, the ambitious, powerful, and power-hungry Zulu chief, would cause trouble, perhaps even civil war. He was worried that de Klerk would make a public show of turning the government over to majority rule while playing one black faction off against another and retaining as much power as possible for the whites. He believed in Mandela, but was worried about some of Mandela's actions: what was the meaning behind some of his power-brokering, and how did it help ordinary people?

Joseph was worried about the breakup of families due to economic conditions. Children were growing up with no mother or father – at least not as a daily influence. Would there be more jobs under majority rule? Would there be education for all? A religious man, Joseph often prayed for peace, for an end to all the violence.

I liked him. He glowed with something special – self-respect, personal pride, a warmth toward others. He embodied many of the things I was seeing on a daily basis in South Africa, in dozens of minor little daily encounters – strength and individual kindness in the face of long suffering, a vision of the future which hourly swung between hope and despair, an endless string of questions, a deep commitment to South Africa. On the truck, someone commented that she thought South Africa would be one of her least favorite countries in Africa. To my surprise, it was becoming one of my favorite.

Again and again here, I am reminded of two of my favorite places in the world: Sicily and home. There is racism, crime, violence, an atmosphere full of change, struggle, a hope which must constantly renew itself, and a very bloody history which these people carry on their shoulders as their own burden and no one else's.

After guarding the truck (and snarling at anyone who suggested I shouldn't feel safe without a man on board to protect me), I went to the Market Theatre Complex across town. I loved it. There were four theatres, a bunch of my kind of stores – second-hand books, second-hand records, second-hand clothes, a couple of coffee houses – lots of street musicians and handicrafts booths. Across the street was a vast open-air market, where merchants sold food, second-hand goods, and the sort of thing that I usually refer to as "something that fell off of a train."

It was so different from what we had so far seen of South Africa – conservative and seemingly old-fashioned, with sharply confined and defined race relations. The Market Theatre's neighborhood was like a tiny piece of Greenwich Village or London's Camden Town. The walls were plastered with notices for black and experimental theatrical productions, gallery showings, and music lessons. People were dressed as if they were on Neal Street in London or Bleeker Street in New York – colorful, creative, individualistic clothes. There were white men with long hair, and black women who looked independent, educated, and self-confident in clothes that would look right at home on West Fourth Street. It was the first place in South Africa where I saw whites and blacks mixing, though even here they didn't precisely *mix*. Nonetheless, they seemed relaxed and good-willed in each other's presence.

There was a dark-skinned woman with Caucasian features and very straight black hair who took my order in a cafe. She spoke with an Afrikaner accent. I wondered how she had been classified. Was she a white person with dark hair and a nice tan? Was she Jewish? Or Hispanic? Asian? Coloured? Cape Malay? When South Africans met strangers during the long years of racial classification, were they ever as confused as I now was?

We drove a long way out of the city that evening, heading south. Peter and I sat up on the side of the truck. When we pulled into a campsite, Stuart hopped out and told the white woman in charge we'd like to stop there for the night. She stared at the truck while she chatted with him; everyone always stared at the truck, since it was a very unusual sight. I watched her watching us. Peter was looking the other way, talking to someone. After a couple of minutes, we left. We went elsewhere and finally camped just around dark. Later on, I was told what had happened. I was also told not to tell Peter. (This continued to be our policy all the way to Cape Town, but I've always wondered if he knew.)

When Stuart had said we wanted to camp for the night, the woman had looked at our truck and asked if we were all white. Stuart had said, no, as you can see, we are 16 white people and 1 black person. The woman had said we couldn't stay then, because this was an all-white camping area. Stuart pointed out that that was illegal in the New South Africa. Realizing she'd been indiscreet, the woman said, well, maybe so, but it wasn't *her* rule. No, by golly, it's just that the people who camped here insisted on it, so what choice did she have?

Stuart told her we had changed our minds and had no desire whatsoever to camp there; and, fuming, he drove the truck away. Ironically, Peter had mentioned just a few days earlier that, despite all the stories about South Africa, he hadn't seen any "bad" people yet. Well, they were obviously still alive and well here. The vote in favor of majority rule had not been unanimous, after all.

On the flip side, as I was standing in line at a bank in some rural town, cashing money for the kitty, a short white man walked up to me and said, quite out of the blue, "I'm not AWB."

"What?" I said, bewildered.

"I'm not AWB," he repeated.

I looked him over. He was Afrikaner. A farmer. He wore khaki shorts and a beard. He looked friendly and earnest. "Um, you aren't?" I said.

"No. I saw you standing here, an obvious foreigner, and you looked at me, and I knew what you saw. Afrikaner farmer, with a beard, wearing khaki. So I just wanted you to know, I'm the *other* end of the spectrum."

It was time to put a stop to this polite, clearly well-meaning, but utterly incomprehensible speech. "Sir, I'm new to South Africa. I'm sorry I looked at you, but I have absolutely no idea what you're talking about."

"Oh!" He smiled, shook my hand, and then explained not only to me, but also (one by one) to half a dozen of the overlanders who wandered into the bank after me, that AWB, the Afrikaner-Weerstandsbeweging, is a right-wing Afrikaner white supremist political party, and that while this area was certainly a bastion of the AWB, he was at the other end of the political spectrum. Whenever he saw strangers, he stepped forward and said so, because he loved South Africa and wanted them to know that not all whites were AWB, that some of them believe in the coming changes. Based on the way the many black farm workers coming to the bank behaved toward him, he seemed to be telling the truth.

And then, of course, there are always people like handsome Donald of the Swadini snake park. I had a feeling he was too concerned about snakes to give a damn about any person's skin color.

Meanwhile, the petty problems of group living simmered along as always. Since it was so cold, I'd been sleeping in a tent since leaving Harare. But Wendy (my new tentmate) and I, who otherwise got along very well, were ready to kill each other after a couple of weeks: my restlessness, her snoring, my hitting her for snoring, her being annoyed at my claiming she snored when she was certain *I* snored, and so on. So I started sleeping outside again, or unpacking a spare tent if the weather was bad. Then someone mistook my hankies for her own (when toilet paper is so precious, you don't waste it with nose blowing), and they disappeared into her locker for two days while my nose was running. Imelda, who already had 8-9 pairs of shoes on board, bought another pair of shoes, which annoyed Jane. Sue wanted to kill Imelda for buying the last available copy of a book she wanted. I bawled out one of the new people for barging into the truck in the mornings while the guards were still sleeping because he was too lazy to get his shaving gear the night before. He'd been doing it for a week, and I think I threatened to kill him if he did it again. He thereafter never forgot to take it to his tent the night before.

All systems normal.

We were lucky to be able to get into Royal Natal Park in the Drakensberg, which limits the number of people they let enter. A 50-kilometer marathon was just finishing up there, most of it taking place straight up and down. The Drakensberg Mountains are steep, raw, rocky, rugged, and incredibly beautiful. Hauling water, I bumped into a middle-aged white woman who had taken part in the marathon. The mother of two teenagers, she had a body like Linda Hamilton in *Terminator 2*. She came round our campfire that night; she and her kids were very interested in taking an overland trip across the border, now that they'd be allowed into those previously forbidden countries. As an overlander, I met a variety of reactions among white South Africans. Some were envious of the places I'd been, hungry for information, and eager to go. Others– the conservative element that was clearly uneasy about the New South Africa – couldn't believe anyone had been to those savage lands and survived. Many of the latter couldn't imagine why I'd even wanted to go. Everyone, however, welcomed us to South Africa and wanted to know what we thought of it.

Since Royal Natal is a hiking park, and since we'd be there for several days, I felt obliged to do some hiking. So I walked to the park center (a kilometer or so away from where we camped) and bought a trail map. I was determined not to climb anything with the word Tower, Peak, Summit, Cliff, Crag, Spire, or Devil in its name.

(This made choosing a route harder than you might suppose.) Sue concurred. We had similar tastes when it came to hiking – slow pace, frequent breaks, and flat or gently rolling land.

Everyone in the gang enjoyed Royal Natal. Something for everyone. Stuart got to work on his engine in peace. Peter got to read in peace. David and Jane got to scale some deadly vertical cliff with a terrible name. The Girls got to wear short shorts and scour steep hills. Sue and I hiked about 15 kilometers of rolling trails.

Fairy's Glen had a beautiful cave-like area of boulders and trickling water overlooking a valley. The climb to Bushmen's Cave provided a close-up view of Bushman cave paintings and breathtaking views of surrounding mountains and countryside. On Otto's Walk, we stumbled across two bushbuck, just five or six yards from us, munching away. We stared at them. They stared back, graceful and wide-eyed. We hiked into the cascades, too, an absolutely gorgeous spot with water tumbling over levels and layers of rock.

After almost seven months of beating my clothes against rocks or scrubbing them with a nail brush or soaking them in rivers, I was *shocked* to discover real washing machines in the camp at Royal Natal. I lost control of myself and washed everything I owned, even things that didn't smell that bad.

We stopped in some tiny little rural town, a wide spot in a dusty road, to do some marketing: middle of nowhere, two shops, a post office, and lots of people staring at us, the most exciting thing to come to town all year. The whites were very nice in this town, treating Peter very politely as I shopped with him, calling him "sir." I had become aware that, since crossing the border, I had been keeping an eye on Peter, feeling defensive on his behalf, and reluctant to see him go shopping, where he'd have to interact with whites. However, Peter had lived his whole life in a post-colonial independent country, so I finally decided that he wouldn't let his self-confidence be undermined by a few white bigots in a dying apartheid system in a country so far from home.

I never attempted to murder any of my fellow overlanders. I did, however, make a genuine attempt to abandon one of them. I'm sure I should feel much worse about it than I do.

Any time we stopped somewhere, we always arranged a time for everyone to be back on board and ready to go, whether it was a half hour from now, or sunrise the following day, or three days from now. Since we were just stopping in this village to buy food, post some letters, and stretch our legs, it was agreed we would all be back in the truck and ready to go at one o'clock. Now, there was no risk of the truck leaving without you. If you were late (and everyone was late sooner or later, sometimes *hours* late if something unexpected happened), we just sat around and waited. No big deal. We might beat the shit out of someone when they finally turned up, or at least glare at them and give them the worst jobs in camp that night, but we never left without anybody.

Well, not until today, I mean.

We all piled into the truck at one o'clock – occupying favorite spots on the seats, grabbing water bottles, getting out the Scrabble set or a deck of cards or the diary or a book, demanding a share from whoever had the best snacks, pulling on sweaters and blankets against the wind that would hit us soon, taking off shoes, squinching sweatshirts into pillows and ruthlessly shoving people out of the way to make enough space to lie down for a snooze, chatting, picking up walkmans, locking lockers, securing overhead storage, and so on. As was the custom, someone said, "Is anyone missing? Are we all here?"

Someone noticed that Imelda wasn't there. She wasn't on the roof, either. A brief query revealed that, five minutes before we were scheduled to rendezvous back here, she had left the truck and wandered off to the post office. Who knew how long she'd be gone?

"Maybe she's in the cab," someone said.

I looked at Jane, who was sitting by the buzzer, ready to signal the cab when we were ready to go. I confess! I gave in! I nodded as if Imelda was in the cab and said, "Yes. Let's go. We're all ready."

Jane pressed the buzzer. We took off. Most people went about their business. One or two people looked doubtful. "Um, *is* she on board?" one of them asked.

"Who cares?" I said as we began rumbling out of town.

"But–"

"Look, this is South Africa. It's very sophisticated here," I reasoned. "She'll find a bus to one of the major cities, and from there, it won't be hard for her to get a flight home. Let's just get out of this town!"

Freedom from Imelda! The long hoped-for dream! I could taste it as we pulled out of town! Free, free, free at last!

Then some fool looked out the back of the truck and said, "Wait! I see her! She's running after the truck!"

Someone pressed the buzzer. The truck came to a stop. We lowered the back door. Imelda caught up. I think someone glared accusingly at me. Most people just shrugged.

That night, when Stuart asked me who signaled we were ready to go while knowing full well that Imelda wasn't on board, I played dumb. I don't think he believed me. He pointed out that it would look very bad on his record if he lost a passenger somewhere in South Africa.

Sadly, I saw nothing of Natal. Drove straight through it. We had lost time, and this was apparently where we were going to have to make it up. By the time we pulled up to the beach outside Durham, I was well and truly ready to get out of the truck, and to beat up half the people on it. However, the warm weather, the beach, and the ocean all restored me. Wendy and I fixed an American barbecue for dinner. Of course, we had to improvise a bit. The marshmallows for the some-mores got rather rubbery when toasted, and there were no graham crackers, so we used chocolate- dipped digestive biscuits. There was no corn on the cob, either, but we made cheeseburgers and baked beans. The Brits had to be carefully instructed in the art of making some-mores. They were slow learners, and most of them thought the whole business was rather disgusting. I wasn't intimidated, though; I've eaten in England.

Darren had heard about a disco in town and got a group together to go. I couldn't see any good reason to leave this beautiful beach on such a balmy night, and I wanted to catch up on my diary anyhow. It turned out to be just as well. Two white guys there harassed the Girls, asking (among other things) if they'd ever date a black guy. Young Jo explained that skin color was irrelevant, and the young men got verbally abusive and soured the evening. That sort of thing reminds me of why I had never previously considered going to South Africa. People like that were in charge of the whole country most of my life. These days, however, it's as pathetic as it is infuriating. Those whites were already living in the past, and a shameful past, too. South Africa was preparing for majority rule, and then the whole continent would be majority-ruled. There would be no place left for white right-wingers and adherents of apartheid. I wondered, as I had once wondered in Kenya, how these people could fail to notice whose country this was now?

Sleeping outside for the first time in a while, I slept incredibly well, much better than I ever slept indoors or in a tent anymore. A warm breeze woke me in the middle of the night, blowing clouds across the moonlit sky, fluttering tent fly sheets and hanging laundry. I got up and checked the truck to make sure the Girls had come home safely. Not only were they tucked in and long-since asleep, but I later learned that I had been sleeping so soundly on the ground that I never stirred when they milled around me (one of them nearly tripped over me) while getting ready for bed. Good thing no one had tried to rob the truck that night.

Our route required us to drive across Transkei, one of South Africa's black homelands. However, it was reputedly in a state of unrest, and it wasn't clear to us whether or not we'd be safe crossing it. Shades of days past. Stuart had made inquiries as we headed south but wasn't satisfied with the answers.

While I paid the owner of the campsite outside Durban, Stuart asked her what she thought about Transkei. She told us not even to *consider* going through Transkei, that it would be *insane.* I was skeptical. I had noticed that that seemed to be the standard reaction of many South African whites when you mentioned going any place where there were bound to be blacks. I'd lost count of how many people in the Transvaal insisted I would *die* if I went to Jo'burg. And how many whites had I met who shook their heads and rolled their eyes because I had been reckless enough to travel in black Africa? I had a feeling we needed to seek more sources before making a decision about Transkei. That seemed to be Stuart's opinion, too.

As I sat on the beach and watched the surfers near Margate one afternoon, I recalled a comment writer Tami Hoag had made in a letter she'd sent me in Harare: what do you suppose inspires people to dress up like seals and go swimming in shark-infested waters? One of the surfers looked like Alexander Gudonov in a very tight wet suit. He was quite good and gave me an idea of what surfing should look like, but the others made it clear why you have to be insane to surf. They spent most of the time looking like they were drowning. Or worse. The way their surfboards flew up in the air, randomly landing on important body parts.... Just watching them wore me out with anxiety.

The campsite was weird. The people who ran it were like Nazi stormtroopers. Upon checking in, we'd been handed two pages of written rules. In addition, there were signs posted everywhere with stern orders and warnings: Pay upon arrival! Don't hang laundry anywhere except designated clotheslines! Keep small children under control! Ten minute limit in the shower! Five minute limit in the toilet! (David got really rebellious and took a book into the bathroom with him.)

We camped up near the bright, shiny, new ablution block. The kommandant – sorry, *camp manager* – came around, took a good look at us, and ordered us to use the shabby old ablution block at the other end of the camp. I assumed it was because we were grubby overlanders. I, of course, ignored this order, so I never saw the other ablution block. Jane did. She told me that the sign on it was faint, but still legible; that ablution block was for non-whites. The woman had seen Peter with us.

Despite such incidents, I really liked most white South Africans. A lot of them were pretty hard to understand, but I found I liked them because they were committed to Africa. Not all of them, of course; news reports, letters, and satirical columns were (and are) full of news of white emigration. Somehow, I never seemed to meet those people. I only met people who were staying. Whatever their political position – and most of the whites I met seemed to believe, either enthusiastically or resignedly, that majority rule was South Africa's true and proper destiny – they weren't going to abandon ship. So many whites living in the rest of Africa seemed to carry British, European, or American passports. It was a kind of backup: they *lived* in Africa, but they were European and could bail out any time they wanted to.

I respected the white South Africans because their identity–paradoxical or anachronistic, some might say – was their own. They've been there a long time, and they're there to stay. More than the whites I met anywhere else, I felt a sense that they *wanted* to integrate into this continent, to be a permanent part of it. Anyhow, for those who've been there for generations (400 years in some cases), where can they go? They're no more likely to go back to the country of their ancestors than I am. They didn't have the handy escape valve of another nationality; they had to be committed to Africa or give it up forever.

LAST STOP, PRISON

We continued asking for information about Transkei and continued not to be completely satisfied by the answers. The general attitude of horror crumbled into critical confusion when facts were requested. I thought we'd be fine. Stuart said he thought so, too, but he thought it would be terribly embarrassing if it turned out he was wrong and one or two passengers got killed as a result.

Well, yeah.

I confess that I seemed to be having trouble with the kitty. Part of the problem, of course, was that Stuart had supplied me with a solar-powered calculator on its last legs. It gave the right answers, but portions of the screen had stopped working, so I couldn't actually *read* the answers. However, far from the kitty falling short, it seemed to be getting fatter, multiplying geometrically. Not only was there always more money in there than I had expected, there was usually *more* more than the more of the day before, if you follow me.

Perhaps I should have been a banker.

David and I climbed onto the roof as the truck approached Transkei. The decision finally reached was that we *would* go through the Transkei, but not on the route originally intended, which was in a more populated area. We sort of slipped through the back door and took some dirt track crossing a remote inland portion of the homeland. Although the road was slow, we were actually cutting down the distance to be crossed in Transkei, so we could probably get across it in one long day.

Transkei looked a lot different than what I'd so far seen of South Africa. It's poor, arid, rocky land. Not particularly beautiful, and not

much good for farming. It's not surprising that the whites were willing
to give up such places when they forced blacks to leave good land and
relocate. The areas of Transkei we drove through were populated by
bleak settlements which resembled nothing else I had so far seen in
South Africa, but which were sharply reminiscent of many poor places
I had seen all across Africa. When South Africans said they were afraid
of their country now becoming a Third World nation, I supposed they
just hadn't been to the country's homelands; they already *were* one.

Everyone who saw us in Transkei waved and then called to their
families, who came running out to shout and greet us. It was a wildly
friendly place, this land that so many people had assured me I'd *die* if
I visited. I was glad to be here. By the end of the day, though, my arm
hurt from all that waving. Everywhere we went, people smiled and
cried, "Where are you from?"

"I'm from Ohio!" I'd cry back.

However, things got a little unpleasant at the checkpoint when
we were leaving Transkei. A black border guard tried to make
trouble for – of all people – Peter, insisting there was something
wrong with his passport (which there wasn't). Fat and swaggering,
the guard was rude and intimidating. Peter was very calm and
polite. Since he knew his passport was in order, he seemed willing
to simply wait for the guard to get bored with this. Watching from
the roof, David and I were surprised. In a truck full of whites, the
guard had chosen to make trouble for the only black man on board,

Tuskless elephants in Addo Elephant Park, South Africa.

a man from an African country which had publicly observed all the sanctions against South Africa's apartheid government. Go figure.

I'd bought a beginning stargazer's book in Kruger. Until this trip, I had never been south of the Equator, and the night sky looked really different from what I was used to. Once dinner was all cleaned up, I'd take my flashlight and my book, go away from camp, and seek out the Southern Cross, the Jewel Box, the Coal Bag, the False Cross, Pegasus, Scorpio, Beta and Alpha Centauri, Pisces, Altair, and Vega. Soon, I'd be leaving the southern hemisphere, leaving South Africa, leaving Africa. So every night I searched for a new constellation, wanting to learn that southern sky before it was too late. Strange as it seemed, soon I would be going home.

Despite all the fancy roads, shiny signs, and big buildings, things happen all the time in South Africa to remind you that, appearances notwithstanding, you are still in Africa.

We camped one night at an apparently deserted campsite. The next morning, an old man found us and started speaking to us in a language we didn't recognize. I was surprised to see anyone there, as there had been no electricity in the ablution blocks, the ladies' bathroom had been locked, and the men's only seemed to be open because the lock didn't work. Unable to communicate with us, the man went away. He showed up again a half hour later. Inexplicably, he could now speak some English. He gave me a bill. Since the exchange rate made it cheap, I opened the kitty and paid without squawking. Then, after we had finished washing and getting dressed, when the truck was all packed up and ready to go, the man opened the locked door to the ladies' bathroom, turned on the electricity to the ablution block, and showed us how everything worked and where everything was. We thanked him and drove away.

David and Jane had to make a call to Britain that afternoon, so we stopped for diesel while they went to the telecommunications office in some little town. David returned 90 minutes later to tell us it would probably only take another hour. We had forgotten where we were, and so had he. I pulled out the Scrabble and sat down.

Addo Elephant Park was set aside after a big elephant-hunting operation that took place early this century. Untold thousands of elephants were killed, not from trophy hunting, but to clear and protect farmland. When 100 or so retreated to this dense scrubland, someone finally came up with the brilliant idea of creating a reserve for them. Probably not out of entirely humanitarian impulses; the scrub was so thick and thorny that it was both painful and dangerous to hunt them down here. Addo now has the densest elephant population on the continent, but it looks much hardier than Chobe or certain other heavily populated parks. Elephants here are pretty safe from poaching, too. Not only because the South Africans are wealthy enough to protect them, but also because the strongest surviving genetic strain in Addo has provided for generations of elephants that *don't have tusks.*

There's not a whole lot of interest in Addo besides the elephants. There are a few hippos, and we did find a giant tortoise wandering around our campsite. We fed him scraps and played with him. He kept mistaking everything on the ground for a lady tortoise – sleeping bags, daypacks, washbowls.

Naturally, we saw lots of elephants in Addo. Probably the most exciting group we saw had a tiny, hairy little newborn with them. They were very protective of him, very suspicious of us. It was hard to see him, since the old mothers kept shoving him around with their trunks to keep him out of sight. He looked dizzy and confused, but very sturdy.

We dined in the lodge that night since, for once, we didn't have to worry about the truck being stripped while we were all off having fun. I found the restaurant a trifle distressing, since after having admired elephants all day, I was now expected to eat in a room with stuffed elephant heads and even one whole stuffed baby elephant. Since the food took forever to arrive, we went through a lot of wine. South African wine is incredibly good – and incredibly cheap, even apart from the great exchange rates we were getting.

How much wine did we have, you ask? So much wine that I actually encouraged David to explain biochemical genetic research to me. I was pretty dazed by the time I decided that it would be really neat to find a phone and call home collect, since dinner *still* didn't appear to be imminent. So, alone and without my flashlight, I wandered out into this dark park full of elephants, hippos, and over-friendly tortoises to look for a phone booth I had seen near the restaurant. It was actually a reasonable hour in the US when I phoned my parents – not that I cared after several glasses of wine on an empty stomach. They had recently returned from the World Science Fiction Convention in San Francisco, a world apart and a million miles away from here.

"Kid," Dad cried (despite the fact that I was now 31 years old), "you were mentioned in the *New York Times* today!"

"That's nice. It's really, really pretty here," I burbled.

"You won the Campbell Award, kid!"

"And today, I saw elephants. Lots and lots of elephants," I warbled.

"You won the Campbell Award, and you were in the *New York Times!*"

"And one of them was this hairy l-i-t-t-l-e baby elephant," I twittered.

And so on.

When I went back to the table, dinner still hadn't been served, but someone poured me more wine. I announced that I'd been in the *New York Times*, and I let someone touch my hem. After a bit, I remembered *why* I'd been mentioned in the *New York Times*. The John W. Campbell Award is presented annually during the Hugo Awards ceremony (literary awards) to the best new writer in the field of science fiction and fantasy. I'd won it for the dozen or so short stories I'd had published in various science fiction anthologies and magazines over the past couple of years. I was pleased, since I felt that this (and not my books) was the area in which I had been challenged and grown as a writer over the past couple of years. Stuart asked what this award meant for me. Money? Fame? Contracts?

I thought it over and answered honestly.

"No. But if I had *been* there, someone might have bought me a drink or two."

"Nothing else?" someone asked, clearly less impressed than they had been a moment ago.

"Well, if I'd timed it right, and if anyone had recognized my name, I *might* have had the signal honor of being thrown out of the Hugo Losers' Party. But," I hastened to add, "I might not be important enough for an honor like that."

"Oh. When's the food coming?" someone asked.

My 15 minutes were over so fast.

After all that wine, I should have felt like hell the next morning, but I felt great. So uncharacteristically chipper, chatty, alert, and cheerful, in fact, that I annoyed the hell out of everyone. This strange behavior persisted until they began worrying that I was coming down with some kind of weird fever.

Even stranger, when we took an afternoon break by the sea that day, I put on my swimsuit and *willingly* plunged into the bitterly cold and dangerously violent surf. People were getting seriously concerned about my mental health by the time we reached Tsitzikama that afternoon, a national park on the seacoast. It's a rugged, rocky, mountainous place where waves pound along the great jagged rocks as far as the eye can see. Deciding we needed a bit of the hair of the elephant, I bought a bottle of something improbably called Creme de Cactus Pear to enjoy around the fire.

Darren decided to sleep in the truck that night, and I decided to sleep out again, so he loaned me his big green army bivouac bag,

Crossing the suspension bridge "at your own risk." Tzitzikama National Park, South Africa.

saying it would keep me warm; the wind can be bitter at night at that season. Sleeping in that thing was one of the most horrifying experiences of my life.

Darren's bivouac bag enfolded me like a Venus Flytrap. It wrapped itself around me like a living thing. I felt trapped inside. I tried to get out. Couldn't. Got a little panicky. Tried harder. I got disoriented and could no longer find the flap to get out. I started beating against the thing and calling for help, but no one could hear me over the pounding of the waves and Dick's snoring. I rolled against someone's tent stakes, but didn't manage to wake anyone up.

I finally escaped by dawn and sprawled across the grass, exhausted and glad to be alive. The gang found me like that when they woke up the next morning. Muddled, confused, unkempt, and fully recovered from yesterday's uncharacteristic amiability, I barked for some coffee and *dared* anyone to make fun of me. (They did anyhow.)

In this, yet *another* hiking park, some of the group decided to climb up to a waterfall. I wanted a day that didn't include the words "climb" or "up", and Sue and a girl called Therese concurred. We wandered off in the other direction, crossed a suspension bridge, and headed for something called Lookout Point.

September 14th:

Lookout Point. I must, in future, remember those words. It means going up. Way, *way*, WAY up. Up, *up*, UP. Ever upwards.

By the time – heaving, sweating, trembling – I realized what I'd gotten myself into, I was already too far up to go back. There comes a point when you're committed (even if it's against your will) and can only go on. I kept seeing signs posted on rocks, and I'd peer nearsightedly at them, expecting them to say something encouraging like "You're nearly there!" or "It's just ahead! Don't give up now!" But no such luck. The South Africans had defaced rocks every 200 meters or so with signs telling me not to deface the rocks.

As I kept climbing, hauling myself up rocks, and dirt, and *more* rocks, and *more* dirt, and then *steep* carved stairs, I became convinced that the whole park was a vast, subtle, hideously cruel revenge plot against foreigners, thought up by the whites here to punish us all for our countries' political and economic sanctions against the apartheid regime.

I bet it began like this. One South African said to another, "I have a brilliant idea, Janni: we'll build a path with a sign to Lookout Point, and make them all believe they'll find something up there, but *really* we'll just keep them climbing upward until they die of cardiac arrest!"

Someone later suggested that the spectacular view at the top made the climb worthwhile.

Gimme a break.

I was melancholy when we finally pulled out of Tsitzikama and headed south, one day closer to Cape Town – and the end of my journey. I ached when I thought of leaving. I couldn't imagine it. Me, who had once barely been able to get through a single day as an overlander. I'd had more trouble than any overlander I had seen. I had been baffled, bewildered, frustrated every step of the way by poverty, culture clash, and my own failings – so many and so immediately obvious out here. I had been exhilarated by the exotic and the ordinary, by friendliness and generosity. I'd seen animals in the wild, which forever changes the way you look at them. I had met my failures one by one and changed not who I was, but how I encountered people and places. All the best challenges were out here, and I was proud of myself. If I could just turn around and head back up the other side of the continent, imagine all I'd learn and discover!

I'd also grown to love the daily life of overlanding. Building a fire, sinking an ax into wood, or cleaning the truck is ultimately a lot easier than writing a book, to be honest. There were days I didn't feel like digging the truck out of a bog or searching for firewood or getting up before dawn, but doing those things had become a lot easier than sitting down with a notebook, typewriter, or keyboard has ever been. I'd even grown to like not washing very often! I only washed more often in South Africa (where it was possible virtually every day) because I didn't really want to be the *only* person on the truck who smelled funny.

It was hard to think about going home and no longer counting on seeing lions and elephants and crocs in the wild just a few hundreds kilometers up the road. The thought of phones and televisions and microwaves overwhelmed me. I couldn't remember what I did with my evenings when I didn't spend them sitting around the campfire.

The Cango Caves are a famous sight in South Africa, but I thought the whole thing would be pretty tedious. Tour buses surrounded the place when we arrived, and there was a huge café, lobby, and ticketing area. I thought I had taken a wrong turn and stumbled into Dollywood. We bought our tickets and followed a guide who delivered a memorized lecture in a dull, sing-songy voice, making feeble stock jokes that suggested to me they needed better writers here at the caves. (Being an out-of-work writer, I thought about applying.) After seeing the "sound and light spectacle" in the main cavern, I decided that not even Dollywood could possibly be this hokey.

Then the guide explained that the guided portion of the tour only goes halfway through the caves. The rest of the tour was self-guided, physically challenging, and not for the faint of heart. I was unimpressed by this hyperbole. Despite the guide's warnings, I couldn't see any point in *not* going ahead, since I assumed the caves might be interesting without the memorized patter.

More than seven months in Africa, and I still hadn't learned to pay attention when someone told me that something wouldn't be easy. I guess I deserved what happened next.

After you leave the guide, there are four tunnels in the Cango Caves, each progressively smaller. I really had to squash my chest to get through a tight crevice in the first tunnel. Having expected the caves to be cold, I had worn heavy clothes. These caves, however, (whether due to natural influences or the numbers of people who tour them) were hot and stuffy. So stuffy that I couldn't get enough air in the smaller tunnels and kept drawing in deep gulps and yawning. I was dripping with sweat by the time we reached the *really* small tunnels.

I reached the moment of truth at the point where you leave a cavern about the size of a classroom, crawl into a hole the size of microwave, and then shimmy *up* a tight, bumpy, 3-meter-long tunnel.

I crawled into the microwave and looked up. Three meters

above me, I could see a hole and a light. I felt the weight of Mother Earth, heavy, rocky, and slimy, pressing down on me. I couldn't draw in any air. For the first time in my whole life, I suffered a terrible attack of claustrophobia. I slid back out in a state of panic and gabbled at Stuart. He said he'd go up first. He did. I crawled back into the microwave. The panic was worse. I slid back out, shaking, wondering what I could do now (since I didn't really relish going back alone the long, slippery way I had come). I told the next person to tell my companions to go ahead without me. I slipped to the back of the cavern. The Girls were there with Darren, awaiting their turn. The Girls were showing the first sign of trepidity they had shown in longer than I could remember. They had changed and grown up so much since Nairobi. They were now tough young women who said their say, did their work, bullied others into doing their work, too, and took charge when it was needed, all without losing the cheerful sweetness that had always made me like them so much. I felt better now, seeing that they were nervous, too.

Ever calm, Darren suggested I wait with them. He was very soothing. I guess what I eventually needed was enough fear-adrenaline to propel me forward. By the time I got to the micro-wave again, I was pumping enough personal chemicals to try once more. It also helped to have people I trusted above and below me, and no strangers around. Darren and the Girls hovered around my horrible little hole, telling me I could do it. David peered down from above, coaxing and goading me up. Mostly goading. He had known it would take a lot to get me to climb up that chimney. I pulled and pushed myself up, ignoring the horrifying feeling of rock pressing into my butt and diaphragm, shouting and cursing at David the whole way. Of course, my being in this horrible situation was in no way his fault, but being angry at someone really helped me get to the next chamber.

The worst wasn't over yet, however.

David asked someone else to come wait for the Girls, so he could "psychologically prepare Laura" for the next part of the journey. Upon being shown a little hole in the wall at the top of the new cavern, I shouted "Mother of God!" and flung myself against something. I think it was the floor.

David, who loves caving as well as rock climbing (he's a very sick boy) was in raptures. He was amazed at how much "real caving" we were getting to do in a tourist spot. While he had certainly been through caves more difficult to traverse than this one, there are apparently also "real caving" adventures that aren't this difficult. I didn't care. I just kept shouting things. Mostly I kept saying that nothing and no one could convince me to climb up into that horrible little hole.

Stuart came back, following the sounds of my shouting. Less patient with my hysterics than David, he explained my options.

"You have 3 choices, Laura. You can go down the way you came up."

"No, no, no!"

"You can go through the next tunnel."

"No, no, no!"

He pointed to the corner. "Or you can sit in that corner and wait to die."

David intervened before I could kill Stuart, suggesting I choose my second option and take the tunnel. I agreed. Stuart led the way, snickering and goading me so much that I wanted to kill him. Indeed, chasing after him, with the intention of getting my hands around his throat, was what kept me going. I followed him, flat on my belly, through this horrendous tunnel called the Mailbox, squirming along beneath tons of rock, thinking only about killing the man in front of me. Next thing I knew, I was sliding out of a little hole, down a smooth wall, and landing in another cavern. Everything would be fine from here on out.

"Now you know how toothpaste feels," Stuart said.

I was so glad to still be alive, and to be out of those tunnels, that I magnanimously decided not to kill him after all.

I rather agreed with young Jo, who fell out of the hole a moment later and said dazedly, "It's like being born."

We camped on a rocky hill overlooking the countryside, then visited an ostrich farm near Oudtshoorn the next morning. Ostriches are big business around there. After being shown around for an hour or two, I decided that ostriches are more interesting than I had supposed, though far less interesting than my guide thought they were. I admired the ostriches, and then I sat down to eat one. If there was a contradiction, I was too tired to explore it. I then browsed through a shop full of ostrich feathers, ostrich eggs, ostrich nests, ostrich leather, handbags, boas, artifacts... Well, you get the picture.

It was at the ostrich farm that I saw one of the most bizarre sights I'd ever seen: ostrich races. They put numbers on four ostriches, and four guys jumped on their backs, and then the ostriches raced along this little ostrich track.

I don't really think it'll catch on.

We went to an ostrich riding rink and were all offered the chance to ride one. After Imelda was thrown head-first into the bleachers, I politely declined. I found it all deeply weird.

The scenery got ever more glorious as we approached the Cape. As South African novelist Alan Paton phrased it: a land beautiful beyond any singing of it. Napping in the truck, I woke up suddenly one afternoon, realizing we had stopped. Darren had seen a lookout point and pulled the truck off the road. Everyone hopped out while I groggily muttered and shook myself awake. David came back a moment later, wearing the biggest grin I'd ever seen on his face.

"What a dreadful place to have to live," he said contentedly. He and Jane were moving to Cape Town for two years for his post-doctoral work. They had shipped their belongings ahead and had used the three-month leeway they had to journey to Cape Town overland from Nairobi. Unlike the rest of us, they wouldn't be leaving Africa after we reached Cape Town.

We spent our last night before Cape Town in an overgrown, deserted campsite chock full of mosquitoes. I think they were the first mosquitoes I'd seen since Malawi – the first that had had the temerity to bite me, anyhow. There were showers, as with most campsites in South Africa. The hot water ran out just as I got there. A memory to take away.

I was in a moody "last time" mode. Last time I'll live in the truck, sleep under African stars, sit round the campfire. Last time I'll flap the dishes after dinner (admittedly, this particular "last" didn't make me at all melancholy).

In honor of our last day on the road, our "Africa all the way" journey, our tens of thousands of kilometers in overland trucks, Sue and I sat in the cab that afternoon and navigated into Cape Town. We drove past a highway exit for the township where Amy Biehl was murdered. There were army tanks and weapons everywhere. The highway ramps were all blockaded. You could see quite a lot from the road, though. The place looked like hell on earth, as horrible as the shanty-towns outside Nouâdhibou in Mauritania.

We were headed for a business school dormitory on Cape Town's Victoria and Albert Waterfront. We found it after a few passes; cities were still confusing to us. I was used to having only a couple of choices when I looked at my map or the road. Intersections paralyzed me with indecision and confusion.

We were clearly a bizarre sight in Cape Town. As usual, people kept shouting up at us: Who were we? Where were we going? What were we doing in this strange contraption? Behind me, I heard the Girls telling someone that we were overlanders, and that the two women in the cab (me and Sue) had come overland all the way from Morocco. Two young white men were still expressing their admiration when we pulled away; in this small world, I would bump into them again a day later at Cape Point, where'd they'd be full of questions about the countries beyond their borders.

I eyed the dormitory complex when we found it. I thought the Breakwater Lodge looked like a prison from the outside. I later learned that it *had* been a prison. We were booked in here for a couple of nights, after which everyone would be going their own way. There was sudden massive confusion on board. We were supposed to off-load immediately. The truck had to be cleaned and prepared for the arrival of a whole new group of overlanders due to arrive in a few days; the crew was taking them into Namibia. Moreover, the engine needed to be replaced, since they'd been encountering serious technical difficulties with it. Indeed, it now seemed to be dead. This was rumored to be the oldest truck in the company's fleet, and I wondered if they should just shoot it. Darren explained the problem to me, but he could have been speaking Egyptian for all that I understood.

I started off-loading my stuff. I unlocked my locker for the last time and gave my key back to Peter, who was collecting them. I went through last-minute rituals, clambering up on the seats to check the overhead racks, climbing around the edges of the truck to lower the plastic sides and hook them shut one last time, double-checking the library for my books, checking the roofseat for anything I might have left up there. Peter and I settled the grocery money for the last time.

Then suddenly, anticlimactically, with no fanfare, ritual, or departing speeches, I was off the truck, as was everyone else, and it was going to become someone else's home.

One day, way back in Morocco, the truck had left us alone in camp somewhere for a few hours. I remember Pippa telling me that the truck gave her security; she didn't like to be separated from it. I didn't understand, since it was only a dusty, beat-up, open-air overland vehicle. *Now* I understood. I felt like crying. I was moving out of the nest. I'd lived in every inch of that truck, or ones just like it, for more than seven months. I'd dug it out of sand and mud and water, I'd pushed it and cursed it and cleaned it, I'd even fallen out of it a couple of times. I'd slept in it, under it, and on top of it. I'd lived, eaten, and traveled in it, been sick in it, played cards and Scrabble in it, written most of my diary in it. All of a sudden, I was moving out and would probably never see it – or anything like it – again.

I stood alone in the parking lot for a moment, staring at the truck like a kid leaving home.

The rooms at the prison were clean, simple, and comfortable. I shared mine with Sue. I slept terribly. Scarcely at all. The bed felt funny. Noises in the hall sounded funny. Sleeping in a closed room felt weird; I kept bumping my head and arms against the wall. I'd slept inside several times in recent months, but tonight I realized I'd be sleeping inside – in beds, in rooms –*from now on.* It somehow upset me.

With the truck broken down, David, Jane, the Girls, and I decided to chip in for a rental car and drive around the Cape. David wanted to drive, and I was happy to let him; I hadn't been behind the wheel of a car since January, and, besides, they drive on the wrong side of the road in South Africa. I have always found that confusing, even after several years of living in England. Accustomed to the lumbering truck, it felt weird and wild to be in a car again, zipping around with the agility of an acrobatic child.

We screeched to a halt just as a street light turned red.

"You can *do* that in a car!" David announced, pleased.

We were so low to the ground, I kept thinking my bottom would drag on the pavement any moment. I was used to looking *down* at everything when I rode.

I botched the navigating – not surprising, if you consider that I hadn't even asked where we were going. Understandably, Jane took the map away from me and took over. We got off the main thoroughfare and entered a grubby neighborhood. It reminded me a bit of certain parts of Chicago, the parts where my father always said, "Lock your door." People were staring at us in our nice car with our little white faces, puckered in confusion, poring over a map of the city.

"I don't think we should be here," I said nervously. "We're the only white people as far as the eye can see."

"It never bothered you in Tanzania," David chided.

"No part of Tanzania ever reminded me of the Bronx," I snapped.

We finally found Table Mountain, our destination, about an hour later. I was thrilled to see a cable car there! I had been requesting a mountain with a cable car ever since hauling my ass up Mount Toubkal in Morocco. Have I mentioned that I *hate* walking uphill? And while I don't really *like* standing in a crowded glass box hanging from a little wire thousands of feet above rocky ground, it sure beats *walking* up those cliffs.

David being macho on Table Mountain.

Table Mountain is *high* and – yes! – as flat as a table on top. The view was spectacular. We could see False Bay, Table Bay, and Robbin's Island, where Nelson Mandela was held prisoner for so many years – a tiny, barren rock out in the bay. There are rock hyrax all over the place on Table Mountain. Very tame, but not too bright. One of them started nibbling on my fingers, apparently thinking they were food.

We drove all over the Cape that afternoon. Not by design, actually. We were trying to get to Cape Point, and we were nearly there when an unannounced roadblock sent us scurrying around the Cape to find another route. I didn't mind, since it was wonderful to see the area: rolling hills, towering mountains, crashing waves on empty shores, lovely villages, beautiful homes in fabulous settings.

There's a lovely nature reserve at the end of the Cape. We paid to get in and drove straight to Cape Point, where I would complete my journey 215 days after I had begun it; end to end, from the shores of Morocco to the cliffs of Cape Point. True to form, as befitted my arrival at the southern end of the continent, Cape Point was at the top of a very long, *steep* hill. So I hauled my ass uphill for my last few hundred meters of my African journey, grumbling all the way.

A cliff overlooking pounding waves hundreds of feet below, the point is extravagantly beautiful and dramatic. Quite fitting for the end of a continent! I was suitably impressed.

David faced south and gave me a geography lesson: "To the left, the Indian Ocean. To the right, the Atlantic. Straight ahead, Antarctica."

And down below, I noted, was certain death. Especially for David, who insisted on leaving the platform and clambering around on rocks leading off into infinity.

I was so thrilled! Here I was! All the times I'd nearly quit, all those miles hauled across desert, mountain, jungle, and savannah... I stared out at the ocean and tried to remember all the different stages of the journey. The bitter bones of a dead cow lying somewhere in the Sahara, the spirit trances of the Ivory Coast, the magical hills of Cameroon, the thick jungles of Zaïre, the glowing smiles of the Ugandans, the vast herds of Serengeti, the scented breezes of Zanzibar, the thundering waters of Victoria Falls, the sky-viewed spectacle of the Okavango Delta, and the tuskless elephants of Addo drifted through my mind.

I remembered myself as I had been, and I thought of the stages I'd gone through, the graceless struggles, the flashes of insight, the slow acceptance not only of everything around me, but also of myself.

Standing at the edge of Cape Point, I realized in wonder that I had done it: I had crossed all of Africa! It had been hard, frustrating, frightening, exhilarating, adventurous, breathtaking, inspiring, and bewildering. I had faltered, fumbled, and failed many times, but I had always gotten back up and kept on going. And here at the end, I realized that that was what counted most.

Having done this, I suddenly knew I could do *anything* I really wanted to, anything I committed myself to. Anything!

Not a bad feeling to carry back downhill.

Desperately trying to set my shorts on fire at the Cape of Good Hope, South Africa.

NO FINAL SEASON

We felt we had to cover all our bases, because people would always ask the wrong questions of me if we didn't, so we then drove to the Cape of Good Hope. Hah! Gotcha! Been there, seen that.

We had an important ritual to perform at the Cape of Good Hope. I needed a ritual, after all. This was my moment! This was it! I had crossed Africa from one end to the other, and I needed to commemorate the occasion.

I had a pair of shorts that had come all the way from Morocco with me, hanging on grimly until the bitter end. They were The Shorts That Would Not Die! They were a very odd color by now (much of it acquired in a clay bog in the Sahara), and they smelled *awful.* The Girls had started begging me several weeks ago not to wear them anymore.

The first time young Kate asked, I had mumbled, "Bug off, I'll burn them later, okay?"

"How about right now?"

"Later!"

"When?" she persisted.

"When we get to the Cape, okay?"

The Girls decided to hold me to it and had actually sent me back to my room for the shorts before we set off in the rental car that day. When we got to the Cape of Good Hope, we hauled my shorts out of the trunk, where the Girls had made me put them. Then we discovered that we had forgotten matches. Unbelievable! How could I burn my shorts and fling their ashes into the sea without *matches*?

One of our new South African friends (the young men from the day before) loaned me a lighter. We took the shorts to the edge of the water and held the lighter to the hem. To our chagrin, we couldn't set them on fire. They were apparently a little too ripe to simply go up in flames.

Perplexed but interested in our quest – for this clearly meant a lot to us – the South African guy then dug a toolbox out of his trunk, opened the hood of his car, and pried apart some cables that had fluid – oil or diesel, I suppose – running through them. This was the kind of friendly help in the face of my illogical foreign behavior I had learned to really appreciate all over Africa. We smeared my shorts with the oily stuff, then tried again.

We got a little brief flame and then some smouldering before they put themselves out. It was nice to know that while wearing them I had never been in danger of immolation, but I felt deflated. It was very anticlimactic. Nonetheless, in true resilient overlander style, I swung them around my head (while a small but growing crowd of absolutely baffled South Africans watched us) and flung them into the raging sea while my friends cheered and took photos.

The shorts rolled back into shore like a Nigerian goat resisting sacrifice. We flung them out to sea again and again until they stopped coming back to shore. Finally, they floated out to sea. Mission accomplished and a continent crossed.

"Should we really leave them in the water?" I asked.

"They're 100% cotton," David said. "Biodegradable. Let's go get a drink."

The group broke up slowly over several anticlimactic days. The worst part of my job as kitty manager was upon me now, since I had to figure out what I owed the prison (since *they* couldn't figure it out) minus the individual phone calls and extra meals none of the overlanders could remember being responsible for. The money had to be sorted out soon; if there was going to be any left over, then I had to divide it up among the overlanders before they all departed for the four corners of the earth.

Eventually the prison warden and I came up with figures which were only about US $150 apart. We faced each other like gamblers now, cards held close to the chest. I raised my figure. She lowered hers. We dickered some more. We haggled fiercely. I tried to imagine doing this in a hotel when I got home and started laughing, which wasn't good strategy. We finally settled on a figure roughly halfway between our two original figures, and I paid the prison bill.

The Girls left for the airport that afternoon. It was a very emotional parting. I had grown so fond of them and was so impressed by how they had grown during their journey. They went home to good jobs, and their cards and letters since then have been full of good news. I said a weepy good-bye to a few of the others, including Sue, who had also landed a terrific new job when last she wrote, and Wendy, whose adventures since then would take another chapter to recount – the last time I heard from her, she had just become the first importer of South African cane liquor to the US. I have no idea whatever happened to Imelda, though I assume she eventually went home, too. Stuart, Peter, and Darren went north to Namibia the same day I flew out of Cape Town. For all I know, they've all long since quit overlanding; but in my mind, they're eternally on the road, looking for a good place to camp up for the night.

David and Jane, of course, stayed on in Cape Town, where they've both been successful in their various pursuits; although they're returning home soon for a year, there is a possibility that they will eventually go back to South Africa.

Saying good-bye to David and Jane the night before I flew out of Africa was the hardest parting of all. I promised I would come visit them after I sorted out my life, which was something that really needed to be done. After all, feeling like you can do anything isn't the same thing as having a plan. I was broke, out of work, at the end of an ambitious journey, and had no idea what I'd do with my life now.

Many of my former overland companions will laugh uproariously when I say this, but it would be dishonest to leave it out: I was even thinking of trying to become an overland driver. With this in mind, I eventually went to see the Operations Director of Guerba when I got back to England. Of course, I wasn't remotely qualified to be an overland driver, since I didn't have the appropriate kind of driver's license and I know absolutely nothing about fixing and maintaining such vehicles. But I could do *anything* now, remember?

The Operations Director was patient and spent a lot of time with me, but he thought I should go home think things over for a few months. After all, I wasn't the first person who'd ever wanted to go straight back to Africa after leaving. Besides, he said, didn't I *write* or something?

Well, I guess he was a smart man. I did indeed think things over for a few months, and while even today the memory is strong and the appeal is alluring, I went on to do other things instead.

I actually tried to quit writing, but finally discovered that, like it or not, writing isn't just what I do, it's what I *am*. And if I'd learned one thing on the road, it was how to accept what I am, like it or not. So I struggled for a while after I came home, wrote a few things that just didn't work, and wrestled with incorporating all the parts of my life into something new. As I had learned on the road, as long as I kept getting back up and forging ahead, all the mistakes, failures, and personal crises were just part of the journey, not the whole story.

More than a year after I finished crossing Africa, months of hard work and searching for something new were finally rewarded with the kind of opportunity that all writers dream about and only a few get. I'm now writing the first novel of a fantasy trilogy which will be released in hardcover in both the US and UK, and which may finally make me a writer that someone's actually heard of!

September 20th:

While I waited around the prison for my airport shuttle this morning, there were new, clean, fresh-off-the-plane, eager overlanders all over the prison; Stuart is pulling out of Cape Town today with his new group. No, they won't be going all the way to Morocco. I think Harare is probably the farthest any of them are going, but I didn't ask. The truck, of course, will eventually go all the way back to Nairobi.

Some of the new overlanders were chatting about water. Gosh, one girl was worried about brushing her teeth with the water in the rooms. Was it safe? What should she do? Another fellow explained that he'd brought his own purifiers for an emergency like this. Someone else assured them that the water here was probably okay, as long as you didn't actually *drink* it.

I started to speak, then changed my mind. I've brushed my teeth with river water, I've drunk purified brown and green water we hauled out of springs in the jungle, and I've done all sorts of other things that, seven months ago, I'd have sworn were crazy and suicidal and that I would definitely never do (not realizing that I'd have no choice). I didn't think I had many reference points in common with these people. (*Yet.*)

I said my good-byes to Stuart, Peter, and Darren when I finally found out that the airport shuttle, having nothing better to do, was simply waiting around outside until I felt like leaving.

Leaving Africa and the life of an overlander behind me, I cried my eyes out on the way to the airport.

The driver noted with a smile, "You're sad to leave Cape Town."

"Yes," I said, crying harder.

When he dropped me off at the airport, he said with apparent sincerity, "Come back. You must come back."

"I will," I bleated.

And I will.

And sure enough, I did.

EPILOGUE:
A BLONDE BACK IN AFRICA

S even months after I left Cape Town, the people of South Africa buried the festering corpse of apartheid and held free elections for the nation's first democratic government. Hundreds gathered in Cape Town to watch the old South African flag being lowered outside Parliament and the new one being raised in its place. The cheering crowd nearly drowned out the soaring voices of the white choir struggling with the words of South Africa's new national anthem, *Nkosi Sikelel'i Afrika* (God Bless Africa); people used to be jailed for singing this hymn.

Only five years earlier, the African National Congress was still a banned organization. Only a month earlier, the independent electoral commission had concluded that it would be impossible to hold elections in KwaZulu-Natal due to the pledge of the Inkatha Freedom Party to boycott and disrupt the process. Only a few weeks before elections, five young ANC supporters were murdered when they entered the township of KwaMashu in KwaZulu to talk peace with the Inkatha. Then Zulu Chief Mangosuthu Buthelezi, Inkatha's leader, changed his mind at the last minute and abandoned the boycott – much to the relief of the rest of South Africa. Among other things, this meant that Zulus no longer had to fear for their lives if they went out to vote; not all Zulus are Inkatha-supporters. Nonetheless, there was still violence on election day, including over a dozen political killings in KwaZulu-Natal, three bombs in Johannesburg, and one bomb in Pretoria; the bombs were blamed on white extremists, yet another faction endangering the delicate balance of the new society.

None of this kept voters away from the polls during the 3-day election process, which was also fraught with disorganization and accusations of incompetence and corruption. And nothing could diminish the wild enthusiasm of a people who were, as Nelson Mandela had said, free at last. Although no one was surprised when Mr. Mandela won the presidency, there were some surprising election results in the Northern Cape and Western Cape provinces, where blacks (who make up the vast majority of South Africa's national population) are a minority. A great number of the Coloureds (South Africa's people of mixed race) of this region voted for the National Party, former President de Klerk's party; this is the white man's political party that uprooted Coloureds from their homes and disenfranchised them. It is, however, the same government which gave many Coloureds a contempt for blacks. As one Coloured woman told *The Economist*: "I hang my head in shame when I say it, but I could never vote for a black."

The long walk to freedom is over, but the distant goal of racial equality and harmony is still so very far away.

Prior to selling my big fantasy novel I had sold a romance novel in mid-1994. Not the kind I used to write, but a really fun, full-length book (written as Laura Leone) which incorporated some of my own observations and jungle experiences from my 1993 journey across Africa. An editor called me up one day to say she'd always loved my writing and now that I was free (she was too tactful to say "broke and out of work"), would I please submit a book to her? (Did I mention that she is also an editor of rare refinement, good taste, and perception?) I agreed to do it when she said the magic words: "Write what you want, and surprise me; just make sure it's a love story and that it's good." (The book is called *Fever Dreams* and will be available in December 1996.)

Upon finishing the novel, I took the money I earned from it and fulfilled the promise I had made more than a year ago to visit David and Jane in Cape Town as soon as I could. I flew out there in mid-January of 1995. Since it's such a long journey, and since I *hate* winter, I sent them a letter announcing that I was staying for nearly a month. (Well, hell, it was *summer* down there; and they're used to having me around all the time, after all.)

Anyhow, my timing on this wasn't the best. For the first year they were down in Cape Town, David and Jane were very eager for visitors, but they didn't get many. By the time I finally arrived, however, they had not (I then learned) been *without* houseguests for over two months. Moreover, they had houseguests at this very moment! Four adults and a young child; they had been there for 3 weeks and were catching that evening's flight back to Europe. Personally, I thought this constant stream of visitors ought to be enough to dim the enthusiasm of even the most hospitable hosts.

Moreover, I learned that Jane had just enrolled in an intensive one-

The house David and Jane were renting when I stayed with them in 1995. Cape Town, South Africa.

year MBA course at the University of Cape Town. I was flabbergasted that someone with a Ph.D. in biochemistry would feel the need to go back to school, but Jane thought the MBA would further her interests in working in the biotech industry. The course, which was extremely arduous and demanding, began one day after I arrived, so I seldom saw Jane again. She was terribly apologetic about it, but several of my friends have been through graduate school, and I fully understood the demands being made upon her time and energy.

Despite everything, though, David and Jane were good hosts, ensuring that we often spent time together in the evenings and got away at weekends.

Oh, and as if all this weren't already a hectic enough situation, we also had to move house while I was there.

Timing is everything in life.

The house David and Jane were renting when I arrived was beautiful. A big rambling farmhouse from the days when this area was farmland, it was now surrounded by one of the older suburbs. The lush garden was surrounded by a high wall, and our street was narrow and quiet. The rooms were open and spacious. I had my own bedroom and bathroom. Upstairs was a 3-room loft; I set up my portable computer in one of the studios up there.

We were in Rondebosch in the southern suburbs of Cape Town,

The famous view of Table Mountain.

a white community of tree-lined streets where blossoming bougainvillea and oleander overflow the walls that the citizens live behind. Our housekeeper came twice weekly to clean and do laundry, and a man came each week to tend the garden. Americans and Europeans may be interested to know that all of this was a life-style readily affordable for the owners of the house, two academics with children; they were currently in England for some yearlong project. Moreover, the rent David and Jane paid for such a house was (when translated into dollars or pounds) equivalent to what many of us pay for a modest one- or two-bedroom apartment.

Cape Town is laid out around Table Mountain, the distinctive landmark which you can see from almost anywhere. The city itself sits on the bay and includes the Castle that the Dutch built, the Company Gardens where food was grown to restock ships rounding the Cape some 300 years ago, the Parliamentary government buildings, the business district, and some very old neighborhoods. Whites live in the suburbs along the water (breathtaking cliffside scenery overlooks the sea on the eastern side, while the flat land on the other side has postcard views of the mountain), in the suburbs behind the mountain (where we were, looking up at it), or else on the peninsula.

The black and Coloured townships are all out on the Cape Flats, a bleak, barren expanse of land north of town. The land there was covered by seawater millennia ago, so now it's all sand. Nothing grows there. It's hot in summer, cold in winter, and always windy. During the

The township of Khayelitsha.

forced removals, the first of which took place around the turn of the century during an outbreak of bubonic plague, non-whites were relocated there, often by the thousands.

Apartheid didn't just separate blacks and whites. It separated all the races of South Africa into five groups – white, black, Coloured, Malay, and Indian. In talking about people there, I usually refer to their race, as people there do. It's a holdover from apartheid, and will probably remain so for some time to come. Due to the national life created by apartheid, a person's race still often tells you a great deal about them – where they live, the education they received, their economic level, their employment, their religion, their language, etc. There are many exceptions, of course, but I want to make it clear why I mention almost everyone's race, lest some reader take offense.

The two racial groups which may not be self-explanatory are the Coloureds and the Malays. Cape Malays are people of Asian origin, frequently Indonesian, who were originally brought over from the Dutch East Indies centuries ago. They are traditionally Moslem, study Arabic in their mosque schools (and did this even during the centuries when it was illegal to do so), and speak English or Afrikans (or both).

The Coloured people were, according to the official apartheid government story, a mixture of the Khoisan (Bushmen) people and various black tribes. What they mostly are, though, are people whose heritage is a mixture of black and white ancestors; but since this was both illegal and An Abomination Against Man And God, it couldn't be the government's official story. They are a very large population in South Africa, particularly in the Cape. They have no tribe and usually speak Afrikans at home, whereas blacks usually speak their own tribal languages at home (Xhosa and Zulu being the two most prevalent).

Like many white families in South Africa, the people who owned the house David and Jane rented employed a housekeeper and a gardener, so taking on the house meant taking on the employees, not only for convenience, but also as a responsibility; they needed the work, and their incomes would seriously suffer if a Right Minded European decided she'd do her own housework rather than leave it to the black maid. Our housekeeper was Elizabeth, a middle-aged woman now living in Khayelitsha, a township originally founded to solve the problem of squatter camps in Crossroads. There are now over 500,000 squatters in Khayelitsha.

Elizabeth was born to a Xhosa father and a mother who was mostly Xhosa but who had enough mixed blood to obtain a legal classification as Coloured. For this reason, Elizabeth's father insisted that all the children be registered as their mother's children and Coloured, because being Coloured was a step up from being black under apartheid. By the same token, he thought they'd have better opportunities for work if they spoke English well, so he always spoke English with them at home rather than Xhosa, to encourage their language ability. As a result, Elizabeth said, her Xhosa was very weak, which she regretted.

She grew up in a small township near Hout Bay, a seaside town 30 minutes or so outside of the city (by car), a beautiful, sheltered bay with lush green mountains rising all around it. Then one day her family and all of their neighbors were forcibly removed to the vast townships on the barren Cape Flats. I don't know whether it was because of her father's or her husband's race, but she wound up in Khayelitsha, a black township.

After Elizabeth started working for the owners of our house, they drove her home one day to deliver a carpet they had given her which she couldn't transport herself, having no car. After seeing her whole family living in a two-room "core house" in the township, they bought the plot and house from the council for her and funded the building of one more room – which was all that the plot had space for. When it recently became legal to do so, they signed the house and plot over to Elizabeth.

There was clearly great loyalty and affection between Elizabeth and the family, who wrote her often from England and who were very concerned that David and Jane and all their guests treat her respect-fully and courteously. I gathered that our absentee landlords were lifelong opponents of apartheid who had found it hard to be living overseas during South Africa's first democratic elections. Anyhow, due to her own self-respect and her close relationship with the family, Elizabeth was comfortable talking to me, asking me questions, and using my first name, whereas I did occasionally encounter non-whites who were very nervous when talking to a white woman.

I was the first American she'd ever met, and she had many questions for me. Most of them were the result of watching American television programs which had recently come to South Africa. Television, one white told me, only got there in a big way a decade ago. Moreover, electricity was a very recent thing in the townships, most of which had only started getting it within the past year. So there was a lot of new exposure arousing people's curiosity about life abroad.

I had to confess to Elizabeth that *The Cosby Show* wasn't a completely representative picture of black life in America, though there are black families that wealthy and educated. I confirmed that, yes, it's true, black people got to America by being stolen for slavery and brought over on sailing ships centuries ago.

She asked if I knew any blacks *personally* and was amazed to learn that two of my college roommates had been black.

"So you all just mix together like that?" she asked.

Much as it would have been nice to paint an idyllic portrait of life in the USA, I tried to explain how things really were at home, from integrated professions, schools, and communities to the most segregated ones, adding that slums were usually all one race, whatever the race in question happened to be – and admitting that it was often black. She asked me what a slum was.

I realized, while explaining urban poverty in America to her, that it's a relatively unknown concept in South Africa. Townships are even poorer than slums, but they're rural or suburban. Almost all non-whites were moved out of city centers long ago in South Africa. Blacks, in particular, were moved as far away from all cities as possible while still keeping them close enough to work there each day.

"Picture townships with tall buildings, running water, paved streets, and electricity in the center of a city," I finally said, "and with many more guns and drugs. That's a slum."

"Are there many such places?"

"Many," I confirmed.

I guess I tarnished the silver of America that day.

The townships were the features of South Africa that I knew about, from TV and newspapers, long before I knew anything else about the country, so it seemed to me that seeing them was as important as seeing the nature reserves, the white suburbs, the famous scenery, the winelands, etc. However, they're not as easy to get to as these other things, since they're basically vast, self-contained, non-white slums set up at considerable distance from cities and towns. Indeed, their location isn't even marked on most maps, and there are no area-specific maps of the townships available to the general public. Yet in Cape Town alone, more than 2,000,000 people are estimated to live in the townships.

Although I had some misgivings about a "tour," I also knew that the townships were places that most South African whites wouldn't venture, and where whites could certainly get killed. Amy Biehl's death was still fresh in my mind. (In October of 1994, three young black men were convicted of murdering the young American woman in the Cape Town township of Guguletu; they were each sentenced to 18 years in prison.) I also considered how many neighborhoods there are in the US which I would *strongly* advise a foreign visitor not to enter without a knowledgeable companion or guide. Since I was unlikely in the next few weeks to meet anyone socially who knew the townships well, I decided that going with professional guides was my best option. Since Christopher Hope, an award-winning South African writer living in London since the '70s, recommended a township tour of Soweto, near Johannesburg, in his book *White Boy Running*, I thought there was even an outside chance that the experience wouldn't suck.

Two local operations ran trips into the townships; I booked with both of them, since I figured they'd be different and since the opportunity to do this is rare in South Africa. There was only one other operator in all of South Africa which, according to my inquiries, took whites into the townships – the one in Soweto. Soweto, by the way, stands for SOuth WEstern TOwnships and is a vast conglomeration of many townships all running together.

Townships have existed in reality ever since the establishment of the white man in South Africa. They began as squatter camps of blacks (and, long ago, of Khoisan people) living near the white communities that employed them. The first of the infamous forced removals in South Africa occurred around the turn of this century, when non-whites were removed from the center of Cape Town (and other towns, too) and shipped far outside of town, to isolated locations. The biggest forced removals and the establishment of the townships on the huge scale of recent decades is primarily due to the Group Areas Act, which divided all of South Africa geographically by color and decreed certain areas (the centers of cities, the suburbs, the best farmland, and, in general, *most* of the land in South Africa) to be "white" areas from which non-whites must be removed.

The Mind of South Africa by Alistair Sparks and *White Tribe Dreaming* by Marq de Villiers are two good books which can tell far more about it than I can here. Another excellent book is *My Traitor's Heart* by journalist Rian Malan, a painfully honest book about the failure of white liberalism in South Africa.

One City Tours, whose motto is "One City For All," was a new company operated by four black men. Our guides were Cinga (pronounced with a characteristic Xhosa click which I couldn't being to simulate) and Siswe. We began our tour at the notorious site of the former District Six. For five generations it was a mixed race community – Coloureds, Indians, Malays, Jews. Overcrowded and crime-ridden, it was nonetheless a lively, popular neighborhood, one that Cape whites often ventured into for music or ethnic food – or prostitutes. As someone later pointed out to me, life must have been awfully strange for the white boys who had often never even met a Coloured woman until they lost their virginity with one. (Malan's book, *My Traitor's Heart*, gives a pretty bleak personal depiction of such an incident.)

Under the terms of the Group Areas Act, which classified Cape Town as white-only, District Six became an illegal neighborhood since it was right in the heart of the city. An estimated 10,000 people were forced out of District Six and removed to townships out on the Cape Flats. Then their homes, streets, and businesses were bulldozed and destroyed.

The liberal Cape whites were appalled by what the national government had done here and so refused to ever purchase, develop, or build on this land. Indeed, the only party which ever had the audacity to do so was the South African government, which erected the Cape Technical College there.

Today, 30 years after its destruction, District Six is a tumbled wasteland – right in the heart of the city – of overgrown grass and weeds, heaps of rubble, and broken bricks. Nothing was left standing except a few houses of worship, which even the government couldn't bring itself to knock down, and a few apartments at the farthest end of the district.

With the new government now changing everything in South Africa, there is a District Six Museum on Buitenkant Street in Cape Town, and plans are being made to do something with the wasteland which was District Six – possibly a memorial park. There will apparently even be some effort made to recompense the people who, like war victims, were forcibly evacuated from their homes and separated from all their family possessions.

A few days after seeing District Six, I met Hermione Suttner, a delightful lady and South African writer. She co-authored a memoir about life in District Six with her housekeeper, Lettie, who had lived in and been removed from the neighborhood; the book is still available in the District Six Museum.

A donated sea container now functioning as a schoolroom. The township of Langa.

From District Six, we drove out to the Cape Flats, far from anything else in Cape Town, and quite a contrast to the beautiful scenery elsewhere in this region: flat, barren, sandy, seemingly endless. As the highway leaves behind an industrial wasteland and enters the township areas, it is lined on both sides by densely-packed shacks and shanties as far as the eye can see. The last time I came through here, in the truck, there were military barricades at most of these exits due to the riots in Crossroads.

We were four whites (a German couple, a Canadian woman named Donna, and me), travelling with our two black guides in a comfortable little mini-van which was the same size as the local bush taxis. Bush taxis are the minibuses, usually blue and quite decrepit, which are the primary mode of transportation for South Africa's (usually) carless non-whites. There had been taxi wars the previous year in these townships between rival companies competing for business; dozens of people were wounded or killed.

The Cape Flats townships were fairly quiet when I was there. However, both Cinga of One City and Aly Khan of Otherwise Tours (my guide the following day) assured me that even on a bad day in the townships, they had taken visitors there who never even knew there was trouble, since trouble was usually confined to a given neighborhood or area. This confirmed my notion that it was best to be with someone who knew the townships extremely well.

When the government first started building townships, they tried building core houses, the sort of two-room brick structure that

Elizabeth had in Khayelitsha. However, they were relocating people too fast to keep up with the demand, and building a whole house, even a badly-built two-room house, takes time and some money. So the apartheid government started building what they called "serviced sites." That's a plot of land (and we're talking plots of land smaller than the one-room loft I rent in Ohio) with a cement water stall; there's a toilet inside the stall and a faucet with running water on the outside. The family moving to a serviced site would then build their own home. The shortage of supplies in the black townships makes for surprising use of cast-off materials. Sea containers are turned into schools, and throw away construction materials make patchwork houses of wood, cardboard, plastic, and corrugated tin.

Even serviced sites couldn't be built fast enough for all the people coming into the townships, especially not when people started migrating here from the homelands to look for work and began squatting in the townships. So the next stage of development was to run water pipes into an area and set up one communal tap for an entire neighborhood. People would claim a plot near this water supply and erect a shanty. Rent due to the government for a serviced site was less than the rent on a core house, and rent on a plot with a communal water tap was lowest of all. Estimates on how many people used a communal tap were vague, as were all estimates about the townships. Cinga said that no proper census had ever been done of the non-white communities, and certainly not of the townships. It was believed, though, that 300 new shacks a day were going up in Khayelitsha alone.

Another of the apartheid government's housing innovations were the vast all-male dormitories for men who came to the cities to work, but who – due mainly to the pass laws – couldn't bring their families with them. Since the abolishment of the pass laws, men are now allowed to bring their families from the homelands. However, with unemployment so high and wages so low, that doesn't necessarily mean a man can move out of the dormitory, which is much cheaper accommodation than a core house or serviced site. So, where 16 men might have shared a toilet, kitchen, and common room before, now as many as 16 *families* might share those facilities, with one family per bed.

Cinga and Siswe took us into one of the dorms where the inhabitants were apparently their friends or relatives and we were clearly expected. I felt very strange wandering through someone's home, and I thought the inhabitants must have found it even stranger that white people wanted to come see their hostel. Since most people were at work, there were only 3 or 4 men there today. A grizzled old man sat in the kitchen/sitting room; a younger man was cooking in the tiny kitchen; another man was relaxing in one of the bedrooms before going out to work the night shift.

The dormitory was made of wood and brick. It was old, and it smelled of long use and too many people. There was a single bare lightbulb in each room – a new innovation, since the townships had only started getting electricity within the past year. The kitchen, which was shared by 16 or more people, had no stove. The tennants cooked on a single bunson burner. No sink. Nothing else. The 16 beds were scattered throughout 3 bedrooms. Each bed had storage below and overhead for personal possessions, of which there were few in evidence.

It was altogether an absolutely depressing place, especially when one considers that this wasn't a starting place from which most people hoped to better themselves. Under the pass laws, this was simply how a man lived; there would never be any work at home near his family, and he had little chance of ever bringing his family here.

Back out in the dusty street, a woman was roasting sheeps' feet on an open fire, scraping soot off with a steel-wire brush, and putting them back on to roast again. The neighborhood people were friendly to me, smiling when I smiled. The children waved and squealed and, like children all over Africa, were full of excitement and curiosity at the strange sight of a white woman in their neighborhood. Moreover, people *thanked* me for coming here, and (when they realized I was foreign) for coming to South Africa.

As I climbed back into the van, I asked Cinga if white South Africans ever take this trip. "No," he replied, "unless they feel embarrassed by foreign friends who have seen more of South African life than *they* have seen, so that they feel they must come. But very, very few." He could only recall two or three.

We drove on to Guguletu, the township where Amy Biehl was killed. Everyone in the Cape remembered the incident clearly, and people often referred to it while I was there. The locals, black and white, simply referred to her as "Amy": "When Amy was killed," they would be begin. It was a cross South Africans bore with sorrow: a foreign white girl who had friends in the townships, who had come to help their people, was killed in a riot there.

Cinga recalled seeing Amy's family come to lay flowers upon the spot where she was murdered. The same spot was so empty and quiet today that it was hard to conjure up the scene in my mind. A little further along, I spotted the first official street sign I'd seen in the townships; the road leading to Guguletu from the township of Langa is called "Valhalla." Now who the hell thought of that, do you suppose?

Cinga and Siswe also took us to a Coloured township, where they pointed out how differently the former government had administered the communities. The Coloured township, poor as it was, was noticeably better off than any of the black townships we had seen. It had real streets, street signs, and street lamps. The people, because of access to slightly better jobs and slightly higher wages, tended to have nicer homes. More of them had been able to purchase their tiny plots, hence there were more homes here that were privately owned and proudly cared for.

We ended the afternoon in Carol's shebeen in Guguletu. When alcohol was outlawed for blacks, enterprising women set up private commercial bars in their two-room houses, selling bootleg liquor and homemade brew, and the shebeen became a fixture of (non-white and non-Moslem) South African life. Carol had no children, but, she said, even she and her husband of 10 years drove each other crazy in these two tiny rooms, and so she had been slowly building a third room in her spare time. She asked me to imagine how whole families managed to live in a tiny, badly built space like her clean, sparsely furnished core house.

Going home to our big, lovely house back in Rondebosch felt strange. It was a relief, certainly, to be in such pretty, comfortable surroundings. But I noticed for the first time how incredibly quiet it was here. The townships, I realized, reminded me of the rest of Africa – not in terms of their desolation, for I had seldom seem such bleakness in the rest of Africa – but in terms of the vibrancy, life, smiles, music, and energy which also lived in those dusty streets. I hadn't felt like I'd been in Africa since arriving, not until today.

The vibrant life which can exist in such a barren, alienating environment is truly a great triumph of the non-white peoples of South Africa. The townships are artificially established communities, and they both look and feel like it. There is no river, no port, no farmland, no trade route, no natural reason for the Cape townships to be where they are – except, of course, for the strange paradoxes of South African life.

My next trip into the townships was somewhat different, as was my guide. There were only two of us with him today – and I would have been alone if I hadn't asked Donna if she'd like to go, too. As we drove out to Athlone, a Coloured business community, I sat in the backseat of Aly Khan's comfortable car and learned more about him. He'd been taking whites into non-white areas for over 7 years. He began this when it wasn't legal and continued doing it secretly even after the white government told him to stop. At one point, the government even launched an investigation into his activities, not believing his stated reasons for bringing people of different races together (i.e. making business in Cape Town harmoniously and profitably multi-racial).

A businessman, Aly Khan lost his job during the South African economic decline in the 1980s and went into business for himself, promoting non-white businesses in the Cape. This led to his developing a sort of field trip for white businessmen which brought them into non-white communities and introduced them to their non-white counterparts – for the very first time ever, in most cases. He became so successful that he started getting a lot of attention for this work, which was when the government tried to shut him down – so he went "underground" with it and kept on bringing whites and non-whites together.

When apartheid restrictions were lifted, he came out into the daylight again and continued his work, this time bringing tourists into the picture, too. He has received several local honors, from the mayor and from business organizations. Among other things, he is credited with instigating new business between white and non-white businessmen to the tune of more than 2 million dollars.

Experienced and knowledgeable, he spoke almost nonstop in a beautifully modulated voice that any actor would kill to have, talking about apartheid, the history of non-white communities in the Cape, and the non-white history of now all-white areas. This trip also rounded out the picture for me, since Aly focused mainly on the Indian and Coloured communities.

In Athlone, Aly introduced us to his friend Ameer, who owned a bustling linen and household supplies shop. The street felt strangely familiar; it was a little like Canal Street in Manhattan, but nowhere near as big or crowded. Aly suggested Donna and I stroll up and down the street, advising us to talk to people, introduce ourselves, take our time.

Donna and I were the only whites here. People looked, of course, but I had the impression we weren't quite as strange a sight here as we were in Guguletu, Langa, and Crossroads. People here were (again) friendly and welcoming. Someone blessed me for coming to South Africa. A fruitseller asked us to chat with him for a moment while he filled up bags with fruit. To our surprise, he then gave us the bags and refused payment.

"If I give to others," he said, "then God will give to me." Then he, too, thanked me for coming to South Africa, and for coming to his neighborhood.

Aly Khan then took us to an "informal business district" in Khayelitsha, the vast black township where Elizabeth lived. A sandy street was lined with shacks on both sides. People were selling clothes, shoes, food, bootlegged audio tapes, and various services. There was no electricity in this street yet, so the local barber used a little generator to power his shavers. Crates of skinny chickens squawked at me. Most of the meat being sold here was in the form of feet and heads of cows and sheep.

Some people were friendly, others seemed uncomfortable with my presence. *Everyone* seemed pretty baffled. A few people standing above me on a structure that looked oddly like half of a highway bridge even looked hostile, but I thought that might just be because they weren't smiling and I felt conspicuous. Certainly no one looked threatening, and some were extremely friendly.

Okay, I wouldn't want to be white and alone here after dark (or alone here at *all* after dark, to be honest), but by day, I felt comfortable. I was sure glad I didn't have to buy supplies here for a truckload of overlanders, though, since the food supplies were minimal and very unappetizing.

Following a suggestion of Aly's, we decided to give our fruit away to some children hanging around another part of Khayelitsha. I had strong misgivings about this, since I had crossed an entire continent full of open-palmed people expecting handouts of any and every kind from anyone with white skin; I didn't want to be part of creating the same situation here. Based on previous experience, I expected to be mobbed the moment we gave the first plum away, and I expected the children to beat the shit out of each other to get the fruit away from each other. I was quite mistaken this time – which taught me, once again, to always expect surprises in Africa. The children watched me wide-eyed and only came forward hesitantly when I made eye contact and specifically offered them a plum. Some had to be nudged forward by an adult, who apparently thought I was doing a nice thing. The children all approached me with solemn eyes, shy smiles, and a breathless whisper of "nkosi" – which I gathered meant "God bless you" in Xhosa. Any child who forgot to thank me was sharply elbowed and reminded by the older kids.

As I *had* expected, they all wanted their picture taken, though it was unlikely they'd ever get to see the photos (though, at Aly's request, I sent him copies of the photos so that he could hand them out next time he was in the neighborhood). Even the shyest or gawkiest African kid turns into a film star when you point a camera at him, giving you dramatic, funny, and photogenic poses as if being paid $400/hour for this. I hope Aly did indeed find a few of them again and give them those pictures.

While I was gallivanting around the townships and David was killing rats and performing biochemical experiments on their dead carcasses in the lab, Jane was struggling with her newly-begun MBA course. It can be hard to work closely and well with people you've only just met, and this MBA program was throwing everybody into the deep end right away. Consequently, we three decided to throw a dinner party at the house one Friday evening, get some of Jane's fellow students together on a social basis, and encourage them to let their hair down and get to know each other. The class was much too big to invite everyone, so we narrowed down the invitation list to a dozen or so people that Jane had already met or been assigned to work with.

I was curious to see these people, who I'd been hearing about since my arrival. I have to be honest and admit that I didn't expect to like everybody at the party. Nothing to do with nationality. I'm a third generation writer, born to an artistic family that unconsciously raised me to think of big business as inherently evil, and big businessmen (and women) as therefore wicked by association. While I know many exceptions to this prejudice of mine, and even love a few of them, it is nonetheless a deep-rooted bias.

Jane had told our invited guests that dinner would be at seven o'clock. That seemed pretty clear to me; but to a handful of Jane's classmates, it was apparently a statement of deep, baffling mystery which couldn't be resolved.

Our first hint of this came around 7:30, when we got a phone call from a couple of guests who apologized for being so late; they were waiting for another invited guest to whom they had promised a lift, and he still hadn't shown up. Jane happened to know that he had arranged a lift with someone else; he had apparently neglected to tell these two people, so she advised them to just come along without him.

At this point, I said, "That does it. If people aren't here by 8:30, we're eating without them. They can just fend for themselves."

Jane thought this was a trifle pessimistic of me; of *course* people would be here by then! She had said dinner at seven o'clock, after all!

Guess what happened? By 8:30, four guests still hadn't shown up. Nor had they called. I was frankly appalled by such rudeness. This wasn't a party where you invite people to stop by "at some point." This was dinner, with a time clearly set.

I had talked Jane into doing a *braai* – a South African cookout where you roast marinated meat. The English, for some reason, seem to have an utter revulsion for cooking outdoors – maybe because of their native climate? – so Dave and Jane weren't all that keen on the idea. They knew, of course, that I was just looking for an excuse to build a fire, not having had the opportunity for too long. I was dismayed to discover that while I hadn't become incompetent in the 16 months I'd been away from Africa, I *had* lost my touch. The fire didn't leap to life just because I asked it to. Jane thoughtlessly shattered my confidence at one point by bringing me a can of fire starter, which I snapped at her to take away. I eventually got the fire going with an excess of fanning and newspaper, and we had beautiful a glowing bed of coals in the backyard over which we cooked really succulent meat. The house, with large rooms which were perfect for entertaining, was well-stocked with food, drinks, munchies, chairs, music, and soft lighting. We had all the ingredients for a great party.

Some of the guests were really nice. Interesting, sincere, and intelligent, shattering my general prejudice about people pursuing big business. I didn't like everyone, though, and I was rude to the people who showed up an hour and a half late. I stuck to my vow to start eating at 8:30 whether all the guests had arrived or not, and I insisted everyone else do the same. When the final four guests showed up, three of them were drunk, noisy, unruly, under-dressed for the occasion, and (to my knowledge) didn't apologize for being so late. I didn't regret not waiting for them, and I didn't interrupt my meal to greet them.

Several of the students enrolled in the MBA program (including one or two of these latecomers), I was told by one guest, were Rhodesians.

"You mean white Zimbabweans?" I asked.

"No. *Rhodesians*. There's a difference." I was about to learn what it was.

Generally speaking, white Zimbabweans are people who live in Zimbabwe, have mentally moved into the modern era, and accept that they live in black Africa. "Rhodesians" have an inflexible colonial mentality that doesn't accept that blacks are now state presidents and not just houseboys you can beat whenever you feel cranky. And, of course, lots of Rhodesians *don't* live in Zimbabwe, because they left either when the war began there, or else when the country *became* Zimbabwe. South Africans call a Rhodesian a when-we, because (they say) every phrase begins with, "When we were in Rhodesia..."

I began to understand what a when-we was, and why some white Zimbabweans are called Rhodesians, when a Rhodesian guest at our party said: "I'm not a racist, but when I eat in a restaurant, by God, I don't want to see a black man eating there, too."

I wasn't even going to tackle that one.

Another of the guests I tried talking to had only one conversational gambit, which was to contradict everything everyone said, no matter what. This could reach ridiculous proportions, as you might imagine.

"What a lovely climate you have here," I said at one point, striving for mediocrity with all my might.

"Nonsense. Rotten climate!" he riposted.

"But it's so sunny and warm," I protested.

"There's no *sun* here!"

"But it was sunny all day."

"No it wasn't. Bloody miserable overcast day today."

"But I was out all day. It *was* sunny."

"No it wasn't."

He thought I was a fool to have crossed Africa and an idiot to have entered the townships. He guaranteed that I couldn't have possibly survived going to Zaïre. I pointed out that I *did* go to Zaïre the previous year and *did* survive. He contradicted me. I gave up and walked away.

I had been wondering who supported apartheid, who had been a part of that architecture, since all the whites that I'd met since arriving seemed to verbally distance themselves from it as much as possible. In some cases this was quite genuine – David's white boss had lived in exile until the dismantling of apartheid, and his boss's sister had been a member of the banned ANC for over two decades. But I felt sure there had to be people whose apparent enthusiasm for the New South Africa was more convenient than genuine. I met one such person at our dinner party. The comments were subtle, but the sum of them was worth noting. I almost pitied this person who so clearly didn't want to believe that the days of white rule were forever over in South Africa.

Fortunately, however, most of the guests were enjoyable people. One of them knew Winnie Mandela's secretary (or something) and passed along some interesting anecdotes. According to the stories I heard that night, she and Nelson still love each other and would rather be together, but their opposing ideologies are just too irreconcilable. Now *that's* devotion to an ideal.

We threw another dinner party a few days later, this time for some of Dave and Jane's rock climbing friends, and had a delightful evening. Two of the dinner guests were a mixed black- white couple. I was aware that their relationship, which even now probably isn't always logistically easy, was illegal and punishable by imprisonment when it began. My curiosity was aroused, but I didn't feel that even being American would excuse my asking personal questions of people I'd only just met. So I did the correct thing – I pumped David shamelessly the next day.

The couple couldn't legally marry under apartheid. They still weren't married now; I supposed they didn't feel compelled to run out and get a license just because the government now said they *could.* They had got round the problem of the rigidly color-coded housing laws of apartheid by moving into a rare remaining Coloured neighborhood in the city ("remaining" meaning that the people were left where they were rather than being shipped out to townships.) For whatever reason, perhaps because Cape Town has long been a liberal city accustomed to looking the other way in many such situations, they lived in relative peace there.

Under apartheid, there was a government office which specifically dealt with the question of racial classification and judged the petitions of people who sought to change theirs. The most common reason for applying for a new classification was falling in love and wishing to marry across the color barrier. Hundreds of people every year changed their classification (and thus their whole lives, in many cases) to marry. The whole subject fascinated me, as did this couple who had defied all of that, and who had also chosen to remain here rather than emigrate. Given how educated, sophisticated, and well-travelled they both were, it was a choice that would have been open to them.

The issue of emigration was an interesting one there, too, and one with many viewpoints. As I mentioned earlier, David's own Afrikaner boss and his wife were prominent scientists who couldn't stand apartheid any longer; so they left, going into exile in England. They came back after apartheid and got excellent positions at the university. One of them heads a research team and is probably destined for even higher postings. Indeed, having been in exile can now *lead* to opportunities; so many people who are now important in the government were in exile, too, and many exiles knew each other overseas.

On the flip side, people who never went into exile have varying views. Aly Khan, for example, refers to exile in those days as the "chicken run," and complains that those people are now returning to jump into opportunities which are only available to them because people like him stayed and slugged it out.

So was going into exile in those days the principled thing to do, or merely the easiest way out? Rian Malan's book, *My Traitor's Heart*, explores this; he tried exile and he tried coming home, and found that white liberalism was a double-edged dagger-in-the-heart wherever he went.

Of course, if exile was the only alternative to prison, the answer becomes easier. Someone in the US recently complained to me about how many of our intellectuals will be out of work due to new educational budget cuts, and how terrible for our society it is, and how we might as well throw all our intellectuals in jail because, after all, what's the difference? Such naivety is precisely the reason I think most Americans should travel more. There *is* a difference, a *big* difference. And as Rian Malan pointed out in an article I read while living on the truck, there's also a difference in police forces. Under apartheid, for example, the South African police usually challenged the right to remain silent by wiring the detainee to a car battery.

Yes, questions of exile, of staying on, and of relationships across the color barrier fascinated me. They remain among the hardest questions there, harder than the so-who-*did*-support-the-apartheid-government-if-you're-all-so-glad-it's-gone question, because the latter has an answer which people merely want to forget, while the former questions never did have answers – and perhaps never will.

Since I wanted to drive out to some of the small nature reserves within day-trip distance of the house, Jane kindly loaned me her car. I'd been practicing driving on the left for several days. The biggest problem was shifting gears with my left hand. I often found myself pressing the clutch and wildly scrabbling about with my right hand at a crucial moment before realizing the gear shift was on the *other* side. Getting used to that, plus the road system, plus the car (which had a stiff gear box that I made frequent mistakes with), plus not ever knowing where I was going made for some interesting adventures. If Jane, a truly intrepid woman, was in the car, she remained remarkably calm. Indeed, when I'd suddenly find myself accidentally in second gear on the highway with a truck barrelling down upon me, she'd smile mildly at my panicked cursing and say, "Come on, Laura. Stay calm."

David was manful about my driving, though if he was sitting in the back seat and thought I couldn't see, he did flinch on occasion. So one day these trusting souls let me take their car out to the West Coast National Park by myself.

One interesting thing about South Africa, commented upon even by South Africans, is that although they are generally a hospitable and friendly people, their service industry has a long way to go. If lost or confused, I could always count on anyone I met in South Africa to cheerfully and eagerly try to help me out. More than once, people went above and beyond the call of courtesy to a stranger. Yet the people whose actual *job* it is to help you out frequently won't do it.

For example, to get from the house to the city center, I usually took the train. The commuter train system is quite good in Cape Town, with frequent trains and timely arrivals. However, on my first day there, when I was getting ready to leave the city and go home, I noticed something odd for a major station with 17 active platforms: there was no schedule posted anywhere in the station, no platform listings, and no loudspeaker announcements. I had no idea how to find my train back to Rondebosch. So I started walking up to uniformed railway employees and asking. Not only did no one know how I could find out which train was mine, no one even made the slightest effort to help me. In fact, the first half dozen employees I approached all stared blankly at me, shrugged, and turned away.

I found the train by pestering ordinary commuters, all of whom tried their best to help me out. They also informed me that if I wanted to have this information on hand for my next trip to the city, I should go to one of the tobacco shops or newstands that sold railway timetables. I did. All the information was in there, very accurate and clear. And not one single railway employee told me about this.

Someone had told me that there was an excellent boat ride at the West Coast National Park: a 3-hour trip out onto the water that was the best way to see the birdlife there. So I approached the National Parks office at the tourist center in Cape Town. They knew nothing about it and refused to call the park on my behalf.

"But isn't your business helping people visit the national parks and booking tours and accommodation there?"

"Yis, ma'am." (South Africans pronounce it *yis*.)

"Then won't you help me book this tour at the West Coast National Park?"

"No, ma'am."

I was reluctant to telephone myself because I had trouble understanding many people's accents, so phones were a serious challenge to me. It always depended on the individual. Some South Africans sound nearly English, and I could follow them easily. Others, whether white or non-white, had strong local accents which took all my concentration to unravel. And when I would say, "Could you speak more slowly, please? I'm foreign and it's hard for me to understand," they'd be baffled. Since English was our mutual language and they could understand *me*, how I could possibly not be following their conversation with complete comprehension?

I don't know. Maybe they've seen more American movies, TV shows, and news broadcasts than I've seen of South African ones.

However, wanting to do the boat trip, I phoned the park.

"I understand you offer a boat trip there," I began.

"Yis..."

"Can you tell me more about it?"

Silence.

"Uh, it's three hours, right?" I said.

"Ya."

"And what else can you tell me about it?"

Silence.

"How much does it cost?" I asked.

The price was finally revealed.

"And when do you go out?" I asked.

"When do you want to go out?"

(I began having flashbacks to Mr. Haji in Zanzibar, but I persisted.)

"Well, a friend who was there recently told me you go out Wednesday mornings. How about this Wednesday morning?"

"Oh. No..."

"Oh. Is some other day better?"

"Well, look, we only take the boat out if we've got six people booked, you see."

"Ah, I see. Of course. Well, how many are booked so far?"

"None."

"Oh, dear. Well, look, we are two persons," I said, since I knew someone who wanted to go with me, "so can we book for later in the week? If someone else calls you in the meantime, then hopefully we'll get six people by that day."

"Well, I don't think so, because we only go out with six people."

"Well, do you think more people will call and book? You went out last week according to my friends, after all."

"More people. Ya."

"So perhaps I could give you my phone number, and if more people book, you can call me and..."

"Oh, I don't think more people will book."

"So you're just not taking a boat out this week, is that it?"

"Oh, no, we're taking a boat out."

"Really? When?" I pounced.

"Well, if we get six people, you see."

"Well, since you're unlikely to get six people all at once, what if you took *our* two names, and if four *other* people call..."

"Well, I don't think anyone else will call this week."

"But it's Monday morning! How can you say... Never mind."

I gave up. I'd just try to spot the birds from the damn car.

The first thing I did after I took Jane's car out of town was get horribly lost. By chance, I eventually stumbled across a place called Table View, a dull, flat, rather dreary seaside white community with one notable feature – the most spectacular view of Table Mountain you could imagine. Lots of postcards have this view printed on them. So I took photos.

I had left the house quite early because I had to drop Jane off at the business school at the crack of dawn in exchange for the car. The business school, by the way, was the same one I'd stayed in at the end of my 1993 journey – the prison! Ah, how that brought back memories... Anyhow, I was hungry now and decided I wanted breakfast. So I stopped at some little roadside place. The waiter – a white man who also seemed to be the chef, bartender, manager, and owner – asked what I wanted to eat.

"Have you got a menu?" I asked.

"No."

"Oh. Well, what have you got?"

"The usual stuff."

"I'm sorry. I'm foreign. I don't know what usual breakfast food is here."

"Oh."

I waited. Nothing happened. Finally I asked, "Can you give me a hint? What do *other* people here eat? What are those people over there eating?"

"Bacon, eggs."

"Uh, got any granola? Any waffles? Any pancakes? Any bagels?"

"No."

"Oh. What else do you have?"

"Toast. Coffee."

I sighed. "Okay. Bring me the works. And coffee. Lots of coffee. Do you have any orange juice?"

"Ya."

"Okay. Please bring me a glass of orange juice, too."

It took some nagging to get my coffee after the juice came. He couldn't believe anyone wanted coffee *and* juice with breakfast.

"I'm foreign," I said stonily, requesting my coffee again.

That was apparently explanation enough.

I took the coastal road up to the park, which is a spot of nature-reserve green on the map, bordered by the sea and surrounded by a *vlei*. I'm still fuzzy on the definition of *vlei*, despite having visited several of them in South Africa. It's a body of water, anyhow, but somehow different from a lake. It's not a swamp, and no one seemed satisfied by my suggestion that perhaps it was a big pond. So a *vlei* is a mysterious body of water with birds on it, okay?

The West Coast is flat and scrubby, barren, and rocky. I found it quite a contrast to the mountainous, lush, beautiful Cape. The two writers I met in Cape Town both had weekend places out here, so the area is not without appeal, but I didn't like it nearly as well as all the other places I'd seen in South Africa.

I convinced the park station (with difficulty) to give me a map and some advice about where to go, paid my entrance fee, and drove Jane's little car down a dusty unpaved road. It was an incredibly hot day, much hotter than it was back in town, and the sun shining into the car burned my arms and legs. The *vlei* was frustrating. There were several beautiful, comfortable bird hides there, but they were so far from the water, and hence far from the wading birds, that even my binoculars couldn't pick out much – probably because this was dry season.

The road got increasingly worse, so I spent far longer in the park than I had intended, barely getting out by closing time that evening. However, it was a really good day. I had met so many people lately that I really needed a day alone, without talking, to get my equilibrium back. And I needed a day out in the country. I *did* get to see some wildlife, though I realized how spoiled I was, since I considered the pickings here dreadfully slim: wildebeest, eland, bontebok, zebra, and springbok. As for the birds, I decided that I'd have to go somewhere with an actual bird guide to figure out what I was seeing.

Strangely, there are some villages in the park – white communities. I fell upon one such village late in the afternoon, thirsty and hungry, and was pleased to find a little supplies shop open. It was obvious the Afrikaners around here didn't hear much English; I was taken for a Captonian, despite a very apparent American accent that people everywhere else noticed immediately. The second village I came upon had more people buried in the cemetery than living in the cottages. The third village looked brand new but seemed to be completely abandoned except for a herd of about 30 eland prancing about. A rather strange place.

I felt great though. The heat, dust, thirst, wildlife, and wind all took me back to happy days on the truck and a sense of freedom I hadn't had in a long time. I was sorry not to be pitching a tent and building a fire when the day ended. Instead, I turned Jane's car south and headed home.

The owners of our rental house had had a sudden change of plans and were coming home sooner than expected, so we had to move out. Dave and Jane had only learned about this after I had bought my airplane ticket, so I wound up being there when they had to move. As it happened, we were merely moving into a little cottage three doors away. That's more trouble, in a way, because you don't hire movers or rent a van for that, you just keep hauling things down the road for a week. David may well be the only man who ever walked down a street in Rondebosch carrying a Maasai spear (bought in Tanzania).

The new house was small by comparison to where we'd been living, and not well set up for guests. We had only one bathroom, and I slept in a combination study-bedroom-dining room. It was a good thing we were all used to living cheek-by-jowl together, but I felt a little guilty now about having made my visit so long.

Only a *little* guilty, mind you.

David and Jane had agreed to co-rent a house in the country with some friends the following weekend. With so much time lost due to the move, Jane decided not to go with us at the last minute and stayed behind to study. So David and I pulled out a map, tested the wind, and set off for De Hoop, a nature reserve up along the east coast, 2-3 hours drive from town (the last half hour on roads resembling those in West Coast National Park).

The house we rented was institutional, but we did have panoramic views of vast, rolling hills. The house was on a farm. When the De Hoop Nature Reserve opened nearby, the farmer had built it to cash in on the weekenders who'd be coming out for hiking and birdwatching. I liked the setting, since it was an ordinary working farm, full of people and animals, rather than a resort. It was also virtually at the gate of the nature reserve, where we spent most of our time.

There was a *vlei* at De Hoop. We walked all the way around it one sunny, breezy morning. De Hoop mostly had bird life, but there was some game there. An antelope ran right past us at one point, and we saw zebra, blesbok, and far too many ostriches. Ostriches are one thing a person becomes very jaded about on the Cape. Dave saw a snake, too – but, mercifully, I did not. De Hoop backs up to the sea, so we poked around in rocky seacaves, wading through the warm water, and then went for a dip in the Indian Ocean. Ohio was covered in eight inches of snow at the time.

At night we cooked big communal meals and sat around the table till bedtime. I slept on the porch, since the bedrooms were all taken and I found the house stuffy anyhow. The farm was thick with dogs, most of whom seemed to live with us. They were mostly sheep dogs, but there was a little dachshund that we named Sausage and were never able to get rid of. After we'd thrown all canine beings outside, we'd invariably discover Sausage hours later, curled up in my daypack or under a couch cushion. At night, he slept (most insistently) inside my sleeping bag.

Our final day at De Hoop, one of David's friends – a really nice man named Trevor – suggested a little rambling stroll to go look at some vultures. Those were his exact words: "A little rambling stroll." So, like everyone else, I failed to take water or sunscreen with me – or a compass or flares or anything else – when we left the house that morning. How was I to know that this "little rambling stroll" would turned into a 4-hour forced march up the side of a mountain?

Well, it was all very well and good for the others. Most of them do that sort of thing for *fun* – hell, David is a caver and rock climber, and two of our companions were tri-athletes. But *I* am a chubby writer who doesn't get enough exercise and is no longer used to the midday African sun. By the time I realized what I'd gotten myself into, going back would have been no better than going ahead. I did see a couple of vultures, by the way; at one dreadful point, as I lay down on a rock on some remote mountainside, so dehydrated I couldn't even sweat anymore, and convinced I was about to die, I saw two of them circling slowly overhead.

"Just resting!" I said loudly and struggled to my feet again.

We rounded off the visit to De Hoop by going down to Cape

Agulhas, the southernmost tip of Africa. Cape Point is actually merely the south*western*most tip of Africa, and I could not leave the *southern*most tip unvisited, despite David's insistence that it was very dull and there was nothing there.

He was quite right. However, I hauled my weary, aching, dehydrated body out of the car, clambered over the rocks, and made him take my picture next to the sign marking the spot.

"Right. Been there, seen that, done that," Dave said briskly. "Get in the car. We're leaving."

I found most people in South Africa very optimistic and ready to face the future. They believed in Mandela, they believed in themselves, and they believed in their country. They all also seemed terrified of what would happen if Mandela died early. He didn't announce his decision not to run for office again until after my departure, so I don't know how that has affected people there. However, his influence will be important long after he leaves office, so people's concerns for his health will probably remain paramount.

A prime issue that frequently came up, among blacks and whites alike, was finding African solutions to African problems. Whether it was white dinner table conversation, Coloured township slogans, Zulu theatre, or corporate promotional videos, everyone seemed to have decided that listening to and taking aid from the West hadn't done Africa much good.

Hence, tourism was becoming a big issue. Did you know that Africa gets less than 2% of world tourism? England, one tiny country, gets something like five times as many tourists as the entire African continent. Gaining something like one more percentage point of world tourism for Africa would create an estimated ten million new jobs. Tourists leave their dollars behind when they go back home, enriching the economy. South Africa is trying to use its business influence to encourage cooperation in East and southern Africa in promoting tourism, regulating and standardizing practices, and making it easy for people to include several countries in their itinerary, thus making Africa a more convenient and attractive destination. It is astonishing that such an extraordinary place, which offers things that cannot be seen anywhere else in the world, has so little tourism – until one considers how consistently difficult and frequently dangerous it is to travel there.

One night in Cape Town, I attended a performance of *Sisters of the Calabash*. A bunch of township Zulu housewives had put together a review of traditional songs and strung them together with their own speeches. It was performed half in Zulu and half in English, with an occasional song

Jackass penguins at the Cape.

in some other tribal language. We were the only whites in the audience. Of the speeches I could understand, there were a number telling the white man to take all his "superior" culture and learning and get out of their way and out of their faces. The audience – multi-racial despite the absence of whites – would cheer and applaud these passages.

If you're wondering how *I* felt in there, the answer is: fine. People smiled at me and spoke to me, including the performers; no one seemed to feel I shouldn't be there.

This theme of finding their own path rather than constantly being told by whites and by the West what to do, how to act, and what to learn was one that seemed to be echoed everywhere I went. "Bring back my calabash," women kept refraining during the performance of the play, and it touched a chord with many people. The show, which had small beginnings, was touring South Africa and winning a lot of recognition.

Of course, there's a lot of conflict between old ways and new ways, too. While I was there, the government was grappling with a huge problem: witch hunts in the Transvaal. Over 70 people had already been burned or otherwise killed, accused as witches, sorcerers, and demons. The newspapers were full of lengthy, detailed articles (which, to my utter dismay, I lost while we were moving house in Rondebosch) about the accusations, the sorcery involved, and the traditional practices. Sadly, apartheid demolished some of the ways of dealing with these panics by ravaging tribal structure, emasculating the power of tribal chiefs, and persecuting witch doctors – all of which had been part of the traditional structure to investigate such accusations and deal with such panics.

The new government had so far been ineffectual in dealing with this witch hunt sweeping across the Transvaal. The whites were extremely curious to see just how the black government would handle the situation. (So, I think, were the non-whites.)

I made good on my vow to go out with a bird guide one day by jaunting off to Rondevlei (yes! another *vlei!*) with a one-man operation called Green Cape Tours. With only one other client that day, and she an avid South African bird watcher, I learned a lot; I was able to start identifying a few species by the end of the day. Further down the Cape, we walked down to The Boulders to sit with the very tame jackass penguins there – so called because their call sounds like a braying ass. Apparently some lunatic had gone nuts with a gun there recently and killed some of them. An easy enough thing to do, since they wander around paying little attention to the people who come down to gape at them daily. There's some controversy over these, the only penguins in mainland Africa, I was told. Some of the people living along the beach complain that the jackass penguins are noisy, and that their nesting shreds up their yards. For this reason, they want them killed off.

People amaze me. I mean, the penguins have been there a long time. It's not as if anyone currently living there moved to that beach and *then* got set upon by the penguins. Why someone who objected to the natural inconveniences of local wildlife would move to that one particular tiny spot, on the entire Cape, bewilders me, as does the notion that it's better to kill a rare group of animals than to get used to their noise and nesting.

We pressed on to Cape Point, where the baboons (the only ones in Africa, I gather, which eat seafood) bully people they catch hiking. They were bullying people on the road today, too, leaping onto car hoods, roofs, and trunks. My guide had some nasty stories about what he'd seen happen on this road to people careless or inexperienced enough to leave a car window partially open. He'd seen a baboon remove a woman's cheek one day! So we were appalled to see a man in front of us actually get out of his car to take a closer look at the baboons. One baboon mother seemed to take this as a sign of aggression and got restless. She was only about 10 feet away from him. And – wait for it ! – this idiot *turned his back on her.*

Nothing happened while we were there, but we were amazed at

such stupidity. The man didn't hear (or didn't acknowledge) our shouts to get back in his car, this was *DANGEROUS*.

This, I assert, is where statistics come from.

Although Rondebosch has many different roads, there's generally only one route between the residential area where we lived and the shopping district if you're on foot. I walked this route almost every day, either going to town to buy groceries, or going to the train station.

I walked through Rondebosch Park one morning, as I did almost every day. For once, there were no gardeners, picnickers, nannies with children, or flirting domestics in the park. It was empty, even though it was 10:30 AM, usually a busy hour here. Far on the other side of the park, I saw a black man. He saw me, but he didn't wave or smile as most people did, he just watched me. I thought he must be another gardener; it was only as I drew near him that I realized that thing in his hand was a big stick, not a rake. Then he moved to block my path.

I wasn't alarmed yet. Since he hadn't greeted me but was obviously trying to get in my way, I assumed he was a beggar, and I stepped around him quite casually.

Having watched me all the time I was crossing the park, he now turned and paced with me as I walked to the road. When he nearly got himself run over in order to keep up with me as I crossed the road, I realized he was pretty determined about following me. Since he hadn't asked me for money, I finally suspected that he intended to *take* it from me. As soon as I reached the sidewalk, I stopped dead. He went about 8 feet ahead before he realized I was no longer at his side. He stopped, turned, and looked at me. I looked right back at him, glaring. We stared at each other for a while.

He finally turned around and slowly, ever so slowly, so v-e-r-y slowly, started walking onward. It was the direction I obviously had to go, because of the layout of the town – unless I went back through the park, which didn't seem very smart.

I walked even slower than he did, keeping a good distance between us. I couldn't believe this! It was broad daylight in a busy neighborhood. It was sheer chance that we hadn't run across any pedestrians or workmen yet. We passed a house that was under renovation, where there were always workmen, some of whom would recognize me because I walked by there often. To my astonishment, they were nowhere in sight. I'd never seen the street so empty before. Nonetheless, there were many cars zipping past us on the busy four-lane road. It wasn't as if he could do anything to me without a witness seeing us.

However, he could probably hit me pretty hard with that big stick before anyone had time to stop their car and help me. Even so, I couldn't believe how *dumb* this guy was, though the teacher of my self-defense class frequently assures me that brains and criminality don't often go together. I mean, of all the people to attack, *I* was not an obvious choice. I was about his size, and I am not a weak, willowy woman. I had made it clear that I had spotted him and was keeping a sharp eye on him. I had maneuvered to walk behind him. I was wearing a daypack strapped firmly to my back, as opposed to carrying a purse dangling from my hand. He'd have to disable me and wrestle the thing off my body, and it wouldn't be easy. There were many cars on the busy road, and a pedestrian was bound to come along at any minute. Yet he kept dawdling, watching me, and fiddling with his stick.

I wondered if I was overreacting. I didn't think so. A beggar would have already asked me for money. I can't even express how very unlikely it was for a black man to try to pick up a white woman on the streets of Rondebosch. The stick clearly wasn't a gardening implement, a construction tool, or a walking stick. Indeed, there seemed to be only one possible explanation for it: a weapon.

After returning from Africa, I had begun training in a very serious self-defense class which combined Indonesian martial arts with urban street fighting. We didn't have belts or uniforms or competitions; we studied defending ourselves against attack in real situations. I now started trying to remember what my teacher had said about facing a stick, bat, or machete while unarmed. I'd need to get the thing away from this guy, or at least disarm him. But how? If he swung at me, I'd have to make sure he didn't get my head. If he only caught my shoulder or torso, it would hurt, but I'd have a chance to leap on him then, because I had a feeling that he'd be slow and clumsy with it. Of course, if I was wrong, if he'd actually *practiced* with the thing, then he'd break whatever he hit.

I was pretty amazed at how calm I was being. My studies seemed to have had some effect; I was thinking instead of just panicking. I was also *really* hoping it wouldn't come to confrontation. It seemed unbelievable to me that this normally busy neighborhood was so devoid of people today!

Then suddenly a white woman about my age appeared out of nowhere. She stared hard at the man, then walked past him to me.

"Is he giving you trouble?" she asked loudly.

"Well, I think so, but I'm not – "

"I've been watching the whole thing," she said rapidly, watching him turn and s-l-o-w-l-y idle down the road to town which I'd have to take. "I saw him spot you in the park, wait for you, and try to cut you off. I saw you spot him, walk around him, speed up and try to get away, and then stop and stare at him. I saw the way he dawdled and watched and waited for you to catch up. He's definitely got his eye on you. Where are you going?"

"Town."

"Of course. Well, he's going to be waiting for you down that road. You mustn't go that way. Take the next road over. It'll get you there, too."

I thanked her, watched her climb into her car, then did as she suggested. A few moments later, her car pulled up beside me.

"Look, I stayed behind to watch him," she said, "and he's realized that you're not going to go down that road after all. He's doubling back now to follow you again. You'd better get in the car. I'll take you to town."

Surprised at his persistence, I thanked her and climbed in. I had a moment of dread: *Oh, God, I'm being rescued from a black man by a white person in South Africa. How did this become my life?*

However, to my relief, she didn't use this as an opportunity to talk about what horrible people blacks were. She simply said that there was seldom any trouble in this neighborhood, but this was obviously a troublemaker, and one had to use common sense about it. She dropped me off in town, adding that she was going to double back and take another good hard look at him, so he'd known she'd seen him. There were a lot of old people strolling around in this neighborhood, she said. Easy pickings.

I decided I'd feel really guilty if I read the next day that some old person had been attacked by a black man with a stick in Rondebosch and I'd done nothing to prevent it, so I walked to the police station. I had another qualm: *Oh, God, they'll all be white, and I'll be responsible for them going out and beating the shit out of every black man they find on the streets of Rondebosch this morning.*

I went inside the station – and saw that all the cops were Coloured. Another qualm: *Oh God, they're going to think I'm a hysterical white woman who freaked out because she saw one black man walking around Rondebosch.*

However, to my relief, they listened intently, took my story seriously, and said they'd send a car out to look for this guy. Feeling like I'd done what I could, I left.

I must say, the white woman's behavior was typical of my experience of South Africans, which is perhaps why I wasn't more frightened. I felt certain that if *anyone* saw us, white or non-white, they would help me. I had been sure the situation would be alleviated the moment I found another pedestrian. Certainly whites do seem to band together when it comes to protecting one another from non-whites, and the private security services which guarantee armed guards at your house within minutes of an alarm testify to their paranoia. However, despite that, and despite the various color issues which one can't help being aware of in such a situation there, I usually found ordinary South African people of every race extremely hospitable, generous, helpful, neighborly, and eager to ensure that I had a good time, didn't get hurt, and got my heart's desire.

Kind of strange, when you think about what they've all done to each other over the years.

After my near-adventure, Jane took great delight for the rest of the week in announcing to people quite suddenly, over tea or at dinner: "Laura was attacked in Rondebosch."

This never failed to make someone choke. Certainly the notion of someone getting attacked who, if not yet a friend, was at least becoming a fixture in people's lives, was startling enough. But that it should happen in Rondebosch, that quiet, liberal, little suburb best-known for the number of schools (many of them multi-racial) it has, surprised everyone – especially considering that I spent so much time wandering around places most whites never went, too.

I had decided that I was obviously missing something in the Bo-Kaap, the old Moslem neighborhood in Cape Town which had not been evacuated during the forced removals. It was a hilly neighborhood of closed doors, closed gates, and shuttered windows that didn't welcome the outsider.

Wanting to know more about a neighborhood that had escaped the forced removals and thus maintained centuries of continuity for a non-white population, I called up Ubuntu Tours, a tiny little company with a grainy brown-paper brochure I'd unearthed a week ago. I and the elderly South African bird-watching lady I'd met previously both booked a walking tour of the Bo-Kaap.

Shireen was our guide, a beautiful Moslem woman with a long, thick, braid of shining black hair, modestly baggy thin-cotton clothes, a sort of many-pocketed hunting vest, a head scarf which served half a dozen different functions during the morning, and a sort of straw pith helmet to protect her face from the sun. She had a soft, contemplative voice and graceful gestures which were initially deceiving, for Shireen was no wilting lily. Highly educated, intellectual, and extremely political, she had recently returned from living in exile, though I don't know if her exile was by choice or out of necessity. She was clearly glad to be back, though fire-eyed and furious about the legacy of apartheid, and relentless in her pursuit to get equal rights for her community under the new government. This included focus on many practical aspects of life – continually nagging the local council to give the Bo-Kaap, full of taxpaying merchants and professionals, the same services they gave to the white communities just a stone's throw away.

In Shireen's company, I finally felt the doors of the Bo-Kaap opening up a crack – literally as well as figuratively, since she took us into otherwise inaccessible buildings, such as the local 300-year-old community mosque, private gardens, and a couple of private homes. She also took us to shrines of some of the earliest religious leaders in the Moslem community here. There are over twenty such shrines on various hills in Cape Town. Six or seven of them are particularly holy, and five of these must be visited on foot at the start of a local Moslem's pilgrimage to Mecca.

The people of the Bo-Kaap are Cape Malay, Malay being one of the former legal racial classifications of South Africa. As the sun rose higher and the day got hotter, we finished off the morning at Shireen's mother's house, high atop what seemed to be the steepest hill in the city. The house and garden were quite large, and her mother had converted the front three rooms into a little tea shop. Traditional Cape Malay tea and food were placed before me: little samosas, little coconut and honey cakes. I gobbled everything, having missed breakfast. The tea shop did a limited restaurant business for small private parties which called ahead, and I've kept the number for when I go back.

Afterward, our driver took us out to a squatter camp at Hout Bay. The land here is better than the sand on the Cape Flats, so about half the people had actually planted gardens outside their corrugated tin shacks – sometimes a fussy bed of flowers, sometimes vegetables, sometimes a wild profusion of greenery, and occasionally some marijuana. One of the local shebeens had a little cast-iron fence and brick walk leading up to the door. It looked startling outside a corrugated tin shack with no windows.

We went into the home of a lady who showed us around. This place had begun as a squatter camp two years earlier, so there were no "core houses" here. Nonetheless, our hostess and her family seemed quite wealthy by township standards. Their shack had five rooms: a sitting room, the kitchen, a bathroom, the parents' bedroom, and their child's bedroom. This had been a serviced site originally, but the family had enclosed the toilet with a tin roof and walls, and then installed a bath tub under the water tap coming out of the side of the cement toilet stall.

Electricity came to this township (called "Our Pride" in Xhosa, and nicknamed Mandela Park by local whites) less than a year ago. Our hostess had obviously been ready for this event; she had two large commercial coolers, like the kind you see at a convenience store, from which she sold cold drinks to locals. There was a small TV and a fancy stereo system in the living room, and plenty of second hand appliances in the kitchen.

Despite all that upward mobility, though, the woman struck me as a lousy housekeeper, since everything seemed rather dirty, and the toilet reminded me of some of the public ones in West Africa. I recalled Carol's spotless little shebeen kitchen in Guguletu, and thought about how incredibly fussy Elizabeth was about cleanliness and tidiness in the house back in Rondebosch (where it was safer to vacate the premises than risk getting in her way). I also noticed that the family's yard, which was twice the size of yards in the Cape Flats, was a junk heap: a barren patch of beaten earth with broken equipment and rusted-out halves of oil drums. Most of the other yards here were well-tended and gardened.

Our hostess strolled around the village with us, introduced us to a few of her friends, and told us the history of the area. She took us into the community center, a big, simple but cheerful structure in the center of the township. Any black woman who can get a job works, of course, but almost all of them have children. The breakup of traditional family structures there has left many of these women without female relatives to look after their children (or else all their female relatives are working, too). Unfortunately, most of these children just run wild from the time they can walk. Some, for a nominal fee ($1 a month or so), are watched by old women who take in children but aren't capable, physically or financially, of doing much caregiving.

For a slightly larger fee (I think it was about $5/month) a child too young for school (they start at 7) could go to the community center here all day, where there were toys, games, and a trained staff to teach, supervise, and feed them. The new government is actively encouraging this sort of development and providing training for these women. One of the women at the center told me a bit about her education. She had successfully completed the first course in day care in Guguletu, and was now scheduled to go back for the second course. I watched her cutting up food for the children while we talked and figured they'd be bouncing off the walls later, since there seemed to be a lot of doughnuts for lunch. Still, the center was a cheerful, busy place, and the children, like children everywhere, were fascinated to see a couple of strangers visiting.

In the end, it was hard to leave South Africa. Hard to leave summer, certainly, when I knew I'd be going back to gray skies, cold temperatures, and freezing rain. Hard to leave such beautiful scenery. We awoke every morning in Rondebosch to see Table Mountain looming over our heads, covered by the white mist known as the Tablecloth. It was even harder to leave behind all the interesting, kind, and wonderful people I'd met. Hardest of all to leave such a vibrant country in the middle of so much change, trying to go where no man has gone before – a truly integrated multi-racial society in Africa. There probably hasn't been a more radical idea on that continent, and many people seemed to genuinely believe in it. The optimism there was perhaps South Africa's single most appealing quality.

Which was perhaps why I so loathed the rare cynics I encountered.

"It's so exciting here right now. Everyone's optimism is contagious," I said to a white person one day.

To which she replied, with a blandly patronizing expression, "Do you think they're really optimistic, or are they just pretending to be?"

"Why would they pretend?" I asked in surprise.

"To save face, of course."

"Who?"

"The blacks, obviously. I mean, here it is, nearly a year after the elections, and nothing's changed. I think everything will go back to normal soon, and all this will be over."

I was so astonished, I was speechless.

Yes, I think the optimism there is genuine. And the fact that that woman thought nothing had changed amazed me, since everywhere I went, people were recounting stories of change to me: people returning from exile, non-whites owning homes for the first time, people getting electricity for the first time, day care centers opening, training programs and rural development, black and white schoolchildren holding hands as they crossed the streets in Rondebosch, people reaching across the color barrier.

No, of course the future of South Africa isn't all bright and rosy, and none of it will be easy. They have a vast, disenfranchised, uneducated, underemployed, impoverished majority. They have economic and environmental problems. Their leader is old, ill, and beset by rival factions in a violent and armed society.

But they also have everything it takes to make a country great, both in terms of natural resources and human resources. The people who have stayed and the people who have returned are committed to the future there. Many people there seemed to genuinely believe they can make it work, and I believe it, too.

Nkosi sikelel'i Afrika.